ROARS FROM THE MOUNTAIN

COLONIAL MANAGEMENT OF THE 1951 VOLCANIC DISASTER AT MOUNT LAMINGTON

ROARS FROM THE MOUNTAIN

COLONIAL MANAGEMENT OF THE 1951 VOLCANIC DISASTER AT MOUNT LAMINGTON

R. WALLY JOHNSON

PRESS

PACIFIC SERIES

Frontispiece: Mount Lamington from the north in late 1967

Mount Lamington is shown here 20 kilometres to the south of Popondetta, Northern District, in what was then the Territory of Papua and New Guinea. The photograph was taken by Mr John R. Horne using a telephoto lens, probably at the end of 1967. The lava dome that grew inside the summit crater, or avalanche amphitheatre, of the mountain after the catastrophic explosive eruption of 1951 is seen largely free of vegetation and is still thermally active.

Published by ANU Press
The Australian National University
Acton ACT 2601, Australia
Email: anupress@anu.edu.au

Available to download for free at press.anu.edu.au

ISBN (print): 9781760463557
ISBN (online): 9781760463564

WorldCat (print): 1145890837
WorldCat (online): 1145891085

DOI: 10.22459/RM.2020

This title is published under a Creative Commons Attribution-NonCommercial-NoDerivatives 4.0 International (CC BY-NC-ND 4.0).

The full licence terms are available at creativecommons.org/licenses/by-nc-nd/4.0/legalcode

Cover design and layout by ANU Press.

Cover photograph taken by Qantas pilot, Captain Arthur Jacobsen, at about 10.40 am while flying from Port Moresby to Rabaul on Sunday 21 January 1951 (see also Figure 5.9a(i)). The catastrophic eruption at Mount Lamington has created a large, expanding, mushroom-shaped volcanic cloud, which then collapsed producing destructive, ground-hugging, pyroclastic flows. Captain Jacobsen provided volcanologist Tony Taylor with prints of the photographs he took that morning, and Taylor included three of them in his report of the eruption (Taylor 1958, figs 10–12).

This edition © 2020 ANU Press

CONTENTS

List of Figures ix
List of Acronyms xiii
Prologue xv
Acknowledgements xxi
About the Author xxv

PART 1. TIDAL WAVE FROM THE WEST
1. Claiming Land for the British Empire 3
2. Colonialism on a Shoestring 27
3. World War and Australian Recovery 51

PART 2. CATASTROPHIC ERUPTION
4. Victims, Survivors and Evacuations 85
5. The Next 10 Days: Disaster Relief and Controversy 135
6. Beginning Disaster Recovery 177
7. Volcanological Analysis and New Eruptions 201

PART 3. AFTER THE DISASTER
8. Resettlement, Myths and Memorialisation 225
9. Lead-Up to Independence 255
10. Living with Mount Lamington in Postcolonial Times 285
References 297

APPENDICES
Appendix A: Correspondence and Reference Collections 339
Appendix B: A Postcolonial Time Series 343

LIST OF FIGURES

Frontispiece: Mount Lamington from the north in late 1967 v

Figure 0.1. Volcano distribution in Papua New Guinea
and the Solomon Islands xv

Figure 0.2. Volcanic features on north-eastern side of the
Owen Stanley Range xviii

Figure 1.1. Coastal surveys by Captain John Moresby 4

Figure 1.2. North-eastern part of Freycinet map of New Holland. 6

Figure 1.3. Shooting at Traitors Bay 6

Figure 1.4. Portrait photographs of Sir William MacGregor (left)
and Lord Lamington (right) in 1899 19

Figure 2.1. Detail from map of the two territories of New Guinea
and Papua 29

Figure 2.2. Map of part of the Territory of Papua 32

Figure 2.3. Detail from geological map of Papua by Evan R. Stanley . . . 35

Figure 2.4. Photograph of Lieutenant Wilfred Beaver during WWI . . . 36

Figure 2.5. Photograph of three 'Taro men' at Sangara 42

Figure 2.6. Map of Orokaiva 'tribes' by F.E. Williams. 44

Figure 2.7. Photographs of Sangara missionaries, L. Lashmar (left)
and M. Brenchley (right) 47

Figure 3.1. Paths of attack during the Buna–Gona campaign 54

Figure 3.2. George Silk photograph of Raphael Oimbari
and Private Whittington 57

Figure 3.3. 'Fuzzy Wuzzy Angels' and American sailors sharing cigarettes 59

Figure 3.4. Minister Ward and Colonel Conlon at Higaturu in 1944 61

Figure 3.5. Detail from geological map by Montgomery, Osbourne and Glaessner 63

Figure 3.6. District headquarters at Higaturu................... 67

Figure 3.7. Higaturu postmarked envelope franked on 1 March 1950..................................... 68

Figure 3.8. Consecration of Bishop David Hand at Dogura 73

Figure 3.9. Military aerial photograph of the summit of Mount Lamington in 1947 75

Figure 3.10. Debris-avalanche hummocks at Galunggung volcano, Java 76

Figure 3.11. Sketch by Murphy in 1948 and silhouette of Mount Lamington.................................. 77

Figure 4.1. Main geographical features of the Lamington area 86

Figure 4.2. Photograph of eruption taken by Kevin Woiwod on 18 January 1951.................................. 96

Figure 4.3. Photograph of eruption possibly taken by Allan Champion on 19 January 1951 98

Figure 4.4. Sketches by S.H. Yeoman of eruption clouds on 20–21 January 1951................................ 103

Figure 4.5. Photograph of eruption cloud on 21 January by Captain Jacobson 109

Figure 4.6. Map of limits of devastation at Mount Lamington 133

Figure 5.1. Healed burn scars on man's back.................. 138

Figure 5.2. Casualties on the Higaturu access road 145

Figure 5.3. Devastated area at Higaturu including destroyed jeeps ... 146

Figure 5.4. Dakota crew preparing to airdrop supplies 151

Figure 5.5. Requiem mass held by Father Justin on bonnet of jeep ... 152

LIST OF FIGURES

Figure 5.6. Dr Fisher and Leslie Topue during fieldwork in the
disaster area 165

Figure 5.7. Aerial photograph of Lamington from the north
on 8 February 1951 166

Figure 5.8. Taylor and Crellin approaching the active crater
on 11 February 1951 167

Figure 5.9a. Headline cuttings representing only a small number
of the many articles that were published on the Lamington
disaster in different Australian and Port Moresby newspapers . . . 170

Figure 5.9b. Four additional newspaper headlines 171

Figure 5.9c. Four more newspaper headlines 172

Figure 5.10. Photograph of Lamington in full eruption 175

Figure 6.1. Rabaul residents visiting Lamington area in mid-1951 . . 181

Figure 6.2. Wairopi and pedestrian bridge over the Kumusi River . . 183

Figure 6.3. Flooding of Kumusi at Wairopi refugee camp 186

Figure 6.4. Bert Speer photograph of evacuation of Wairopi camp . . 188

Figure 6.5. Twin babies at Ilimo refugee camp 189

Figure 6.6. Lamington lament words and music
in Balob songbook 191

Figure 7.1. Taylor and assistant undertaking fieldwork near
shooting taro 202

Figure 7.2. The Hendersons at a charred tree trunk 203

Figure 7.3. Destroyed and stranded jeeps at Higaturu 205

Figure 7.4. Three parts of a pyroclastic flow 206

Figure 7.5. Shallow-pocket eruption from Popondetta airstrip 209

Figure 7.6. Shallow-pocket eruption on 11 February 1951 210

Figure 7.7. Pyroclastic flow of 5 March 1951 in Ambogo River
valley 212

Figure 7.8. Avalanche on northern side of lava dome 216

Figure 7.9. Fully grown lava dome in Lamington avalanche
amphitheatre 216

Figure 7.10. Sketch map of summit dome and avalanche amphitheatre 217

Figure 7.11. Three-part evolution of catastrophic eruption of 21 January 1951 221

Figure 8.1. David Hand and Sydney Elliott-Smith at Saiho hospital . . 231

Figure 8.2. Opening of the Mount Lamington Memorial Cemetery in 1952 242

Figure 8.3. Paul Hasluck speaking at the opening of the memorial cemetery 243

Figure 8.4. Tony Taylor being presented with the George Cross 245

Figure 9.1. Part of the CSIRO land use map 258

Figure 9.2. Land use 'units' in the Lamington area 260

Figure 9.3. Wind directions at Port Moresby above and below 5,000 metres 262

Figure 9.4. Kururi cone on the Managalase Plateau 264

Figure 9.5. Volcanic features of Mount Victory 266

Figure 9.6. Oblique aerial view of summit area of Lamington 268

Figure 9.7. Drawings of the Sumbiripa myth by Maine Winny and Louise Bass 272

Figure 9.8. Local names for Lamington peaks drawn on old milk label. 273

Figure 9.9. Plate boundaries in Papua New Guinea 279

Figure 9.10. Seismometer and radio link equipment on Lamington in 1972 280

Figure 10.1. Digital elevation model for the Mount Lamington area. . 291

LIST OF ACRONYMS

ABC	Australian Broadcasting Commission
ANGAU	Australian New Guinea Administrative Unit
ANU	The Australian National University
BMR	Bureau of Mineral Resources, Geology and Geophysics
CSIRO	Commonwealth Scientific and Industrial Research Organisation
DASF	Department of Agriculture, Stock and Fisheries
DDS-NA	Department of District Services and Native Affairs
GA	Geoscience Australia
GIS	Geographic Information Systems
GPS	Global Positioning System
IAVCEI	International Association of Volcanology and Chemistry of the Earth's Interior
IMS	Information Management System
IUGG	International Union of Geodesy and Geophysics
LMS	London Missionary Society
MRA	Mineral Resources Authority
NGRU	New Guinea Research Unit
PAMBU	Pacific Manuscripts Bureau
PNG	Papua New Guinea
PUB	Papuan Ultramafic Belt
RAAF	Royal Australian Air Force
RSPAS	Research School of Pacific Studies
RVO	Rabaul Volcanological Observatory

TPNG	Territory of Papua and New Guinea
UN	United Nations
UPNG	University of Papua New Guinea
US	United States
USGS	United States Geological Survey
VEI	Volcanic Explosivity Index
WWI	World War I
WWII	World War II
WWSSN	World-Wide Standardized Seismograph Network

PROLOGUE

Almost 3,000 people, possibly more, were killed in January 1951 by a catastrophic volcanic eruption at Mount Lamington in what is now modern-day Papua New Guinea (Figure 0.1). This tragic event could be regarded as the deadliest natural disaster in Australian history because the Australian Government was the colonial power at the time and had responsibility for the safety of its subjects under trusteeship arrangements (Downs 1980). The Australian administrator of the Territory of Papua and New Guinea in 1951, Colonel J.K. Murray, referred to a 'scene of disaster unparalleled in Australian history' (Murray 1968, 21). Such statements do, however, require some clarification and modification.

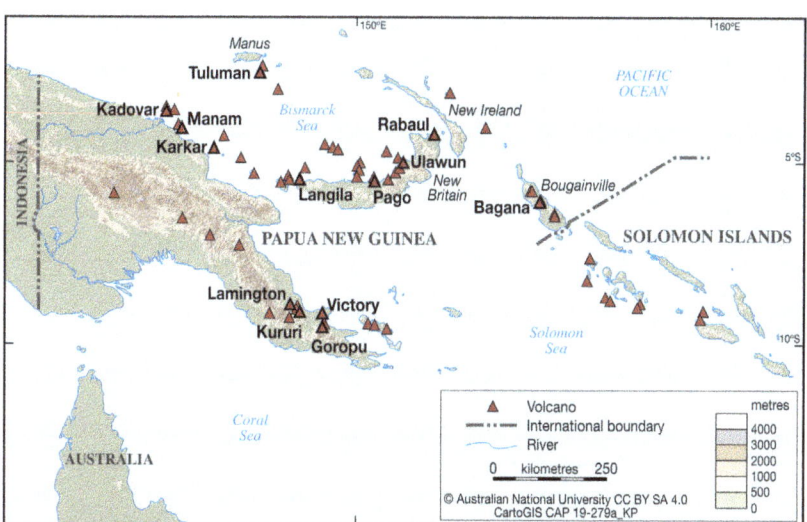

Figure 0.1. Volcano distribution in Papua New Guinea and the Solomon Islands

The triangles in this map represent volcanoes that are known, or believed, to have been in eruption during the Holocene epoch starting at 10,000 years BC. The map has been adapted from those published by Simkin and Siebert (1994, 58) and Siebert, Simkin and Kimberley (2010, 75; see also Johnson 2013, xxiii–iv for further details). Named volcanoes are those referred to in the main text.

First, most of those who perished in the volcanic eruption were local Sangara people, one of a larger group of preliterate Papuans whom the colonists called the 'Orokaiva'. This means, arguably, that the catastrophe at Lamington was not truly an 'Australian' one, and given also that only 35 white people—expatriates from Australia—were killed by the eruption. Second, the volcanic eruption at Mount Lamington was a sudden-impact, geophysical type of natural hazard—a group of phenomena that also includes earthquakes, tsunamis, landslides, tropical cyclones, severe storms, coastal surges and flooding. These are in contrast to the slower-onset and longer-lasting natural hazards of widespread, deadly diseases and related pandemics. At least 15,000 Australians are thought to have died from the 'Spanish' influenza pandemic in 1919 after it was introduced to Australia by soldiers returning from service during World War I in Europe (see, for example, the centennial article by Curson and McCracken 2019).

The term 'natural disaster' is still used widely today, but it too requires some clarification. The expression carries the implication that the cause of the disaster, or blame for it, is solely the impact of a natural hazard or, in insurance terms, an 'Act of God'. However, people affected (if not killed) by disasters may live in highly hazard-vulnerable environments by their own choice and, perhaps, even know and accept that there was some risk of future destructive natural impacts. Orokaiva communities, for example, flourished by developing gardens on the rich volcanic soils of Mount Lamington. How this advantage was balanced against the natural hazard risks identified through their experience and traditional stories about the nearby mountain is an example of community risk-management that is addressed today by many 'at-risk' societies elsewhere in the world and at different times of history.

The Lamington eruption of 1951 is well known in volcano science because of the outstanding landmark report published in 1958 by G.A.M. 'Tony' Taylor, a volcanologist employed by BMR, the Australian Government's Bureau of Mineral Resources, Geology and Geophysics (Taylor 1958). BMR Bulletin 38 is an insightful, well-written and informative account that is still referred to in many, more modern, volcanological research papers, and in textbooks dealing with the so-called '*peléean*' and 'vulcanian' types of volcanic eruption seen at Lamington in 1951. Taylor's scientific account is, in contrast, quite stark in dealing with the disaster management aspects of the eruption that, at the time, were both controversial and well publicised. This omission may have been deliberate to concentrate on the volcanology rather than on the conflicts and disputes of the public controversy.

'Relief' and 'recovery' are two of the four traditional sectors of the disaster management spectrum. The two other parts, which are just as (or even more) important, are 'prevention' and 'preparedness'—that is, what can be done by communities and authorities to reduce disaster-risk before a natural hazard actually strikes, and what can be done before the effects of the disaster escalate to facilitate rapid and effective evacuation of lives and immediate protection of property. All four of these sectors provide the context for this study. Emphasis is given to the prevention and preparedness aspects of the disaster because the primary purpose of this book is to determine why so many Orokaiva were killed in 1951.

A large part of this study is an examination of the abundant colonial literature extending from 1874 to 1950 and, in particular, the shorter, pre-disaster period from 1906 to 1951 when Australia was the governing colonial power (1951, by coincidence, was the jubilee year of the creation of the Commonwealth of Australia). This concentration on colonial records is not purposefully made to identify colonialism as the sole cause of the disaster and so to assign blame for it, but rather to determine how, and how many, disaster-vulnerability factors came to be created at Mount Lamington before the 1951 eruption. Inevitably, the book is about making historical judgements while recognising that perceptions of the past can shift, depending on the historical distance between an event and one's own contemporary standpoint.

This book, then, represents a synthesis of selected information from many different sources on the disaster management story of the Mount Lamington eruption of 1951, including peer-reviewed publications, folios in government archives, periodicals, newspapers and magazines, as well as diaries, memoirs and the records of correspondence and of interviews with eyewitnesses and their descendants. A major challenge, therefore, and in common with other attempts at writing compressed histories, has been not so much what to include but rather what to leave out. Much informal or 'grey-literature' information is of high quality, but different opinions and judgements had to be compared and assessed, not without some subjectivism where conflicts of fact or interpretation arose. Such are the challenges of memory and historical accuracy. Of archival necessity, this history is also one seen almost entirely through an Australian lens. It includes a few records of the experiences of individual Orokaiva, which are given some emphasis where appropriate, but many of these records were produced by European people anyway as a result of listening to their Papuan informants. Some of the information in this book was used summarily in a single chapter on the Lamington eruption of 1951 in a previous book by the author (Johnson 2013).

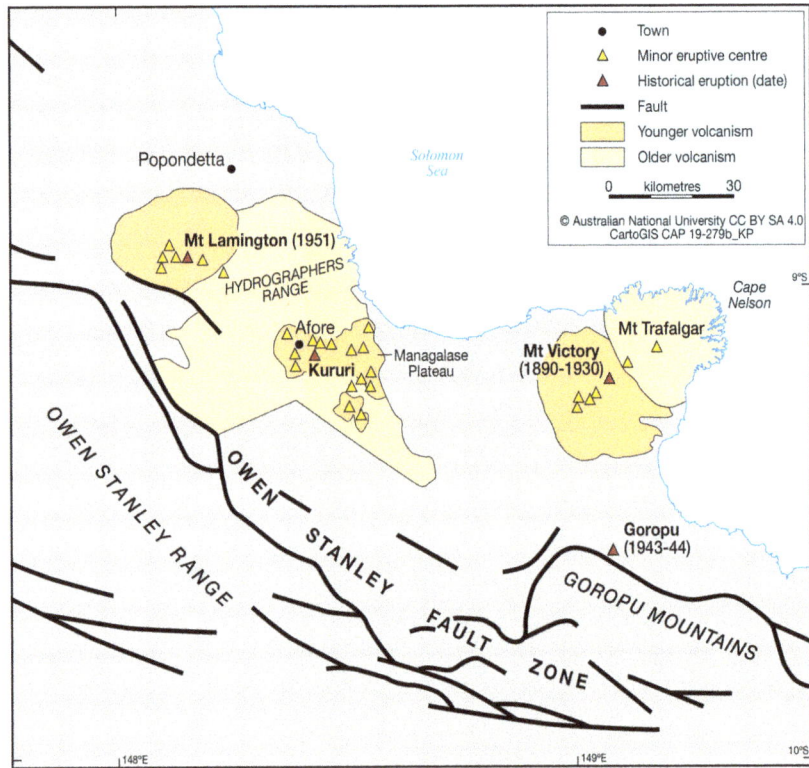

Figure 0.2. Volcanic features on north-eastern side of the Owen Stanley Range

Quaternary volcanic areas and minor eruptive centres are shown here for the north-eastern side of the Owen Stanley Range in eastern Papua. The map is adapted from those of Davies and Smith (1971, fig. 1) and de Saint Ours (1988, fig. 1). The distribution of minor eruptive centres, following de Saint Ours, is largely schematic but is more accurate for Mount Lamington and Mount Victory in Figures 9.2 and 9.5, respectively.

An unexpected consequence of conducting the research for this book has been the intrusion of other volcanoes in the Lamington story, most notably Mount Victory, an active volcano similar in geology to Mount Lamington and only 100 kilometres to the east-south-east of it (see Figures 0.1 and 0.2). Other historically 'intrusive' volcanoes include distant Rabaul in East New Britain and Goropu to the south of Mount Victory.

PROLOGUE

The final chapter of this book deals with the postcolonial period—that is, with events following Papua New Guinea's independence on 16 September 1975. This epilogue-like chapter is included, necessarily, because of the attention that Mount Lamington volcano and the Orokaiva people received after 1975 by a range of people, including outside investigators representing different, mainly academic disciplines—from the social sciences to the earth sciences. It includes also those people—both Orokaiva and Australian—not wishing the disaster to be forgotten, notably the friends and family of those who suffered there. Memorialisation and remembrance are, therefore, key aspects of this disaster management story.

ACKNOWLEDGEMENTS

Many people and organisations have contributed to this book. The manuscript was written during tenure of an honorary associate professorship in the Department of Pacific Affairs, College of Asia and the Pacific, at The Australian National University (ANU) in Canberra, and I sincerely thank ANU staff for all of their considerable support. Specific ANU people whom I must acknowledge—both alphabetically and with gratitude for their interest during this research—are, first, Papua New Guinea (PNG) aficionados Bryant Allen and Robin Hide, both of whom agreed rather courageously to review the first draft of the manuscript. Chris Ballard, Colin Filer, Ewan Maidment and the late Hank Nelson are also acknowledged for their long-term interest in my work at ANU. Two formal referees, including Brigadier Alan Hodges AM, are thanked for providing reviews of the manuscript that was submitted to ANU Press. The skill of Karina Pelling of CartoGIS Services at ANU in preparing the maps and other line illustrations for final publication is also gratefully acknowledged. Rani Kerin and Emily Tinker are thanked for their professional copyediting of the final manuscript, and the ANU Press Publication Subsidy Committee is thanked for partially offsetting copyediting costs, as is the ANU Department of Pacific Affairs.

Two people who have been almost as obsessive about the 1951 Lamington disaster as I have been are John R. Horne of Dunedoo, New South Wales, and the late Albert Speer of Sydney. Horne's correspondence with me and others, plus several unpublished reports by him on matters dealing with Mount Lamington, Mount Victory and the history of the Northern District in general, extend back to the 1960s. Albert Speer was a valuable source of information about the 1951 eruption and its aftermath. He introduced me through correspondence and his extensive network of personal contacts to many of the people listed in Appendix A in the Correspondence Files.

My interest in the Lamington disaster began in the late 1960s when I first joined the Bureau of Mineral Resources, Geology and Geophysics (BMR) as a junior geologist. Volcanologist Tony Taylor supervised the geological fieldwork I undertook, with others, on the young volcanoes in what was then still known as the Territory of Papua and New Guinea. BMR is now called Geoscience Australia, or simply GA, and it still holds the many photographs, now digitised, of Lamington volcano and its 1951 eruption that were used by Taylor in his BMR Bulletin 38. Elizabeth Fredericks, the cataloguing and intellectual property librarian at GA, is thanked most sincerely for her diligence and promptness in supplying copies of the GA photographs used in this book.

GA also holds a copy of a Rabaul Volcanological Observatory (RVO) 'Information Management System' (IMS) that was prepared during a technical upgrade of the RVO following the volcanic eruption at Rabaul in 1994. This searchable IMS is owned by the PNG Government through RVO and it contains many digitised papers on Mount Lamington and the 1951 eruption, and indeed on other PNG volcanoes and volcanic eruptions. I gratefully acknowledge the work on the IMS that was completed by the GA library manager, Chris Nelson, and his staff, supported by Shane Nancarrow, and for their ongoing interest in continuing to develop the IMS. Ewan Maidment, former executive officer of the Pacific Manuscripts Bureau at ANU, played a vital role in the early development of the IMS.

Colleagues in PNG who have been notably helpful during this research are: Hugh Davies, formerly of the University of Papua New Guinea; Maclaren Hiari of Popondetta; Chris McKee of the Port Moresby Geophysical Observatory; and Jonathan Kuduon, the late Herman Patia and Steve Saunders, all of the RVO, East New Britain Province, together with Ima Itikarai the head of RVO. Hugh Davies, in addition, reviewed a late draft of the manuscript and provided valuable suggestions for improvement.

The staff of the National Archives of Papua New Guinea (Port Moresby), the National Library of Australia (Canberra), the National Archives of Australia (Canberra), the Australian War Memorial (Canberra), the Fryer Library at the University of Queensland (Brisbane) and the Baillieu Library, University of Melbourne, are all thanked for their considerable professional assistance in locating research material.

Particular thanks must be extended to the many people who have corresponded with me over many years (see Appendix A). Some of these people were survivors of the 1951 eruption; others came to the Lamington area during the relief and recovery phase; still others came later, both before and after PNG's independence in 1975. The list of correspondents, some of whom are now dead, includes, in many cases, their relations and friends. These people were all generous in providing information, opinions and views—more than could be expected in responding to a pestering researcher in distant Canberra. I was privileged to experience their generosity and willingness to explore issues for which I required insight if not solutions. There were some differences of opinion between correspondents, family loyalties and rivalries were on display occasionally, and a few people did not remember too well or were tricked by memory.

Every effort has been made to acknowledge the people who took the photographs and produced other illustrations presented in this book and to obtain appropriate permission from them and publishers. This was not possible in a very few cases; I apologise for any omissions and if sources have been identified incorrectly.

ABOUT THE AUTHOR

Wally Johnson is an honorary associate professor in the Department of Pacific Affairs, College of Asia and the Pacific, The Australian National University. He worked for many years for the Australian Government's geoscientific agency in Canberra, Geoscience Australia, first as a volcanic geologist and research scientist and later in senior management roles as a division chief. Most of his research career has focused on the volcanology of Papua New Guinea, much of which was undertaken in close association with colleagues at the Rabaul Volcanological Observatory, headquarters of the national volcanological service of Papua New Guinea. Johnson was secretary general of the International Association of Volcanology and Chemistry of the Earth's Interior (IAVCEI) from 1991 to 1999. He is an honorary life member of IAVCEI and an honorary fellow of the International Union of Geodesy and Geophysics (IUGG). His previous book with ANU Press was *Fire Mountains of the Islands: A History of Volcanic Eruptions and Disaster Management in Papua New Guinea and the Solomon Islands* (2013).

PART 1. TIDAL WAVE FROM THE WEST

Melanesia has been invaded by a huge tidal wave from the West in the form of colonisation and Christianisation. Like any tidal wave, the West came mercilessly, with all the force and power, toppling over our earth, destroying our treasures, depositing some rich soil, but also leaving behind much rubbish. This Western tidal wave has also set in motion chain reactions within ourselves and a thirst for a better future.

— Bernard Narakobi (1980, 8)

1
CLAIMING LAND FOR THE BRITISH EMPIRE

Captain Moresby and the Binandere (1873–74)

A 'basilisk', according to Wikipedia, is a legendary reptile mentioned in European bestiaries and reputed to be 'King of Serpents'. It is said to have the power to cause death with a single glance. *Basilisk* was also the name of a British Navy paddlewheel steamer, carrying sails, of 1,031 tons. It was captained by John Moresby and was used to survey the coastline of south-eastern New Guinea island, beginning in 1873 and returning to complete a second phase of mapping in 1874 (Moresby 1876). Such a ship's name might intimidate some English-speakers, but not the Binandere people on the then little-known part of the north-eastern coast who had their own language and life experiences. They may, nevertheless, have been impressed both by the great size of HMS *Basilisk* and by the strangeness of its white-skinned crew of 178 officers and men who had appeared on their coastline. This 'first contact' between the colonising British Empire and the indigenous Binandere, also spelt Binandele, and the many encounters that followed elsewhere, were not in the least peaceful. Further, the invaders had the advantage of rifle power.

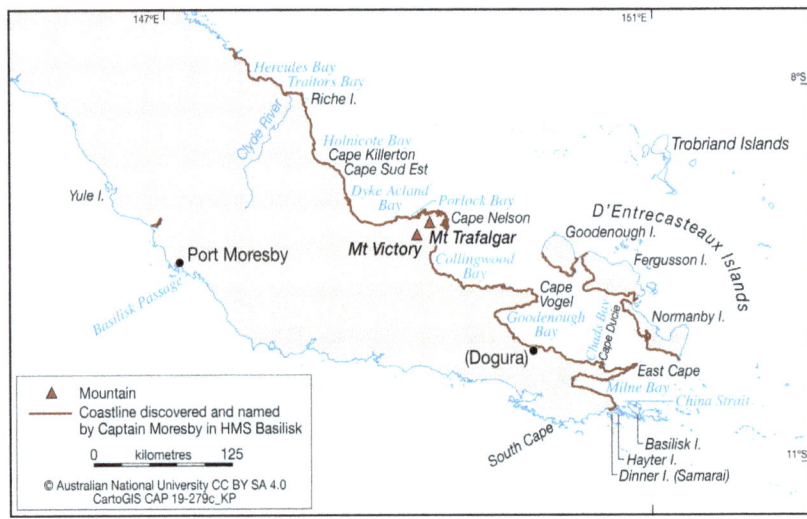

Figure 1.1. Coastal surveys by Captain John Moresby

The coastlines of south-eastern New Guinea surveyed by John Moresby in 1873–74 are shown in this map together with a selection of place names taken from the chart published by Moresby (1876; see also Whittaker et al. 1975, plate 44). The *Basilisk* survey started in the west on the south coast, near where Captain Moresby gave family names to both the main harbour of Port Moresby and to an inner one, Fairfax Harbour. The name of the *Basilisk* was given to both a passage through fringing reefs and islands into Fairfax Harbour and to an island on China Strait in the extreme south-east. Headquarters of the Anglican mission at Dogura were later built on Goodenough Bay. The mountain known later as Mount Lamington is 40 kilometres south-west of Cape Killerton but was not recorded by Moresby.

In 1874, Captain Moresby named two bays along the north-eastern coast of south-east New Guinea that border the mainly flat country occupied by the Orokaiva. The first one he called 'Dyke Acland, after my revered friend the late Sir Thomas Dyke Acland, [Baronet]' (Moresby 1876, 272). The second bay, to the north-west, was named Holnicote Bay after an aristocratic estate in Somerset, England, that was once owned by Sir Thomas. Captain Moresby's naval and English loyalties had come to the fore a few days earlier in the coastal survey to the east when he applied the name 'Cape Nelson' to a 'lofty promontory' (269). Two conspicuous and 'picturesque' peaks on the promontory, or peninsula, were called 'Victory' and 'Trafalgar', and the bay to the east of them was named after Lord Collingwood (Figure 1.1). All of these names were proud reminders of the British victory over the Franco-Spanish fleet at the Battle of Trafalgar in 1805.

Moresby did not recognise Mount Victory as an active volcano, or the volcanic nature of either Mount Victory or Mount Trafalgar, but he did say that the mountains 'descend to the sea in open grassy and wooded slopes, which have all the appearance of English parkland' (Moresby 1876, 271)—a hint, perhaps, of some homesickness. England and the Empire were in any case predominant. Moresby also gave no indication of any volcanoes existing inland from Dyke Acland Bay.

The French voyager Bruny d'Entrecasteaux had sailed off the same north-eastern coast in 1793. He encountered and named the D'Entrecasteaux Islands but went north to the Trobriand Islands (Figure 1.1) and then north-west, staying well offshore from the mainland (Duyker and Duyker 2001). No detailed coastal mapping was undertaken by d'Entrecasteaux, and two coastal points located and named by him—Cape Sud-East and Riche Island—were later discovered by Captain Moresby to have coordinates that plotted inland. Moresby, however, kept the names of these points as a courtesy to d'Entrecasteaux. This coastline is shown blank on the first published map of Australia by Freycinet in 1811 (Figure 1.2).

Captain Moresby was further up the north-east coast on 8 May 1874 when he encountered the mouth of a large river, which he called rather patriotically 'the Clyde', but which a few years later was given its local name of Mambare or Mamba. It is the largest river in this belt of coastal country. The captain here also came across 'a beautiful bay running up to a sandy beach, fringed with groves of a kind of fir tree, admirably adapted for firewood, of which we were now much in need' (Moresby 1876, 275). They anchored, 'rather glad that no villages were at hand' (275).

Wood collection by crew members of the *Basilisk* had begun the next morning when 'a large number of armed natives' (276) landed from canoes and were seen from the *Basilisk* stalking three officers on the beach. Moresby and Sub-Lieutenant Shortland immediately took rifles to the shore in a dinghy. The concealed warriors broke cover, an advancing frontline armed with spears followed by a supporting line of men carrying clubs. Moresby 'fired with a snap-shot at the leading savage' (276; Figure 1.3). He missed the man but hit his shield, and the noise and effect of the fracas was enough to send the alarmed attackers into retreat. The *Basilisk* sailed away on the following morning, 10 May, now carrying about 40 tons of the acquired wood. The name 'Traitors' Bay' was given to this first-contact location by the British voyagers. Equally, however, the Binandere would have been justified in calling this place of attack Wood-theft Bay or even Invasion Bay.

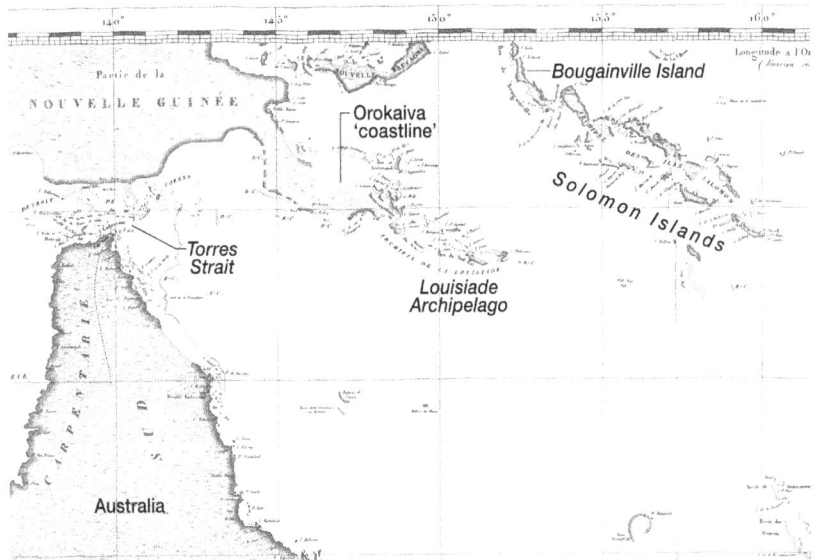

Figure 1.2. North-eastern part of Freycinet map of New Holland

This is an annotated detail from the 'General Map of New Holland', one of 14 charts from the Baudin expedition of 1800–04 (Freycinet 1811). The whole of the coastline of the Australian continent had been mapped by this time, as well as the islands of Torres Strait, the Louisiade Archipelago, Bougainville Island and Solomon Islands, but not the coastline along the north-east coast of south-eastern Papua, which is shown blank. This detail was provided courtesy of the National Library of Australia, Canberra.

Figure 1.3. Shooting at Traitors Bay

The published caption to this illustration reads 'Attack of Natives, Traitors' Bay, North-East New Guinea' (Moresby 1876, between 276 and 277). This digital image was provided courtesy of the National Library of Australia, Canberra.

Moresby's coastline survey of south-eastern New Guinea was regarded as a success by the British, given that this part of New Guinea's shoreline had long been neglected because of its dangerous reefs, shoals, currents and strong south-east trade winds. Further, navigating through the numerous islands extending eastwards from the tip of New Guinea had been risky. Ships trading between Australia and China avoided the area even though this entailed a lengthening of the voyages. Moresby's discovery of China Strait, however, just off the eastern tip of New Guinea, alleviated this necessity. In celebration of his significant discovery, Moresby had raised the Union Jack on 24 April 1873 on Hayter Island—named after the senior lieutenant on the *Basilisk*—and made a declaration of formal possession by Britain 'in the name and on behalf of her most gracious Majesty Queen Victoria' (Moresby 1876, 208). He 'discovered' Milne Bay and named Dinner Island after a meal he had there, which would later become known more famously as Samarai. The coastline mapping by the *Basilisk* officers, led by Lieutenant L.S. Dawson in 1874, would be used on the British Admiralty's navigation chart that was first published in 1886 (Dawson and Officers 1886) and reproduced in many subsequent editions.

Moresby was not the first British naval commander to sail in the coastal waters of south-eastern New Guinea. HMS *Rattlesnake*, under the command of Captain Owen Stanley, accompanied by the *Bramble,* had sailed westwards along the south coast of the island in 1849. Stanley noted that mountains behind the coast to the north 'seemed piled one above the other to an enormous height … [and were] intersected by tremendous gorges' (quoted in Goodman 2005, 244–45). The mountain axis seemed to follow the coast and appeared like a giant backbone to the island. The mountains eventually, and indeed inevitably, inherited the name 'Owen Stanley Range', although Stanley himself was fearful of disembarking from the *Rattlesnake* and exploring any further because he imagined that 'the natives are warlike, very numerous, well armed and very treacherous' (Goodman 2005, 245). This magnificent mountain range can be seen also from the north-east coast, forming on clear days a spectacular backdrop to the mainly flat country occupied by the Papuans. Mount Victoria is a nearby high point in the Owen Stanley Range that reaches over 4,000 metres above sea level. No inland volcanoes were sighted from the *Rattlesnake*.

Powers in Europe other than Britain were, by the 1870s, taking their own imperialistic interest in New Guinea island (Gordon 1951; Whittaker et al. 1975). The Dutch had already claimed the western half of New Guinea, west of 141°E, and the navies of Germany, Russia and France were becoming, or had already become, familiar with New Guinea's surrounding waters and smaller islands. The self-governing colonies of Australia accordingly were rather sensitive to, if not fearful of, the potential threat from these foreigners—especially from the Germans—and urged creation of a British New Guinea as part of the Empire. The tropical islands were being regarded by Australian colonists as a strategic bulwark or 'shield' for Australia's defence from potential invaders—and unwanted migrants—further north in Asia (e.g. Hunt 2017). There was also interest within the self-governing colonies of Australia in the British settlement and development of the agricultural potential and mineral resources of New Guinea, particularly its gold. The British Government in London in the late 1870s, however, was not yet in favour of accepting eastern New Guinea as a new colony of the Empire, and it resisted these pressures from the Australian colonies—and from the Christian churches too.

Tsunami from the West (1873–1900)

Arrival of the colonists

British imperialism had emerged from the experience of centuries of written history, Christianity, gunpowder-fuelled militarism, the Scientific Revolution, the Enlightenment and the Industrial Revolution—including development of wood-fuelled paddle-steamers. A few Europeans arrived with a modicum of sensitivity and insight, but the great remainder included, according to one list, 'immoral settlers, misinformed missionaries, ruthless officials, paternalistic administrators, racist expatriates, and self-interested capitalists' (Trompf 1987b, 6). All of these influences had, until 1874, bypassed the people in the isolated north-eastern part of south-east New Guinea. The Christian-influenced, British imperialists, however, would soon attempt to dominate the people on this north-eastern coast and to change those aspects of their behaviour judged to be 'uncivilised'.

European white men caused breakdowns of traditional life in Melanesia and in Australia. A modern-day Melanesian philosopher, Bernard Narakobi, likened their arrival to invasion by a huge 'tidal wave' or tsunami (Narakobi 1980, 8). This wave of colonisation and Christianisation came forcefully and destructively, forever changing established cultures and depositing 'much rubbish' (8, see also quotation at the beginning of Part 1 of this book). However, as Narakobi observed, the Western tidal wave also triggered changes of thought among the Melanesians and a desire for a better future.

Black peoples had arrived in New Guinea island much earlier than the Europeans, having made their Pleistocene sea crossings from South-East Asia to the combined Australia–New Guinea, or Sahul, continent by 40–50,000 years ago (Pawley et al. 2005; Summerhayes et al. 2010, 2017; Golson et al. 2017). Early arrival of black peoples to the New Guinea region is thought to have started in the western coastal areas of the island, but eastward migrations eventually led to occupation of isolated valleys in mountainous terrain and along scattered island chains. This was well before the melting of ice from the Ice Age caused rising sea levels and the creation of different Australian and New Guinea landmasses, separated by channels such as the one now known as Torres Strait. How long people took to reach the eastern 'tail' of New Guinea is unclear. Post-glacial sea level rises may have flooded archaeological evidence for possible settlements on or near shorelines—such as along the north-east coast of Papua surveyed by Captain Moresby.

Australian Aboriginal people, in general, formed mobile hunter-gatherer societies, moving through large tracts of land that were not conducive to agriculture. The Melanesians of New Guinea, in contrast, typically combined their foraging and hunting with gardening and animal husbandry. They could achieve greater population densities this way because of the availability of foods such as yams and sweet potatoes, but those higher densities in some circumstances placed them at-risk in settled areas that were geophysically hazardous. Agriculture in the valleys of the New Guinea Highlands dates back to about 10,000 years (Summerhayes et al. 2010, 2017; Golson et al. 2017).

The Melanesians also generated an extraordinary diversity of numerous non-Christian religions, languages, dialects and discrete cultures (Pawley et al. 2005; Pawley and Hammarström 2018). Their religions had their own theologies, prophets, rituals and ceremonies together with a capacity to develop new cults or movements when the need arose, such as when white men arrived with their new ideas and wealth in the form of 'cargo' (Trompf 1977, 1987a, 1987b). The languages of New Guinea island comprise a 'Papuan' or Trans–New Guinea phylum consisting of at least

347 languages according to one linguist (Ross 2005), and there are many others for which the data are too slender to make possible assignments to the phylum.

Christian missions in the 1870s were committing to vigorous proselytising among the dark peoples of 'heathen' New Guinea following the evangelical revivals of the seventeenth and eighteenth centuries in Britain (Chignell 1913; Tomlin 1951; Tomkins and Hughes 1969; Wetherell 1977, 1996; Langmore 1974, 1989). The London Missionary Society (LMS), in particular, was already interested in the establishment of a Protestant mission base on a protected natural harbour on the southern coast of New Guinea. The main part of this harbour had been called Port Moresby in 1873 by the captain of the *Basilisk*, and its inner part received the name Fairfax Harbour after the captain's father, Admiral Sir Fairfax Moresby (e.g. Stuart 1970). The first European LMS mission station was established on the shores of the harbour when Reverend and Mrs W.G. Lawes arrived in the following year, 1874. Lawes and, later, his exuberant and unconventional colleague James Chalmers were dedicated to the establishment and development of LMS mission stations eastwards along the south coast of New Guinea to the eastern end, where the highly influential Kwato Mission was established (Langmore 1974; Wetherell 1996).

The first Christian missionaries in Papua were not white men but brown Pacific Islanders. They played an essential role at both Port Moresby and at Kwato as an advanced guard for their later European colleagues. The Pacific Islanders at Port Moresby were originally from the Melanesian Loyalty Group. They had settled at Hanuabada village before the arrival of the Lawes, and previously had been missionaries in the nearby Torres Strait Islands. The approach of the Pacific Islanders to evangelisation seems to have been somewhat different to that of the Europeans who preached from the gospels. The white men taught about a forgiving god of love, as witnessed by the presence on Earth of Jesus Christ, his own son, who was reputed, whether in truth or myth, to be a mild if not meek person but who nevertheless whipped the moneylenders in the temple at Jerusalem.

The Loyalty Island missionaries, in contrast, plus others from Polynesian islands, appear to have preferred the tougher stories of Jehovah and the Old Testament conception of a god of wrath. Perhaps they recognised, too, that this was a more effective way of engaging their warrior-like Papuan brothers in the process of Christian conversion. John Bruce, magistrate and schoolteacher in the Torres Strait Islands, said after two earth tremors had been felt on Murray Island in 1899, that the local islanders had concluded 'God had been very angry'. Bruce wrote that:

> The South Sea teachers know the kind of God to depict to the native far better than the white missionary does; his God of Love is beyond their comprehension. They look as if they believed in Him, but converse with them, and you find the God of Wrath is their ideal of what God is. (Haddon 1901, 80)

This is not the only time that the 'wrath of god' is used as an explanation for the impact of geophysical hazards, including volcanic eruptions, nor the last time that inaccurate interpretations would be made by Europeans about the true nature of indigenous black religions (e.g. Trompf 1987a, 2006).

A Torres Strait magistrate, Henry Chester, raised the Union Jack at Port Moresby on 4 April 1883, thus repeating the ceremony of colonial intent undertaken by Captain Moresby 10 years earlier on the tiny offshore Hayter Island. This was a timely prelude to 1884 when the whole of New Guinea island, and adjacent islands, were partitioned by the imperial powers in Europe. Britain established a Protectorate over south-eastern New Guinea, which was administered initially by a special commissioner. Germany took north-eastern New Guinea, and the Dutch kept the western half of the island. The southern boundary of German New Guinea at latitude 8°S marks roughly the north-western limit of the people known as the Orokaiva who thus came under British control. The main administrative and trading centre for the British would be Port Moresby on the south coast, meaning that reaching the isolated north-eastern coast by land from Port Moresby was impractical owing to the barrier of the towering Owen Stanley Range. Therefore, government and administrative officials, missionaries, miners, traders, curious travellers and Australian recruiters requiring native labour for the Queensland sugar plantations used coastal vessels to sail eastwards, through China Strait, and then westwards round to the north-eastern coast. These vessels included the familiar SS *Merrie England*, a screw steamer boat of 260 tons gross, which was used frequently by the administrator, his officers and visiting dignitaries.

Another significant year for the Empire and New Guinea was 1888. British New Guinea in that year was declared a full possession of the Crown—not merely a Protectorate. Sir William MacGregor became its first administrator and, later, lieutenant governor (Joyce 1971). MacGregor was an energetic explorer of the country under his control and a determined and resolute leader. He also imposed an organisational and management structure on the colony during his 10 years in the role of administrator, during which he was accountable to the British-appointed governor of Queensland based in Brisbane. A series of British and, later, Australian colonial administrators held a general belief in a policy of economic and social development of their indigenous subordinates, if not inferiors, but they had no patience with cannibalism, sorcery, headhunting, skull collection, infanticide, inter-tribal warfare, anti-white cargo cults, polygamy, traditional dancing leading to too much fornication and debauchery, and certainly no acceptance of physical attacks on whites—especially fatal ones.

Meeting the Orokaiva

A dominant geographical feature of the belt of country along the north-eastern coast of New Guinea is the so-called 'northern rivers' area where four main rivers in the north-west drain off the Owen Stanley Range. These meander in their lower courses north-eastwards towards the sea through an extensive swampy basin that runs parallel to the coast, and that easily becomes flooded especially during monsoonal times. The Mambare and Kumusi are the two largest of the four rivers, but the smaller Gira and Opi were no less important. All of them were used by the colonists as highways of access to the interior and to the peoples who live there.

William McGregor visited the coast near the mouth of the Mambare in 1890 in the *Merrie England*, near where John Moresby had landed 16 years earlier. MacGregor was also in 1894 the first foreigner to ascend the Gira and Opi, and to take a steam launch as far as he could up the Mambare and Kumusi rivers. MacGregor encountered river-shore villagers who were prepared to trade, but he was also confronted by armed parties whose behaviour may have been welcoming, propitiating, intimidating or perhaps simply a 'testing' of the unknown—he could not decide (MacGregor 1890; Williams 1930; Joyce 1971; Nelson 1976). The Orokaiva in any case soon gained a reputation, in the minds of the colonists, as exceptionally savage warriors known for their fearsome raids on traditional enemies and for having little compunction about attacking, retaliating and killing the invading whites.

Village people on the Mambare shouted out 'orokaiva!', which the foreigners thought was some sort of greeting, or perhaps a password or statement of presence, for those who came in peace. The word was later used by white travellers throughout the district and was soon adopted by them for all of the local people along this north-eastern belt of south-eastern New Guinea. 'Orokaiva' in that context actually refers to a loosely related group of peoples sharing a broad yet common culture but having different languages and dialects. The people encountered by both Moresby and MacGregor along the Mambare were in fact the Binandere, a name subsequently used by academic linguists for all of the languages of Orokaiva country (e.g. McElhanon and Voorhoeve 1970; Pawley 2005). The Binandere family of languages belongs to the ancient 'Papuan', or non-Austronesian, family of languages signifying, but not proving, that the Orokaiva, or at least their predecessors, may have occupied this country for many thousands of years, possibly even back into the Pleistocene.

British New Guinea was split into geographical 'divisions', each of which was administered by a resident magistrate responsible only to the administrator. The resident magistrate was the representative of British law and its enforcement, as well as the head of all executive and administrative affairs in his division, and much else besides. The early resident magistrates tended to have exuberant, independent and adventurous personalities, and were provided de facto by the administration with a considerable amount of local power, especially in difficult postings that were distant from Port Moresby. They created uniformed constabularies of armed native police composed of selected men, some from parts of the colony that were distant from divisional headquarters. Resident magistrates also needed to acquire some knowledge of the nature of the strange people and cultures they were administrating and attempting to change. This proved to be a challenge for some of them, and a test of patience too. Some of the resident magistrates of a more racist persuasion were found to be rather free in their use of firearms in controlling and killing the fractious and aggressive Orokaiva.

MacGregor observed from Dyke Acland Bay in late 1893 the inland landscape just west of the newly named 'Hydrographers Range' in the Northern Division. It was flat and swampy country:

> Bounded by an extension of the [range], which extends away into the interior in a series of nearly detached hills, from a few hundred to two or three thousand feet high. These are forest-clad, but many clearings have been made, apparently for cultivation purposes. (MacGregor 1893, 2)

This description of gardens on higher ground immediately west of the Hydrographers Range probably refers to cultivation by the mountain Sangara group of Orokaiva, in which case the ground would have been the northern slopes of what later would be called Mount Lamington—and much later identified as a volcano.

Gold prospecting

Australian gold prospectors in the 1870s and 1880s had had some success south of the Owen Stanley Ranges and in the islands east of the south-eastern end of New Guinea, and they turned their attention to the northern side of the range after MacGregor's trips up the northern rivers in 1894 when gold 'colours' were found in the Mambare (MacGregor 1894). George Clarke and others from the Cairns Prospecting Association reached the Mambare in July 1895, but the Binandere people were not welcoming and Clarke was killed by one of them. This was the start of years of deadly clashes in the northern rivers area between Orokaiva warriors and the invading prospectors and administration officers (Nelson 1976; Wetherell 1977). Successful prospecting for the alluvial gold did not come easily: 'There's a lot of gold in New Guinea, but there's a lot of New Guinea mixed with it', said the prospectors (Nelson 1976, 120).

The administrator was on the north coast with the *Merrie England* in 1895 when he heard of Clarke's killing. He headed for the Mambare River, assessed the unstable situation there, and evacuated the remaining miners. The administration could not, and did not, retreat in such circumstances, and the *Merrie England* was sent on for police reinforcements. MacGregor first, however, accompanied by his government secretary, John Green—and by some of the gold prospectors—took the opportunity of exploring part of the Musa River area while waiting for the return of the reinforcements. The Musa drains into the south-eastern shore of Dyke Acland Bay near Porloch Bay, about 150 kilometres south-east of the mouth of the Mambere (Figure 1.1; see also Figure 2.2).

The administration party was in a launch on the Musa River travelling back downstream in September when they encountered a raid by the Orokaiva—a powerful, 'almost spectral' flotilla or 'armada' of canoes moving fast and impressively upstream in the dawn light (MacGregor 1895, 27). There were between 30 and 40 large canoes, each full of warriors—about 400 in total—and all decked out in war gear. Each of two men in the largest canoe in the centre, who evidently were leaders, were covered with paint and plumes and they held banners made from white feathers fixed on to spears.

The flotilla made its way silently and purposefully past the MacGregor party, ignoring the foreigners, although one warrior did call out 'orokaiva' 'in a low hollow tone' (MacGregor 1895, 27). MacGregor collected additional police from the *Merrie England,* which by now had anchored in Dyke Acland Bay, and the next day he went back up the Musa with his armed reinforcements. There they saw gardens devastated by the raiders, and abandoned canoes with roasted human legs, arms, ribs, heads, backbones and so on, some partly eaten, plus the body of young girl, her skull smashed and her body prepared for cooking. There were also neatly made-up parcels and packets of human flesh, and prepared coils of human intestines. Swift and deadly retribution for the warriors of the flotilla was judged by the administrator to be appropriate and fatal shootings followed. John Green 'felt no mercy as he fired', remembering the body of the young girl and her smashed skull (Nelson 1976, 96).

MacGregor next appointed John Green to be his government agent on the Mambare to protect the gold prospectors, and to bring the north-western Orokaiva, the Binandere people, under government control. The Binandere had by this time, in late 1895 and after George Clarke's killing in July, established a reputation as indiscriminate and fierce killers, so Green's task was certainly a challenging one. Green suffered fatal consequences himself at the Tamata Government Station on the Mambare on 14 January 1897 when he and eight others in his administration group were killed by the Binandere. A retributive, dominating and effective response was provided by MacGregor against the perpetrators.

The prospectors persevered even in these circumstances and, by 1890, had been rewarded by significant gold finds in the Yodda Valley, an upper tributary of the Mambare (Nelson 1976). A goldfield was declared, attracting further interest from those new alluvial miners who were prepared to put up with the Orokaiva, the considerable supply costs of being so far inland, and poor food and tropical diseases—malaria, dysentery, dengue fever and blood poisoning through tropical ulcers and untreated wounds.

Anglican Missionisation (1891–98)

The trident of British imperialism consisted of administration officials supported by armouries, evangelistic missionaries carrying the gospels and private enterprise requiring profitable investment. All three in British New Guinea, as elsewhere, depended on reaching an acceptable and pragmatic equilibrium by means of political process. The Christian missions and missionaries themselves, however, had different approaches to evangelisation.

MacGregor was a crofter's son brought up in Scotland where he was influenced by the Presbyterian Church of Scotland. MacGregor in British New Guinea, however, was more concerned about establishing effective alliances with all of the Christian missions whether Protestant or Roman Catholic. He was a strong supporter of missionisation and, indeed, was obliged to be so in practical terms because missionary work provided not only, hopefully, a pacifying role through the spiritual teachings deriving from a god of love, but also education—reading, writing and arithmetic—through mission schools, as well as improved physical health through nursing services and hospitals. MacGregor had trained as a medical doctor, so he brought to the task of administrator a scientific approach to his observations and recording.

The local impact of Christian teaching was already evident early in MacGregor's rule when the administrator and his officers swept through a score of villages on the north-eastern coast of Papua, north of Milne Bay, in late 1888. This was a response aimed at capturing offenders following a killing of a European trader at Chads Bay near Cape Ducie. MacGregor asked Komodoa, the headman at Polotona village, if he had been involved in the attack, and he received the reply: 'No! too much fear God' (Wetherell 1977, 29). Such a view of Christianity may well have originated from the Pacific Island missionaries on Milne Bay and is much the same kind of 'wrath of god' reaction recorded later by John Bruce on Murray Island after earth tremors were felt there. The kind of commonsense pragmatism displayed by Komodoa at Chad's Bay, however, had not yet emerged from the un-evangelised Orokaiva further to the north-west.

The Roman Catholics in 1885 had already established the Sacred Heart Mission on Yule Island north-west of Port Moresby, later extending their influence among the people on the nearby coast and mainland interior. Similarly, the LMS Kwaito Mission was well established by 1890 on the shores of China Strait and Milne Bay. Three other church missions by 1890 had also reached an agreement, facilitated by MacGregor, that separate 'spheres of influence' should be defined for south-eastern New Guinea (Langmore 1974, 148, note 14). The Anglicans would proselytise in a belt of paganism on the isolated north-eastern coast, extending from Cape Ducie in the east—named by Captain Moresby after the Earl of Ducie— to the border with German New Guinea, or the 'Old Protectorate', in the north-west. Their territory, therefore, included all of Orokaiva country. The Wesleyan Methodists would take the D'Entrecasteaux Islands plus a narrow strip east of Cape Ducie, and LMS influence would continue to extend from Kwaito, westwards along the south coast of New Guinea towards the border with Dutch New Guinea, excluding Sacred Heart territory.

The founding fathers of Anglicanism in south-eastern New Guinea were Reverend Albert Alexander Maclaren and Reverend Copland King (Chignell 1913; Tomlin 1951; Tomkins and Hughes 1969; Langmore 1989). They decided in 1891 to establish their mission headquarters at Dogura, Bartle Bay, on a remote stretch of coastline west of Cape Ducie (Figure 1.1). The mission was built on a terrace above the shoreline looking northwards across the waters of Goodenough Bay—named by Captain Moresby after a British naval colleague, Commodore James Graham Goodenough—to the Wesleyan territory in the D'Entrecasteaux Islands, and southwards to the imposing backdrop of the Owen Stanley Range. Primitive living quarters and a chapel were built, which were precursors to eventual construction of a cathedral. The setting had a romanticism that evidently appealed to the Anglicans and to the images of famous cathedral settings in England (Wetherell 1977).

The Anglicans at Dogura were, overall, High Church or Anglo-Catholic in preference, although Reverend King himself classified as Low Church. They adopted Roman Catholic traditions, giving emphasis to the dogmatic and sacramental aspects of Christianity on the continuity of the church from the Middle Ages and in its sympathy with other churches of Catholic Christendom—that is, Tractarianism (Langmore 1989, 320). The confessional was used, and some priests were celibate. There were impressive colourful vestments for ceremonial and other occasions, and an acceptance of episcopal authority. They preferred the full rituals of worship including the use of incense and, most importantly, participation in the holy eucharist and its common association with the controversial doctrine of a magical transubstantiation, whereby the bread and wine of the eucharist changes to the actual body and blood of Jesus Christ. These rituals differed from the less visual theatre of the chapel services preferred by the nearby, less mystical, Wesleyan Methodists on Dobu Island. The Wesleyans, nevertheless, could influence powerfully and emotionally in the best evangelical tradition, by preaching on both the forgiveness of God and the mythical terrors of the Devil—damnation and the punishment of Hell for unrepentant sinners. Missionaries as a whole tended to be strict and dominant towards the Papuans, as they wished to impose Christianity on their poor brethren, but some also wished to escape the confines of their own European culture and so were empathetic towards the Papuans. This 'dominance' versus 'escapism' tension was experienced by other Anglo-Catholic missionaries in south-eastern Papua (Garland 2000).

Dogura is at the south-eastern extreme of its appointed Anglican territory and not too far by boat eastwards round East Cape to the harbour at Samarai and to their counterparts of the LMS Kwaito Mission in the Milne Bay area. Dogura is also, however, more than 320 kilometres in a direct line to the mouth of the Mambare River and is much further by sea after taking navigational detours past the headlands of Cape Vogel and Cape Nelson. The immediate presence of pacifying missionaries in the troubled conflict zone between the Binandere warriors and gold prospectors up the Mambare River would have been advantageous to the administration, but the Dogura missionaries were unable to provide immediate help for several more years yet.

The influence of the Anglicans along the coast to the west was slow because of inadequate staff numbers and weak funding support from their mother church in England. They did not use Polynesians as 'advance-guard' missionaries in the same way as the LMS and Methodists (Wetherell 1977, 98), but rather gave an early preference for local Papuans becoming trained as teachers, pastors and priests. Coastal mission stations, however, gradually became established, including at Wanigela at the foot of Mount Victory and at Sefoa near Tufi on Cape Nelson. Reverend King himself eventually, in 1900, transferred to a dangerous mission station, Mamba, in the Mambare River area. He there learnt and documented the Binandere language as a means of attempting to evangelise through words and ceremony the warring Orokaiva in those distant parts of the Anglican's appointed territory.

Figure 1.4. Portrait photographs of Sir William MacGregor (left) and Lord Lamington (right) in 1899

The Second Baron Lamington served as governor of Queensland from 9 April 1896 to 19 December 1901 (Joyce 1983). His full name was Charles Wallace Alexander Napier Cochrane-Baillie. Both digital images are reproduced here courtesy of the State Library of Queensland, Brisbane.

Reverend Montagu John Stone-Wigg became the first Anglican bishop of New Guinea in 1898, the year that MacGregor left British New Guinea. MacGregor, at the end of his term of office, and in assessing the effectiveness of the four different missions, declared publicly that the Wesleyan Methodists 'have fully maintained without flagging the zeal and industry with which they began, with the result that there is perhaps no more successful mission than theirs [in British New Guinea]' (MacGregor 1898a, xxx). The Anglicans evidently did not fit this same description, and MacGregor seemingly would have liked some Wesleyan-like assertiveness and energy in penetrating new fields that required pacification. Here, then, was a challenge for the inaugural Anglican bishop. Stone-Wigg was the son of an English gentleman, educated at Winchester private school and then at Oxford University. He arrived in Australia at Brisbane in 1891 and served as bishop in New Guinea until 1908. He was able to assist in enhancing the effectiveness of the Anglican mission, in part because of influence from his being so well connected with the higher echelons of society in Australia.

Stone-Wigg, on his first episcopal visit to New Guinea, was in the company of both Lord Lamington, the governor of Queensland, and Sir Hugh Nelson, the Queensland premier. This visit coincided with Sir William MacGregor's last official tour of duty in 1898, and the four travelled around the coast of the possession together in the *Merrie England* (MacGregor 1898b; Wetherell 1977). 'Lamington' thereafter starts to appear as a name in reports and on maps for the mountain west of the Hydrographers Range, but it was not recognised yet as a volcano.

Eruption at Mount Victory (1880s–90)

William MacGregor was on the *Merrie England* in 1890 on one of his earlier voyages to the north-eastern coast of south-eastern New Guinea when he recognised that Mount Victory on the Cape Nelson peninsula was an active volcano (MacGregor 1890). He was not, however, the first European to do so, as Reverend James Chalmers and others on board the *Governor Blackall* on 24 October 1885 observed, and Chalmers later noted briefly, that the mountain—it was wrongly called 'Mount Nelson'—was:

> Very distinct, and had all the appearance of a crater on its east side, and certainly there were more on board in favour of its being a living volcano than against it. Heavy clouds hung over the top, and at various places long jets of steam appeared to rise. (Chalmers 1887, 102)

Five years later, in late July 1890, Mount Victory seems to have had a different appearance, as MacGregor wrote that the mountain had 'great masses of bare rock' near its summit. Further:

> Its sides were scored and marked by brown lines from near the summit to its base; these at first looked as if caused by lava running down the mountain, but the closest inspection could detect no presence of lava, so that it was concluded that these lines had been caused by recent great earthslips … a few days later we had the opportunity in the early morning of seeing numerous columns of steam rising, some from the very tops of the of the two crests of Mount Victory … [where] vegetation is very scant … Flame was not at any time seen by us on Mount Victory, nor could we obtain from the natives any information regarding it. (MacGregor 1890, 14)

MacGregor and others saw the volcano again in following years (MacGregor 1893, 1894; see also Moreton 1894). These included Queensland geologist A.G. Maitland (1892a, 1892b) who, in May–October 1891, travelled with the administrator on the *Merrie England* along the coast to the D'Entrecasteaux Islands, but not past Collingwood Bay, beyond which he might have observed volcanoes other than Mount Victory.

The effects of the eruption at Victory were substantial. Reverend Arthur K. Chignell at Wanigela Mission in 1909 wrote:

> It is not every man who can boast of an active volcano in his backyard, but there it is … always with white steam, or spirals of darker smoke ascending from a dozen fissures in its rugged crown. The elder men in Wanigera [Wanigela] will tell you of a time when the 'burning mountain' burst asunder, and sent flaming streams of lava flowing down to the sea, and they remember how the people dwelling on the higher ground made haste to build new and safer homes more near the shore, and how from that time onwards travellers and huntsmen have been careful to keep away from the slopes of Keroro [Victory]. (Chignell 1911, 1–2)

Dr W.M. Strong was a medical officer and a resident magistrate along the north-eastern coast between 1908 and 1912, and he told a similar story to Chignell's about the still active volcano and its recent eruption:

> I visited the upper slopes of it in 1911, and could quite clearly see steam rising from vents at the top. Reliable native accounts show that some forty years ago there was an extensive eruption—one or more villages were overwhelmed—and the Awanabairia people, who then lived on its slopes, fled to their present home at Lakwa. (Strong 1916, 409)

There is also reference to the disastrous eruption through much later anthropological studies of the Miniafia people (Wakefield 1989). The Miniafia had lived in the Cape Nelson area on Collingwood Bay but some of them survived the eruption and escaped, taking up unoccupied land at the base of Cape Vogel peninsula to the east. One group or phratry, the Asabuworoto, although demoralised and disorganised, was able to maintain their identity as a social unit even though, importantly, those who knew their 'origin story' had been killed in the eruption.

Little else is known about the eruption at Mount Victory, but the above quotations are sufficient evidence for a conclusion that the outbreak was an explosive, ash-producing one of substantial size and impact. No literate observers, however, are known to have witnessed and recorded the eruption, or indeed any explosive eruptions following it. Even the year of the Victory eruption is uncertain. Earlier voyagers, such as Moresby in 1874, Chalmers in 1885 and Finsch in 1884–85 (Moresby 1876; Chalmers 1887; Finsch 1888), do not refer to the devastation recorded by MacGregor, so possibly the eruption took place in the late 1880s or even in early 1890 (e.g. Horne 1974b). The duration of the eruption—whether days, weeks or months—is also unknown. The 'brown scores', 'earthslips' and 'flaming streams' may refer mainly to hot pyroclastic flows or *nuées ardentes*. This well-known volcanological term was first introduced to science by a French volcanologist following the devastating eruption at Mont Pelée that destroyed the town of St Pierre on Martinique Island in the Caribbean in May 1902 (Lacroix 1904). This type of explosive eruptive activity came to be called *peléean*, a term that would be used internationally for several decades afterwards, including, notably, for the disastrous eruption at Mount Lamington on 21 January 1951. Victory and Lamington volcanoes, therefore, may have been built by similar kinds of eruptions.

Coastal Orokaiva living on and near the western side of the Cape Nelson peninsula would have seen the eruption from Mount Victory and would have suffered from it where ash fallout affected their gardens and fishing grounds. The extent to which the eruption was also observed in other more distant and mountainous parts of Orokaiva country 100 or so kilometres to the north-west is also unknown. The eruption cloud, however, could have been seen from what became known as Mount Lamington if it was high and persistent enough, and if visibility was unaffected by long periods of poor weather. Falls of volcanic ash in the Lamington area are not out of the question either. There is, therefore, the possibility that these mountain Orokaiva may have known from this volcanic experience what a 'volcano' and an 'eruption' were in practice, although not necessarily in name.

1. CLAIMING LAND FOR THE BRITISH EMPIRE

Between the Eras (1898–1907)

The year 1898 marked the end of MacGregor's historically memorable, decade-long rule, but British administration of New Guinea continued for several more years. The two subsequent British New Guinea administrators were the lesser-known Sir George Le Hunte in 1898–1903 and then Captain Francis Rickman Barton in 1904–07, and there were even lesser-known acting administrators between these main periods of government service. In 1907 Barton handed over the role of acting administrator to an Australian, John Hubert Plunkett Murray, who began a notable and sustained period of rule as administrator or 'Australian pro-consul', lasting 32 years (West 1968; Nelson 1986).

Conflict and bloodletting between the Orokaiva on the one hand and the foreign gold miners and administration officers on the other had not ceased by the first year of the new century. There was still trouble on the northern rivers in 1900 where the extent of the auriferous ground was known now by the miners—mainly in the headwaters and tributaries of the Mambare, including the valley hosting the Yodda Goldfield, and further north-west in the Gira River, the Gira Goldfield (Nelson 1976).

In early 1900, the resident magistrate for the Northern Division, Belgium-born W.E. Armit, undertook the first government patrol from Tamata on the Mambare to the upper Yodda. He constructed a road and killed many Orokaiva while doing so, characterising the Binandere attackers as 'treacherous, truculent, aggressive, cruel, and cunning … and [they] lie abominably … It will be necessary to teach these tribes a salutary lesson' (Armit 1900a, 98). Armit's comments about the patrol and the killings are recorded historically in his official reports. They were received with 'great uneasiness' by Administrator Le Hunte who asked Armit for more details and a fuller explanation (Le Hunte 1900, 92). Armit, in reply, was largely unrepentant and stated that he and his police had killed 54 Orokaiva over a period of a month, including two women who were carrying 'spare spears for their husbands' (Armit 1900b, 93). Reverend Lawes called Armit 'a shooter of blacks' (Wetherell 1977, 35; see also Nelson 1976, for further information on Armit).

Reference is made to Mount Lamington and to the agricultural value of its slopes in the administration's annual report for 1904–05: 'the soil is of volcanic origin … and is uniformly good thus giving an area … of the finest agricultural land … This land is perfectly situated for the culture of cocoa (*cacao*)' (Administrator 1904–05, 4). This information evidently came from C.A.W. Monckton, the resident magistrate of the Northern Division at the time. Monckton, a New Zealander, first became a resident magistrate in 1897 under MacGregor's rule (e.g. Lutton 1978). Monckton admired MacGregor and seems to have been rather similar in some ways to the administrator: energetic; intelligent; adventurous; a willing explorer of new, difficult country; and not averse to using force and firepower to quell Papuans judged to be difficult and non-conforming. Monckton's years of official service as a resident magistrate included long periods in both the Northern and North-Eastern divisions. The square-jawed and heavily moustachioed Monckton later showed himself to be an engaging writer and literary raconteur by publishing two successful books in Britain in the early 1920s (Monckton 1921, 1922) and another in 1934.

Monckton advocated, quite openly, a 'shoot-and-loot' approach to the colonial domination of Papuan groups who continued to fight among themselves (Monckton 1921, 208). He was, however, highly supportive of the Papuan armed constabularies who served both him and the administration's interest in tribal pacification. The constables in turn provided Monckton with a loyalty reminiscent of a Roman 'Pretorian guard', although the full extent to which the police themselves used Monckton for their own purposes is still not entirely clear (Nelson 1976). Monckton also recruited Orokaiva warriors, especially the fierce Binandere whom he judged as having the qualities needed for such police work.

In 1903, the acting administrator, Anthony Musgrave, instructed Monckton to explore the possibility of establishing a road—a new supply route—between the coast at Oro Bay and the inland goldfields by surveying the northern and north-western slopes of Mount Lamington. Monckton, who would be accompanied by a government surveyor, referred to the challenge as the 'Lamington expedition'. He warned the surveyor, Mr Tooth, about the difficulties ahead: 'You can't make an omelette without breaking eggs, and you can't take an expedition past Mt Lamington without some one being killed on one side or the other' (Monckton 1921, 297). Monckton had had previous experiences with the local peoples of the Lamington area; he had used the constabulary force to intervene in a bloody conflict between the Dobudura and the Notu peoples, a general conflict that also involved the nearby warring Sangara.

Monckton participated in an even more challenging expedition in 1903. This one was instigated by Acting Administrator Judge C.S. Robinson and, like the Lamington expedition, the aim was to discover better access between the coast and the goldfields in the north-west interior (Monckton 1905, 1921). The Robinson–Monckton party, including police, travelled from Porloch Bay on the south-eastern edge of Dyke Acland Bay westwards and inland, south of the Hydrographers Range and then south of Lamington, managing to reach the government station of Papaki in the goldfields. However, this was arduous country. No road could be built south of Mount Lamington and, instead, the Yodda Road or, more realistically, the Yodda 'track', was constructed in 1904 under Monckton's direction to the north of the mountain. The road had to be built well north of the upper slopes of Mount Lamington to avoid as much as possible the numerous gullies and creeks that cut into the northern piedmont area of the mountain. Further, the road had to cross the wide Kumusi River at Wairopi, also spelt Wairope ('wire rope'), the name emerging after construction was completed of a metal hawser and a travelling block for loads. Mount Lamington evidently was not recognised yet as a volcano.

Judge Robinson was impressed by the energetic work of the resident magistrate on his 1903 expedition, and indeed by Monckton's martial abilities in general. However, in the same year, Monckton was suspected of responsibility for the 'Paiwa massacre' in which the resident magistrate's loyal Binandere-sourced policemen bayoneted recalcitrant Paiwa people to death in hand-to-hand fighting, an action supported in principle by Judge Robinson (e.g. Wetherell 1977). The acting administrator even named a prominent peak in the Owen Stanley Range in honour of his resident magistrate. Mount Monckton is more than twice the height of the mountain named after Lord Lamington, and is only 30 kilometres south-west of it, on the other side of the Kumusi River (see, for example, Figure 2.2).

A final achievement of the British administration was accomplished, also in 1904, when a government station was completed at Kokoda in the northern foothills of the Owen Stanley Range. The station was built on a small plateau directly west and in full view of Mount Lamington, overlooking the Yodda Valley and its alluvial gold diggings to the north-west. The station, in picturesque mountainous country, was a showpiece of the Papuan field service (e.g. Murray 1912; Nelson 1976). The Yodda Road thus became an important communication link from the coast not only to the Yodda Goldfield but also for Kokoda. According to Monckton (1934, 41), the road was 'a sanctuary for any and everyone; the wildest tribes only visit it in peace to trade food and goods to passing travellers'. Even Hubert Murray, who was not an admirer of Monckton, wrote later:

> The Wasida and Sangara have been particularly active in forming markets along the road which leads from Buna Bay to the Yodda Goldfield, and in supplying carriers with taro and other food in exchange for articles of trade, such as tobacco, and glass bottles, which are much prized for the manufacture of razors. (Murray 1912, 105)

The importance of a road from the coast to Kokoda and Yodda would be demonstrated clearly in later times when major historical events demanded its use both as a military route and as a disaster relief lifeline. The Yodda Road arguably can be regarded as the most significant historical legacy of Monckton, the 'reprobate magistrate' (Lutton 1978, 48), and of surveyor Tooth.

2
COLONIALISM ON A SHOESTRING

The Papua Act and the New Anthropologists (1904–14)

The 1898–1907 period was one of significant global political change. The British Empire itself was transforming. Canada had already become an independent dominion and the six former colonies in Australia became federated on 1 January 1901, creating the new Commonwealth of Australia. Political pressure mounted for the end of British rule in New Guinea so that Australia could take over its administration. It did so after the *Papua Act of 1905* came into force in 1906, when the Australian-administered 'Territory of Papua' came into existence, and when an Australian Royal Commission provided policy directions for Papua. The name 'New Guinea' for the former British colony was lost, and Australia had changed within only a few years from a group of colonies dependent on a colonial power to a colonial power itself. British traditions continued, however, including in relation to racial attitudes.

Great Britain regarded the vast southern continent of Australia as terra nullius or 'nobody's land' after Captain Cook landed on its eastern shores in 1770. Thus began a history of tragic relationships with traditional Aboriginal groups whom Britain, and the new Australia, believed had no claims to land ownership. That view prevailed despite the richness of Aboriginal culture—its commitment to the spiritual aspect of 'Country', the geospatial aspect of much of its art and mapped songlines, together with an oral history of the Dreaming. Versions of this Australian racism also came to Papua, remaining there for many more years, including during the colonial rule of Hubert Murray and despite accusations from parts of the white community that Murray was too 'pro-native'. Other critics said he was too benignly paternalistic towards his childlike subjects.

Hubert Murray, a trained lawyer, had first come to British New Guinea in 1904 as its chief judicial officer. He was appointed acting administrator of the new Territory of Papua in 1907 and became confirmed in the position in 1908, beginning a distinguished 32-year-long career as one of the British Empire's great colonial governors (West 1968). Murray's new administration would recognise and control native landownership through legislation; advocate and administer a liberal land system, including provision of leases for white settlers; encourage a system of native indenture especially on new plantations; and promote a policy of protecting life and property in general (e.g. Stanley 1923).

Very early in his administration, Murray shifted from the 'shoot-and-loot' type of resident magistrate that had been epitomised by Monckton, Armit and others, to a style that can described more as the 'look-and-consider' type. One of Murray's early policies was to manage the 'peaceful penetration' of areas where the administration had not yet secured a presence, insisting that his officers patrolled regularly. This required of Murray's so-called 'outside men' 'bushmanship, endurance, and a calm confidence to advance peacefully' (Nelson 1986, 3). The policy certainly contrasted with that adopted during British New Guinea times, but it did give rise to a disrespectful catchphrase among some administration officers of the new regime: 'When you're dead you may shoot' (West 1968, 9). Murray also supported a decision to split the former Northern Division into two in 1908–09: the Kumusi Division in the south-east and the adjoining Mambare Division in the north-west (Figures 2.1 and 2.2). This presumably was as an attempt to bring about more effectively his policy of peaceful penetration among the Orokaiva, and despite the additional administration and administrative costs involved.

Figure 2.1. Detail from map of the two territories of New Guinea and Papua

This detail is from a population map that was drafted in 1921 in Melbourne and published in 1923 in the context of the two territories of New Guinea and Papua now being administered jointly by Australia following the Treaty of Versailles in 1919. White signifies inland areas in both territories where there is no population data. Three divisions are mapped for those parts of south-east Papua occupied by the Orokaiva north of the Owen Stanley Range— namely, Mambare, Kumusi and North-Eastern (see also Figure 2.2). Yellow signifies only estimated inland populations, whereas pink refers to an actual count or census in more coastal areas. Kumusi and Mambare together have a total counted population of 15,721, plus an estimated 1,075 for Mambare in the west. The entire map was reprinted and included as a separate insert in a limited commemorative issue of a book on the explorations of Ivan Champion (Sinclair 1988).

From the beginning Murray was also interested in following the results of the newly emerged science of anthropology and in engaging with anthropologists for advice. Anthropology grew out of British imperialism and the need to understand more fully the native peoples one was subjugating, and as part of Western intellectual ambition to discover the origins of, and evolutionary relationships between, different human cultures globally. Leading British anthropologists had been taking an interest in the New Guinea region ever since the Cambridge University expedition to Torres Strait and southern New Guinea in 1898 (Haddon 1901). They continued their interest in the years ahead, not so much in direct fieldwork but in communicating with administration officers and missionaries. Bishop Stone-Wigg was interested in anthropology, as were other Anglicans, such as Reverend A.K. Chignell (1911, 1913) who was based for many years at Wanigela Mission. One general historical conclusion, however, is that 'the Anglicans' appreciation of the Papuans was more romantic than scientific', especially in comparison to the other more pragmatic missions in Papua (Langmore 1989, 112). Administration officers also became much more involved in anthropological work.

Recruits who followed the new employment opportunities offered in the Territory of Papua service included Wilfred N. Beaver and E.W. Pearson Chinnery, each becoming resident magistrates in the adjacent Kumusi and Mambare districts, as well as L.A. Flint and C.T. Wurth, who collaborated with British anthropologists such as A.C. Haddon. They collectively produced reports that form the foundation of a documented Western understanding of the Orokaiva, including notes on Orokaiva magic and myths (ANU 1968; Beaver 1913–14, 1914–15, 1918–19; Chinnery and Beaver 1914–15a, 1914–15b).

Wilfred Beaver wrote the following:

> The Sangara people living round the slopes of Mt Lamington say that the spirits of the dead go to a place called Haugata (one of the peaks on the mountain), where there are many ghosts who live in trees. (Beaver 1913–14, 69)

This is the first known record by a European that the summit area of Mount Lamington was regarded, by the living, as a special place for the dead and, therefore, was of greater significance than just being a mountain. Perhaps it was, by implication, also a place to be avoided. Beaver's record is, in any case, just one example of the respect and reverence that communities worldwide show to lofty mountains close to where they live, and in some cases—such as the Sangara people—to the spirits of the ancestors who live there. The gods of the Ancient Greeks had Mount Olympus and the spirits of the Sangara had Mount Lamington.

The year 1914, when Beaver's words were published, was one of optimism and excitement in Port Moresby (e.g. Davies 1987). Hubert Murray's economic and social developmental work in Papua was being supported by the Australian Government and there was private enterprise investment in the establishment of European-managed plantations and use of native labour. Further, discovery of commercial quantities of oil was expected. A mining company was developing copper deposits in the Astrolabe Range near Port Moresby, and a loan had been received from the Australian Government to establish a light railway from the mine to the port. A reticulated water system had been established in Port Moresby. This, however, was interrupted in 1914 by outbreak of World War I (WWI).

The war led to challenges for the ongoing development of the Territory while the Australian Government focused its efforts and resources on supporting the fighting in distant Europe. Many young Australians, who might otherwise have been recruited to positions and jobs in Papua, went to Europe to support the British Empire's war against the Kaiser and the Germans, and Australians who were working in the Territory of Papua also volunteered for war service. The Australian Government took full advantage of the outbreak of the war and promptly invaded German New Guinea, thus ridding itself of the perceived German threat and, in so doing, acquiring the war-prize asset of a well-run colony, including its extensive plantations (e.g. Lyng 1919; Hiery 1995; Hunt 2017).

A large Australian military force entered Blanche Bay, Rabaul, on 12 September 1914, capturing the radio station at Bitapaka after some resistance, and then claiming the German's well-laid-out and picturesque capital town of Rabaul (e.g. Mackenzie 1987; Stone 1995). However, Australian military personnel occupied Rabaul during what became for them a wartime backwater, militarily speaking. The military administered the whole colony until the Treaty of Versailles of 1919, after which an Australian civil administration took over under a mandate from the League of Nations.

The Australians soon discovered that the colony of German New Guinea and its economy had been run more successfully than had their own in Papua. The German colony had received a greater subsidy from the German Imperial Government, and its exports were greater too, particularly of copra. The Germans had encouraged tropical agriculture rather than mineral extraction; had opened the door to cheap, Asian, skilled labour; and had fixed native labourers' wages at a much lower rate. One Australian commentator summarised the treatment of native labourers in German New Guinea as 'pay them badly; tax them heavily; treat them severely' (Lyng 1919, 235). This, however, was despite the relatively enlightened and strong sense of justice shown by the German governor, Dr Albert Hahl.

Figure 2.2. Map of part of the Territory of Papua

This annotated detail is from an early map of the Territory of Papua that was included by C.A.W. Monckton (1934) in his third and final book published in Britain in 1934. Note the proliferation of names of important British people and historical events used for geographic features, including those of high peaks such as mounts Victoria, Monckton and Lamington. Mount Victoria is shown at 13,500 feet, the highest point on the Owen Stanley Range. The Mambere and Kumusi divisions were known together as the Northern Division on earlier maps. The digital image forming the base of this figure was provided courtesy of the National Library of Australia, Canberra.

There were now two separate Australian administrations of side-by-side territories (Figure 2.1). One capital was Port Moresby, the other Rabaul. Amalgamation of both territories into one administration—and even, indeed, a tripartite amalgamation including the British Solomon Islands—seemed logical, but this was prevented by the conditions of the mandate. It was opposed anyway by other people for other reasons (see, for example, Mair 1948). There were inevitable comparisons to be made, and differences to be stressed, between the two territories, some of them petty, even mutually hostile. This resulted in competitive opinion and debate between the respective white communities and administrative officers in both territories. Papua tended to emerge from these exchanges as the proverbial 'poor relation' in comparison to New Guinea, at least in the eyes of the new, white 'New Guineans', some of whom were not supportive of the more liberal attitude of the white 'Papuans' towards the indigenous local people. There were even different lingua franca in use: Pidgin English or Tok Pisin in New Guinea, and Police Motu in Papua.

Government Geologist in Lamington Country (1911–18)

From the outset Murray looked for ways of developing income and ensuring greater economic self-sufficiency for the new Territory. Development of an agricultural sector was clearly important, and so too were, if possible, discovery and extraction of natural resources such as gold, copper and oil. Engines on ocean-going ships were becoming oil-burners, replacing sail, wood and coal, and the navies of the world were oil-hungry too. The year 1911 was, therefore, a fortunate one for the Territory because hydrocarbon seepages were discovered in the Lower Vailala River area on the Gulf of Papua west of Port Moresby (e.g. Rickwood 1992). This oil discovery eventually triggered considerable interest from petroleum companies who employed investigative geologists to discover the true economic potential of the area.

The Territory of Papua also employed its own geologist, an Australian, 25-year-old Evan R. Stanley, who arrived in Port Moresby in January 1911 (Davies 1987). His principal task was to determine, as far as possible, the geology of Papua as a whole—a formidable task bearing in mind the difficulties of access to its inhospitable mountains and forest-covered basins. Stanley inevitably became involved with the work of the oil company geologists in the west, but he also mapped in the east, notably in 1916 when he undertook a major, and quite remarkable, geological expedition northwards from the coast at Rigo, across the Owen Stanley Range to the headwaters of the Kumusi and Musa rivers (Stanley 1918). They also had to return to Rigo on foot by the same route. The aim was not only to report on occurrences of gold in the headwaters of the rivers, but also on the reported presence of edible earth in the Mamama valley just south-west of Mount Lamington. A major challenge in undertaking such geological mapping was that the quality of the topographic maps was so poor. This meant that Stanley's expedition party had to carry unwieldy topographic surveying equipment into the field so that Stanley could triangulate to peaks and create base maps for his geology.

Stanley reached the Mamama at the south-west foot of Mount Lamington and reported the following:

> Mount Lamington and the Hydrographers are very prominent features on an east and west range above the ninth parallel reaching altitudes of 5,500 feet and 6,280 feet respectively. They are bold and rugged, having been subjected to severe denudation, causing sharp, steep gullies. (Stanley 1918, 76)

Stanley recognised that both Lamington and the Hydrographers together consisted of young volcanic rocks and he assigned a Pleistocene age to them (Figure 2.3). He did not report that Lamington was, in fact, a volcano—whether extinct or potentially active—in its own right and geologically separate from the older Hydrographers Range.

Geologists have since quibbled over why Stanley, who was clearly an outstanding pioneering geologist and insightful report writer, did not reach this conclusion. Perhaps his non-use of the word 'volcano' was simply a reporting oversight. There are, however, good reasons why he was prevented from making a clear identification. First, the southern flanks of the mountain are indeed steep and heavily incised. The south-west directed streams there cut deeply into the flanks of the eroded mountain, delivering sediment into the Mamama, a tributary of the Kumusi, and then northwards around the mountain towards the north coast of Papua. Further, Stanley had no access to aerial photographs, or any views from the air, as the first aircraft to fly in Papua would not do so for several more years. Stanley would almost certainly have used the term 'volcano' had he climbed the mountain from its northern side and identified a north-facing crater and other youthful volcanic features in the summit area, although, from the ground and at a distance from the north, the 'crater' would have appeared just as one of the heads of the stream system of the Ambogo River. However, it remains a cold fact of history that Stanley did not make the volcano identification in his reports, neither in his classic *The Geology of Papua* (1924) nor on its accompanying coloured geological map (Figure 2.3) where he acknowledged the input of oil company geologists A.G. Maitland, J.E. Carne, A. Wade and others. Subsequent Australian geologists working in Papua did not make any correction to that view either—at least up to 1951.

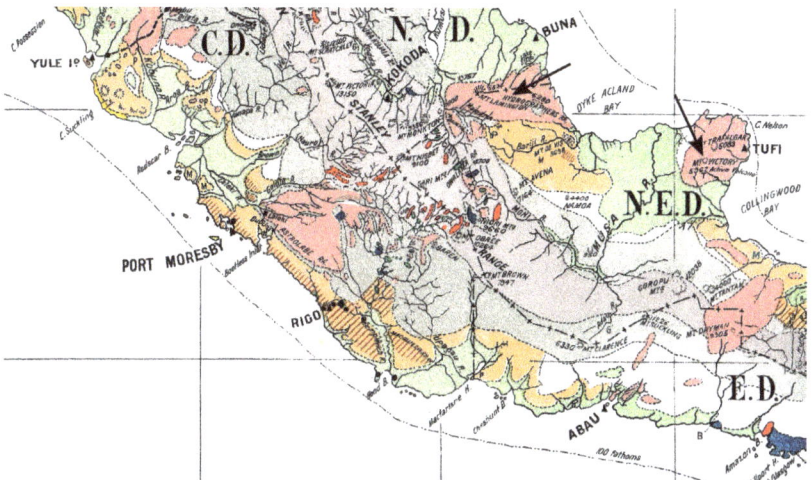

Figure 2.3. Detail from geological map of Papua by Evan R. Stanley
This is part of the geological map of Papua published by Stanley (1924). Young volcanic areas including Mount Lamington and the Hydrographers Range (see left-hand arrow) are shown in pink. Mount Dayman is not a volcano and is an error made earlier by A. Gibb Maitland after viewing the mountain from the north coast. Mount Victory (right-hand arrow) was identified at this time as the only active volcano in Papua. ND stands for the Northern Division, and NED for the North-Eastern Division. Government stations at Kokoda, Buna and Tufi are shown by the filled triangles.

Stagnant Economics (1918–29)

Postwar recovery was stagnant in both Papua and Australia, and there were changes in Territory administration staff as a result of the long and disruptive war in Europe. The Kumusi and Mambare divisions were combined back into a single Northern Division in 1918–19, evidently because of the additional resources and staff needed to run two separate ones in the post-WW1 era (Figure 2.2). There had been a loss of former administration staff in the war, including the experienced Wilfred Beaver (Figure 2.4). The similarly talented E.W.P. Chinnery also served in the war—in Britain as an observer lieutenant in the Flying Corps—and, unlike his former colleague Beaver, he survived it (Fortune 1998). Chinnery undertook anthropological training with Haddon and Rivers at Cambridge University and then filled new positions in the Territory of New Guinea, including that of government anthropologist in 1924—another loss to the Territory of Papua.

Figure 2.4. Photograph of Lieutenant Wilfred Beaver during WWI
Lieutenant Wilfred Beaver, 60th Australian Infantry Battalion, Australian Imperial Force, died of wounds in Belgium, 26 September 1917. Photograph supplied courtesy of the Australian War Memorial (reference number DAOF088).

Evan R. Stanley continued his work as government geologist throughout the war years and shortly afterwards, and in 1921–22 was a key member of the Commonwealth Scientific Expedition to the Territory of New Guinea, where he undertook pioneering observations in the active volcanic arc along the southern margin of the Bismarck Sea (Stanley 1923). Stanley died, however, in Adelaide, Australia, in 1924, aged only 39, from blood poisoning supervening on a facial pimple. His government geologist position was not filled, evidently because of lack of funding related to the postwar global financial downturn. Further, the Australian Government in 1929 (i.e. about the time of the Wall Street Crash and the triggering of the Great Depression of the 1930s) withdrew its interest in development of an oil-extraction industry in Papua (Rickwood 1992). Oil companies, however, continued their commitment to oil prospecting in the Territory, particularly in the west, but an economic pay-off was still many years away.

Agriculture, then, still appeared to be the most immediate economic opportunity in Papua in the years immediately after WWI. Attracting European settlers to Papua was difficult, however, because of postwar labour shortages, low produce prices and high shipping costs (e.g. Crocombe 1964). The emphasis, therefore, was shifted to indigenous cash cropping under the *Native Plantations Ordinance of 1918* and *1925–52*. 'Native plantations' were established by the administration in the Northern Division for the enforced production of coffee, some cocoa, and the ubiquitous coconut. Sixteen coffee plantations were eventually created on the northern and north-western flanks of Mount Lamington in a roughly triangular area between the summit of the mountain in the south, Waseta in the west and a place called Popondetta in the north (Crocombe 1964; Miles 1956). A European controller of native plantations was based at Higaturu and produce collected from the different widespread plantations was required to be carried to Higaturu, Popondetta and Buna for pulping and shipping. The plantation and transporting work was hard for the labourers, the profits minimal and the enforced scheme was not regarded as successful. There was some interest in the district in the leasing and development of larger European-managed plantations of rubber.

White planters joined the European community in Papua that grew after WWI, including the presence of more white women in Port Moresby. Tensions between the different aspirations of the white colonisers—whether government, missions, town business or rural plantation managers—remained, many of the differences of opinion relating in one way or another to the treatment of indigenous Papuans. Some Europeans were still blatant and quite aggressive racists. Others of a more liberal persuasion were content to operate under the 'benign paternalism' banner that still carries the notion of colonial superiority and condescension and Papuans being treated like children—'helping the natives' to develop was all very well but not, say, at the expense of European investment and commercial profits. The Anglican mission had given early and strong support for the development of Papuan priests and pastors on the basis that a god of love and forgiveness does not discriminate on the basis of colour or race. There was, however, 'a gulf fixed between the missionaries who gave a Papuan priest the name "Father", and the planters and townspeople, who gave him the name "boy"' (Wetherell 1977, 302). Some white people would not take confession with black priests.

Racism was both deeply embedded societally and legally institutionalised. Some laws were strongly discriminatory. Hundreds of pages of laws under the heading 'Natives' are listed in Volume 4 of the *Laws of the Territory of Papua 1888–1945* (Papua 1945a). Verbal abuse by a 'native' towards Europeans could result in a jail term, but only being 'whipped with a strap' if the offender was under 14 years of age. Native labourers on plantations could not be absent from their quarters or make noise after 9.00 pm (such as beating on drums and dancing). Papuan men were given a dress code: they must wear a loin cloth; clothes must be clean and dry; shirts could be worn—like white men—but only by Papuans such as mission teachers, medical orderlies and policemen. Thus, shirtless Papuan men were quite common (Papua 1945b).

The *White Women's Protection Ordinance* was passed in January 1926 providing the death penalty for rape or attempted rape upon a European woman or girl. 'It was a piece of legislation discriminatory in its provisions, harsh in its penalties and startlingly out of character with Murray's "native policy"' (Inglis 1974, v). Murray evidently had 'bowed before the strong and concerted pressure of the most influential [European] men in the town [Port Moresby], those who had tried to engineer his dismissal a few years earlier' (Inglis 1974, 147). European residents in Rabaul in the Territory of New Guinea considered adopting similar legislation in 1936, but the 1937 volcanic disaster at Rabaul delayed this and the attempt was abandoned soon after. The ordinance was abandoned altogether only in 1958.

Old racial prejudices remained unchanged in Papua but, at the other extreme, there had been remarkable progress globally in the fields of engineering and technology that would assist Papuan development. Much of this progress was a flow-on from the military competitiveness of WWI. Aircraft usage began in Papua following the first flight of a flimsy seaplane, a Curtis Seagull, over the harbour at Port Moresby in 1922 (e.g. Sinclair 1978). Building Territory-wide road and railway systems was not feasible because of the generally mountainous and isolated terrain, whereas aircraft services could provide much greater travel efficiencies once suitable landing strips in both territories had been constructed. Aircraft usage grew in tandem with the introduction of telegraph and wireless radios for communication that could be used during extended administration patrols. Geologists also could use aircraft overflights of prospective terrains as well as wireless radios during fieldwork, whether on land or during coastal surveys, such as the one undertaken by Stanley (1923) along the southern margin of the Bismarck Sea in 1921–22.

Competitive advantage for the Mandated Territory of New Guinea emerged strongly after abundant alluvial gold was discovered in 1922 in the Wau-Bulolo area in the new Australian administered territory. This discovery was near the southern border with Papua beyond which individual gold miners had struggled to make fortunes on the Yodda and Gira goldfields. Gold extraction in the 1930s on the Morobe Goldfield at Wau-Bulolo was undertaken quite differently to that done previously in Papua. Extraction there involved enhanced dredging technologies, aircraft for haulage and greater financial investment (e.g. Nelson 1976; Sinclair 1978; Waterhouse 2010). Economist Ross Garnaut wrote:

> For a period in the 1930s, New Guinea Goldfields and Bulolo Gold Dredging were amongst the most highly capitalised companies on the Sydney Stock Exchange. The former's initial capital raising in 1929 had been the largest ever on the exchange. Gold increased in value during the Great Depression when the value of almost all other commodities fell … between 1931 and 1938, the mass of airfreight in New Guinea was larger than in any country on earth. (Garnaut 2009, 4)

Papua could not compete with this. Nevertheless, aerodromes or landing strips were built in the Northern Division at the main civilian centres of Kokoda, Yodda, Buna and Ioma. More would follow as the next world war took hold.

Government Anthropologist in Lamington Country (1914–37)

Hubert Murray was fully occupied with the developmental challenges facing Papua during the postwar period, and also had to manage outbreaks of so-called 'cargo cults' in different parts of the Territory. Similar cults appeared elsewhere in Melanesia and, indeed, in many parts of the world where colonialism was changing the nature of traditional societies. A.C. Haddon wrote:

> An awakening of religious activity is a frequent characteristic of periods of social unrest. The weakening or disruption of the older social order may stimulate new and often bizarre ideals, and these may give rise to religious movements that strive to sanction social or political aspirations. (Haddon in Chinnery and Haddon 1917, 455; see also Worsley 1970)

Cults originate mainly where a self-designated leader acquires inspirational messages and instructions from spirits or ancestors living in the supernatural world. His followers or disciples then undertake prescribed rites and rituals in the villages aimed at improving their future way of life in one way or another. These may include the acquisition of material benefits, like the 'cargo' owned by white people that appears magically from the ships and aeroplanes of the Europeans. Some cults contained latent anti-colonial sentiments, or elements of extortion and sorcery, so colonial governments had to keep watch on how they developed. The speed at which the cults first appeared and then spread, possibly through intermediaries, was noted by the Europeans. There is a tendency, however, in some cases, to overemphasise the role of external forces such as colonialism. Some cults may be indigenous and revivalist in that they tried to renew old social orders based on the traditional principles of life (Opeba 1987).

Anthropologists E.W.P. Chinnery and A.C. Haddon in 1917 reported internationally on five 'new religious cults' in Papua, three of which swept through Orokaiva country (Chinnery and Haddon 1917). One of these was the Baigona or Snake Cult that began at the summit of Victory volcano, probably around 1911, and was first reported in 1912 (see also Williams 1928; Worsley 1970; Opeba 1987). A large snake called Baigona took a local prophet called Maine to the summit, cut out his heart and cooked it in a fire. The heartless Maine was initiated into the rights of Baigona and given medicines that would cure all diseases. He was instructed to appoint 'Baigona men' and to spread the knowledge widely. Maine's prophecies and beliefs seemed to have been concerned mainly with agricultural and curative knowledge and was more of a fertility cult than one aimed at acquisition of 'cargo' (Opeba 1987). The killing of snakes was prohibited because this was thought to result in heavy rain and subsequent flooding in rivers near villages. The cult was stopped by authorities in 1914.

The other two cults in Orokaiva country were Kava-Keva and Kekesi, which broke out on, and spread out from, the coastal area between the Gira River and Buna (Chinnery and Haddon 1917; Worsley 1970; Opeba 1987). These cults evolved from the same social situation and both were considered to have derived from the powerful spirit of the garden crop, taro. Both were characterised by special taboos on the killing and eating of particular foods. They were together called the 'Taro Cult' and its principal proponents were 'Taro men' (Figure 2.5). The cult or cults ran throughout much of Orokaiva country including the Mount Victory area where the Baigona Cult had begun a few years earlier, and at more or less the same time starting in about 1919 only a few years after the end of the Baigona Cult. Kava-Keva means 'giddy, mad' referring to the characteristic shaking fits and head-jerking paroxysms known as 'jipari' (Chinnery and Haddon 1917; Worsley 1970). Emergence of the cults may have been influenced to some extent by the new cash crop gardening requirements imposed by the administration through the *Native Plantations Ordinance*.

Whether the Baigona Cult originating at the summit of Mount Victory was, in some way, a response to the large explosive volcanic eruption in the late nineteenth century is unknown. Intriguingly, there were unconfirmed reports by Europeans that volcanic activity continued at Mount Victory into the twentieth century and even that beacon-like summit 'glows' had assisted navigators up to the 1930s (Smith 1981). Anthropologists who reported on the Baigona Cult, however, make no connection between any coeval relationship between the origins of the cult and the deadly explosive eruption at Victory volcano.

Figure 2.5. Photograph of three 'Taro men' at Sangara

F.E. Williams gave the following description of this photograph: 'Three Sangara men. Man in centre wears hornbill beaks (percuo) and gana on breasts. Note streamers of cuscus fur. They are three Taro men on a visit. Man in the centre was apparently not quite himself, acting as if drunk' (Williams 2001, 92). This image was kindly provided by Jan Hasselberg who copied it from a print in the collection of Williams' photographs held by the National Archives of Papua New Guinea, Port Moresby. The photograph is published here courtesy of the Archives.

Hubert Murray responded to the ongoing need for bridging the wide gap of misunderstanding between the European colonisers on the one hand and the Papuans on the other, by creating positions for government anthropologists in his administration. An Australian, Francis Edgar Williams, was appointed to the position of assistant government anthropologist in 1922. Williams' work was needed primarily to serve the interests of the administration rather than to undertake the kind of independent anthropological research accomplished in universities, but he became acknowledged as one of the most talented anthropologists of his generation (e.g. Schwimmer 1976; Young and Clark 2001; Farquharson 2002). Williams and Murray worked well together, as both men shared a humane concern for improving the quality of life of Papuans. Williams, however, believed that traditional clan leaders and chiefs should be used by the administration wherever possible and should be appointed as village councillors rather than converted Papuan Christians, such as mission teachers and pastors, who were not sanctioned by the local people. Conversely, Murray preferred that the administration did not interfere with traditional life because of the risk of destroying it, even though the missionised Papuans might well have done so anyway. Murray was not a supporter of the 'Indirect Rule' policy used in other British colonies such as in Africa.

Francis Williams undertook 14 months of fieldwork in two periods in the Northern Division in 1923–25, which included an assessment of the Taro Cult. He had previously investigated the worrisome 'Vailala Madness' Cult in the Gulf region of western Papua (e.g. Williams 1976), but the Taro Cult in comparison seemed benign. Williams wrote two books on the Orokaiva, both published in London (Williams 1928, 1930), and his outstanding and numerous photographs were displayed after his death in 1943 in an exhibition in Australia and in an accompanying book published in 2001 (Williams 2001). Williams confirmed what earlier anthropologists had observed: that the Orokaiva were 'a more than usually quarrelsome and disunited group of people … [engaging in] tribal feuds, dispersals, and migrations … in a veritable whirlpool of strife, migration, and counter-migration' (Williams 1930, 2, 8). They were hostile and resistant towards Europeans.

In 1923–25, Williams attempted to identify and map the cultural diversity of the people who collectively had been called 'Orokaiva' by the British. He stressed the considerable difficulties and uncertainties in doing so, yet boldly and pragmatically produced his now well-known 'rough and ready' map of the different tribal groups (Figure 2.6). Some of these so-called 'tribes' on the map are separated from each other by straight lines—like the suburbs of a Western city—rather than being mapped as large clusters or concentrations of hamlets separated by poorly populated areas. The Sangara people, for example, are mapped in a trapezoidal area well to the north-east of the summit of Mount Lamington, whereas in fact they live more directly to the north and north-west of it. The so-called 'Wasida' people are not easy to define as a cultural unit and, therefore, mapping their distribution is even more difficult.

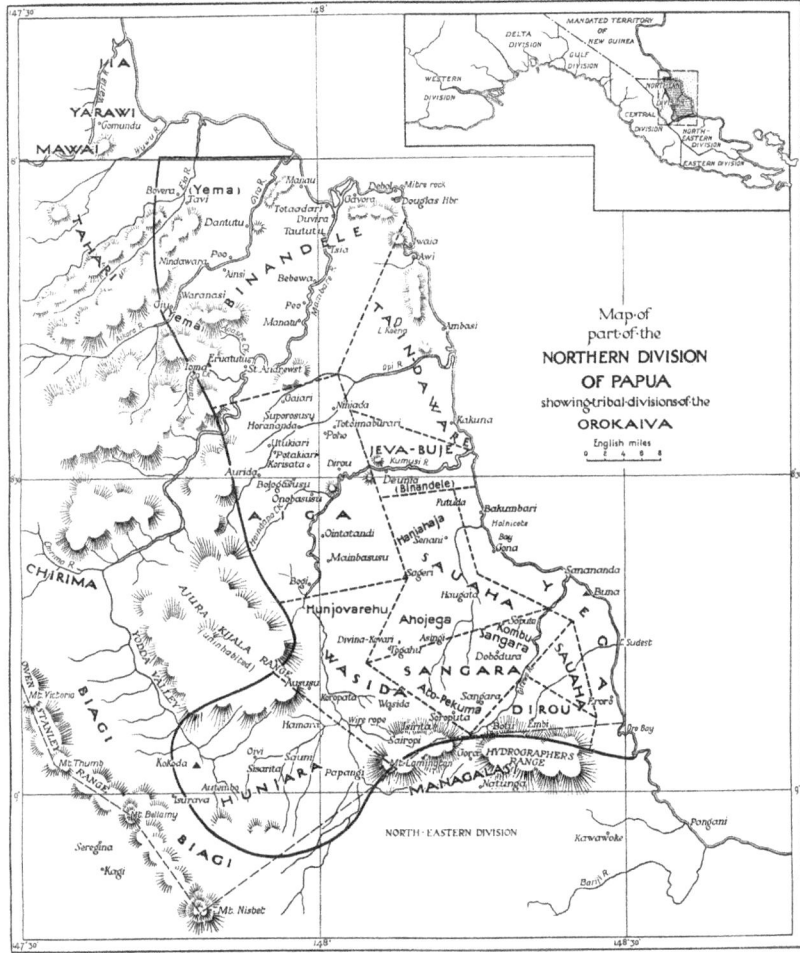

Figure 2.6. Map of Orokaiva 'tribes' by F.E. Williams

This is Williams' map of 'tribes' in the Northern Division (Williams 1930, unpaginated foldout at the end of the book). Note that Binandere-speakers (Orokaiva) also live in the coastal area of the adjoining North-Eastern Division. Anthropologists much later suggested that the 'Wasida' people, unlike the Sangara, were not sufficiently well defined to justify being identified as a separate 'tribe'. Anthropologists also stressed even further the problems of identifying cultural groups in this area (e.g. Rimoldi 1966; Schwimmer 1969).

A correct feature of Williams' map is the southern boundary of Orokaiva country, which runs through the summit of Mount Lamington, separating the Binandere-speaking Orokaiva tribes to the north from the Koiarian-speaking people to the south, who are labelled 'Managalas' on the map. This boundary was confirmed by later, more detailed mapping of Papuan languages (e.g. Wurm, Voorhoev and McElhanon 1975; Pawley 2005). About 15 different languages are now believed to comprise a 'Binanderean' group whose speakers occupy the long strip of coast running north-westwards from Cape Nelson into the Morobe area of former German New Guinea (Pawley and Hammarström 2018).

'Mountain Orokaiva' is a name that has been applied collectively to the populations, or 'socio-political units', that live mainly on the northern and north-western flanks of Mount Lamington (e.g. Rimoldi 1966, 3–4). It derives from usage by the Orokaiva themselves who distinguished 'inland people' (*periho*) from both 'river people' (*umo-ke*) and 'salt-water' or 'coastal people' (*eva'embo*). The mountain or inland Orokaiva lived in numerous hamlet-sized communities based largely on clan affiliations, rather than in larger villages. They were swidden agriculturalists, using fire and digging sticks for the breaking of new forest land and in the long-term rotation of previously occupied land (e.g. Keesing 1952).

Williams was impressed with the northern area of mountainous Lamington, writing that:

> This piedmont area, formed by the northern slopes of Lamington and the Hydrographers, is closely populated and, in comparison with others, closely cultivated; and here the innumerable garden clearings, relieving the close monotony of the bush, make it possible to take in the beauty of the surroundings. With its comparatively bracing climate and the charm and opulence of its scenery, this region may be counted among the most fortunate of Papua. (Williams 1930, 12)

There can be little surprise, therefore, that this beguiling place was later chosen by Europeans for both an Anglican mission station and as a centre for provincial administration of the Northern Division.

Roars from Lamington (1922–40)

Stations for the administration and the Anglican mission had been established along the central Orokaiva coast by the beginning of WWI in 1914 (Langmore 1989). The main administration station was at Buna from where government foot patrols departed for the interior, and the Anglican mission itself developed coastal stations at Ambasi, Gona and

Eroro. One of the early Anglican missionaries and craftsmen to work in the Anglican diocese was the down-to-earth and pragmatic Englishman, S. Romney M. Gill. He served with the mission from 1908 to 1954, thus overlapping with the year of the Mount Lamington eruption of 1951 (Wetherell 1977; Garland 2000).

Gona became the most important of the places for coastal missionisation, as well as acting as the starting point for inland incursions to the populous and fertile areas in the Sangara district on the northern and western slopes of Mount Lamington. Mission work in the Sangara district was begun in 1922 by a layman, Henry Holland, and by a Papuan schoolteacher, Andrew Uware (Tomlin 1951; Tomkins and Hughes 1969; Wetherell 1977). This originally involved taking in supplies and equipment to Sangara by foot track using carriers, but Holland eventually built a trafficable road through the swamps south of Gona and then up the ridges to Sangara where mission buildings were constructed. All of this work, together with a strengthening of the Gona Mission Station, was supported from the beginning by Henry Newton, who, also in 1922, had been consecrated the third bishop of New Guinea (1922–36).

Holland next—and after the work at Sangara had been firmly established—began a mission station at Isivita on the north-western side of Mount Lamington. This new venture involved two-hour treks each way between Sangara and Isivita along a twisting track over forested ridges and gullies. The Isivita Mission was dedicated to St Michael and All Angels. Holland moved there in 1928 leaving nurse Margery Brenchley and teacher Miss Lilla Lashmar in charge of the work at Sangara (Figure 2.7). The work of these three missionaries continued in this difficult area until the outbreak of World War II (WWII). The resident magistrate in Buna at one stage was concerned about the safety of the two women at Sangara because there had been so much inter-clan fighting in the surrounding villages, and suggested that a policeman be stationed at Sangara for a time. Bishop Newton, however, responded that the two women were quite capable of looking after themselves. Further, Sister Brenchley was reported as saying that her 'only concern was the number of broken heads that she had to mend' (Tomlin 1951, 132).

Figure 2.7. Photographs of Sangara missionaries, L. Lashmar (left) and M. Brenchley (right)

These photographs are taken from the plate opposite page 7 in the book by Tomkins and Hughes (1969). They are reproduced here courtesy of the Anglican Board of Mission, Australia.

Brenchley, Holland and Lashmar were adventurous spirits. In 1935, they organised an ascent of Mount Lamington whose peaks rose up behind them in challenging and tempting fashion in the view south from Sangara. Lashmar wrote about the ascent in a letter dated 19 May 1935 that was published by the Australian Board of Mission in Australia (Lashmar 1935). The trip took about a week and they were accompanied by a group of local men who carried their camping equipment and provisions. Lashmar recorded hearing 'roars' at the summit of the mountain. The Reverend J.W.S. Tomlin wrote the following version of the ascent, and of the 'roars', including quotations from original writings by Sister Brenchley:

> Mr [Henry] Holland, the Head of the Sangara staff, and the two ladies, Miss [Lilla] Lashmar and Miss [Margery] Brenchley, 'had often gazed at the blue peaks rearing their heads above the clouds to the south of Sangara, and longed to climb them. Mt Lamington had not been climbed to our knowledge, and the natives warned us it was not safe to attempt as the ground was soft, the earth shook, and a roaring noise could be heard at the top. We asked if the natives ever went up there, and they said "Oh, no! It is the home of the departed spirits!" However, just after Easter, the weather being fine and the two stations quiet, we determined to make an attempt. Mt Lamington is nearly 9,000 feet [sic] high, and the expedition, including five boys as carriers, took nearly a week … the view [during the climb] was magnificent … the Ambogo River

> rushed and tumbled its way over the boulders through the deep ravine.' As they neared the top, the ground, as predicted, became very spongy and walking was difficult. There was also a great roar at the summit, the roar of a mighty waterfall in the chasm below, but the boys began to talk together in whispers. 'Sister, listen,' said one, 'That big noise not river'. Yes, the fear of the spirits was still very real to him. (Tomlin 1951, 132–33)

These words are of interest for several reasons. First, there is no specific mention of the 'roar' being of volcanic origin, or of the mountain being a volcano. Tomlin's book was 'in press' in 1950. He added a short footnote on page 133 at proof stage noting that: 'This was written before the great eruption of Mount Lamington'. Tomlin also speculated that: 'The natives … may have inherited their fear from some remote eruption, but no-one dreamt that it would ever burst out again with such violence' (Tomlin 1951, 218). What was the origin of the roar? Had there been any reporting of the roars at any time to administration officers who then passed the information to any trained geologists or seismologists for their opinion?

This last question is of particular relevance because, surprisingly, in 1939 a geologist in the Dutch Indies published a scientific paper in the international literature on the geological structure of New Guinea island, stating that both Lamington and Victory were 'active volcanoes' (van Bemmelen 1939, 23). The source of this information, however, is unknown and there are no credible reasons to infer that it must have derived from the missionaries' climb of Mount Lamington. The year 1939 was, in any case, a diversionary and pivotal one internationally. Another world war broke out in Europe following the rise of Nazism in Germany, and the Japanese had already, in 1937, initiated the Pacific War when they invaded China and began progressively working their way southwards through South-East Asia towards New Guinea and Australia.

Philip Nigel Warrington Strong had been consecrated the fourth bishop of New Guinea in 1936. His bishopric in the years ahead covered two particularly tragic events that would have a destructive impact on the missions on and near Mount Lamington (Strong 1981). However, there were still celebratory times for the Anglican mission, as they had achieved much in the years since WWI, despite significant challenges including resource difficulties. New mission stations had been created, numerous Papuans had been baptised into the faith, Papuan teachers and pastors had been trained, and ordination of the first Papuan priest, Peter Rautamara, had taken place in December 1917. In 1938, Bishop Strong ordained Holland as a priest to the mission after a special course of instruction because of his great contribution to the mission's work in the Sangara district. Then, in 1939, there were celebrations when a new Cathedral of St Peter and St Paul was consecrated at Dogura where the power of the Church and the imagery and doctrine of the Anglo-Catholic eucharist and other ceremonies could be demonstrated to the full. Meanwhile, more pressing non-religious concerns were being faced in Rabaul to the north in the Mandated Territory.

The Australian invasion of German New Guinea in 1914 had removed a military threat, but Australia inherited a volcanic problem in its place. Blanche Bay is a complex caldera system that contains active volcanoes, most notably Tavurvur and Vulcan, which had been in near-simultaneous eruption in 1878—that is, well before the Germans built and occupied the town of Rabaul at the northern end of Blanche Bay in 1910. Tavurvur and Vulcan were again in twin eruption in 1937, causing more than 500 deaths and covering much of the town and surrounding areas in volcanic ash (Fisher 1939a; Johnson and Threlfall 1985). Rabaul town was evacuated temporarily, and the eruption led to the creation of the Rabaul Volcanological Observatory. A judge and a geologist, respectively, played key roles in the evacuation and in the building of the observatory. Each of these men in different but important ways would later apply their firsthand volcanic experience at Rabaul in the Northern Division of Papua.

Judge F. Beaumont 'Monte' Phillips had to assume the role of acting administrator of the Territory of New Guinea in Rabaul on the evening of Saturday 29 May 1937, because the administrator, Brigadier-General W.R. McNicoll, was on a tour of inspection of the Morobe Goldfield and the appointed acting administrator was ill. Judge Phillips witnessed the twin eruptions and their effects and became responsible for informing the Prime Minister's Department in Canberra of the volcanic disaster. He also organised the evacuation of the town including the dispatch of a radio message to the captain of a passenger vessel, the *Montoro*, requesting a return to Rabaul for evacuation of hundreds of town residents. Phillips was appointed CBE for this work (e.g. Quinlivan 1988).

Norman Henry Fisher was a government geologist at Wau in the Morobe Goldfields at the time of the Rabaul eruption; later, in 1937, he became involved with post-eruption volcanological investigations in Rabaul led by Dr C.E. Stehn, director of the Netherlands Indies Volcanological Survey. The recommendation to build a volcanological observatory for eruption early warning purposes was included in a report on the future of Rabaul (Stehn and Woolnough 1937). In 1939, Fisher travelled to Java and received further volcanological training from Dr Stehn. He then became the resident volcanologist at Rabaul and supervised the construction and instrumental equipping of the observatory, which began operations in 1940 (Fisher 1940). Fisher published on the active volcanoes of the Territory of New Guinea but not at this time on those of Papua (Fisher 1939a, 1939b).

These were also the last years of Hubert Murray's long rule as administrator of the Territory of Papua. His health deteriorated and he died of lymphatic leukaemia at Samarai on 27 February 1940 (*Papuan Courier* 1940; West 1968). Many tributes were paid to Murray on his death, Judge H.G. Nicholas, for example, stating admiringly that:

> Murray made Papua a shining illustration of the British doctrine of trusteeship and set a standard in the treatment of native races which has been acknowledged to be the highest throughout the British Colonial Service and by Commissions of the League of Nations. (Nicholas 1940, 5)

Others commented on the effects of the long duration of Murray's administration during which he had had to cope with several phases of development and change, noting, perhaps, that he may have focused too much in later life on the policies he had established earlier in his career (West 1968, 275). Certainly, there had been difficult times for Murray given that he had had to manage the economic fallout of two world wars and an intervening global depression. Further, support from the Australian Government for Papuan development was not as great as it might have been in a more ideal world. There is, therefore, some justification for the historical conclusion that Australia's work in Papua up to the time of Murray's death—and indeed for some years after WWII—represented 'Colonialism on a Shoestring' (Bashkow 2006, 2).

3
WORLD WAR AND AUSTRALIAN RECOVERY

Pacific War and a Retreating Australia (1941–42)

Japanese military expansion in the Pacific reached a pivotal point on 7 December 1941 when aircraft attacked and bombed Pearl Harbour, Hawaii, triggering the entry of the United States into the Pacific War. The strong momentum of the Japanese advance southwards through East Asia continued, and the Japanese captured the Australian-held town of Rabaul, Territory of New Guinea, on 23 January 1942 (Wigmore 1957). Rabaul would be the stepping-off point for Japanese advances even further south, including overland towards Port Moresby (McCarthy 1959). The Australian Government and the Administration of the Territory of Papua therefore made preparations for further attacks. Australian civilian administration ceased in February 1942 in many parts of the Northern and North-Eastern divisions of Papua, leaving the Orokaiva to cope with the subsequent invasion of yet another dominating foreign power. The Australian war in the two territories would now be run from military headquarters in Port Moresby.

The Australian Military Intelligence Section soon began releasing 'terrain studies' of the South-West Pacific area. One of these geographic intelligence reports was for the northern coast and plains of the Northern Division of Papua. It contains the following bald descriptions of the still isolated and underdeveloped missions at Sangara and Isivita on the slopes of Mount Lamington (AGS 1942a, appendix G, gazetteer, 6, 10):

> Sangara Mission. Consists of a group of houses, one European house with iron roof. All other houses, including church, of native material. Approx. 10 houses.
>
> Isivita. 12 houses. Pop. 120 approx. Village and Mission Station. V.C. [village constable] and Cllr. [councillor] speak very little English.

Plantations listed in the terrain study included Sangara Rubber Estates, which was also called Mason's, consisting of 300–400 acres of cleared ground planted with young rubber trees up to three years old, as well as government coffee plantations that were scattered throughout the Sangara district, 100 acres in all (AGS 1942a, appendix G). The coffee shrubs were about 'man high'—that is, soldier high. There were also numerous, small, village-owned plantations, of both coconut and rubber, and each mostly less than an acre in extent. Four plantations in the vicinity of Sangara and Higatura are plotted in one of the accompanying maps (AGS 1942b). There is no mention of Mount Lamington being a volcano.

Missionaries were still stationed at Isivita and Sangara, and at Gona and Eroro on the coast. Bishop Strong on Saturday 31 January 1942 said in a radio message to mission staff:

> As far as I know, you are all at your posts and I am very glad and thankful about this. I have from the first felt that we must endeavour to carry on our work in all circumstances no matter what the cost may ultimately be to any of us individually. God expects this of us … The Universal Church expects it. (Tomkins and Hughes 1969, 27)

Advances and Betrayals (1942–43)

The Japanese Army landed from naval troop carriers at Sanananda between Gona and Buna on the north coast of Papua on the night of 21–22 July 1942 (e.g. McCarthy 1959). They soon occupied nearby parts of the Northern Division that had been abandoned by the Australian civil administration in February, capturing any Europeans who were unfortunate enough to have stayed behind. Orokaiva villagers now had to choose which side 'they felt offered the best opportunity for themselves and their families, keeping their own livelihoods safe while also serving the interests of their colonial masters' (Grant 2014, 114)—that is, whether the newly arrived masters were the Japanese or the recently departed Australians.

European missionaries escaped into the bush from their missions at Sangara and Isivita but, together with others from Gona, were eventually handed over to the Japanese by some Orokaiva people (Tomlin 1951; Tomkins and Hughes 1969; Grahamslaw 1971b). Seven of the missionaries, with others, were executed at Buna. These included Reverend Henry Holland as well as Miss Lashmar and Nurse Brenchley who had written about their ascent of, and hearing the 'roars' from, Mount Lamington in 1935. They were beheaded by sword. Their remains were never found and were presumed to have been thrown into the waters of Dyke Acland Bay. Betrayal by the Orokaiva and execution of innocent civilians by the Japanese are key elements of the story that emerged subsequently, but so too was an opinion reached much later that the two executed mission priests—Reverend Holland and Reverend Vivian Redlich—had been murdered by the Orokaiva rather than by the Japanese (Hand 2002). Further, a young Papuan teacher and evangelist in training with the mission, Lucian Tapiedi, who was not Orokaiva, had been killed by an axe that was said to have been wielded not by a Japanese soldier but by an Orokaiva.

Japanese soldiers in their thousands soon swept westwards along the Yodda Road north of Mount Lamington, and then began their southwards land advance towards Port Moresby, along the tortuous footpath and deeply ravined terrain of the Kokoda Track. They were eventually repulsed by Allied forces, under the overall command of US General Douglas Macarthur, in fighting that has been made legendary through numerous military histories (e.g. Milner 1957; McCarthy 1959; Mayo 1974; Hall 1981; Paul 1989; Gailey 2000; Ham 2004; Fitzsimons 2004; Grant 2014). The Japanese were forced back along the Kododa Track and the Yodda Road to the north coast of New Guinea island. They became entrenched at Buna, Sanananda and Gona in a strong, well-designed complex of mutually supporting defensive positions and concealed by dense tropical vegetation, but were eventually defeated in January 1943 after attacks on different fronts (Figure 3.1). These attacks involved exceptionally bloody battles. The attacks also involved the creation of new jeep tracks and trails that extended the network of land links to the original Yodda Road north and east of Mount Lamington, which survived in the years immediately after the war. The Japanese in Papua as a whole inflicted more than 8,500 casualties on the Australian and American troops between July 1942 and January 1943, and themselves lost about 13,000 (McCarthy 1959). Lamington seems to have remained volcanically silent as a backdrop to this devastating warfare.

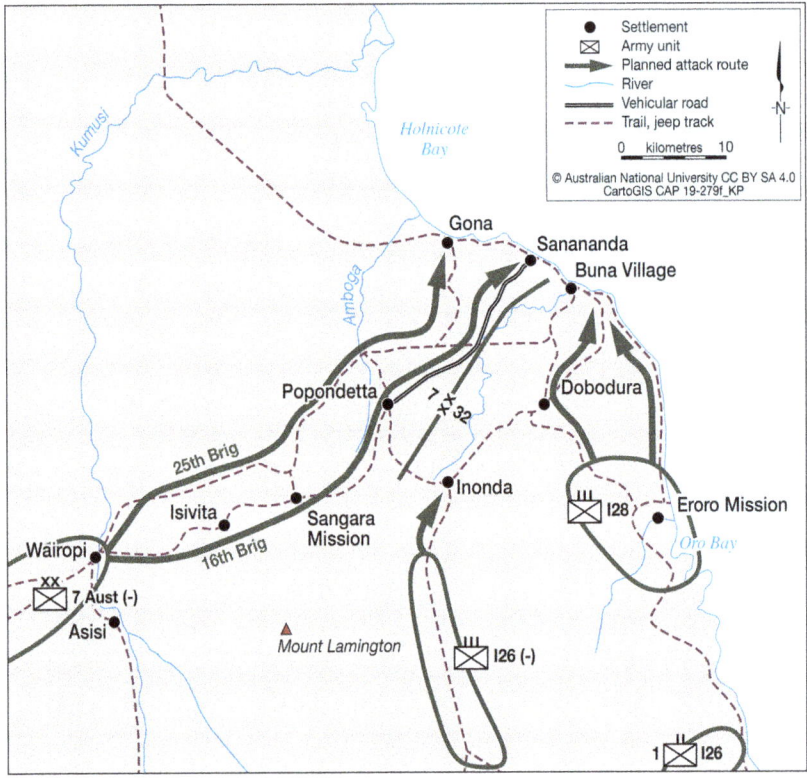

Figure 3.1. Paths of attack during the Buna–Gona campaign
This map of Allied troop movements north of Mount Lamington during World War II is adapted from the one published by Milner (1957, map 7, 127).

There was war in the air too, the presence of bombers and fighter aircraft necessarily involving construction of new airstrips in the Northern Division, built first by the Japanese and then in particular by the occupying Allies. One of these airstrips was constructed in mid-November 1943 at Popondetta by the American 2/6th Field Company using numerous Papuan labourers who cut a swathe through the kunai grass (McCarthy 1959). The airstrip was built quickly at the south-western end of a vehicular road that ran through to the coast (Figure 3.1). It permitted the aircraft landing of soldiers, field guns, jeeps and ammunition that were put to immediate use against the Japanese at the coast.

The Papuans of the Northern Division witnessed the mechanisation and destructive violence of the military conflicts between the invading foreigners. Many Orokaiva endured the consequences of war, including the military thefts of food from their subsistence gardens and enforced conscription. Some escaped into the bush where they suffered malnutrition and death (e.g. Waddell and Krinks 1968). Others served the Australians loyally, including those men who became members of the Papuan Infantry Battalion. Villagers also rescued Allied airmen shot down by the Japanese and helped return them to their operational bases.

Men from the villages were conscripted by both the Japanese and the Allies to serve as carriers, guides and labourers, and many were poorly treated. Some were stretcher bearers for injured soldiers or escorts for them (Figure 3.2). Many displayed considerable endurance and solicitude towards wounded Australians whom they carried to safety (e.g. Kokoda Initiative 2015). The grateful Australians gave them the well-meaning, and now legendary, sobriquet of 'Fuzzy Wuzzy Angels', which nevertheless still hints at the racial condescension that was part of even the best of wartime relations where they existed. Importantly, too, the war effort would result in a substantial increase in awareness in Australia of Papua and Papuans, not least recognition that the Allies may not have defeated the Japanese had it not been for the essential work undertaken by the 'Fuzzy Wuzzy Angels' even where they were under compulsion to do so (e.g. Grant 2014).

One piece of evidence that the Allies required the service and support of the Orokaiva, in particular, is seen in the following racist quotation warning Australian soldiers of the difficulties in crossing the swamp basins of the Northern Division: 'It is probable that the local natives know and use a number of tracks across it, and where natives can lead, men on foot can follow' (AGS 1942a, appendix F, 5)—a slip of the pen, perhaps, in which 'men' should have been written as 'soldiers'. Racism and the need to exert white supremacy were rife, and young white Australian soldiers who came to Papua for the first time had to be reminded of their racial superiority, of the control structure that existed before the war and of the need to continue that colonial domination. Anthropologist F.E. Williams in 1942 wrote an instruction manual for the new soldiers entitled *You and the Native*, encouraging such an attitude of racial superiority (see, for example, Grant 2014). These prewar mores of white colonial society were strange to the newly arrived young soldiers who, in any case, made their own minds up about such views, particularly if they experienced firsthand the compassion of the 'Fuzzy Wuzzies' as stretcher bearers.

The Australian Army's Australian New Guinea Administrative Unit (ANGAU) played a central role in the Allied war effort in the territories of both Papua and New Guinea (e.g. Mair 1948; Grahamslaw 1971a, 1971b, 1971c; Downs 1980; Grant 2014). ANGAU officers were mainly prewar government men such as resident magistrates, district officers, patrol officers and other officials—F.E. Williams, for example, became an ANGAU officer. There were, according to one ex-ANGAU officer:

> Delicate problems of seniority and of difference of philosophy between former Papuan and former Mandated Territory officials … the petty animosities of small closed communities survived and smouldered in war as in peace. (Ryan 1973, 315–16; see also Ryan 1968)

Further, ANGAU officers had no, or very little, expertise in specialist fields such as agriculture and education—nor in anthropology, following the death of government anthropologist F.E. Williams in an aircraft crash in 1943. One of ANGAU's primary roles in 1942 during the Papuan campaigns was to recruit from Orokaiva the males required as carriers, stretcher bearers, labourers and guides. This was undertaken aggressively at times, on occasions leaving villages bereft of men. ANGAU's most important role in 1943 was the reinstatement of Australian authority, civil administration and local development in areas no longer occupied by the Japanese. Duties at this time also included the arrest of those Papuans who had abandoned their allegiance to the Australians and who were accused of betraying or murdering Europeans during the Japanese occupation.

In December 1942, ANGAU Officer Captain Thomas Grahamslaw was instructed by headquarters to resume duty as a civilian district officer in the Lamington area of the Mambare District, which by then had been deserted by the Japanese (see, for example, Fitzsimons 2004; Grahamslaw 1971c). His suggestion that Higaturu—just south of where the Sangara Mission had operated before the war—would be a suitable place for the temporary district headquarters was accepted by those in authority in Port Moresby. New administration offices at Higaturu were constructed. ANGAU staff also restored the Sangara coffee plantation and machinery that had been damaged by the Japanese (Mair 1948). The Higaturu headquarters soon became permanent, thus representing a shift from the former government administrative centre at Buna and its steamy coastal climate, to the more pleasant air of the cooler mountains. Higaturu and Sangara, however, are only about 10–11 kilometres from the summit area of Mount Lamington.

Figure 3.2. George Silk photograph of Raphael Oimbari and Private Whittington
Wartime official photographer George Silk took what has become a famous photograph—reproduced in many war histories—of a young Orokaiva man escorting a wounded Australian soldier, Private G.C. Whittington, near kunai at the Old Strip, Buna, on Christmas Day 1942. Raphael Oimbari, the Orokaiva escort, was not identified and named from the photograph until the 1970s (Grant 2014). Whittington later died of his wounds. Photograph supplied courtesy of the Australian War Memorial (reference number AWM14028).

Chief Justice of Queensland Sir William Webb was appointed in 1943 to lead a Commission of Enquiry into wartime atrocities that affected Australians (e.g. Redlich 2012). The enquiry, which took place after the Japanese defeat at Buna in January 1943 but before resumption of full civil authority in the Lamington district, determined the cases of eight of those murdered by the Japanese in the Sangara–Popondetta area, including four female missionaries. The killings were determined to be 'atrocities' and to have been undertaken, in the case of the women and a child, with 'fiendish brutality' (quoted in Redlich 2012, appendix 5, 146).

The trials of Papuans who were accused betrayers and Japanese sympathisers were held at Higaturu. ANGAU Officer Captain W.R. 'Dickie' Humphries, a former resident magistrate, conducted the proceedings, or at least most of them (e.g. Palmer 1992; see also *Pacific Islands Monthly* 1951a). The subsequent public hangings of five Papuans from tree branches, followed by 17 more, also took place in the Higaturu area (Grahamslaw 1971c; Nelson 1978; Newton 1985; Bashkow 2006; Grant 2014; Stead 2018). Gallows were specially constructed for the 17 condemned men who were hung two at a time from early in the morning until late in the afternoon in front of thousands of local people. Those hung were civilians and should have been judged by Australian civil law and not by the military, but the army at the time appears to have had a strong desire to re-establish and exert Australian authority. The retributive hangings ensured the maximum controlling impact possible, even though the Australian Cabinet in Canberra evidently did not become aware of them, and of other hangings, until well after the events took place.

American forces in their thousands were stationed at this time in the Oro Bay and Dobodura area, although they were dissuaded from attending the hangings (Grahamslaw 1971c). A major military port was developed by the Americans at Oro Bay as a forward Allied base and an inland road system sprang up for the machinery and materials needed for construction of the airfields at the great Dobodura air base (McCarthy 1959). Buna was later developed by the Australians as a military port for build-up of the supplies needed for Allied attacks on the Huon Peninsula to the north, which was made possible by aircraft flying out of Dobodura and by heavy bombers flying from Port Moresby.

Both American and Australian troops in the Northern Division could be generous towards the Orokaiva, sharing cigarettes and gifting them tobacco, food, clothing, tools and so forth (Figure 3.3). The Americans, in particular, ate and fraternised with the Orokaiva locals who concluded that some of the Americans must be 'returned ancestors' (e.g. Schwimmer 1969). Some of the US soldiers deployed to the New Guinea theatre of war were 'coloured' African-Americans who, although they experienced racial antipathy during their military service (e.g. Hall 1995; Bashkow 2006), were seen by the Orokaiva and others as wearing the same clothing, eating the same food, occupying the same housing and working in tandem with their white-skinned compatriots.

Figure 3.3. 'Fuzzy Wuzzy Angels' and American sailors sharing cigarettes

American sailors share cigarettes with Papuan carriers in this WWII photograph reproduced from an article by Porter (1951c, 7) in which it was attributed to the 'Wide World'.

The Orokaiva witnessed the vast resources that the foreign troops deployed and controlled, and saw technical achievements being displayed on a colossal scale. They were being presented, probably for the first time, with good reasons for looking at the outside world, and those who governed them, in a new light. Indeed, the few years of the 1942–45 foreign war may have had a more enduring impact on them, and their landscape, than the much longer period of prewar colonial administration by the British and the Australians (e.g. Moss 2017). Old Orokaiva ways, or *iji matu*, were disappearing and a 'new day' or *iji eha* would develop and be influenced within a few years not only by a strong postwar expansion of Australian interest in Papua as a whole (e.g. Legge 1956), but also by the impact on the Orokaiva of the eruption at Lamington volcano (e.g. Schwimmer 1969, 62, 70). Meanwhile, a quite different volcanic eruption well to the south-east of Lamington was receiving some attention at the end of 1943.

Goropu Eruption and New Geological Mapping (1943–44)

An ANGAU unit including Lieutenant David Marsh was active in north-eastern Papua in 1943 and was based at Tufi at the northern end of the Cape Nelson peninsula. Its members patrolled the coastline of Collingwood Bay, including the Wanigela area to the south where the Reverend Dennis Taylor was based at the Anglican mission. Taylor had joined the mission at Dogura in 1937 but soon transferred to Wanigela where he stayed throughout the war. In 1942, his wife and child, and other European women, were led by him to safety on foot southwards over the arduous Owen Stanley Mountains, but Taylor immediately returned to the Wanigela area, near Mount Victory, where he resumed his mission duties (Tomkins and Hughes 1969).

An unexpected volcanic eruption surprised people living on the Cape Nelson peninsula when four columns of 'smoke' and ash were seen by coastal villagers in October 1943 in the hills south of Victory volcano, as well as other unexpected clouds in November (NAA 1943–45; Marsh 1944; Baker 1946; see also Johnson 2013, for a general review of the eruption). Earthquakes had been felt in the Tufi area during the previous two years. The 'smoke' in the hills south of Tufi was from new volcanic vents in a gently sloping area known locally as Waiowa at the northern foot of the Goropu Mountains in the Owen Stanley Range alongside a major geological fault, where eruptions had never been reported previously and where no volcano was known to exist (see Figure 0.2).

A much larger eruption took place on 27 December 1943, producing a 5,000-metre-high cloud of volcanic ash that caused great concern at Wanigela on the coast to the north-north-east. Reverend Taylor reported that:

> People were screaming and running in all directions and kids and babies were crying and wailing, [and] the place was in a panic … It was a most awe inspiring sight to see this great mass of smoke, a greyish orange and purple colour just billowing overhead [sic] and sort of rolling over itself and accompanied by the sound of the roar of hundreds of mighty furnaces. No wonder the people were frighted [sic]. Jack and I were scarred [sic] stiff. (Taylor 1943, 1)

Figure 3.4. Minister Ward and Colonel Conlon at Higaturu in 1944
Australian Minister for External Territories E.J. Ward (second from the right wearing a solar topee) and his adviser, Colonel Alf Conlon (on the right), meet Orokaiva men at Higaturu in April 1944. Photograph supplied courtesy of the Australian War Memorial (reference number AWM 072668).

There were additional eruptions on 13 February and 23 July 1944 and a fourth and final one is thought to have taken place on 31 August. However, the exact number of eruptions during the entire eruptive period, and any significant differences between them, are unknown because no systematic visual observations were made and the eruptions were not studied at the time by either volcanologists or geologists. Lieutenant Marsh, however, visited the area during its activity, taking photographs and reporting his observations of the volcanic blast effects on the destroyed forest surrounding the craters (Marsh 1944, 2005–08).

In 1944, Dennis Taylor and his family were transferred from Wanigela to Sangara to re-establish the work of the Anglican mission (Strong 1951; White 1991). Higaturu and Sangara were now becoming established as twin settlements for the representatives of both State and Church in the district on the flanks of Mount Lamington. There was even a visit to Higaturu by Australia's minister for external territories E.J. Ward. Ward and his adviser Colonel A. Conlon visited Higaturu in April 1944 (Figure 3.4). Head of the army's Directorate of Research and Civil Affairs, Conlon was principally a headquarters adviser on Australian transitional policy in the two territories for General Sir Thomas Blamey, the commander-in-chief of the Australian Army (Sligo 2013). Although a rather controversial figure, Conlon nevertheless emerged as a skilled adviser with the ability to relate to men in power, and the directorate was influential in what today would be called 'post-conflict operations'—that is, management and implementation of military government policy and civil affairs. He also 'had a genius for recruiting talent' to his directorate, whether scholars, lawyers, public servants, poets, anthropologists or scientists (Sligo 2013, viii). One such scientist was the oil company geologist Martin F. Glaessner who was chief palaeontologist for the Australian Petroleum Company and who, during the war, undertook volunteer work for the directorate.

In 1944, the directorate published a 'Geological Sketch Map of Eastern New Guinea', together with set of explanatory notes produced by three oil company geologists including Glaessner (Montgomery, Osbourne and Glaessner 1944). The map was based on extant geological information and included data collected by the Australasian Petroleum Company, and other companies, over a period of many years (see, for example, Anglo-Persian Oil Company 1930). Goropu was identified on the map as an 'active volcano' as a result of its inaugural 1943–44 eruptions. Another feature is that the extent of the area shown for Mount Lamington and the Hydrographers Range is different to the one mapped by Stanley (1924). The three geologists, however, again restricted the age of the volcanic rocks to the Pleistocene and did not distinguish any difference in geological age between Lamington and the Hydrographers (Figure 3.5). How the area of volcanic rocks came to be remapped is unknown, but, speculatively, wartime aerial photographs may have been available to the geologists for additional geological interpretation of an area where there had been heavy fighting.

The bibliography in the report published by Montgomery, Osbourne and Glaessner (1944) includes the geodynamics paper published by van Bemmelen (1939), but they did not refer to his brief claim of Mount Lamington being an 'active volcano'. Nor did they revise this omission in two further papers published six years later (Montgomery, Glaessner and Osbourne 1950; Glaessner 1950; see also David 1950). The reason for the omission is unknown, but possibly they had doubts about the veracity of the claim. Many years later, van Bemmelen could not recall from where he obtained his information about Lamington being an active volcano (van Bemmelen 1982). He thought it might have been from his colleague Dr C.E. Stehn, director of the Netherlands Indies Volcanological Survey, who had undertaken investigations in Rabaul after the 1937 eruption. However, according to Dr N.H. Fisher, who worked with Stehn in Rabaul and who later (in 1939) visited Java to undertake volcanological training from Stehn, this too seems unlikely. Fisher said that Stehn did not mention anything to him about Lamington being an active volcano (van Bemmelen 1982).

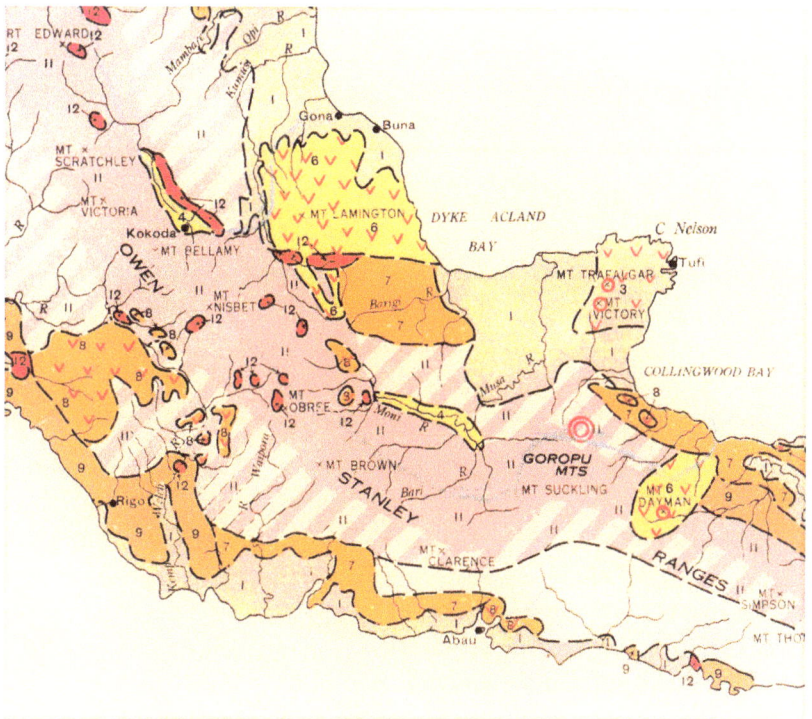

Figure 3.5. Detail from geological map by Montgomery, Osbourne and Glaessner

The distance across this part of the geological map by Montgomery, Osbourne and Glaessner (1944) is about 270 kilometres. North is to the top. The 'v' pattern on a yellow background and numbered '6' represents 'Pleistocene volcanic deposits'. The open circles represent the 'dormant and extinct' volcanoes of mounts Victory and Trafalgar, and the double concentric circles represent 'active volcanoes' — Goropu is the only one so identified. Mount Dayman is shown as a volcano, but this is an error that stems back to the work of A.G. Maitland (1892a, 1892b).

Territory Administration and the Bureau of Mineral Resources, Geology and Geophysics (1945–50)

The Allies advanced into the Territory of New Guinea after the Buna–Gona battles, gradually overcoming the Japanese presence. The Japanese had built a defensive complex of caves and tunnels in the volcanic deposits at their naval headquarters at Rabaul and they were contained by regular aerial bombing while Allied troops moved north to the Philippines and Okinawa (Dexter 1961; Long 1973). The final battles of the European theatre of World War II (WWII), including the German surrender to the Soviet Union and the Western Allies, took place in late April and early May 1945. Japan signed the surrender on 15 August 1945—V-J Day—just days after the disastrous atomic bombings at Hiroshima and Nagasaki on 6 and 9 August. Photographs of the lateral blasting of the buildings and infrastructure of both cities were terrifying images of the power of atomic energy and what would happen if ever it was used again in warfare. The struggle for supremacy in the Atomic Age between the US and the Soviet Union also began in 1945, and Australia again aligned itself with the US and its anti-Communist politics.

The concept of a decolonising British Empire was evolving resolutely by 1945 towards a new Commonwealth of Nations that encapsulated increased self-governance of former British territories. The old colonies would now be treated as free and equal member states. Further, the United Nations (UN) had been created in 1945, replacing the ineffective League of Nations. These global trends were reflected in a policy speech made by Minister Ward in July 1945 to the Australian Parliament in Canberra, the month that Labor Prime Minister John Curtin died and his position was taken over by J.B. Chifley. Postwar events were changing significantly in the two territories of Papua and New Guinea:

> The Government is not satisfied that sufficient interest had been taken in the territories prior to the Japanese invasion, or that adequate funds had been provided for their development and the advancement of the native inhabitants. Apart from the debt of gratitude that the people of Australia owe to the natives of the territory, the Government regards it as its bounden duty to further to the utmost the advancement of the natives, and considers that that can be achieved only by providing facilities for better health,

better education, and for a greater participation by the natives in the wealth of their country and eventually in its government. (Mair 1948, 207–08, quoting from *Commonwealth Hansard* 1945, 4050–55)

A provisional government was foreshadowed by Ward for the two former territories of New Guinea and Papua. There would be only one administration, which was the arrangement that ANGAU had used during the war. The new UN Trusteeship of the Territory of Papua and New Guinea (TPNG) was, therefore, an administrative union between the former Territory of Papua, which had been a possession of the Crown, and the Territory of New Guinea, a Mandated Trust Territory (Papua 1945a; New Guinea 1945; Hasluck 1976; Downs 1980). There would also now be a single administrator based in Port Moresby but accountable to the Australian Government in Canberra. This arrangement was for some years a union only in theory until it became established in Commonwealth of Australia law in July 1949.

The different Australian administration officers, or *kiaps*, who had worked in the separate administrations before the war now had to adjust to the new structure and responsibilities created after it. Officers were called district officers, assistant district officers and patrol officers, as they had been before the war in the Mandated Territory. The Papuan title of resident magistrate created under Hubert Murray was abandoned, and the title district officer would soon change to district commissioner. ANGAU had demonstrated that the two territories could be managed as a single entity in wartime conditions and despite the internal competition or even animosities between the prewar 'New Guinea' and 'Papua' officers. Many of those same officers now had to collaborate and cooperate in managing the new Trust Territory as a whole and to communicate across the old boundary between the two former territories. This included the two-way link between Port Moresby, the new capital, and distant Rabaul, the former capital of the old Mandated Territory.

Colonel John Keith Murray was appointed as the new TPNG administrator by the Australian Government in October 1945, following in the tradition of the colonial vice-regal and pro-consul style of administrator established by William MacGregor and Hubert Murray (e.g. Mair 1948; Downs 1980; Sligo 2013). Colonel Murray had been foundation professor of agriculture at the University of Queensland, a member of Conlon's Directorate of Research and then chief instructor at the army's School of Civil Affairs in Canberra. He was a strong supporter of Ward's policy and became administrator at a critical and difficult time when Australia was attempting to implement its new postwar policies for the combined former territories. This work was in the face of opposition from influential people both in Port Moresby and Canberra, some of whom thought the ex-military man was not sufficiently reliant on Canberra politicians and public servants (Hasluck 1976). Perhaps, too, his habit of conducting his ceremonial duties dressed in full 'vice-regal' uniform conveyed too much of the flair of an old-style British governor. Other critics were sardonic towards Murray, calling him 'Kanaka Jack' because of his favourable practices towards local people, although others used the appellation with genuine affection (Nelson 1982, 176). Murray, in any case, was well respected for his hard work, practicality, uncompromising integrity and scientific appreciation of issues. Bishop Phillip Strong at Dogura, for example, was one of Murray's strong supporters. Murray stayed as administrator for more than two years after the defeat in December 1949 of the Australian Labor Party who had appointed him. The new government in Canberra was a coalition of the Liberals and Country Party under Prime Minister Robert G. Menzies.

The TPNG administration's postwar headquarters for the Northern Division were at Higaturu, adjacent to the reoccupied Sangara Mission and about 10 kilometres from the summit of Lamington. About 4,000 Sangara people, most of whom were still dependent on subsistence agriculture, were thought to live in the surrounding area in villages and hamlets. Higaturu itself was accessed by a short connecting track south-east from the principal road between Popondetta and Wairopi and running westwards to Kokoda. By 1950, the Northern Division was under the control of District Commissioner Cecil Cowley, whose headquarters were in a simply constructed, single-storey building alongside an assembly area where the Australian flag could be flown on special occasions (Figure 3.6). There was also, by this time, a post office, hospital, doctor, staff accommodation, Department of Works and Housing support, technical training centre, police barracks, parade ground and gaol. Higaturu had radio communication with Port Moresby and with other stations. The nearest airstrip was at Popondetta about 10 kilometres to the north-east and about 21 kilometres from the summit area of Mount Lamington. Mail could now be sent out from Popondetta by small aircraft (Figure 3.7). This was quite unlike the government postal service before the war when a police runner carried mail to Kokoda and exchanged his mail package with a counterpart runner from Port Moresby, each runner then returning to his point of origin.

Figure 3.6. District headquarters at Higaturu
This photograph of district headquarters at Higaturu and the parade ground in front of it was taken by Kevin Woiwod. It was provided courtesy of the Woiwod family.

Agricultural development by the administration was re-established in the Northern Division by staff of the Department of Agriculture, Stock and Fisheries (e.g. Godbold 2010). The European agricultural extension officers, or *didiman*, by 1950 were F. 'Fred' Kleckham and Grainger 'Blue' Morris. They lived with their families in simple staff quarters in the small and undeveloped cluster of housing at Popondetta where Jack Scurrah also ran a trade store for Buntings Pty Ltd. The agricultural officers created an experimental station near Popondetta for the testing and development of new types of crops in the district. The large, company-owned Sangara Rubber Plantation was to the south-west along the main road past Double Crossing on the Ambogo River, and was managed by European staff. Awala Plantation was further west along the road and was owned and run by the Searle family.

Figure 3.7. Higaturu postmarked envelope franked on 1 March 1950

This is a rare copy of a Higaturu postmarked and registered envelope using Australian postage stamps and franked on 1 March 1950. Princess Elizabeth, who became Queen Elizabeth II in 1952, is shown in the second stamp from the left (between the kangaroo and the horseman). This image of the envelope was provided courtesy of Munro Kennedy and Max Hayes.

No geologists came to Sangara–Higaturu after the war and before 1951, but they did come eventually to the new TPNG. An Australian national geological survey, the Bureau of Mineral Resources, Geology and Geophysics (BMR), was created in 1946 for an ambitious program of systematically mapping the geology of the Australian continent, including TPNG (Wilkinson 1996). Recruitment of suitably trained staff to BMR was difficult, however, until new postwar graduates started to become available from the universities. An oil company geologist, A.K.M. Edwards, was eventually appointed resident geologist in Port Moresby in 1949 when a geological office was established there.

BMR also had the responsibility of re-establishing volcanological services in the new Territory, but the volcanological observatory at Rabaul did not become operational again until after G.A.M. 'Tony' Taylor arrived there in April 1950 (Fisher 1976). Taylor's volcanological responsibilities now covered the whole of the new Territory and not just the Mandated Territory of New Guinea, as his predecessors had in prewar times. His priority was to establish instrumental monitoring of Rabaul volcano, but in December 1950 he also inspected Bagana volcano after some particular powerful explosions earlier that year (Taylor 1956).

Return of the Anglican Mission (1945–50)

Re-establishment of the Anglican mission stations at Sangara, Gona, Isivita and Eroro had also been taking place (Tomlin 1951; White 1991; Tomkins and Hughes 1969; Hand 2002). An early task was disinterring the remains of three of the Anglican mission workers who had been murdered during the war, and reburying them at Sangara thus establishing the Martyrs Cemetery. The three 'martyrs' were Mavis Parkinson, a teacher at Gona Mission; Sister May Hayman, a nurse at Gona; and Lucian Tapiedi, a young Papuan teacher from Milne Bay whose statue can be seen today in London at Westminster Cathedral (Hand 2002).

Reverend Dennis Taylor worked from 1944 onwards rebuilding the Sangara and Isivita stations (Strong 1951, 1981). This included the repair and reconstruction of St James Church and a schoolroom at Sangara. Taylor 'was a man of few words, but immense resource and ability … an experienced bushman [who] had a great capacity for organising, improvising and getting things done' (White 1991, 6). His wife Lesley, a mission teacher, returned in 1945 and became involved increasingly in raising their growing family of four children. Dennis Taylor was assisted at Sangara by Reverend John Rautamara, a Wedauan from the Dogura area whose father, Peter, in 1917 had been the first Papuan to be ordained as an Anglican priest. John Rautamara 'was a big man in every way, physically, intellectually, and spiritually [and] was a splendid athlete' (Hand 2002, 35). He was also an inspirational preacher who seemed to have had a special affinity and vocation for the Orokaiva (e.g. Tomkins and Hughes 1969).

Margaret or 'Peggy' de Bibra was a well-qualified teacher who arrived at Sangara in 1947. Her task was to re-establish mission education including—and initially by herself—a secondary school that was later named the Martyrs Memorial School. Miss de Bibra came from a distinguished Tasmanian family, was a first-class honours graduate from the University of Melbourne and had given up a position as headmistress of an Australian high school to become a missionary teacher at Sangara. She was joined in 1948 by another trained teacher, Nancy White, who took over duties in the primary school allowing de Bibra to concentrate on the secondary school (White 1991).

Reverend David Hand arrived at Sangara from Dogura in 1948 as acting priest-in-charge while Dennis Taylor and his family went on furlough. This was Taylor's first long break from mission work since 1937. Hand was met at Sangara by John Rautamara and Peggy de Bibra who soon became his close colleagues and friends. Hand was born in Australia but raised in England where his father, Canon W.T. Hand, was also an Anglican churchman. David Hand developed a strong commitment to Christian evangelism among the Orokaiva and especially the Sangara people. He took his guardianship responsibilities seriously, developing a fatherly concern and deep affection for the Orokaiva. Hand also seems to have had a forceful, commanding, even formidable personality and, where necessary, could use his 'stentorian voice' (White 1991, 20) to good effect. Both Peggy de Bibra and David Hand became godparents to one of the Taylors' children. Hand admired Miss de Bibra greatly and had considered proposing marriage to her (Hand 2002).

Several other Anglican missionaries arrived at the mission stations of Sangara, Isivita, Gona and Eroro in the postwar years up to the end of 1950. L.J. 'Rodd' Hart and teacher Miss Madeleine 'Maddy' Swan came separately to Sangara, and became engaged to be married. Reverend Robert G. Porter, Sister Pat M. Durdin and Mrs Barbara Lane were based at Isivita. Canon James Benson returned to Gona Mission after surviving three years as a Japanese prisoner of war at Rabaul (e.g. Chynoweth n.d.). He was joined by Reverend W.A. 'Alf' Clint, Sister Nancy A. Elliot and schoolteacher Elsie Manley. Sister Jean Henderson in January 1946 went as a nurse to Eroro Mission near the coast and just inland from the deserted American base at Oro Bay (Figure 3.1). She helped to build a hospital using bush materials and the concrete base of an old American bakery (Henderson 2007). Dr Blanche Biggs joined the Eroro staff in 1948, the first of a 27-year period of service in the area (Kettle 1979). The priest-in-charge at Eroro was Reverend J. Luscombe Newman, but he and his family went on leave and the relieving priest in January 1951 was Reverend John Andersen (Henderson 2007).

Relationships between the Anglican mission and administration were not particularly smooth. The activities of both agencies among the Orokaiva were not well coordinated, meaning that consistent development policies were made difficult (e.g. Waddell and Krinks 1968) and, presumably, some confusion was created in the minds of the Orokaiva. One example of a difference of opinion was in the area of secondary education. The mission believed that what the administration and European business community wanted 'were clerks, interpreters, store-boys [and] "boss-boys" … to assist the smooth running of the white man's administrative or money-making machines' (Tomkins and Hughes 1969, 81). The mission, and Reverend Hand in particular, strongly articulated the view that secondary education for Papuans should take a more enlightened approach, embracing a future in which responsible government of the country may include the Papuans themselves. Two Anglican historians later asked the question of whether Hand and the mission had, in 'those years of intensive white exploitation, 1947–51, a clearer idea of the future needs of a people, almost entirely living by subsistence agriculture in small villages, than did the government of Australia or the traders' (Tomkins and Hughes 1969, 82). Such were the kinds of pressures, from both sides of this particular argument, that Administrator J.K. Murray had to manage at the time.

Another related example of such conflicts swirled around the mission-inspired Christian Co-operative Movement at Gona Mission, which was started by Canon Benson and implemented by Reverend Clint (Benson 1949a, 1949b, 1949c; Tomlin 1951; Tomkins and Hughes 1969; Garland 2000; see also Crocombe 1964; Dakeyne 1966; Waddell and Krinks 1968; Horne 2017). There was an emphasis on the cooperative growing of cash crops including, especially, rice in specially prepared fields. The administration had been encouraging secular cooperative movements elsewhere in the Territory because they were community-inspired, unlike before the war when compulsion was applied (e.g. Legge 1956). These secular cooperatives involved people from different villages tending common cash-producing crops but not necessarily involving concurrent work. The Christian Co-operative Movement was different, however, because the work was communal—that is, people working together at the same time—and because of its accompanying religious ceremonies that included prayers in the fields and gardens, ceremonial blessings by the bishop and tools being treated with particular reverence.

The Anglican-based movement spread effectively to other parts of Northern Division and began to generate large sums of money. The administration became concerned about these developments, as well as the perceived cargo cult–like character of the movement. These were also Cold War times, and there were additional concerns about the actual meaning of 'cooperatives' and their relationship to communism. Were they Christian 'communes' in the communist sense, despite their non-atheistic nature? Reverend Clint had left-wing ideological connections, and had been associated with the Christian Socialist Movement in Australia. The administration appointed cooperatives officers and took over the running of the Northern Division cooperatives, thus reducing the influence of the mission. Clint fell ill in 1949 and left for Australia, resuming his cooperatives work there with Aboriginal groups (e.g. Cunningham 1974).

Canon Benson also opposed a postwar pilot scheme for Australian soldier settlement on lands in the Sangara area. He argued that 'the Papuan Infantry Battalion [also] had fought and died to save Australia, etc. All right then I say, Let the Papua Infantry Battalion boys go and take up land in Australia', and told villagers that 'whatever government or white man comes here don't sell your land. Do not sell your land!!' (quoted in Tomkins and Hughes 1969, 105). Senior members of the mission such as Benson and Hand therefore took seriously their responsibilities as the caring shepherds of their Orokaiva flocks, as one might expect from such committed missionaries in these difficult years of uncertainty and rapid external change.

David Hand was on a clear path of promotion in the Church of England hierarchy when, on St Peter's Day 1950, at the age of only 32, he was consecrated as diocesan coadjutor (i.e. assistant) bishop to Phillip Strong at Dogura Cathedral. A striking, all-male 'end-of-Empire' photograph was taken of the event outside St Peter and St Paul Cathedral on 29 June—the old British Empire in Papua captured in an instant (Figure 3.8). The whole event was a memorable day for the young bishop who was photographed with five other mitre-wearing bishops. The ceremony also included some less than serious moments that Hand himself recorded, somewhat teasingly, at the expense of the administration and the justice system (see Hand 2002, 40–43). Helmeted Colonel J.K. Murray was in the full attire of administrator for the theatre of the day, wearing also a ceremonial sword that, in the highly charged atmosphere of the occasion, he forgot to unbuckle before entering the cathedral. His Honour Justice Ralph T. Gore was attending the ceremony as chancellor of the Diocese of New Guinea. He wore his full-bottomed judge's wig, which he had to lift at times to mop his perspiring bald head because of the tropical heat. Judge Gore, Administrator Murray and Bishop Hand would, together with others in the photograph, play much more serious roles in the aftermath of the 21 January disaster at Mount Lamington.

Figure 3.8. Consecration of Bishop David Hand at Dogura

Bishop David Hand's consecration was held at Dogura Cathedral on Thursday 29 June 1950, St Peter's Day. This image is reproduced from the photograph published by White (1991, 38). Bishop Strong and Administrator J.K. Murray are facing each other in conversation left of centre in the front row; Bishop Hand is third from the right in the front row; Justice Ralph Gore is at the right-hand end of the same row; Ivan Champion is in the back row, first on the right from the left-hand candlestick; and Archdeacon Romney Gill is in the middle of the photograph, behind and just to the right of Administrator Murray. All of these named European men were involved seven months later in the 1951 disaster relief and recovery at Mount Lamington. The two Papuan priests carrying the processional candle sticks are Reverend Peter Rautamara (looking at the camera between Strong and Murray) and his son Reverend John Rautamara (looking to his left) who died at Sangara during the 1951 eruption. The names of all those shown on the photograph are listed by Wetherell (1977, fig. 30). The photograph is reproduced here courtesy of the Anglican Board of Mission, Australia.

Discovery of Volcano-Related Information from 1947–48

Europeans who lived in and visited the Higaturu–Sangara area commented on its impressive scenic setting: the great blue mountains of the Owen Stanley Range to the south and multi-peaked Mount Lamington in front of them. The schoolteacher, Miss de Bibra, for example, wrote that Lamington:

> Lies behind us and consists of four or five sugar-loaf peaks [that, at times, are shrouded] in gossamer scarves of mist … We have always loved her for her beauty and nearness. (White 1991, 45–46)

Other people using non-prose referred to the peaks as 'the Marx Brothers', naming them after the popular American vaudeville team who appeared on radio and in films (e.g. *South Pacific Post* 1951a). Lamington, however, despite its natural features, was still not yet recognised as an active and threatening volcano.

There was no opportunity for any geologist or volcanologist to inspect Mount Lamington in the immediate postwar years, but aerial photographs were taken over the area in 1947–48 and any qualified geoscientist would have interpreted the youthful volcanic nature of the mountain by inspecting them. Volcanologist Tony Taylor, in particular, later pointed out features that were consistent with Lamington being a geologically youthful volcano, unlike those of the older Hydrographers Range to the east (Taylor 1958). Young lava flows were identified clustered around the summit of the mountain (Figure 3.9). These lavas, when extruded, had not been fluid or voluminous enough to flow very far but, rather, had accumulated as bulbous 'lava domes' and short stubby flows known technically as 'coulées'.

Another important feature that can be identified on the aerial photographs of Mount Lamington is a summit volcanic crater. This was not a complete crater or 'hole' in the normal sense of the word but, rather, was an amphitheatre-like depression that faced towards the north. The amphitheatre-shaped headwall was drained by the north-flowing Ambogo River in the west, and in the east by the Banguho River that drained more towards the north-east. Both rivers flowed across the broad, populated, piedmont area that slopes away from the summit. The headwall of the amphitheatre must have been enlarged by erosion caused by these rivers and their upper streams, and by rock avalanches from the headwall. The debris was then transported by the rivers down what Taylor (1958, 7) referred to, appropriately, as 'the avalanche valley'.

Figure 3.9. Military aerial photograph of the summit of Mount Lamington in 1947

This oblique aerial photograph of the summit of Mount Lamington, together with the Hydrographers Range in the background, was taken towards the east in 1947 by the US Air Force as part of a trimetrogon series of photographs distributed by the US Army Map Service (Taylor 1958, fig. 2). The labelling in white was added by Taylor. Buildings at Higaturu can be seen on the extreme left. Note also the Ambogo 'avalanche valley', the small summit crater containing a small lava dome or 'tholoid', and youthful lava flows and lava domes clustered south-west of and around the summit. Photograph supplied courtesy of Geoscience Australia (negative number G/3342).

Many volcanoes have avalanche amphitheatres. They are created where large slabs or sections of a volcano disintegrate and slide away from the summit of a volcanic cone, at times catastrophically, like giant landslides. Some of the depressions so formed are described as 'horseshoe-shaped'— that is, open at one end. The headwalls are indeed generally curved, but the two walls that trend downslope can be quite straight, in some cases diverging from each other, but gradually reducing in height away from the volcano. An excellent example is found at Galunggung volcano, Java, which was mapped by a geologist of the Netherlands Indies in the 1920s (Escher 1925; see also Siebert 1984, fig. 1). A particularly striking feature of this Javanese example is the large area of hummocky topography downslope and south-east from the avalanche amphitheatre (Figure 3.10). These are volcanic 'debris-avalanche deposits' created by the disintegration of the volcanic cone, their gravitational transport downslope and redeposition at the foot of the volcano.

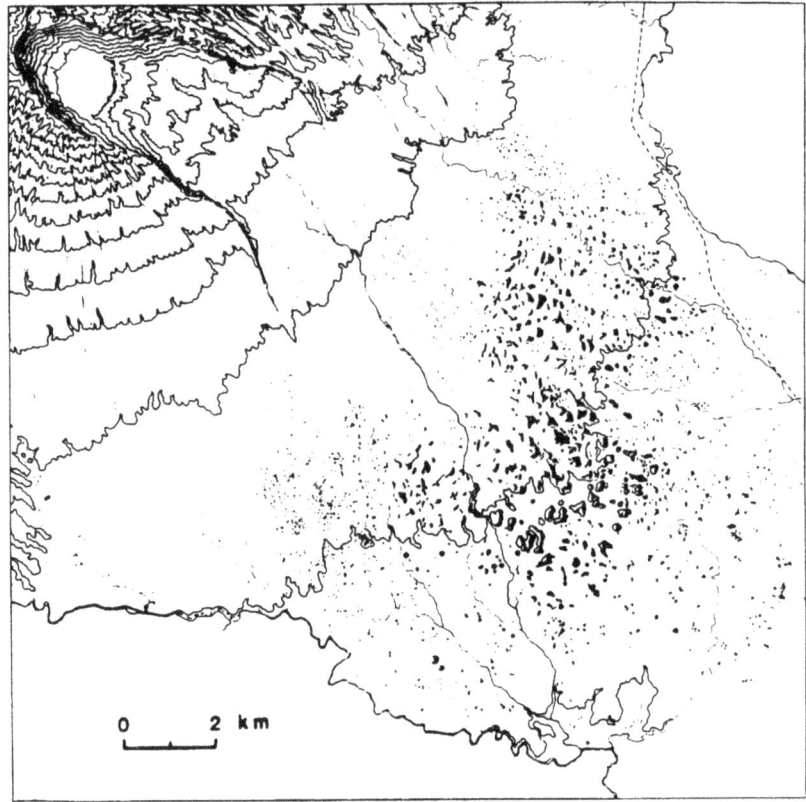

Figure 3.10. Debris-avalanche hummocks at Galunggung volcano, Java
Debris-avalanche hummocks are seen forming the 'Ten Thousand Hills of Tasikmalaya' downslope from the avalanche amphitheatre at Galunggung volcano, Java (Escher 1925). North is to the top of the map.

The summit 'crater' of Mount Lamington was observed from the north and at close quarters by an administration officer, John J. Murphy, during an ascent of the mountain from Higaturu on 29 May 1948. The purpose of the climb was to determine whether pines were growing high on the upper parts of the 'Lamington Mountains'. Murphy reported on the details of his climb in a memorandum dated 8 February 1951—that is, not until after the major eruption of 21 January 1951—and he included a sketch (Figure 3.11) of the northern side of the summit area as it was in 1948 (Murphy 1951, 1). Three peaks were named on the sketch, these names evidently being provided by the Orokaiva men who accompanied him. Murphy wrote:

I noticed no evidence of volcanic action in recent times though the crater itself was unmistakeable as of volcanic origin. There were no signs of any activity at all in the way of earth tremors, fissures or heat, although two land slides [sic] were present on the steep Northern slope of Arunguho [Arungaho], though these were probably caused by rainfall. (Murphy 1951, 1)

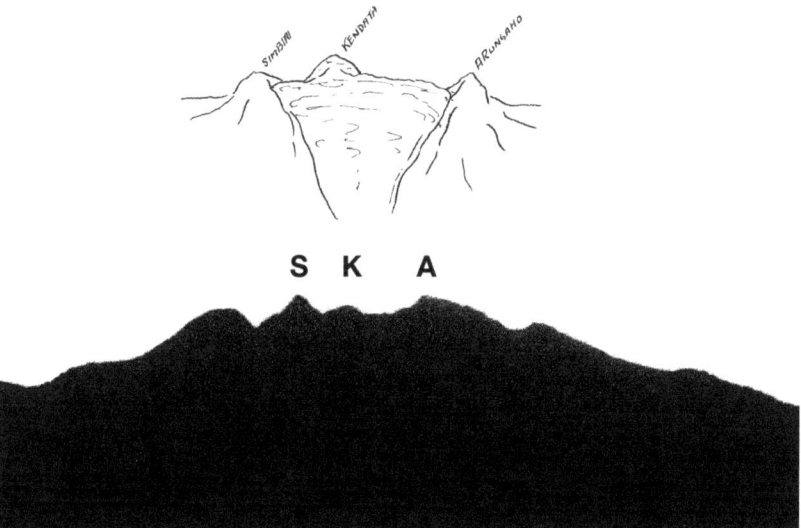

Figure 3.11. Sketch by Murphy in 1948 and silhouette of Mount Lamington

The top sketch of the volcanic crater at the summit of Mount Lamington was drawn by administration officer J.J. Murphy close-in from the north during an ascent of the mountain on 29 May 1948. The names shown are just some of the many that have been given to the peak or peaks of Mount Lamington. The lower silhouette profile of Mount Lamington and its peaks is adapted from an underexposed photograph taken from the north before the eruption of 21 January 1951. The photographer is unknown. S, K and A refer to the three peaks shown in the upper diagram. Note also the volcano-like, truncated, conical form of the rugged mountain.

The three peaks in the sketch are remnants of old lava domes. The highest of these—named 'Kendata', which is a village name—can also be seen on the 1947 aerial photographs where its truncated northern side forms the precipitous southern wall of the crater (Figure 3.9). Another peak, called 'Simbiri' on the sketch but spelt 'Simberi' in Murphy's memorandum, possibly refers to Sumbiri, or Sumbiripa, the name of a spirit who lives on the mountain and who would gain much notoriety in later years. All three dome remnants form part of a stronger buttressing of the volcano's central part compared with the less-resistant outer flanks of the mountain. They create an irregular profile that gives the false impression of an old eroded volcano rather than one of the youthful morphology of bulbous lava domes or lava flows. Taylor (1958) later noted that thermal areas could be seen clearly on the aerial photographs, grouped around the southern flank of the highest dome, but not visible from the northern side.

The short, rugged southern side of Mount Lamington that was seen by E.R. Stanley in 1916 contrasts strongly with the broad, extensive, piedmont side to the north. The south- and south-west-flowing creeks on this southern side eventually drain into the upper parts of the north-flowing Kumusi River system, as do streams on the western flank of the mountain. Similarly, creeks on the eastern side of the mountains form the Girua River that drains northwards between Lamington and the Hydrographers Range. The volcano as a whole, therefore, has a strong north to south asymmetry caused by far greater sedimentation in the north compared to the south, and evidently enhanced by the north-facing disposition of the summit crater first described by Murphy. Further, the volcano may have grown on a surface sloping gently from the foothills of the Owen Stanley Range to the north coast, which may have created a propensity to collapse gravitationally and preferentially in that same direction.

Murphy observed that:

> Local history says that this crater [Figure 3.11, upper] once formed a large lake which burst through its walls on the Northern side releasing its waters which swept down and devastated several Higaturu villages and caused great loss of life. My informant puts this catastrophe at forty years ago, and it was no doubt the basis for the superstition with which Lamington Mountains were regarded by the natives. (Murphy 1951, 2)

Such a crater-wall collapse at Lamington is geologically feasible although the young date of just 'forty years ago' is questionable, if not unlikely. This disinterred information in any case did not gain significance until after the catastrophic volcanic eruption of 21 January 1951. Murphy, however, had identified the mountain clearly as a volcano, thus complementing suspicions interpreted after the 1951 eruption concerning the 'roars' from the mountain noted by the Sangara missionaries in 1935.

The hydrological hazards of the Lamington area were better known before 1951 than any threats deriving from volcanic eruptions. This is hardly surprising in a region where tropical annual rain can fall at any time of the year, but particularly in the monsoon or 'north-west' season. Further, large cyclones can form in the Coral Sea south of the Owen Stanley Range and their outer parts can release torrential rain onto the range and in Orokaiva country, causing rivers to swell rapidly. Anthropologist F.E. Williams, for example, wrote that:

> The clear stream of yesterday is transformed overnight into a brown swirling flood, sweeping down masses of forest wreckage and rising over its banks to cover the surrounding country … The rapidity with which the flood-waters sink is somewhat surprising when we consider the very gradual fall of the ground. (Williams 1930, 13–14)

The occasional flood, however, noted Williams (1928, 112), 'is rather welcomed than feared' after it recedes, as it may provide hunters with opportunities for collecting stranded frogs, fish and small game from the forest.

The Orokaiva themselves have hydrological legends, one story involving an eastward-draining river that used to flow under Mount Lamington (Horne 1974a). The 'tunnel' then closed after an 'upheaval', the water from west of the mountain began to flow into the Kumusi and the east-bound river diminished in size. Williams (1930) referred to a catastrophic flood and to a legendary being called 'Kokowaio' who was identified with the lake or lakes at Embi. Kokowaio, or Gogowairo, was 'a strange creature … It was more like a gigantic turtle than anything else, and its back was covered in long grass instead of hair' (Austen 1951, 2). The beast rescued 'a boy and girl, the sole survivors of a flood which led to the formation of lake Embi … [and who still] exercises some sort of control over the lake, which is regarded as a place full of danger' (Williams 1930, 277). There is some consistency between this creation legend for the lakes and the known sediment distribution north of Mount Lamington. This is because some Lamington-derived sediments have been transported north-eastwards, perhaps as mudflows, around the northern side of the Hydrographers Range. These appear to have dammed streams flowing from the northern side of the range, thus forming Embi Lakes.

Another, perhaps more important, Lamington legend was recorded in 1948 in a local, unpublished patrol report written by a Higaturu-based patrol officer, H.M. Corderoy, and published later by the anthropologist Cyril S. Belshaw (Corderoy 1948; Belshaw 1951b). This version of the story, consisting of only one short paragraph, was also told in a different form after the 1951 volcanic eruption and it achieved some considerable prominence once 'Sumbiripa' emerged as the name of the man concerned. It also refers to the creation of the Lamington 'hills':

> Long ago a man, a woman and a dog went up into the area which was then flat land with no hills. The man wished to have intercourse with the woman and she consented, thereby doing wrong. They did not return to the village but lived in the area. The people did not see them again but periodically used to ask how they were by shouting into the bush. First they learnt that the dog had died, then the woman, then the man (the man's spirit told them the last fact). The hills appeared and it was always cold and wet on top. It is not good for the people to go into the area. (Corderoy 1948, 10)

After the 1951 eruption at Lamington, Higaturu-based District Officer O.J. Atkinson wrote to the administration about his experience with earth tremors in the Northern Division at both Higaturu and Buna from 1948. He had felt many of the tremors, but they all seemed to come from the east, rather than locally. Further, he recorded that shortly before leaving Higaturu in 1949 an old man told him a story that had been handed down from his forefathers 'that Lamington would erupt again' (Atkinson 1951, 1). Atkinson recorded also that in 1940 at Buna he was informed that some people in the Waseta area of Mount Lamington had killed their pigs and others were about to do so. News had been spread that there was 'going to be an eruption, that the whole countryside would be smothered, and they would lose all their pigs, gardens and lives', so they might as well kill their pigs themselves (Atkinson 1951, 1). These stories taken at face value are evidence that the mountain Orokaiva did have a belief in the volcanic dangers of Mount Lamington. What precisely was meant by the English words 'erupt' and 'eruption', however, whether there were directly equivalent words in the Orokaiva language at the time, and what errors were made in Orokaiva-to-English translation, are unknown. Even an Orokaiva version of the word 'volcano', for example, does not appear in one Orokaiva dictionary compiled after the eruption (Larsen 1984), and other linguists tracing language development in proto-Oceanic society noted tentatively that Melanesians may well have 'had no separate concept for "volcano", regarding it simply as a mountain that produces fire' (Osmond, Pawley and Ross 2007, 81).

The extensive piedmont of fragmental volcanic deposits on the northern footslopes of Mount Lamington contains geological evidence for past *nuées ardentes* of the kind that were first seen, recorded and named at Mont Pelée in the Caribbean in 1902 (Taylor 1958). Deposits from such 'glowing clouds'—which today are called 'pyroclastic flows' or 'pyroclastic density currents'—produced by eruptions at Mount Victory in the late 1880s, were almost certainly seen by William MacGregor, but by 1950 they had not yet been observed and recorded at Lamington, including in local legends. A broad generalisation that can be made today is that the structure of Mount Lamington is such that pyroclastic flows tend to be directed preferentially northwards from the north-facing crater area, downslope towards the sea. People living on the northern footslopes in early 1951 had no knowledge of such destructive volcanic phenomena, but they would soon face them and experience their terrible consequences.

PART 2. CATASTROPHIC ERUPTION

At 10.40 hours on Sunday, 21st January, the volcano produced an explosion of great magnitude. A large mass of ash was projected rapidly into the stratosphere to form a huge expanding mushroom-shaped cloud. The base of the column began to expand laterally as clouds of incandescent ash swept down the slopes of the mountain and laid waste more than 90 square miles of country.

This tremendous release of energy was awe-inspiring and terrifying to the people living on the slopes of the volcano, and almost immediately large numbers began to flee. Such was the velocity of the enveloping cloud, however, that only those on the extreme edge of the subsequently devastated area were able to escape.

— G.A.M Taylor (1958, 24–25)

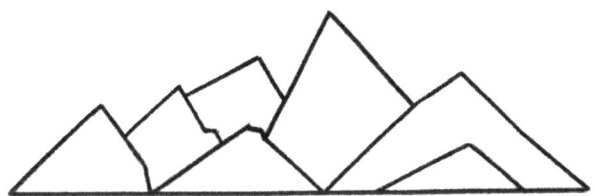

4

VICTIMS, SURVIVORS AND EVACUATIONS

Vulnerability on the Mountain in January 1951

Life on the mountain for the Orokaiva in the third week of January 1951 may have re-equilibrated somewhat after the traumas of World War II (WWII), but memories of the hangings at Higaturu would never be forgotten. The mountain Orokaiva were settled in their communities and hamlets in the Sangara–Higaturu area on the lower northern slopes of Mount Lamington, and in the north-western sector bounded roughly in the north by the road between Wairopi and Agenahambo, a sector that was called the 'Isivita District' by some people (Figure 4.1). Populations in both places were quite large by Papuan standards, as they had been long before the arrival of white men. This was because of the fertile, well-drained soils, and cooler, more pleasant climate than at the coast. This summary helps to define a primary disaster-vulnerability factor: too many people settled in a volcanically hazardous place.

Europeans had settled in the area in the 1930s, initially for the purposes of Christian prosyletisation among the large Orokaiva populations, although the mountain settlements had been visited by government patrols and others since the beginning of the century. The rich agricultural land during that time had also attracted commercially orientated European planters, and there were now both European-owned and local 'native' cash cropping plantations held under a range of different land tenure conditions. Therefore, there had been only about 20 years of direct, settled, interaction between the Orokaiva and Europeans, and this had been interrupted by the war. The Europeans had brought peace, at least to the extent that the deadly, inter-tribal clashes of pre-contact days had been eliminated. Postwar growth was now being provided by new medical and educational services from a district headquarters at Higaturu and at the nearby Anglican mission at Sangara. Further, government agricultural services in the area were being provided from Popondetta by officers of the Department of Agriculture, Stock and Fisheries.

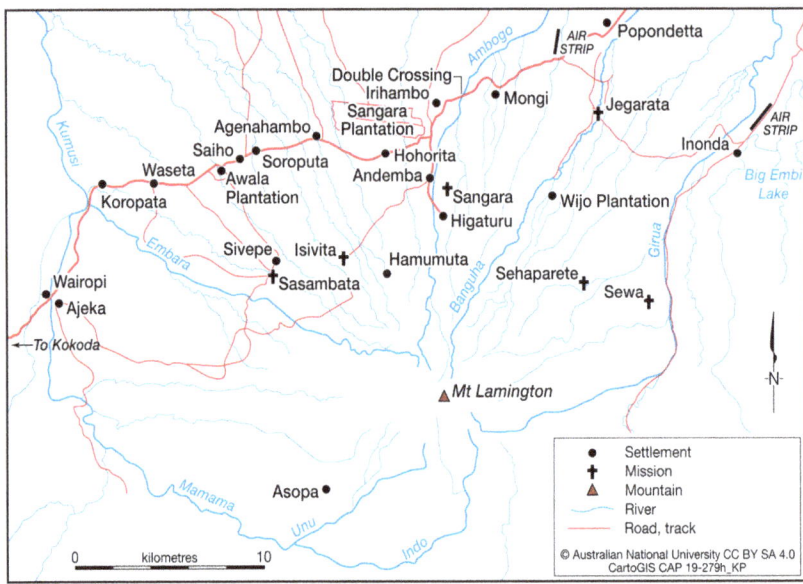

Figure 4.1. Main geographical features of the Lamington area
The principal geographical features of the Lamington area prior to the 1951 eruption shown here are based on the map published by Taylor (1958, fig. 52). Only very few of all the tracks used in area are shown. This map also forms the basis for Figure 4.6.

The European population was small—just a few dozen—but the much larger Orokaiva one was still under the control of postwar colonialism. This was centred on Higaturu, now the administrative headquarters for an economically important division in the new Territory of Papua and New Guinea. Colonisation seemed to be working reasonably well, at least in comparison to the years between the two world wars and during the Great Depression when Hubert Murray struggled to achieve any significant economic development for the Territory of Papua. This apparent improvement, however, can be regarded as a further disaster-vulnerability factor: growth and development of what was already a heavily populated area.

There existed still the situation of a strong colonial power in charge of, and controlling, a largely preliterate people through the immediate triple presence of representatives of the State, Church and the commercialised white planter community. Structural racism still existed, racial dependencies had been created and the Orokaiva were still, in one sense, 'controlled' by their elitist colonial masters. There were also beliefs and perceptions among at least some of the Orokaiva that the white-skinned expatriates were a valuable source of modern knowledge and that they had an ability to generate material wealth. The Orokaiva could see for themselves the results and power of European engineering and technology, and of medical and agricultural science, although not of other sciences such as geology, geophysics and volcanology. Some of the Europeans also seemed to worship a rather powerful and universal God. Thus, there existed a willingness among the mountain Orokaiva to listen to, and to be led by, the Europeans, as well as them holding a trust for, or reliance on, the foreigners' decision-making capabilities. These local dependencies, then, can be regarded as another disaster-vulnerability factor. Nevertheless, Orokaiva cultural relationships at the family, kinship, clan and 'village' levels were still strong at this lower stratum of the racially layered society. This, in turn, reflected an innate community strength and self-reliance that would be displayed to the full after the catastrophic volcanic eruption on 21 January 1951.

A final disaster-vulnerability factor is the situation in which few people in January 1951 in the Mount Lamington area itself—whether Orokaiva or European—appear to have had sufficient, or indeed any, knowledge that the mountain on which they lived was a potentially active volcano. The situation might have been different if government geologists or volcanologists could have been employed in the Lamington area by the administration after the death of geologist Evan R. Stanley in 1924, but budgetary constraints, the Great Depression and WWII seem to have prevented this. There was no obvious potential for resources such as gold and oil in the Lamington area, meaning there was no obvious motivation to give the area any economic priority for geological surveying in the first place.

Six Days of Growing Threat

European life near the mountain

The week of Monday 15 to Saturday 20 January 1951 was one of great uncertainty for the inhabitants of the Lamington area. Strange and unexpected physical changes were taking place at the summit of the mountain and were evolving unexpectedly. Several Europeans who were there during that week later wrote about these changes, thus providing volcanology with a useful record of the geophysical phenomena that preceded the catastrophic volcanic eruption of Sunday 21 January. Margaret de Bibra, for example, produced a particularly valuable summary of the events up to the Sunday morning, extracts of which were published later (Taylor 1958; White 1991).

January was not a typical month for people in the Higaturu and Sangara area. It was, firstly, the time of school holidays, meaning that local students who boarded at the Sangara Mission had returned to their respective homes in the Northern Division. The hard-working Margaret de Bibra took this opportunity to arrange a special training course for local schoolteachers who then came to the mission from outlying areas. Bishop David Hand was in Australia on a deputation in search of staff and finance for new proposed missionary activities by the Anglicans in the New Guinea Highlands (Hand 2002). Similarly, Sister Nancy White, who was normally based at Sangara Mission, was on furlough in Victoria, Australia (White 1991). Rodd Hart and Madeleine Swan had married and were taking their honeymoon at nearby Jegarata. Administrator J.K. Murray was also away from his base in Port Moresby. He was undertaking one of his regular tours of the Territory during the second week of January, and was due in Rabaul, East New Britain, at the end of the week. Judge F.M. Phillips remained in Port Moresby, acting as administrator in Murray's absence, and S.A. 'Steve' Lonergan was the acting government secretary for the administration in the capital. Volcanologist Taylor was at the volcanological observatory in Rabaul for the whole week.

The postwar European communities on the plantations near Mount Lamington and at Higaturu by this time had created their own social life. T.G. 'Hendy' Henderson was the manager of Sangara Rubber Plantation where he lived with his wife, Toby, their son and a daughter, Mary Rose. Assistant managers were F.W. 'Stevie' Stephens and John R. Gwilt, who were accompanied by their wives, Laura and Heather, respectively. Australian Bill Schleusener was a young single assistant at the plantation. Another European family, the Searles, ran their own smaller rubber, coffee and cocoa plantation at Awala further along the road towards Wairopi. The Searle family were Cledwyn, or 'Clen', and Jessie Lilian, known as 'Pat', and their children Peter and Rhonwen. All of these plantations depended on Papuan labour.

Laura Stephens wrote that at Sangara they:

> Lived a normal, happy, busy life on the plantation. There were plenty of social happenings in our small community, as Higaturu was nearby and a flourish[ing] Government Station, with 36 European personnel and many natives both in Government Service and in their own villages, and working around on other estates. We were going up to Hibaturu [sic] very often, for the various little social events which a small community indulges in; and the Higaturu people used to come down to the plantation to visit the various people who lived here. The [previous] Christmas … was very bright, ending with a new years party in fancy dress, at which nearly everybody from the near and far districts attended. At that time, no one suspected that the nearby range of mountains known as the Lamingtons, were abnormal in their appearance, nor, at that time, had any earth tremors or rumblings been noticed. (Stephens 1951, 1)

New administration staff had arrived at Higaturu by January 1951, including three cadet patrol officers. Pat Searle recalled that:

> The Commonwealth Bank had recently opened a branch … there were several new Patrol Officers on the station at that time we had barely met … The Australian Commonwealth Government had sent several men to Higaturu to build a new permanent station to replace the old war-time buildings. A large new hospital was already built and in daily use. (Searle 1995, 234)

Two Australian children—Erl, who had just celebrated his 16th birthday, and his younger sister, 12-year-old Pamela—had returned home to Higaturu from boarding school in Australia and were staying with their parents over the holidays (Cowley and Virtue 2015). Their father was Cecil F. Cowley, the district commissioner for the Northern Division. Cowley first came to Papua in 1927 as an engineer for the Anglo-Persian Oil Company, but in 1929 became one of Sir Hubert Murray's 'outside men' in the prewar administration of the Territory (e.g. *South Pacific Post*

1951b). He served with the Royal Australian Air Force and then with the Australian New Guinea Administrative Unit during WWII. Cowley's wife was Amalya, née Franceschi, a former professional violinist. Both Amalya and daughter Pam played their violins at Higaturu.

The most senior public servant in Higaturu at this time was W.R. 'Dickie' Humphries, who had presided at the Higaturu trials and hangings of the accused Orokaiva in 1943. He was now director of labour for the administration and had recently been appointed a member of the Territory's first Legislative Council (e.g. *Pacific Islands Monthly* 1951a). Humphries was on recreation leave visiting his daughter, Letty, her husband, Maynard Locke, their small daughter, Marion, and a recently arrived baby. Maynard Locke worked at Higaturu for the Department of Education as an education officer. The educational facilities at Higaturu included the technical Commonwealth Rehabilitation and Training School.

Dr Pal or Paul Martin was the doctor at the Higaturu hospital. He was a postwar immigrant to Australia from Romania, and was one of several European doctors recruited to the Territory after the war by Dr John Gunther, director of public health, at a time when European medical qualifications were not being recognised in Australia (see, for example, Sinclair 1981). Martin lived at Higaturu with his wife, Olga, and three-year-old son, Pinky. Other former European doctors included Max Sverklys and Olgerts Ozols, both based in nearby Morobe District.

Agricultural officers Fred Kleckham and 'Blue' Morris and their families were still based at Popondetta. A new arrival was an anthropologist from The Australian National University, Marie Reay, who had started academic studies of the Orokaiva and was living at the government resthouse in Waseta. Acting Assistant District Officer S.H. 'Bunny' Yeoman was stationed at the Sub-District Office in Kokoda, and the Kienzle brothers were at their nearby Yodda Valley property (Kienzle 2013). Both of these locations were well to the west of Mount Lamington but were in full view of the changing mountain.

Administration Patrol Officer Geoff Littler was at Higaturu headquarters during the first half of January 1951 when Mount Lamington seemed to be in its normal peaceful state. He was about to be transferred to distant Ioma to relieve the patrol officer there, W.W. 'Bill' Crellin, who was anxious to take recreation leave after first visiting headquarters at Higaturu (Littler 2005). However, Littler did not reach Ioma until Thursday 18 January. This late arrival meant that Bill Crellin did not arrive at Popondetta until the evening of Saturday 20 January, too late to proceed to Higaturu that same day. Each of the patrol officers in later life was grateful to the other for providing the circumstances that prevented their deaths at Higaturu on Sunday 21 January.

Monday 15 to Wednesday 17 January

Monday 15 January is regarded as the first day of the volcanic 'unrest', although there may well have been signs of change on the mountain before this. Visibility is not always good during the 'north-west' season, meaning that clouds can cover the summit area of the mountain at different times of the day. Earlier volcano-related earthquakes beneath Mount Lamington would have been recorded had there been a seismograph on the mountain. A few people did say they had felt small, localised earthquakes before 15 January (Taylor 1958). Further, and notably, Sister Pat Durdin at Isivita Mission on the evening of 1 January 1951 had written to her family 'that there was a strange light in the sky and wondered if it had anything to do with volcanic activity' (Kettle 1979, 139).

Several people on the Monday morning saw landslide scars on the inner faces of the peaks, which they described as 'brown streaks in the forest of the steep slopes' (Taylor 1958, 19). This is the first indication that the upper parts of the volcano were gravitationally unstable. The attention of Toby Henderson on this Monday was drawn by their Papuan cook at Sangara Rubber Plantation to a white vapour or smoke rising from the base of the Lamington peaks (Henderson 1951, 1; Taylor 1958, 19). The cook was not believed initially when he said that this was a 'bad omen', but he was from the Tufi area and apparently had witnessed the Waiowa or Goropu eruption of 1943. The ground in the crater area had evidently become hot and was starting to kill off areas of vegetation. Cloud concealed the mountain later in the afternoon.

Unrest increased slightly on Tuesday and the vapour column was seen from Higaturu for the first time. More extensive landslides moved down the slopes of the inner peaks and John R. Gwilt observed from Sangara Plantation that the vegetation had been removed from the inner slopes by late afternoon (Gwilt 1951). A 'swarm' of earthquakes was felt widely in the area at 4.00 pm, and Amalya Cowley counted 30 shocks at Higaturu from then up to 8.00 am the next day (Cowley 1953, 1). More powerful shocks were felt at Isivita north-west of the crater where the movement was described as the 'whole earth rocking' (Taylor 1958, 19).

The mountain became visible at 10.30 am the next morning, Wednesday, when:

> The first spiral of dark grey ash or smoke was noticed rising very high into the sky in a perfectly straight line but not from the top of the mountain—it seemed to come from the valley in between the hills leading up to Lamington and the mountain itself. (Cowley 1953, 2)

The volcanic emissions increased in volume and density throughout the day. Earthquakes were now being felt with monotonous regularity in the area. No luminous effects, however, such as volcanic glow from red-hot rocks or lava, were observed in the column that night.

These first three days, 15–17 January, were just the beginning of the escalating geophysical unrest. How much news about the worrisome events had been sent out during this period by different people in the district to other parts of the Territory, including to administration headquarters and to the media in Port Moresby, is still unclear. District Commissioner Cowley would not have wanted to appear nervous and indecisive to his superiors in distant Port Moresby, but he had no experience of managing volcanic crises or evacuations, and there was no government disaster plan for the Lamington area. The evolving situation was a quandary, and an extremely difficult one administratively because of the considerable uncertainty and the absence of any reliable volcanological prognosis. Would any evacuation apply just to the people in the immediate Higaturu–Sangara area, perhaps even just to the Europeans, or would it apply to all of the thousands of mountain Orokaiva who lived on and near Mount Lamington, particularly those closer to the summit crater on the north-western side of the mountain? Amalya Cowley, writing many years later in her memoirs, recalled that:

> All this time Cecil … was in contact with Port Moresby … no one seemed to be in a panic. Personally, I was terrified but kept calm despite how I felt. From the first moment of the eruption (Wednesday morning) Cecil was sending reports of it to the authorities in Port Moresby. He radioed asking for a full scale evacuation. He also asked for a volcanologist to come over and examine the mountain, but neither eventuated. (Cowley and Virtue 2015, 90; see also Cowley 1953)

Thursday 18 January

Many people on this day became aware of the eruption for the first time. Sister Jean Henderson, for example, at Eroro Mission on the north coast, heard in the morning a large explosion and saw black smoke appearing. Local people 'hopped on top of the houses to get a better view and they said "we think a drum of petrol must have exploded at Higaturu"' (Henderson 2001, 4). Sister Henderson and others were travelling by boat that morning to Gona, and they recognised while at sea that Lamington was in fact a volcano in eruption. Father Benson at Gona warned them that tsunamis might be expected along the coast and advised the visitors to return to Eroro and to warn coastal villages of the threat. Sister Henderson thought that a volcanic eruption may mean that mission staff at Isivita and Sangara would come to Eroro, so she 'had some beds made up' (Henderson 2001, 4).

The rate of cloud emission increased markedly and by nightfall it was described as 'gushing forth at a great rate' (Taylor 1958, 20). The cloud colour ranged from black to grey and there were spasms in the emission activity at the crater. The Cowleys previously, in the early hours of Thursday morning, had heard a roaring from the mountain, and once daylight arrived and visibility had improved, they saw through a telescope set up outside their house a newly built hill from which the ash column was emerging and in part flowing over the sides (Cowley 1953).

Earthquakes became more numerous and by midday were almost incessant at Higaturu. They were also being felt at both Isivita and Waseta. Some people were becoming alarmed. Photographs were taken (Figure 4.2). John Gwilt at the Sangara Rubber Plantation reported:

> That night in a clear moon-lit sky, flashes of light, more brilliant than lightning, were visible in this vast column, with noises that sounded like thunder; up to this point there did not seem to be any subterranean rumblings, although there were plenty of earth tremors. (Gwilt 1951, 1)

Sleep that night was difficult for some people.

District Commissioner Cecil Cowley sent the following radiogram from Higaturu to the Department of District Services and Native Affairs (DDS-NA) in Port Moresby in the early afternoon of 18 January:

> CONTINUOUS EARTH TREMORS COMMENCING EVENING 16TH AVERAGE SEVENTY PER DAY STOP LAMINGTON COMMENCED ERUPTING 11 OCLOCK THIS MORNING 18TH STOP SIX SPIRALS VERTICAL STOP LANDSLIDES PLENTIFUL IN VIEW ALSO STREAM FLOWING DOWN STEEP RAVINE SAND COLOURED STOP DIFFICULT DETERMINE EARTH WATER OR LAVA STOP VAST SMOKE BILLOWING WHOLE NORTHERN MOUNTAINSIDE 2 PM STOP ESTIMATED DISTANCE FROM HIGATURU EIGHT MILES STOP CONSIDER NO NEED ALARM BUT YOU MAY CARE INVESTIGATE BY AIRCRAFT STOP WILL KEEP YOU INFORMED STOP SUGGEST RADIO CONVERSATION 4.30 PM TODAY.
> (Deputy Administrator 1951, 3)

The proposed afternoon radio-telephone call took place at about 4.00 pm between Cecil Cowley in Higaturu and Sansom, a DDS-NA officer in Port Moresby. A radio-telephone service monitor, Mr Jefford, accompanied Samson and he also listened in to the conversation. However, radio static—evidently caused by the volcanic eruption—interfered significantly with the clarity of the conversation. The crux of an important issue that emerged later was whether Cowley during that call had asked for a volcanologist, accompanied by Sansom, to come to Higaturu to provide the district commissioner with professional advice (Deputy Administrator 1951; Phillips 1951c). A 24-hour radio communication link was established at this time for emergency communication between Higaturu and Port Moresby.

Cowley's radiogram to Port Moresby also formed the basis of an international telegram that was sent in the evening by Judge Phillips from the administration to the Department of External Territories in Canberra and hence to the minister, Percy Spender (Administration 1951a). That evening, the acting administrator, Judge Phillips, decided that he would go to the Lamington area himself to assess the situation. He arranged to fly down to Popondetta airstrip the next morning on an Avro Anson aircraft that was already on charter to the administration (Deputy Administrator 1951).

Among the newcomers to Higaturu Government Station were three cadet patrol officers. Two of these, Athol J. Earl and Ian James, wrote quite different kinds of letters on 18 January to their respective parents in Australia:

Things have been happening here the last two days. We started off yesterday with earth quakes, they were not very bad but frequent, every three to five minutes this went on all day and on the Lamington Mountains behind us we could see great land slides. The quakes kept up all last night and this morning great rumblings commenced. At about ten o'clock it blew its top and we now have a volcano just behind us. Great masses of smoke have been belching out ever since and the lava can be seen running down the mountain side. We have looked at it through a telescope and you can see rocks, and so forth being tossed into the air. The native[s] from all around here deserted with all their belongings, however I notice they had started to come back tonight. Earth quakes are still continuing and great rumbling is going on … The District Commissioner has been on the radio to Port Moresby and we have an emergency crystal ready if anything happens. Tomorrow a plane is being sent out to view it from the air and see how it is going. Who knows what's going to happen? Higaturu may be wiped off the map. (Earl 1951, 1–3)

As I write the whole house is shaking and loud rumblings can be heard now and then in the distance. On the night of the 16th we experienced small earth tremors which continued right through the night up till now … On the morning of the 18th, this morning, smoke began to rise, and by the time darkness fell tonight it was gusting forth at a great rate … the smoke was mostly rising into the air, at times it was a very vivid black, but other times it was fairly light-covered … There was a flow of something on one of the ravines, but we are unable to make out whether it is water, lava or earth … There is no need for alarm here, as we are quite a few miles from it, and it does not look as if it is ever going to throw up flames … It is absolutely safe here and we are really lucky having a bird's-eye view of the fun and games going on on the mountainside. Wouldn't be surprised if a geologist or a vulcanologist came out to have a look. (James 1951, 1–2)

Another young man at Higaturu was Kevin Woiwod, a carpenter working for the Department of Works and Housing at this time. Woiwod was an enthusiastic amateur photographer, developing his own negatives at his accommodation at the government station. He developed prints of photographs taken that day of the eruption cloud. The letters from the two patrol officers and the Woiwod photographs would be mailed from Higaturu in time to catch the aircraft mail-pickup at Popondetta on the next day, Friday. Woiwod evidently sent his photographs to a local newspaper, or newspapers, and these were later published in Australian newspapers (see Figure 5.9b).

Figure 4.2. Photograph of eruption taken by Kevin Woiwod on 18 January 1951

This photograph of the eruption cloud at Lamington volcano was taken by Kevin Woiwod on Thursday 18 January, presumably near or at Higaturu. It appeared later in published newspapers (see, for example, Figure 5.9b(iv)). This uncropped and digitally enhanced version of the Woiwod photograph is from a loose print in the papers of Ivan Champion held in the Fryer Library, Brisbane, where it is wrongly attributed to Allan Champion and given the wrong year (Champion 1950).

Friday 19 January

News of the eruption on the previous day, Thursday, appeared on the front page of the *South Pacific Post*, a weekly newspaper published every Friday in Port Moresby (*South Pacific Post* 1951a). The news article was entitled 'Mt Lamington Erupts' and it highlighted the statement that: 'The District Commissioner, Mr C.F. Cowley, reports that there has been no loss of life, nor is there any immediate danger' (1). It also stated that emergency contact would be maintained with Port Moresby through the Department of Civil Aviation radio network and that Judge Phillips would be flying down to Higaturu that day.

Light-coloured ash was seen in the morning lying on the summit peaks of Mount Lamington. The spasms in the crater emissions had become more pronounced and were becoming more visible to people over a wider area. Anthropologist Marie Reay at Waseta made a note in her diary that in the morning she saw 'a great column of smoke rising from the direction of Isivita. Mt Lamington had erupted for the first time in recorded history' (Reay 1951, 1). Some local people from Isivita came down to Waseta and spoke with her and said that they had not seen or heard of Mount Lamington having been in eruption previously. According to Reay, they explained the cause of the eruption by saying:

1. might be kerosene or benzine start fire in the mountain.
2. might be god punishing the people—jesus christ died for we and we no do what god says.
3. atiti—might be spirits. (Reay 1951, 1, original lower case)

Acting Administrator Judge Phillips arrived at Port Moresby airport, Jackson's Strip, at 7.30 am, but his scheduled Avro Anson flight to Popondetta was delayed because of mechanical difficulties (Deputy Administrator 1951). He arranged, while waiting for the repairs to be completed, for his wife to take, at his own expense, a seat on a Norseman aircraft that was also going to Popondetta so that she could see a volcano in eruption. Mrs Phillips arrived before her husband at Popondetta airstrip where a crowd had gathered, some of them to farewell Allan Champion and his family. Champion had just completed his term as deputy district commissioner at Higaturu.

Judge Phillips eventually arrived at Popondetta having made an aerial inspection of the column of vapour from Lamington, which at first seemed to him like 'an unusually high tower of cumulus cloud' rising 20–25,000 feet high, but in places it had slightly greyer 'folds' and there was a slow upward movement of the column (Deputy Administrator 1951, 4). Phillips, after landing at the airstrip, engaged the district commissioner in a discussion about the eruption. Cecil Cowley expressed surprise on having seen both the administrator and his wife arrive at Popondetta. He had expected instead a volcanologist and Samsom to disembark from the aircraft, as requested on the radio the day before.

Figure 4.3. Photograph of eruption possibly taken by Allan Champion on 19 January 1951

A strong emission of ash from Mount Lamington is seen in this photograph taken from Higaturu presumably before 20 January. This digitally enhanced copy is from a paper print held in the papers of Ivan Champion in the Fryer Library, Brisbane, where it is attributed to Allan Champion (1950). The reverse side of the print reads: 'Mount Lamington erupts before the final devastation. Allan Champion 1950 [1951]'. However, the name of the photographer and the date of the photograph are both uncertain. The photographer could have been Kevin Woiwod and the print may have been carried out of the area when Allan Champion left from Popondetta airstrip on Friday 19 January (see also Figure 4.2).

Judge Phillips later recorded his impressions of the eruption cloud, as seen during his short time at the airstrip:

> It was not moving violently at all, but rising so gently and slowly that one had to look at it for an appreciable time to detect movement … it was not spasmodic and did not emerge in violent bursts: in short, it looked as if the initial force of the volcano had spent itself and as if the forces underneath had found

sufficient outlet. The appearance of that column reminded me of that of the column from the volcano that erupted at Vulcan Island at Rabaul in 1937, several days after the actual eruption, when the Vulcan column was beginning gradually to subside. (Deputy Administrator 1951, 5)

Phillips also noted at Popondetta airstrip that:

> The ladies present appeared understandably anxious, particularly Mrs. Cowley, who at moments seemed to break down, but Mr. Cowley was cool and confident, and tried to calm his wife's nervousness … Mrs. Cowley came to me and said that she was thinking of her children and did I not think there should be an immediate evacuation … I said that I did not think an immediate evacuation was necessary but added that, if the volcano got violent, she should 'get into that jeep and go to Kokoda', or words to that effect. (Deputy Administrator 1951, 5, 7)

After providing this advice, Judge Phillips flew back with his wife to Port Moresby for the weekend. The eruption at Lamington escalated that afternoon.

Amalya Cowley had an interest in radio broadcasting that stemmed from her wartime ambition to be a radio announcer at a radio station in Canberra—'she had a beautiful speaking voice', recalled her daughter Pamela (Cowley and Virtue 2015, 55). This interest had continued at Higaturu where she responded to a request from the Australian Broadcasting Commission (ABC) radio station 9PA in Port Moresby for information about the eruption (Cowley 1953). At 3.45 pm on Friday 19 January, Amalya Cowley sent a radiogram to the ABC (Correspondent 1951), the first half of which read:

> CORRESPONDENT COWLEY STOP LAMINGTON BELCHING STEADILY CONTINUOUSLY MAXIMUM INTENSITY MIDDLE FRIDAY AFTERNOON THIRTY FOUR THOUSAND FEET HEIGHT FIVE MILES LENGTH BASE GRAY BILLOWING COTTON WOOL VIOLENTLY AGITATED CLOUD STOP MORNING CLOUD WHITE WITH DULL RED BLACK SPEARLIKE BLOW TORCH THROUGH CENTRE TO HALF HEIGHT STOP NO NOISE OCCASIONAL DISTANT RUMBLING STOP. (Correspondent 1951, 1)

In strong contrast, the second half of Amalya Cowley's radiogram focused on a legend about Mount Lamington:

> LEGEND SUMBIRITA MANS NAME KAMIKARI MEANS SHUT IN STOP THE IMPRISONMENT OF SUBITITA SWEETHEART DOG FOUND ENTRANCE TO BOWL NEAR SUMMIT STOP SUMBIRITA LOVE OVERTURES PREVAILED AGAINST SWEETHEART PROTESTATIONS STOP MOUNTAIN CLOSED ENTRANCE WITH STONES IN ANGER STOP BOWL ROSE SLOWLY SUMMIT DOG THROWN OVER SIDE TEST POSSIBILITY ESCAPE CRUSHED DEATH STOP TRAPPED SWEETHEART DIED LINGERING DEATH STOP NEIGHBOURS VISITED BOTH CALLED OUT FOR EXPLANATION WEEKS LATER SUMBIRITA ADMITTED RESPONSIBILITY GUILT CALLED AGAIN MONTH LATER NO ANSWER END LEGEND. (Correspondent 1951, 1)

This version of what would become a frequently told story about Mount Lamington and the legendary Sumbiripa, or Sumbirita, is of interest in that it matches, more or less, the mountain myth recorded in 1948 by H.M. Corderoy, although Sumbiripa and the wife are not named specifically in the earlier version. A point of interest, too, is the timing of Amalya Cowley's record—that is, in the same week that Lamington becomes recognised unequivocally as an active volcano. The story had been told some time earlier to Cecil Cowley by 'a village chief at Higaturu' (Cowley 1953, 2). It is not clearly a volcano-related story, however, unless 'bowl' refers to a crater or volcanic vent, or—even more speculatively—if the bowl was inverted and it refers to a mound or 'dome' of formerly viscous lava.

District Commissioner Cowley, meanwhile, was at Higaturu without the volcanological expertise he had hoped for and requested. In addition, his superior, the most senior officer in Port Moresby—the acting administrator of the Territory—now believed there was no need for concern about the likely course of eruption. There would be, decided the administration, no evacuation. This was despite the fact that there were people remaining in the Lamington area, such as the anxious European women at Popondetta airstrip, who felt otherwise. Cecil Cowley had been provided with a 24-hour emergency radio link with Port Moresby should the situation worsen, but this assumes that electrical interference from the volcano would not again produce radio static and thus affect the clarity of any voice exchanges.

4. VICTIMS, SURVIVORS AND EVACUATIONS

Volcanologist Tony Taylor recorded briefly that he had heard about the Lamington volcanic activity from a radio broadcast on Friday 19 January, but he did not state specifically that this was the *first* time he had heard of the mountain's unrest (Taylor 1951). The statement, however, contrasts with a detailed record made by Taylor's volcanological colleague and friend John G. Best, who, writing mainly from memory 37 years later, said that Taylor had told him he had heard about the Lamington events from radio broadcasts as early as Monday 15 January, and that Taylor had approached the district commissioner in Rabaul, on the north-eastern tip of New Britain, about the matter (Best 1988). The district commissioner in Rabaul was J. Keith McCarthy, a well-known former 'New Guinea' officer from before the war who had lived through the volcanic eruptions at Rabaul in 1937 (McCarthy 1971a, 1971b). McCarthy, however, was uncertain about what should be done concerning the Lamington reports, according to Best, as there had been no request from anyone in authority in Port Moresby for the services of a volcanologist. Further, Mount Lamington in the distant and former Territory of Papua was not known, either by him or Taylor, to be an active volcano.

There was also some confusion about whether the reports of volcanic activity were actually for Goropu or Victory in the Tufi area, which were known to be active volcanoes, rather than for Mount Lamington. Then there was the practical problem of Taylor travelling at short notice from Rabaul to Popondetta by air—especially the availability of a seat on an aircraft to Lae or Port Moresby and then to Popondetta. As the administrator himself, Colonel Murray, was due to arrive in Rabaul on Saturday 20 January, he could be asked directly for a decision (Best 1988). Murray was touring plantations in the Gazelle Peninsula and Duke of York Islands, and on Saturday was scheduled to open an extension to club rooms of the East New Britain Ladies Club, followed by a 'ball in the evening and presentation of debutantes' (*South Pacific Post* 1951a, 2). Tony Taylor met the administrator on the Saturday; Murray agreed that Taylor should inspect Lamington volcano and, further, that he should accompany him on a return flight to Lae leaving early on Monday morning.

How reports of the volcanic unrest at Lamington came to be broadcast by the ABC as early as Monday 15 January, as stated by Best, is unknown. Was Best's memory and reporting of the facts correct after so many years? Could Amalya Cowley have had a general agreement with the ABC to send news items from Higaturu that she thought might be of interest to listeners, bearing in mind her interest in radio broadcasting? If so, had she sent earlier messages to Port Moresby that week? Whatever the case, Taylor did not leave Rabaul until the morning of Monday 22 January. Would Taylor arriving at Higaturu any earlier have made any difference anyway in terms of what would happen next?

Saturday 20 January

Saturday was a clear day, enabling many observations to be made of the escalating volcanic activity. The active area in the old crater had enlarged, and there were, according to Margaret de Bibra, as many as four or five active vents. Mission mechanic Rodd Hart at Jegarata village directly facing the open crater area reported that the sounds that had been emerging from the mountain for three days were like those of a 'gigantic underground railway' (Hart 1953, 1). Wallace Kienzle in the Yodda Valley noted in the morning that 'the activity was most marked with what appeared to be no longer than 3–5 minute intervals between fresh burst[s] of energy pushing those fresh clouds up in a practically continuous stream' and that a wind carried the top of the eruption column at 25–30,000 feet towards the south (Kienzle 1951, 1).

Later, Mr Yeoman made a sketch of the 'bent' eruption cloud (Figure 4.4) and recorded that the column during the day, as seen from Kokoda, had the:

> Appearance of [a] black wall with straight face towards the sea, turning over at the top of the wall and back towards the Managalasi. Behind the sea face and beneath the bent over column of smoke the sky was pitch black—like black night. Through the field glasses, the billowing smoke had something of the appearance of a cauliflower and was similar to an oil fire. The smoke was illuminated from within by huge, curved, red flashes of light. (Yeoman 1951, 1)

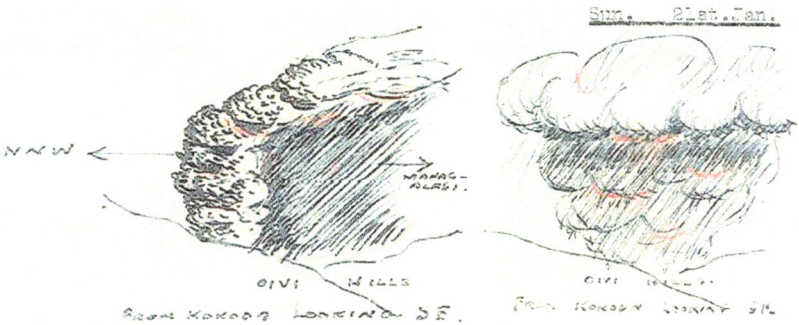

Figure 4.4. Sketches by S.H. Yeoman of eruption clouds on 20–21 January 1951
These are Assistant District Officer Yeoman's sketches of the contrasting eruptions at Mount Lamington on Saturday 20 January (left) and Sunday 21 January.

The monsoonal winds of the 'north-west' season were causing this heavy ash fallout on southern side of the volcano in country occupied by the Koiari-speaking Managalasi and Omie people. The nature of the destructive effects south of the mountain during these first six days has not been recorded by Europeans, but clearly the damage at least to gardens must have been substantial. The Omie live high on the south-western slopes of Lamington and called the mountain Huvaemo, attributing special spiritual powers to her (Modjeska 2009). Historian and novelist Drusilla Modjeska much later collected a story told to her by the Omie, which she used in her book *The Mountain*:

> Before the eruption, there had been signs that the mountain was angry. Cassowaries and bandicoots came into village, wild boars came close to the houses. There were great storms with lightning in the sky, and though rain fell, the rivers ran dry, the water pulled back up into the mountain. When the water returned it was hot. (Modjeska 2012, 140)

No ash fell to the north of Mount Lamington on the more populous country of the mountain Orokaiva during the preceding six days. Ash fall might have taken place there during the 'dry' season when south-east trade winds blow, which is not to say that the Orokaiva were any the more fortunate. Hypothetically, however, some fallout might have influenced decisions to leave any ash-affected area. Much worse was to follow for the Orokaiva in any case.

Reverend Robert Porter, Sister Pat Durdin and Barbara Lane were at Isivita Mission during this time and, by Saturday, were concerned about the safety of local people living nearby, and of themselves (Anonymous 1951f; Porter 1951a, 1951b, 1951c). They were closer to the active crater than were people living down the mountain at Higaturu, Sangara and Waseta, and they felt many of the earthquakes more strongly. The previous day, Barbara Lane had suggested to Porter that he contact the district commissioner for advice, but Porter delayed, 'half influenced by the fear that he might be thought too "jittery"' (Anonymous 1951f, 18). Porter, however, changed his mind on the Saturday:

> Lamington now looked very fierce. The [active] crater now seemed to be much more on our side … The smoke was much denser than before, and indeed was hardly like smoke at all. It was just a grey mass which seemed to curl out of the ground like toothpaste squeezed from a tube … The people were terrified and several from the villages of Hamumuta, Pinja, and Popondota came to live on the mission station. I wrote to the [district commissioner] to ask his advice about any further people coming on the station. Fr. [Dennis] Taylor came to us in the afternoon to see how we fared and to re-assure us that all would be well. (Porter 1951b, 1)

Reverend Taylor's reassurance derived from his personal volcanological experience of the explosive eruption at Goropu in 1943–44 while stationed at Wanigela Mission south of Tufi. He said that, in comparison to what was happening now at Lamington, Goropu 'was far more severe, but yet there had been no loss of life' (Porter 1951a, 25). Taylor had earlier expressed a similar opinion to the Cowleys at Higaturu (Cowley and Virtue 2015). This declaration by the priest-in-charge at Sangara Mission, therefore, was in accord with the view of the acting administrator, Judge Phillips, who on the previous day had made an assessment, based at least in part on his own previous experience with the eruption at Rabaul in 1937, that there was no reason for concern. The representatives of Church and State in the Lamington area were in apparent agreement that no evacuations were necessary at this time. District Commissioner Cowley sent policemen out with messages to communities and churches—where there would be services the following day, Sunday—informing people they would be told if any further action was necessary.

This final and crucial decision not to evacuate was made by four European men, primarily by Judge Phillips and Reverend Taylor—one of them a lawyer and the other a priest—and secondarily by their subordinates,

Cowley and Porter. Phillips and Taylor were attempting to appear knowledgeable and authoritative about volcanic eruptions based on their respective personal experiences at other volcanoes, and, therefore, to appear in control of the volcanic crisis. Local people, women in general, and the white planter community seemed to have had little influence. The concordance of Phillips and Taylor on this matter is all the more striking in recalling that the administration and the mission had had their differences, if not conflicts, in the postwar years up to 1951.

Porter's description of the Lamington eruption column being a 'grey mass' curling out of the ground is volcanologically significant because it is indicative of a densification of the ash cloud and, thus, the potential for overloading of the ash column. These are conditions that can lead to collapse of a heavy eruption cloud and to the creation of hot, surface-hugging flows of ash and gas that will move outwards and downslope gravitationally. Such flows may have formed at times on the Saturday, but, if so, they were small, did not travel far, and were not reported unambiguously (Taylor 1958). Further, no new extrusions of viscous lava domes were observed taking place in the crater area, and this too would have some later significance among the volcanological community.

Reverend Taylor came to Isivita that Saturday afternoon accompanied by two local schoolteachers, George Ambo and Albert Maclaren Ririka (e.g. Anonymous 1951f; Patience 2001; Johnston 2003). Both men were enrolled as participants in the course for teachers being run by Margaret de Bibra at Sangara, but had come with Reverend Taylor to assist the mission staff at Isivita who were having to cope with an increasing number of people arriving in the hope of some kind of reassurance if not protection. Reverend Taylor meanwhile, and fatefully, returned to Sangara Mission that afternoon. George Ambo and Albert Ririka however—and equally 'fatefully'—stayed overnight at Isivita. George Ambo later became the first Papuan bishop of New Guinea and Albert Ririka an ordained priest.

Cecil Cowley had been in touch with Port Moresby by radio-telephone at about 3.00 pm. The conversation was again interrupted by strong radio static evidently caused by the volcanic activity, and Cowley could not complete a message concerning the state of the volcano. Several operators tried to hear the message, but Cowley is reported to have said 'not to mind, it was not very important … [and that] he will try again tomorrow morning' (Deputy Administrator 1951, appendix C, 2).

Amalya Cowley had been having sleepless nights at Higaturu because of the threatening seismic and eruptive behaviour of Mount Lamington. She was encouraged by her husband, and by the Stephens, to spend the night at Sangara Rubber Plantation, and she reluctantly agreed, comforted that her daughter Pamela would be accompanying her (Cowley and Virtue 2015). Cecil drove them to the plantation and returned to Higaturu to stay on duty that night. Erl remained with his father at the government station. The plan was that Amalya Cowley and Pamela would be picked up the next morning and driven back to Higaturu. That night, the number of felt earthquakes appeared not only to decrease but also to do so fairly abruptly after about 8.00 pm, and they may have ceased altogether by Sunday morning (Taylor 1958, fig. 12).

Spectacular luminous effects were seen after nightfall that were later judged to be characteristic of the more vigorous phase of the eruption up to that time (Taylor 1958). Wallace Kienzle noted from Yodda at night that he was:

> Able to see what appeared to be fireballs bursting in the mass of the clouds above 10,000 feet. These were not visible as long streaks of flame but only as short tails immediately prior to bursting in a red glow. Definitely not to be compared with lightning. (Kienzle 1951, 1)

John Gwilt at Sangara observed after nightfall that:

> A new phenomena appeared in the shape of whirling stars reaching the full length of the column, intermittently mixed with brilliant flashes of light; these whirling stars gave the impression that they were [being] seen through a dense fog. (Gwilt 1951, 2)

Agricultural officer 'Blue' Morris at Waseta noted 'horizontal flashes' as well as 'flaring patches of blue light' like the spasms of flame seen when a gas jet backfires (Taylor 1958, 22). Margaret de Bibra at Sangara Mission set down her experiences of that eventful week on the following morning, expressing her deep concerns about the 'new' volcano.

Climactic Explosions on the Sunday Morning

Aircraft and ash cloud close encounters

Two Qantas Empire Airways aircraft were in-flight and uncomfortably close to Mount Lamington at the time of the devastating eruption at 10.40 am on Sunday 21 January. Their occupants obtained spectacular and frightening views of the enormous and rapidly changing cloud including the lateral movement of its base (Qantas 1951; *Pacific Islands Monthly* 1951b; Taylor 1958; Sinclair 1986). Captain Arthur Jacobson was flying a Douglas DC3 'Dakota' aircraft at a height of about 2,900 metres on a normal 'Bird of Paradise' flight from Port Moresby to Rabaul via the Kokoda Gap. He was above a layer of cumulus cloud and saw to his starboard side a continuous column of black ash rising from the crater. The column penetrated another layer of cloud above him at about 4,300 metres, above which the cloud was expanding greatly (see Figure 5.9a(i)). Then, at about 40 kilometres north-west of the volcano, and at 10.42 am, he observed:

> Dark mass of ash shoot up from the crater and rise, within two minutes, to 40,000 feet [more than 12 kilometres], forming a huge expanding mushroom-shaped summit. The base of the column expanded rapidly as if the 'whole countryside were erupting'. (Taylor 1958, 24)

The Qantas aircraft was in danger of being engulfed by the enormous eruption cloud, so Captain Jacobson put the sedate Douglas into a fast descent reaching a speed of about 215 miles per hour (350 kilometres per hour). However, even then the DC3 'was unable to draw away from it for at least five minutes … and the apex of the explosion [by then] had reached a height of approximately 50,000 feet'—that is, more than 15 kilometres (Qantas 1951, 9). Photographs were taken from on board the DC3 that later became widely reproduced in different publications (Figures 4.5 and 5.9a(i)).

> **Extracts from letter by Margaret de Bibra, Sunday 21 January 1951 (White 1991, 45–47)**
>
> We have a volcano! Just at our back door too. Mt Lamington … lies behind us and consists of four or five sugar-loaf peaks. We have always loved her for her beauty and nearness … [but now] she has changed from fairy queen to a wicked witch, and the gossamer scarves of mist [seen in the early mornings] have turned into smoky outpourings of some bubbling cauldron …
>
> For days we had earth tremors; at first occasional ones such as we [had] experienced before, and then they became almost continuous and the face of Lamington became scarred with great patches of bare earth, caused by landslides. Then one morning—January 18th—after a night of continuous tremors, smoke appeared. At first there was only a little. Then it came pouring out in great thick puffs high into the sky, wreathing and curling in awe-inspiring cauliflower shapes …
>
> ***
>
> What do the people think? We are carrying on our work as usual, though we run out from time to time to watch it …
>
> The Papuans?—well, most are calm, many are apprehensive and some really frightened, especially those whose villages are near the mount. It is all understandable, in fact it is to their credit that there is no panic. Lamington has not been a volcano within the memory of living man, nor in the legend of the people. True, Lamington is feared as the home of spirits, and no local man—even Christian—will venture to the top. As one of our Church Councillors said, 'The mountain people do not understand. They are afraid. We understand a little and we are afraid too. Our fathers did not know of it. The trembling of the earth yes, but not the fire. At night it is like a torch and we do not understand the sign.'
>
> What will it mean? … How will it affect the faith of new Christians? Can we make them understand what a volcano is, or will it be a return to old fears and superstition? … Will you think of the people here, particularly the Managalas people, and those near our stations of Sewa and Sehaperete [on the distant northeastern side of the mountain]? Pray for them and for us, that out of this good may come, and as the dead mount came to [the letter ends abruptly at this point].

The second Qantas aircraft in the area was a smaller De Haviland DH84 'Dragon' being flown by first officers Ross Biddulph and Fred Barlogie on a charter flight from Lae to Popondetta (Qantas 1951; Henry 1951; Horne 1976; Sinclair 1986; Bullard 2017). Two government officers from the Department of Agriculture, Stock and Fisheries were on board. They were accompanying D.H. Urquhart, a cocoa expert and a representative of the Cadbury's chocolate company. The aircraft was approaching Popondetta airstrip and about to land when they saw the fast eruption cloud advancing towards them, appearing as if the entire side of Mount Lamington had blown out. They saw Higaturu Government Station being enveloped and blotted out. Biddulph banked the aircraft steeply and flew away at full speed from the advancing cloud that he estimated, by roughly calculating the speed of its shadow on the ground, to be twice that of the Dragon aircraft. He headed back to Lae, but not before Urquhart had taken low-level and close-up photographs of the threatening eruption cloud. The negatives of these photographs have not been found although at least one photograph was published in Australian newspapers (Horne 1976). One of the many stories about the cause of the eruption was that an aircraft flying close to Mount Lamington had dropped a bomb on the mountain and then flown away (Belshaw 1951b). That mistaken aerial bomber may have been the Dragon piloted by Biddulph.

The basal expansion of the cloud noted by the pilots took place when the rapidly moving and ground-hugging ash flows descended the flanks of the volcano, particularly the northern flank. The flows eventually came to a halt, however, and dumped their load of hot ash and lava fragments. The remaining, strongly heated, clouds of light ash, gas, vapour and air then rose up from the hot area of devastation as if, falsely, from innumerable surface vents. This caused a 'draw back' of the clouds, thus seeming to reverse the direction of flow.

Figure 4.5. Photograph of eruption cloud on 21 January by Captain Jacobson

The dark volcanic cloud from Mount Lamington is seen here between two levels of cumulus cloud in this starboard view from the Qantas DC3 flight flying northwards. Hot lateral flows of ash and volcanic gas are beginning to emerge from the base of the cloud, especially on the right, down the southern side of the volcano as shown by the arrows (Taylor 1958, fig. 11). Photograph supplied courtesy of Geoscience Australia (negative number GB/1886).

Observations of the ash cloud from the ground

On the morning of Sunday 21 January, Patrol Officer Jim Sinclair and Medical Officer Dr Olgerts Ozols were about 270 kilometres north-west of Mount Lamington. They had been patrolling the area of the Buang villages of south-west Morobe Province and were about to walk back to their headquarters at Mumeng on the Lae-Wau road, when, wrote Sinclair:

> At about 10.45 a.m. on Sunday I was lying on my canvas bunk, reading, when I was hurled from the bunk to the black-palm floor by a convulsive heave of the entire resthouse. The impact half stunned me, and as I was lying on the floor I felt a series of deep rumbles, and a little later a dull, grinding shudder that seemed to run up the long pilings of the house from the very centre of the earth. Olgerts, who was outside, rushed up the sapling ladder. 'Something very bad has happened, Jim', he said, 'Listen to the people.' From the village came the screams of women and the frightened wails of children. But there was no further movement of the earth, and after some discussion we dismissed the occurrence as a more than usually severe 'guria' or earth tremor. (Sinclair 1981, 77)

They were told about 'the volcanic eruption of terrible force in the Northern Division of Papua' on reaching Mumeng that evening and did not report seeing the Mount Lamington volcanic cloud. The volcanic explosion was heard in other distant places, including Finschhafen and even at Talasea on the north coast of New Britain (Crane 1971).

Views of the high eruption cloud from Lamington on the Sunday morning were seen by people at Kokoda and in the Yodda Valley, about 48 kilometres west of the active crater. Witnesses there were well placed, theoretically at least, to see the laterally directed ash flows racing northwards down the slopes of Mount Lamington, except that the wind direction seemed to have changed from the previous day and was now blowing towards them, 'thus we lost what I would call a profile view of yesterday', wrote Wallace Kienzle (1951, 1). The higher parts of the ash cloud were now being driven by high-level winds that were different in speed and direction from the normal, low-level 'north-west' season winds at this time of year. The cloud by mid-morning had become darker and was moving closer towards them in the Yodda Valley, streaks of lightning were evident and, by 10.55 am, the cloud was almost overhead. Hot black ash began to fall on roofs. The Kienzle family at their Mamba property had been relaxing after breakfast when the house shook violently and an intense rumble was heard. House servants 'screamed and ran for cover and, as the sky turned black and blocked out the sun, they panicked even more, believing the end of the world had come' (Kienzle 2013, 255).

The *kiap*, Bunny Yeoman, reported the same darkening and ash fallout at nearby Kokoda Government Station, and noted the same electrical phenomena he had seen on the previous day (Yeoman 1951). He also wrote that lights had to be used in houses because of the darkness produced by the now enveloping cloud. Yeoman later provided a rough sketch of the shape of the cloud while it had been approaching Kokoda, which contrasts markedly with the one he drew of the 'bent' ash column the previous day (Figure 4.4, right).

Wallace Kienzle and some reluctant helpers set off from Mamba to see what could be done down the road towards Mount Lamington and to check on their storerooms at Kumusi River and Sangara:

> As he came closer to the scene, he saw first-hand the shocking devastation. The rivers and creeks flowed black with ash, and in among the debris, the charred bodies of victims floated grotesquely. Wallace stopped and collected what bodies he could, stacking them by the side of the road. He [later] grabbed supplies like blankets and basic food items from the trade stores at Mamba, and he handed these out to the stunned survivors, many of whom were badly burned. (Kienzle 2013, 255)

The view southwards from Eroro Mission on the coast, 40–50 kilometres north of the Lamington disaster area, was equally impressive, as recalled by Sister Jean Henderson. She was on her way to work in the hospital wards that morning when:

> There was a mighty explosion, several, not just one but quite a few … large black clouds filled the sky and there was a darkness … and as I watched, unbelievably the large dark clouds began to roll back. At the edge of the black cloud was a brilliant golden light, fantastic to watch. The Papuans were terrified, and they were worried because they had young families living and working with the Government [at Higaturu] and with the Sangara mission station. (Henderson 2001, 4)

Sister Henderson also wrote that, on Thursday 18 January, local people at Eroro thought after hearing a large explosion and seeing 'black smoke' that 'a drum of petrol must have exploded at Higaturu' (Henderson 2001, 4). She later recalled that a patrol officer, possibly Murphy, had told her previously that Mount Lamington was a volcano.

People at Eroro Mission escaped any volcanic fallout from the distant eruption, but the situation was much more devastating for those at Isivita Mission, which is about 9 kilometres north-west from the active crater itself and slightly closer to it than even Higaturu Government Station. From Isivita Mission on the morning of Sunday 21 January, Mount Lamington had the same fierce appearance it had had the previous day; however, at 10.15–10.30 am the irregular rumblings gave way to a sustained and uniform roar that increased in volume. Then 'to our horror we saw this grey mass of thick smoke moving swiftly towards us at ground level' (Porter 1951a, 25; see also Porter 1951b, 1951c; Anonymous 1951f; Strong 1951; Patience 2001). Part of a lateral flow of ash and gas was about to envelop the mission.

Reverend Porter, Sister Durdin and Barbara Lane retreated for safety to the main mission house, crowding in as many local people as possible, but they were surprised when the threatening, ground-hugging flow of ash stopped suddenly in the mission grounds. The missionaries discovered outside a remarkably sharp, demarcation line between green grass on one side and thick volcanic debris on the other, a boundary seen also at other places just outside the area of devastation on the flanks of Mount Lamington. People at Isivita on the 'green' side of the line had escaped the flow of ash, but not so those on the other side of the 'draw back' line, as recorded by Reverend Porter:

> The mass of smoke gradually lifted, and I went outside to observe the situation. Dozens of terrified people were running on to the station, covered in pumice. Their two eyes emerged from completely grey bodies. I ran up to Isivita village (200 yards from the station) and urged all and sundry to come to the station. They did not require much urging. The poor dears were terrified and there were pitiful scenes. (Porter 1951a, 25)

Porter returned to his own house by which time the mission house was filled to capacity, and people were beginning to fill other houses on the station:

> The next phase was about to begin … The heavens now proceeded to pour down everything on us. Pumice fell again, sand, and small stones. But the most terrifying thing of all was the darkness which now descended on everything. The sun was completely blotted out, and at 11.30 a.m. it became darker than any night I have ever known. The blackness was relieved only by fierce streaks of lightning, followed closely by deafening bursts of thunder … Sister Pat [Durdin] prepared dressings for the first burns case which had just come in … It was now [at 1.00 pm] that the most pitiful and awful scenes of all were witnessed. People with the most terrible burns imaginable began to stream in for treatment. (Porter 1951a, 26)

Porter at this point urged those who were well enough 'to get away as far as possible from Lamington, and as quickly as possible, and they needed no second bidding' (26). He told them to make for Sasambata downslope west from Isivita but he later found out that most of the evacuees had gone down to Agenahambo village on the main road between Popondetta and Awala. Porter then returned to the mission house to do what he could to assist Barbara Lane and Sister Durdin:

> The entire floor was covered with people in utter agony. Some had almost the whole of their skin burnt off. It hung from their hands like discarded gloves, and their agonising cries were awful to hear. The best we could do was make dressings from lint and vaseline and apply them to their charred bodies. About forty were treated at the Mission, but there must have been many who could not reach us. Soon Sister was busy with the morphia, which must have been a blessed relief for these unfortunates … In the mid-afternoon our first case died. (Porter 1951a, 26)

A large grave was dug in anticipation of more deaths to come.

Awala Plantation evacuation

Awala Plantation was several kilometres north-west of Isivita and the devastated area, and so was spared the disastrous impact of the ash flows. However, it did experience severe ash fall from the higher-level, westward-drifting cloud, leading to damage of its plantation crops of rubber, coffee and cocoa, and to slow evacuations along the Waseta–Popondetta road. Clen Searle, the owner-lessee of the Awala Plantation, which adjoined the road, had had a long association with the Awala area, including during WWII when he trained as an army commando and was given advanced telecommunications equipment and training for surveillance of Japanese movements in the Northern Province (Searle n.d.). Searle, before the war, had been a radio engineer at the Amalgamated Wireless Australasia radio station in Port Moresby (Searle 1936). He now had his own radio communications equipment at the plantation.

Pat Searle was at Awala Plantation on the Sunday morning preparing for a lunch to be attended by 13 guests, including Dickie Humphries and the Locke family, together with the Hendersons from Sangara Plantation (Searle 1995). The Hendersons would also be driving out along the road to pick up their daughter, Mary Rose, who since Friday had been staying at Awala Plantation with the Searle children, Peter and Rhonwen. Other Europeans in the Awala–Waseta area on this Sunday morning were agricultural officer Blue Morris, who was normally based at Popondetta, and anthropologist Marie Reay, who was staying at the Waseta Rest House. Blue Morris was in the area, on this Sabbath day-of-rest, working with hulling equipment that was being provided to local rice growers on nearby native plantations.

Many years later, Pat Searle recalled in some detail the effects of witnessing the 'huge thick black cloud' that was advancing towards them at Awala. It was 'starting to fill the whole of the heavens' (Searle 1995, 236), and it triggered the spontaneous evacuation of people from the plantation once the fallout of ash began. The Searle family, together with Mary Rose Henderson, took a jeep—its canvas roof now covered with corrugated iron sheets for protection—and drove westwards along the Kokoda Road towards Waseta, which is about 4 kilometres further from the volcano. Some plantation workers had already left Awala on a tractor-trailer, but many others had to escape on foot. Then:

> Quite suddenly we were in a complete blackout, so dark it was impossible to see a hand in front of your face. Severe thunder and lightning had long started when the heavens opened up, showering tons of stones, dust and debris on the world we had known. The air became stifling, it was almost impossible for Clen to see the road, with the jeep lights so very dim in such intense blackness and falling ash and we stopped in the darkness … Very, very slowly, we moved on again at a snail's pace. (Searle 1995, 237–38)

To their surprise they came across Blue Morris at the roadside in a bush hut, 'his tractor going full bore running the rice thresher! He said work had continued there, being the best solution to what was still happening' (Searle 1995, 238). There is no record of the conversion that Clen Searle had with Blue Morris, the sole government employee in the Awala–Waseta area at that time; however, after arriving at the Waseta Rest House at about 1.00 pm, Searle decided to return to Awala to radio government authorities in Port Moresby about the critical situation. He had problems doing so as the usual weekday circuit in Port Moresby was closed each Sunday, but he used a different radio crystal, got through to the Port Moresby airport, and then asked for the weekday circuit to be opened immediately. The 'outside world' had been contacted.

Ongoing activity at the volcano later in the afternoon was interfering with radio communications, so Clen Searle temporarily transferred the radio and its aerial to Waseta for further traffic the next morning, setting up the aerial in a mango tree that, by coincidence, he had used in July 1943 in sending coded messages to army headquarters in Port Moresby. The Searle family group, now including Marie Reay, spent that night at Waseta.

Blue Morris had decided earlier to drive westwards from Waseta to the Kumusi River to see what was happening in the general Wairopi area, possibly to check whether evacuation was still possible in that direction. He took with him the two young European girls, Rhonwen Searle and Mary Rose Henderson, perhaps in the hope of getting them over the river and finding transport to evacuate them to Kokoda. The rivers crossed by them 'all came down swiftly from the upper areas of Mt Lamington, and some were warmed by hot mud, and as they flowed covered thickly with ash the fish were gasping and dying, floating to the surface in great numbers' (Searle 1995, 241). A load of fish and eels was gathered and brought back to Waseta Rest House where the hungry evacuees all sat around, with their helpers, and enjoyed a fish feast (see also Morris 1951).

Fish populations had been reduced in the rivers and, perhaps more important economically, the ash fall damage to crops had been substantial, such as at Awala Plantation:

> All was an ashen grey: all colour obliterated by the pervasive ash on every leaf and bough. The coffee trees stood like grey cylindrical bottle brushes about two metres high, the lateral branches angled down from the familiar horizontal. The ground was covered inches deep in ash. There was not a sound except for the breaking of

> the rubber tree branches … The incremental weight of the ash accumulated on every leaf was devastating: rubber wood is known to be quite brittle and susceptible to damage in windstorms.
>
> [Also] … numerous trees in the rainforest kept falling to the ground … the constant wrenching and the tearing off of great branches from trunks of many trees made loud and continuous noises. There might be a momentary pause, but the noise of their falling would start again, as the branches, heavily weighted with ash from the eruption during the many hours of darkness, plunged below, finally crashing to the ground. (Searle 1995, 239–40)

Most importantly, however, the many hundreds of people living on this north-western flank in the so-called 'Isivita District' were without homes and gardens because of the damaging ash falls. Most of these people had escaped the deadly ground-surface flows of ash down the northern flank, but they became refugees congregating at, or near, the road west of Awala Plantation and towards the Kumusi River.

Sangara Plantation evacuation

People at Sangara Rubber Plantation about 9 kilometres east of Awala and along the road towards Popondetta were also having to manage extreme volcanic conditions (Stephens 1951, 1953; Gwilt 1951; Schleusener 1951; Cowley and Virtue 2015). Sangara Plantation was much more extensive than the one at Awala. Its main buildings near the road were less than 5 kilometres north of the now destroyed Higaturu and only 2 kilometres from the northern edge of the devastated area. The plantation also had a larger staff, both European and Papuan, and, like the people at Isivita Mission, they endured the shock of seeing burnt people who were escaping from the edge of the volcanic devastation emerge onto the main road.

Laura Stephens, who was hosting Amalya Cowley and daughter Pam, recorded the drama:

> I was just about to announce that [morning tea] was ready when a terrific explosion occurred. The noise was loud and sharp, almost like a series of detonations right along the range … But this was different [to a normal explosion]. Instead of reaching its peak and then dying down, the explosion kept growing and coming toward us at a terrific rate. I called out in alarm to my husband … 'Come quickly', I said. 'The whole range seems to have disintegrated and is coming this way!'. He came in, looked for a few seconds, and then

4. VICTIMS, SURVIVORS AND EVACUATIONS

said quietly, 'Come, all of you. We are getting out. Don't stop to pack anything'. We left everything as it was and went outside to a truck, which fortunately was parked in the compound.

> … the cloud was spreading and coming on. It enveloped the sky and hung over us like a great umbrella. It was black and opaque, and the noise it made was like a huge roaring and hissing, so loud one could hardly hear oneself talk. We drove in semi-darkness to the Manager's [Mr Henderson's] and to the other Assistants' houses [including the Gwilts] and picked them and some servants up … Each moment it was getting darker, and the cloud was coming nearer in a rolling movement with that indescribable hissing noise … [The truck became stuck] and we stood there simply waiting for death that we knew was inevitable, once the cloud reached us. (Stephens 1953, 219–20)

The experience was no less terrifying for Mrs Cowley and her daughter Pam, who recalled waiting 'for this nightmare to engulf us. I panicked and started screaming, "I'm too young to die!" till Mr [Stephens] told my Mother, "Stop that child screaming"'. Amalya Cowley calmed Pam, took her face in her hands and said gently: '"Don't look Pammie. Put your head on my shoulder. We're going to God"' (Cowley and Virtue 2015, 96–97). Then, however:

> While we were standing, we looked up, and the rolling movement of the enveloping lethal gas seemed to halt for a split second—then it rolled back! It was an amazing phenomenon. At that moment, it seemed nothing less than a miracle, and we thanked God for the respite, then discussed further means of escape. (Stephens 1953, 220)

The laterally cascading ash flow had indeed stopped close to them, perhaps just 2 or 3 kilometres away, and about halfway between the plantation and Higaturu. The flow had dropped its load of hot ash and rocks, and now was reversing its direction by drawing in air from its surrounds, just as observed at Isivita Mission in even closer circumstances. Laura Stephens wrote that:

> It was still roaring and hissing, even on its backward journey. Even where we were, breathing had become difficult. There was a heavy sulphurous smell in the air, and it was dry and hot. (Stephens 1953, 220)

> **Slightly edited extracts of letter by Bill Schleusener to his parents, 21 January 1951 (Schleusener 1951)**
>
> <u>10.30 a.m. Sunday.</u> Things are crook and I'm writing fast—just 5 minutes ago I nearly went thru the roof with noise of a bang—God knows I think a mountain must have blown away—a pall of smoke, the like of which it's impossible to describe came forth at at least 100 [miles per hour] sideways and has absolutely covered everything—I saw it sweep over Higaturu and No 1 Plantation and heading this way, but with a slight north [unfinished]
>
> <u>Now 11.30.</u> A little more calm now—I left off back there to stem a tide of panicking locals and had a spot of bother until I was heeded by the mob. The cloud ... [was] rolling along toward [us] jet black ... Finally got mob to wait and not 5 mins after down came the muck—mud galore which lasted nearly 20 mins, and you want to see my station—there's nothing standing, or what is isn't apparently worth two bob.
>
> Then the cloud came, filled with lightning and thunder and the locals scared almost white, screeching and asking me what to do—Hell, I hadn't a clue myself—however I packed 'em in the store, under the store, and here we are coughing like blazes. After mud (my house not the best protection with leaf roof—hence store) came grit and gravel and now there's inches of it over everything—a white grey colour. I've women 'n kids stacked in with pieces of wet calico over each one's face, and outside the powder is coming down. I've heard of a dead world, but this is the first I've seen—no wind or noise now, just a thick fog, a frightful bloody smell and we're just waiting for the muck to clear—I've been to inspect a couple of creeks and they're just grey slush.
>
> <u>12.45 p.m.</u> Perhaps a little calmer again state of affairs now. I've packed the workers to their houses with strict instructions what to do if there's any more ... just what's going on I don't know cos can't see a thing—God what desolation ...
>
> <u>2.45 p.m.</u> Fog seems to be dispersing, but not the locals. I've dozens hanging about now—one worker has come from No. 1 [plantation]—news from Higaturu I can't count on, but I think it's pretty well wiped out ... Many of the No. 1 workers are around with their goods and chattels ready to blow, but I'm not moving yet ...
>
> <u>4.50 p.m.</u> now. Just received note from returnees (local Orokaivas)—Higaturu is apparently gone, and most Europeans dead—the road between Sangara [plantation] and Higaturu missing so nobody has been up. Villages on the road wiped out, dead and dying all over the shop in hundreds, and trucks are apparently carrying the wounded to Popondetta ... The workers won't go to their rooms so I've got 'em by the score about the store for the night—which I hope will be calm. Daytime panic one thing, but night another. I'm finding it hard to credit that people at Higaturu are no more!

They decided to escape north-eastwards along the road to Popondetta even though the rolling flow had seemed to be moving in a similar but parallel direction, off to one side:

> And the nightmare drive began. For about five miles, we were pelted with mud and pumice ... My husband [Steve], who was driving the truck, was the most uncomfortable of all. The windshield had become caked with about two inches of pumice in the very early

part of the drive, and he had to stick his head out of the side door, where he was soon half-blinded with the mud in his eyes. At frequent intervals along the road, we stopped and picked up fleeing natives with their wives and children. By the time we got to Popondetta, there wasn't an inch of unoccupied space on the whole truck. (Stephens 1953, 220)

Bill Schleusener was a junior European employee at Sangara Rubber Plantation. He was living in his own locally made house in the cocoa area of the plantation and missed the speedy evacuation of his colleagues to Popondetta. Schleusener was in his mid-20s and still single at the time. He had the remarkable experience of writing down in a letter to his parents, and in memorable style, his impressions and thoughts about the eruption and its impacts as they happened (Schleusener 1951).

Popondetta Disaster Centre and the Second Eruption

Popondetta in the afternoon was becoming crowded with arriving Europeans—the Hendersons, Stephens, Gwilts, Cowleys and Miss Margaret Rae—and, increasingly, by many injured local people. Margaret Rae had been staying overnight with the Hendersons and had been visiting her fiancée, Terry Hoolihan, who was on the staff of Works and Housing at Higaturu. Accommodation at Popondetta was limited to the family homes of the two agricultural officers, Fred Kleckham and Blue Morris, and the manager of the local Buntings store, Jack Scurrah. There was no radio communication at Popondetta and there were no medical facilities either—neither mission nor administration—although Marjorie Kleckham had had training as a nurse. A European woman, Mrs Gleeson, was due to give birth at Higaturu at any time and Marjorie Kleckham was 'to do the confinement' (Kleckham 2010, 45). However, Dr Martin at the Higaturu hospital had advised Mrs Kleckham to stay at home in Popondetta and not to return to Higaturu until Monday morning (see also Kleckham 2003). Mrs Kleckham had three of her own children, one a baby whom she was still breast feeding.

Two other Europeans also escaped to Popondetta that day. They were Rodd and Madeleine Hart who were still on their honeymoon away from Higaturu at Jegarata Mission 'in a sort of Peter Pan house—almost in the treetops' (Benson 1955, 6) and about 5 kilometres south of Popondetta.

Jegarata is on the Banguho River, which drains from the crater area of the volcano and is on a direct line of sight. The Harts saw from Jegarata the black eruption cloud spreading out into a gigantic mushroom shape, and they quickly left the mission when the cloud was overhead. They later recorded:

> It was now about half an hour since the eruption had begun. Suddenly we saw emerging from the dust haze in the distance a tongue of grey pumice-like dust … [as a] cloud which moved forward with great rapidity in our direction. The people with us and ourselves were experiencing difficult with breathing and beginning to cough. We made off down the road to Popondetta leaving all our belongings behind us. (Hart 1953, 1)

They had been facing south-westwards almost in direct line with the central axis of the northward-advancing front of ground-hugging ash flow that, as at Sangara Plantation, fell short of them by a few kilometres (Figure 4.1). The Harts did not record any 'draw back' clouds but they might have seen them if they had stayed.

Marjorie Kleckham at Popondetta later told her own story of the eruption:

> We were out in the rubber patch fixing the small trees, and also showing the children the volcano and explaining it to them. Suddenly there was a terrible explosion, it came up like a huge mushroom of smoke, gradually this spread over the whole area … As we were standing there taking photographs of the eruption a boy came running with a note from Jack Scurrah, it was just 'It looks as if Higs' gone [i.e. Higaturu is gone]'. Then we saw Jack coming down the road towards us. He and Fred had a talk and decided to start walking to Higaturu to help, as soon as the dust cleared.
>
> I had to prepare food for everyone, got all the bandages and medical supplies I could collect together. Get the machinery cleared out of the sheds, spread tarpaulins across the floors of the shed and make an emergency war hospital for people. I … also collected all the 44 gallon drums I could find and sent boys with every available bucket to carry water to fill these drums and tubs. It was very fortunate I did this; the streams ran hot and filled with mud and dead fish and other animals. When I had this much under control, I went into the house and started cooking pastry and scones. A truck [the one driven by Mr Stephens] arrived from Sangara rubber estates, the windscreen was inches thick in

mud—the people on the back had the pandanus floor mats over their heads; they and the mats were also covered in mud … Fred and Jack had met this truck, but they had kept on walking into Higaturu. (Kleckham 2010, 46)

The European women from Sangara Plantation who had arrived at Popondetta stayed there with Mrs Kleckham and Mrs Morris, but the European men turned the truck around and headed back along the road towards Sangara and Higaturu. This required great determination as they were driving back towards the still active volcano and were not to know what further eruptions might bring, nor indeed what they would find in the disaster zone. They soon encountered, however, Reverend Dennis Taylor who had been brought by mission boys to a place close to the road called Monge, or Maungi. Reverend Taylor had been able to escape from the devastated area:

> He was very badly burned all over his body, but his fortitude was amazing. All he could say was that he had left his family [at Sangara Mission] to go for help and that someone should try to get to them. (Stephens 1953, 221)

Taylor was brought back in the truck to Popondetta for what little medical care could be provided by Mrs Kleckham and Mrs Hart.

Meanwhile, the truck and the European men had gone back towards Sangara. It was joined in time by two other vehicles, and the drivers began travelling back and forth along the road in a shuttle, picking up survivors and bringing them to Popondetta. The old Yodda Road had become an emergency 'lifeline'—of sorts:

> A steady stream of burned and shocked people began staggering and crawling in [to Popondetta] … The groans of the living and the wailing of those who recognised their dead are something I shall hear to the end of my days …
>
> The men brought us harrowing tales of the sights along the road toward Sangara and Higaturu district … All along the road trees had fallen, and those that had not fallen were entirely bare of foliage. Often the trucks had to stop to clear the road of victims who lay where they had fallen in their attempt to escape the cloud. At Andemba … heavy timber across the road made it impossible to get farther … Over everything lay an unearthly silence, broken occasionally by the rumbling of the mountain. Bodies lay piled in the villages, on the ground, and in the houses. (Stephens 1953, 221–22)

The rescuers who entered Andemba village on the side road leading in to Higaturu were Rodd Hart, Fred Kleckham, Jack Scurrah and Elliott Elijah, a Trobriand Islands cooperatives officer who worked with Fred Kleckham at Popondetta (Murray Administrator 1951k; Crane 1971). The group had to work at great speed as ash was still falling and there was the ongoing fear of a further eruption, as would in fact take place later that evening. Their priority was to find survivors. No burials could be undertaken, and they were unable to enter Higaturu itself. Their courageous visit to Andemba village would later be the subject of unfortunate mis-reporting to the news media in which Elliott Elijah's behaviour became a topic of criticism that proved to be unjustifiable.

Fred Kleckham and Rodd Hart drove in a mission jeep all the way back along the road to Awala having failed to get into Higaturu (Searle 1995). Use of radio communications from Higaturu was out of the question so Clen Searle's radio set at Awala was seen as the only option. Messages were sent out by them from Awala to Port Moresby, advising of the deadly disaster, although, by this time, the authorities—and especially aviation authorities in Lae—were becoming aware of the seriousness of the situation in the Lamington area. Captain Jacobson had earlier reported by radio his ash cloud encounter to Qantas officers in Lae who 'immediately prepared an aircraft in case a request for assistance came through' (Qantas 1951, 9–10). Further, Captain Biddulph and his passengers in the Qantas Dragon aircraft, which had no radio, had arrived back in Lae by 12.50 pm giving further news of the eruption to aviation authorities (Sinclair 1986). The administration in Lae was also informed and the district commissioner of Morobe, H.L.R. 'Horrie' Niall, arranged for the administration vessel *Huon* to sail from Lae on the Sunday evening arriving the next morning at Cape Killerton. Authorities in Port Moresby also were now aware of the need to organise a medical response and began making arrangements for a Department of Health team to reach Popondetta as soon as possible on the following day. The Australian Red Cross Division in Port Moresby was asked to 'stand by' for assistance, particularly in relation to the care of evacuees reaching Port Moresby from the disaster area (e.g. Ahearn 1951a; Wardrop 1951b).

Captain W. 'Bill' Forgan-Smith was Qantas chief pilot for New Guinea. He and his crew took off for Popondetta in a large Douglas C47 from Lae at 4.18 pm following instructions from the Department of Civil Aviation in Port Moresby 'to the effect that Higaturu had been off the air since 10.30 that morning, that Mount Lamington had erupted and that the area was covered in volcanic dust' (Qantas 1951, 10). The relief aircraft was loaded with drums of water, sacks of rice and flour, cases of meat and medical supplies (Sinclair 1986). They:

> Flew in perfect weather to Cape Ward Hunt, but from here on, dust haze and a heavy cloud of dust at the actual volcano had made it almost dark … We circled Cape Killerton at about 300 feet, but could see no Europeans. We flew on down the coast for about 10 miles, but observed nothing … [and then decided] to follow the track [inland] to Popondetta. As we progressed we could see hundreds of natives all walking towards the coast with their belongings on their backs; the dust was very thick and all was a greyish colour. (Qantas 1951, 10)

The welcome sound of the aircraft was heard above Popondetta at about dusk. However, the optimism was short-lived:

> We beckoned frantically for them to land, but apparently they took our gestures to mean we were all right. I shall never forget how my heart sank when that plane departed. (Stephens 1953, 222)

Marjorie Kleckham wrote later that she had even, in desperation:

> Grabbed a bundle of the babies napkins [in order to form the words] 'Please land on the ground' … I felt so elated that I might be able to get some of the badly burned people out … [but] they flew away. I've never felt so deflated as I did at this, there were all these people needing special treatment and there a big plane flew away empty of passengers. (Kleckham 2010, 48)

The captain had indeed misread the waving of the desperate Europeans at Popondetta. Although the small airstrip was still green and serviceable, he noted that there were no SOS signs or symbols on the ground (Henry 1951). Mrs Kleckham's longer request to 'Please land on the ground', written using babies' nappies, may well have been impractical. Nevertheless, the crew dropped a 'bundle of loadsheets', the reverse side of which contained the message that a government trawler would arrive at Cape Killerton at noon the next day (Qantas 1951, 10). The aircraft then headed back to Lae. Those on the ground were left to work out how best to endure the night ahead of them. Was the Popondetta airstrip now unsuitable? Did the aircraft's departure mean that all outside help would now come from the coast? How best could the Europeans deal with the dead and injured at Popondetta?

A decision was made to shuttle the injured by truck to the coast at Cape Killerton. Stevie Stephens was one of the drivers. 'The truck carried several loads of the injured there and left them in the care of some mission people until the cutter could arrive next day' (Stephens 1953, 222). Other European men were still down the road at Sangara Plantation, collecting what extra supplies might be required back at Popondetta. The Awala group was still at Waseta where Pat Searle noted that:

> Around 8.30 pm noises began again with the constant growling of thunder, while the lightning was frightening in its intensity, lighting up the night sky too often and for too long. Once more the heavens opened with further weighty onslaughts of ash and debris, the heaviest for several hours, while eight or more of us sat under a fragile sago-frond roof! (Searle 1995, 241)

The precise time of the start of this second major eruption is unknown—some people said it was about 9.00 pm or even later, some earlier—which is not surprising given the night-time conditions and the attention of survivors being focused on coping in a disaster zone and so not closely timing events. Nevertheless, a radio schedule arranged by Clen Searle for 8.45 pm could not take place because of the electrical disturbance caused by the eruption (Taylor 1958). The second eruption also caused great concern, especially for people worrying whether it was to be a repeat of, or even greater than, the one in the morning. The night-time darkness and the volcanic noise added to the fear and apprehension of those still alive in the disaster area. The pyrotechnics of the second eruption were spectacular even at distant Gona, on the coast, as recorded by Elsie Manley:

> It was more fearful than the first, for it showed up more … Here at Gona it was like shells bursting overhead; no noise, just the sight of them bursting like rockets; more smoke, rumblings loud and long, and terrific lightning. (Manley 1951, 5)

John Gwilt also witnessed the second eruption—which he thought may have started forcefully at about 9.30 pm—from the back of a truck leaving Sangara for Popondetta. His description of his southward view as the truck progressed north-eastwards later proved valuable to volcanologist Tony Taylor in deducing that the second major eruption, though powerful and terrifying, was different to the one at 10.40 that morning:

> The eruption was plainly visible in the bright moonlight … the column was now racing towards us from behind; ahead and above us was the moon … the column which appeared to be infinitely

> wider than the previous one in the morning … [had] a dull red half-circle of what appeared to be a large blood red moon shape, stationary over what I considered to be the direction of the crater. This moon-shaped light was penetrating and visible as seen through dense smoke … [and] was visible on numerous occasions as we climbed from lower to higher ground. Shortly after, a wind blowing approximately from sou' sou' east, and at a height of several thousand feet … was forcing the canopy above us in the direction of the moon … Some minutes after the moon was covered by the canopy, a wind arose approximately nor' nor' west again checking and rolling back this vast canopy … the wind had folded the canopy again for the second time that day towards Mt Lamington; we arrived [at Popondetta] in moonlight. (Gwilt 1951, 4–5)

Stevie Stephens was at Cape Killerton with a truck when he saw the second major eruption towards the south. Laura Stephens wrote:

> It appeared that the cloud, visible through the intermittent flashes of lightning, had enveloped Popondetta. [Stevie] stepped on the gas as hard as he could and returned to meet a party of us—women and children from Popondetta—on the road. We too had feared that the cloud might reach Popondetta and had started out on foot toward Killerton. However, it didn't travel that far, and the men bundled us back into the truck and took us to Popondetta once again. (Stephens 1953, 222)

The second eruption, but evidently not the earlier one at 10.40 am, was also heard by Bishop Phillip Strong and others at about 9.00 pm on the coast far to the east at Dogura. They 'heard a loud report as of an explosion which seemed to be high up above us like a shell bursting overhead' (Strong 1981, 212). Boys in the dormitories thought it was a coconut falling on the iron roof, and others thought that someone must have been dynamiting for fish. Bishop Strong recorded in his diary for 21 January that he vaguely recalled someone saying that Mount Lamington was a volcano, just as Sister Henderson had recalled.

Meanwhile, inland Popondetta remained a de facto 'relief' centre overnight. Despite the absence of proper medical services:

> All the women worked tirelessly all day, all night, and into the next morning. All we had for treatment of burns was tins of dripping [i.e. cooking fat]. Every native was given a place to lie down in the shelter of a roof. The women (European women) put dripping on

> all of their burns and Jack Scurrah did a marvellous job of keeping us supplied with food from the trade store. He also had his staff making buckets full of hot Bovril and lacing it with Rum to ease the native's [sic] pain. We had no morphia, nothing except Rum and Whisky to give them to ease their pain. We got this from the trade store. (Kleckham 2010, 47)

Urgent notes had been sent by runners from Popondetta to both Sister Nancy Elliot at Gona Mission on the north coast and to Sister Jean Henderson at the Eroro Mission near Oro Bay to the north-east, asking for medical supplies and assistance. The missionary at Gona, James Benson, recalled them receiving a note from Madeleine Hart: 'Dennis Taylor here badly burned; come at once with plenty of dressings. Haste.—Maddy' (Benson 1955, 6). Sister Elliott and some young men soon left Gona carrying medical supplies and walked through to Cape Killerton where they saw some of the growing number of bewildered evacuees who had arrived there. A truck was available for the onward journey to Popondetta, but the driver refused to go. Father Benson recalled the driver's words:

> Me! … me go back to that hell where the spirits are so angry they are slaughtering their own people—whole tribes of them; what would they do to me, a Buka man? No! I never go back there. Besides, there is no petrol in the truck. (Benson 1955, 6)

Sister Elliott, accompanied only by Simon Peter Awado, then walked all the way through to Popondetta (see also, for example, Manley 1951; Tomkins and Hughes 1969; White 1991). They arrived at about 3.00 am, shortly after Reverend Taylor had died of his burns. Their morphia supplies were given to people in most need of them.

Sister Jean Henderson at Eroro received her note for assistance the next morning (Monday): 'Mt Lamington blown up, all lives feared lost, medical help needed urgently and drugs' (Henderson 2001, 4). She prepared some dressings and drugs, picked a team of medical workers, and set off by road, not knowing what to expect; they took picks and shovels in case they had 'to dig people out'. Father John Anderson, the relieving priest at Eroro, also left for the disaster area that morning. The Eroro group met distressed local people close to Popondetta and, on arrival, found that 'thousands of people had assembled' (Henderson 2001, 5; Henderson 2007). Father Benson, who had come up from Gona, told them of the death of Dennis Taylor.

There had been little sleep for those who had spent the night at Popondetta. A realisation of the scale of the disaster, and of a large number of dead and injured, had gradually become clear. Grieving had begun and trauma had set in. Amalya Cowley had asked Stephens for 'the truth as far as he knew it about the fate of Higaturu and its inhabitants' and had to accept that both her husband, Cecil, and son, Erl, were unlikely to have survived (Cowley and Virtue 2015, 102).

Some vague hope existed at Popondetta regarding the arrival of the relief vessel at Cape Killerton that was now on its way from Lae. Trucks were once more in action and some reliable information was obtained 'that help for the injured could be secured more rapidly by aeroplane than by cutter, so the survivors had to be brought back to Popondetta' (Stephens 1953, 222). However, these hopeful signs were not available to those still stranded, isolated and dying at the Isivita Mission on the volcano close to the active crater and who, potentially, were much more vulnerable to the effects of the second eruption.

Isivita Mission and Blue Morris

Reverend Porter reported that, at Isivita, the second eruption started shortly after 9.30 pm when, after a pause, a constant and regular roar began that was much louder than the one in the morning, and there 'seemed to be noises like exploding fireworks just above the roof':

> Then falling matter began again—not only dust and sand this time, but quite large stones. I urged Mrs Lane and Sister [Durdin] to get under the table, which would at least give some protection if the roof fell [in]. The noise by this time was deafening. I am sure not one of us believed we would survive this second blast. It was even more terrifying than the first, the only difference being that the darkness of the night relieved the darkness that accompanied the eruption. We 'sat it out' underneath the table, praying continually. But yet it passed, and we found ourselves still with the roof on and still sound in body. Of course, there were no casualties from this one, and so we just spent the night talking, and longing for the dawn. I have never known a night to pass more slowly. (Porter 1951a, 27)

The missionaries roused themselves at first light on Monday 22 January 'amidst the smell of death all around us':

> Eighteen people had died in the Mission House that night. We carried them all out and laid them on the lawn at the end of the church. As we lifted several of them we could feel the burnt flesh coming away on our hands. It was a terrible sight to see those eighteen poor charred bodies laid in a row. Immediately we set to work to dig more graves. (Porter 1951a, 27)

A note arrived at Isivita from Rodd Hart who advised the missionaries to leave just as soon as possible, and they accepted that evacuation was now the best option. The Isivita villages were deserted and only seven burn victims remained with them. The missionaries found, to their surprise, that their jeep could start and so they began to move slowly down the mountain track, Albert Ririka in front cutting away the worst of the fallen trees. They met Blue Morris 'who seemed somewhat surprised to see us alive. He was on his way through the villages looking for survivors, and what a grand job he is doing!' (Porter 1951a, 27; see also Morris 1951). Blue Morris advised them to go down to Waseta rather than all the way to Popondetta. They were able to use Clen Searle's radio at Waseta for messages to their families. 'It was here that we first learned of the Sangara and Higaturu tragedy, and, though we were to an extent prepared for it, yet the final confirmation stunned us' (Porter 1951a, 27).

Later that Monday, Blue Morris drove back up to Isivita and then beyond to villages within what he called 'the blast area' (Morris 1951, 4). Trees had been blown down but lay in different directions, only some of the trunks pointing towards Higaturu. Blue Morris found the body of a man at Hamumuta village, later describing its condition in some forensic detail and noting that most of the dead man's thigh had been 'eaten away by a dog and several fowls' (Morris 1951, 5). He also noted the nature of the volcanic deposits around and under the body and deduced that the man had been killed by the Sunday morning eruption rather than the one in the evening. Morris kept moving on until a 'column of smoke broke in a billow' fairly close to him. This unnerved him and he:

> Ran away and forgot to make any observations until I put my hand on the ground, going under a tree at Hamumuta. The ground had a constant even vibration—immeasurably slight; I checked to see if it was [just] myself, but it was not. (Morris 1951, 6)

Blue Morris's later report was basically an observational one in volcanology, even though Morris was himself an agricultural officer by training. Morris provided short descriptions of the eruptions of Sunday 21 January as he saw them from the Waseta–Awala area. He also gave particular attention to the different volcanic materials that were falling at different times, as well as the thicknesses of the deposits they produced on the ground. For example, Morris at about 11.00 am first felt 'drops of slightly damp mud' and had the impression 'the first drops of rain had collected sufficient dust to make a damp mud' (Morris 1951, 2). Heavier pellets were like mudstone and could be broken by squeezing. Other more water-rich drops were so wet that they splattered when they landed on the ground. Morris still later observed that the ash fallout was a dry, 'dark grey powder, granulated like sugar, but not gritty' (2). The evening eruption, in contrast, produced walnut-sized stones:

> They were of a crystalline nature, very much like granite in appearance, and appeared to have been fused by heat. Some were flat on the base and honey-combed, others were irregular, but all were very light in weight. (Morris 1951, 3)

Assessing the Observations

Volcanologist G.A.M. Taylor arrived at Popondetta on Monday 22 January. He had not witnessed any of the extraordinary eruptive activity on the day before, or on any of the previous days, so one of his tasks was to gather as much scientific information on the eruption as possible. He did so by interviewing many of the mainly European eyewitnesses who had survived, asking key observers to provide their own written accounts of what they had experienced. Reports, letters to family and photographs all comprised a valuable collection of information of what had happened up to and including Sunday 21 January. Taylor spent much of the next two years collecting additional information obtained from his observations of ongoing eruptive activity, field studies of the eruptive products and researching reports on similar eruptions elsewhere in the world. All of this additional work, however, built on the foundation of the reports by eyewitnesses, none of whom had training in geoscience or in volcanology and its use of technical terms. Several key points can be highlighted from the eyewitness observations.

1. Perhaps the most valuable attribute of the observations is the record of a gradual build-up of volcano unrest that began at least one week before the climactic eruption of Sunday 21 January. The volcanic disaster was, therefore, heralded, at least in retrospect. However, the authorities were unclear on how to interpret the warning signs and did not know how to manage the escalating crisis.

2. A notable aspect of the observations of the eruption clouds, starting on Saturday 20 January, if not before, is of the clouds being heavy or 'densified' with ash, so much so that Reverend Porter, for example, referred to 'a grey mass which seemed to curl out of the ground like toothpaste from a tube' (Porter 1951b, 1). The heavy ash column on Sunday morning was unable to sustain its upward motion but rather carried the potential for gravitational collapse.

3. The high rising eruption cloud on the morning of 21 January was described as 'cauliflower' or 'mushroom' shaped, but these shapes changed when the eruption column collapsed—that is, when the base of the cloud expanded and hot, laterally directed clouds of ash, volcanic gas and vapour spread out on all sides of the volcano.

4. Dramatic, if not terrifying, descriptions were given by survivors of the fast, ground-hugging, ash clouds advancing towards them, particularly at Isivita, Sangara Plantation and Jegarata. These volcanic clouds were recognised as being the principal cause of the numerous deaths in a main area of volcanic devastation on the northern flank of the volcano. The term 'blast' was used commonly in descriptions of this deadly impact. Volcanologists now use the more general term 'pyroclastic flows', where 'pyroclastic' means 'fire-broken'. Smaller 'flows' of indeterminate material—landslide, water or lava—in the crater area were also recorded for Thursday 18 January.

5. One of the more striking aspects of the descriptions by some local eyewitnesses was the way in which the pyroclastic flows, although advancing threateningly towards them, suddenly stopped and then, almost miraculously, drew back, reversing their direction of flow and leaving behind a sharp 'draw back' line on the ground. This reversal of direction, and indeed of fortunes, takes place where pyroclastic flows come to rest, dumping their loads of ash and debris. New clouds then rise quickly from the hot, newly deposited surface materials. Colder surrounding air is drawn in, which pushes back against, and in a direction opposite to, that of the original flow. Some volcanologists have used the informal, and not especially popular, descriptor of

'phoenix clouds' for this now well-known phenomenon of ash clouds 'rising again' from pyroclastic flows that have stopped well away from the main source vent of the eruption. A phoenix in Greek mythology is a long-lived bird that cyclically regenerates itself obtaining new life by rising from the ashes of its predecessor.

6. Blue Morris's descriptions of the volcanic materials deposited by the eruptions of 21 January are also noteworthy. Some parts of the eruption clouds were wetter than others and some of his descriptions refer to what geologists call 'accretionary lapilli', which are formed by the wet accretion of small ash particles by rain drops. Also, the larger, drier fragments he described from the evening eruption were probably of pumice containing visible crystals of what petrologists call 'phenocrysts' and that probably were mainly of the light-coloured mineral feldspar.

7. John Gwilt's observations on the Sunday evening from the back of the truck on its way to Popondetta are also significant. Tony Taylor later concluded from Gwilt's report that no significant pyroclastic flows, like those in the morning, were produced by the second, night-time, eruption, otherwise Gwilt's view of the 'blood-red half-circle' over the crater would have been obscured by the flows as they raced down the northern flank of Mount Lamington, emitting great clouds of ash from their surfaces. This means also that there could have been no 'draw back' effect creating a phoenix cloud or clouds as in the morning eruption.

8. Formation of the devastated area on Mount Lamington was accompanied by dramatic changes in the shape of the mountain itself, changes that became apparent only when visibility allowed suitable views in the hours and days ahead. Even the occupants of passing aircraft were unable to see the new summit crater because of the pervasive volcanic clouds covering the summit area. The height of the mountain had been reduced by several hundred metres and a huge crater, about 1 kilometre in diameter and open to the north, could be seen at the head of the Ambogo River. The impression gained by early observers was that the northern side of the volcano and its summit had been blown out explosively towards the north as a result of the catastrophic eruption. This, they thought, created a forceful 'lateral blast' like that of an atomic bomb, that resulted in the area of total devastation and the destruction of Higaturu and Sangara Mission

to the north. Thus, one newspaper inaccurately, but understandably, and perhaps misquoting Taylor, reported that:

> A segment … has been blown right out of the mountain. A chasm, varying in width from three-quarters of a mile to one and a half miles, runs straight from the crater towards the stricken town of Higaturu. Mr Taylor estimates that at least 2,000 feet of the 5,000 foot mountain was blown off in Sunday's big explosion. (*South Pacific Post* 1951b, 1)

However, Laura Stephens, who appears in print as a careful and accurate writer, observed that 'the whole range seems to have disintegrated and is coming this way!'. The term 'disintegration' is of some interest and may be appropriate if the new, enlarged crater formed as a result of collapse rather than by an outwards explosive blast.

9. Visibility was not good throughout the Sunday but survivors gained a clear impression that a large area on the northern flank of Mount Lamington had been devastated, particularly those survivors who attempted to gain access to the area on the Sunday and Monday. Jack Scurrah's minimalist statement on the Sunday morning that 'It looks as if Higs' gone' encapsulates that impression rather well. Thousands of people, in fact, had perished in settlements within what was called an area of 'complete devastation' including those at the government station at Higaturu and Anglican mission at Sangara.

The full extent of the devastation, including destruction on the southern side of the mountain, was not realised until later when volcanologist Tony Taylor mapped the area in detail. Taylor noted that the central area of complete devastation was surrounded by a much narrower zone of 'partial destruction' defining the limits of the heat effects (Figure 4.6). People died in the central area but had some chance of escape in the peripheral zone. Not shown on Taylor's famous map, however, is the extent and thicknesses of the air-fall ash that fell over a much wider area, causing considerable damage to gardens, homes and plantations that had escaped the impact of the pyroclastic flows.

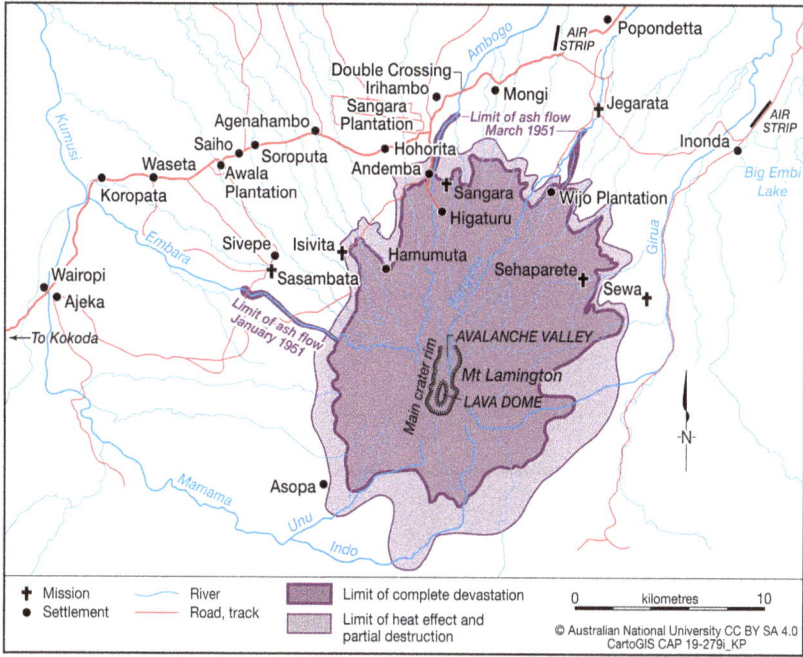

Figure 4.6. Map of limits of devastation at Mount Lamington

The limits of complete devastation, and of heat effect and partial destruction, as mapped by Taylor (1958, fig. 52) are here superimposed on the map shown in Figure 4.1.

> **Acknowledgement by G.A.M. Taylor (1958, 12)**
>
> As a measure of the morale and calibre of the people who inhabit these isolated communities of the Territory, I should like to draw attention to the fact that little more than an hour after the catastrophic eruption of 21st January and long before the news of the event had reached the outside world, a handful of survivors from the marginal settlements found their way into the dust-fogged area of devastation and began to evacuate the wounded.
>
> Finally, I wish to pay tribute to the courage and fortitude of all those who worked in the Lamington area during the emergency. Long hours, arduous duties and an abiding fear of further eruptions were all met with an infectious spirit of courage and self-sacrifice which was an inspiration to those whose duty lay in the area.

5
THE NEXT 10 DAYS: DISASTER RELIEF AND CONTROVERSY

Monday 22 January: First Arrivals by Air and Sea

Residents in Port Moresby 'awoke to a blanket of grey, gritty dust laying inches thick over everything. The air was so full of pumice dust that by 8 a.m. the opposite side of the bay was blotted out', reported the *South Pacific Post* (1951b, 1). The ash was from the strong eruption at Lamington on the previous evening and it was carried to the Territory's capital by the high-level east–west winds. Visibility was also poor at Port Moresby airport, Jacksons Airstrip, which had to be closed temporarily. It was open, however, for the later arrival of evacuees from Popondetta via Lae, and to ensure support for the required emergency relief effort into Popondetta, although much of this came from Lae.

Outside assistance for the still-living victims of the Sunday eruption in the Lamington area arrived in force from Port Moresby and Lae on the morning of Monday 22 January. The government trawler *Huon* had sailed from Lae on the previous evening and it arrived at Cape Killerton on the coast near Popondetta at around dawn (e.g. Blaikie 2006, 2007; Martin 2013). On board the *Huon* were administration and medical personnel and emergency supplies. The personnel included the district commissioner of Morobe District, H.L.R. 'Horrie' Niall, as well as patrol officers J.D. 'Des' Martin and R.W. 'Bob' Blaikie, together with Dr Max Sverklys, an Australian nurse Sister 'Rusty' Maclean and about six

Papua New Guinean police. The party did not know what to expect, but after landing at the beach at Cape Killerton, unloading and then driving by truck to Popondetta they started to appreciate the impact and horror of the disaster. They encountered on the road a jeep and trailer being driven from Popondetta by Rodd Hart and heading to Gona carrying the body of Reverend Dennis Taylor in a coffin built by Father Benson who had arrived at Popondetta from Gona (Strong 1951).

Qantas aircraft carrying relief personnel and supplies began landing at Popondetta airstrip early on Monday (Qantas 1951; Henry 1951; Sinclair 1986; Bullard 2017). One aviation historian later wrote that these first flights into Popondetta represented the beginning of an:

> Amazing, inspiring and superbly-coordinated work of rescue and evacuation … [in which] the air companies of PNG, and in particular Qantas, played a vital part … One hundred and seventy-five rescue personnel … were flown in during this period. One of the principal needs was for clean drinking water, as all the streams in the area were heavily fouled with pumice dust. In total, the DC3s made 143 flights to the disaster area, carrying over 265,000 kilograms of supplies. Dragons made 117 flights, carrying over 53,000 kilograms. Virtually every Qantas pilot took part. (Sinclair 1986, 118–19; see also Civil Aviation 1951)

Senior administration personnel and their support staff began arriving early on the Monday by air, mainly from Port Moresby. Judge Phillips in Port Moresby had attempted to fly into Popondetta on the previous day, Sunday, but his aircraft had to turn back because of poor weather and the pervasive eruption cloud that could be seen 'coming towards Port Moresby, its upper part or layer extending, at 20,000 feet or so, many miles ahead of its lower layer. We flew under the upper layer, but were pressed westward by the lower mass' (Deputy Administrator 1951, appendix C, 1; see also Phillips 1951a). Phillips, however, flew into Popondetta the next day, Monday, at around midday, and found that Ivan Francis Champion, acting director of District Services and Native Affairs, and medical support staff led by Dr John T. Gunther, director of Public Health for the Territory, had arrived at the airstrip already and had begun organising the relief effort (e.g. *South Pacific Post* 1951b).

Ivan Champion had established a strong reputation as a government explorer in Papua when, in 1928 as a young patrol officer, he accompanied Charles H. Karius in a crossing of New Guinea island from the headwaters of the Fly River in the south to the Sepik River on the north coast, later publishing a successful book on the crossing in London

(Champion 1932). Champion's reputation and fame continued to grow when, in 1938, he led the great Bamu–Purari patrol through the Papuan side of the formidable central cordillera of the Highlands area. He passed by impressive mountains whose volcanic origin had been recognised by earlier explorations undertaken by Champion's fellow officer and friend Jack Hide (Sinclair 1988). Champion's leadership skills, knowledge of local conditions throughout the Territory and many years of experience within the Papuan colonial administration would be applied successfully during the relief and recovery phases of the Lamington eruption in 1951.

The other senior administration officer at Popondetta, Dr Gunther, had been in Finschhafen on the Sunday of the eruption, but had flown into Popondetta the following morning. Gunther took on the overall responsibility for dealing with the medical and health aspects of the disaster, both immediate and subsequent, and so worked closely with Ivan Champion and others (Gunther 1951a, 1951b, 1951–52). He quickly set about assessing the disaster area on the ground. The Searles at Waseta were surprised to see Gunther arrive there by road from Popondetta later that afternoon after:

> Quite a dangerous journey through constant ash and debris devastation, and possibly quickly rising rivers, to come so far to us … coming into the huge area of death and destruction, urgently arranging the first emergency supplies so badly needed. (Searle 1995, 245)

Popondetta was confirmed by Champion and Gunther as the forward rescue, relief and evacuation centre for the area, as well as the main medical casualty centre, at least for the time being. Radio communications were established with Port Moresby and Australia. The *Huon* relief party from Lae reached Popondetta from Cape Killerton later on Monday and saw the extent of burns on the survivors who had been brought to the small settlement. Dr Sverklys and Sister McLean joined other Europeans who had already been attending to the victims still alive at Popondetta. Mission sisters Pat Durdin from Isivita and Jean Henderson from Eroro had also joined the medical team. Caring for the burnt people who had survived the trauma of the night at Popondetta was a priority. These casualties were mainly Orokaiva whose burns on their backs and on the backs of their legs were particularly severe, a result of their skin not being covered by clothes as they attempted to run from the encroaching ash cloud (Figure 5.1). Blood plasma for burns treatment was in short supply on this day but much of what little there was in Port Moresby had been brought to Popondetta. Severe cases were evacuated as soon as possible to Lae Hospital and some to Port Moresby.

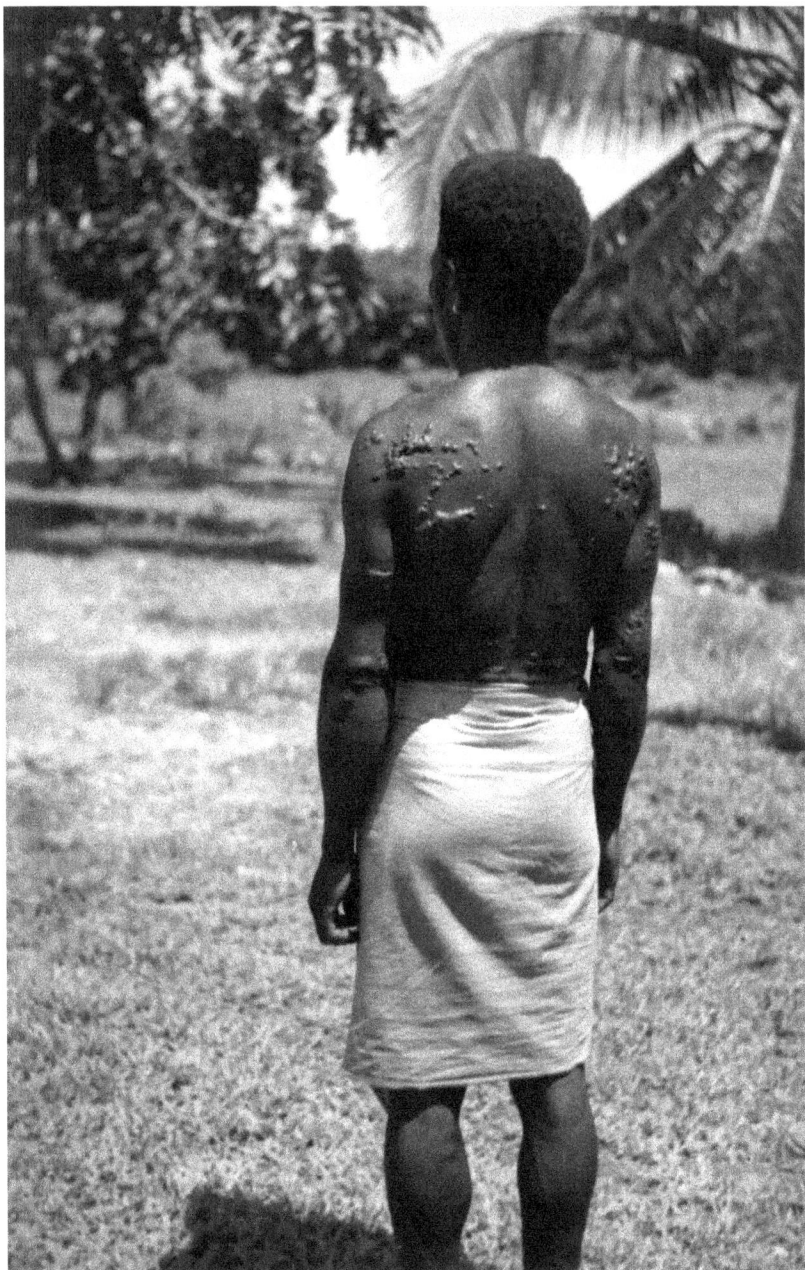

Figure 5.1. Healed burn scars on man's back

Healed burn scars inflicted by the 21 January ash flow are seen here on the back of a survivor (Taylor 1958, fig. 77). Photograph supplied courtesy of Geoscience Australia (negative number GA/8201).

Ivan Champion established an Administration Field Group at Popondetta and immediately gave written instructions to subordinate officers W. Crellin, A.A. Roberts, F.P. Kaad and I. Holmes, and, two days later, to J.R. Foldi:

> You are hereby instructed to do any act you may consider bona fide necessary to assist in the alleviation of suffering and the functioning of the Administration Field [Group] in the area under its control. (I. Champion 1951)

Other tasks begun by administration staff were identifying further casualties, collecting and burying the dead, and planning for the care of the survivors. Numerous survivors and evacuees had assembled in different areas, notably at Waseta and Popondetta, at Cape Killerton on the coast, at Inonda in the north-east and at Eroro on the coast. Assistant District Officer Kaad and Patrol Officer Morris went to Waseta to identify and establish an evacuation camp for the hundreds of refugees in that general area. A site was soon chosen at Wairopi on the low, western bank of the Kumusi River. Patrol Officer Bill Crellin was placed in charge of the refugees at Cape Killerton and Assistant District Officer Ian Holmes went to the Inonda airstrip to collect survivors there (Phillips Deputy Administrator 1951).

Death statistics for the relatively few Europeans in the devastated area emerged quickly, as seen, for example, in a rough, undated, initial listing of 35 'missing' people that is preserved in the archived papers of Ivan Champion (Anonymous n.d.). All of the 28 Europeans at Higaturu Government Station and the seven at Sangara Mission Station were not only 'missing' but also had perished. Those Europeans at Popondetta, Jegarata, Sangara Plantation, Isivita, Waseta and Awala had survived.

Surviving European women and children in Popondetta were flown to Port Moresby via Lae, many of them departing without their husbands who remained to assist in the Lamington disaster area (Wardrop 1951b). Mrs Cowley was leaving behind her dead husband and son. She became hysterical and had to be sedated by a doctor who had come over on the aircraft (Cowley and Virtue 2015). The European evacuees were held up at Lae airport, at least until Mrs Evelyn Murray, wife of the administrator and president of the Red Cross Division in Port Moresby, contacted Qantas who facilitated their departure to Port Moresby, arriving at 3.30 pm. Thirteen distressed women and children were met at Jacksons Airstrip by volunteer lady members of the Australian Red Cross in Port

Moresby, who arranged refreshments and emergency accommodation and supplies for them (*South Pacific Post* 1951d). Newspaper reporters in Port Moresby needed to find out more about the disaster, and the European women who arrived in Port Moresby by air on this Monday became the first eyewitnesses of the eruption to report on the disaster and its effects to the general public in both the Territory and in Australia. Mrs Cowley was admitted to hospital.

Administrator Colonel J.K. Murray had left Rabaul by air for Port Moresby at 6.30 am on the Monday and volcanologist Tony Taylor was on board with him (Taylor 1951). They were in-flight over New Britain when they heard about the catastrophe that had taken place at Lamington on the previous day. Their aircraft was diverted to Lae because of the temporary closure of Port Moresby airport, but only after they first had flown close to the disaster area. At Lae airport, Taylor met Mrs Kleckham, who had been evacuated from Popondetta, and she told him something of what had happened in the Mount Lamington area (Taylor 1951).

Murray and Taylor flew on to Popondetta from Lae on a smaller Drover aircraft, arriving later that afternoon. Murray took over from Phillips as administrator and Champion was put in charge of the relief operations. Murray and Taylor flew over much of the disaster area in their slow Drover aircraft and saw the extent of the devastation, including on the south-western side of the mountain, as well as the damage to buildings at Higaturu Station and Sangara Mission (Phillips Deputy Administrator 1951). Thousands of trees had been felled creating a blow-down zone in which the tree trunks pointed generally away from the centre of the volcano. The flight, recalled the pilot, Captain Forgan-Smith, was an emotional one for the administrator who could see for himself the catastrophic impact of the eruption on people and communities—both Papuan and European—in the disaster area (Sinclair 1986).

That night, the administrator sent an international telegram from Popondetta to the Department of External Territories, Canberra, and hence to Minister Spender:

> HAVE FLOWN OVER HIGATURU WHICH HAS BEEN FLATTENED BY BLAST INCLUDING MOST BUILDINGS AND TREES. RESCUE ARRANGEMENTS IN HAND WITH IVAN CHAMPION IN CHARGE AND ADEQUATE STAFF. CASUALTIES EUROPEAN AND NATIVE UNCERTAIN BUT CONSIDERABLE. VULCANOLOGIST TAYLOR IN

AREA. INTENDS [sic] STAYING HERE MYSELF. FURTHER EVACUATION ARRANGEMENTS BY SEA ROAD AND AIR IN HAND AND ON VULCANOLOGISTS ADVICE HAVE ORDERED EVACUATION UNESSENTIAL PERSONNEL FROM AREA TWICE THAT HAVING RADIUS KNOWN PRESENT. (Murray Administrator 1951a, 1)

This message to Canberra was the first of many that would be made by telephone and telegram in succeeding days and involving, particularly, exchanges between senior bureaucrats S.A. 'Steve' Lonergan, the Territory's acting government secretary in Port Moresby, and J.R. 'Reg' Halligan, secretary of the Department of External Territories and his staff in Canberra. Media releases were written by the department, thus making news of the eruption and disaster a major item in Australian newspapers and radio stations.

The radius of the closed area mentioned in the administrator's telegram was 16 miles. This represents a large area, meaning that Murray and Taylor were taking few chances at this stage. No records are available of the scientific discussions that were held that day between the administrator and the volcanologist, but Taylor, in his reports after the early aerial inspections that day, almost immediately began using the term '*peléean*' for the type of eruption that had caused the Lamington catastrophe. Mont Pelée on Martinique Island in the Caribbean had caused similar devastation on 8 May 1902, which was only one day after Soufrière volcano on the neighbouring island of St Vincent, about 150 kilometres away, had produced a similar volcanic eruption. Did this mean that other volcanoes in Papua—and indeed elsewhere in the whole Territory— would join Lamington in eruption? Victory volcano to the east was one potential candidate, and the administrator that evening sent a warning radiogram from Popondetta to district headquarters at Tufi on the Cape Nelson peninsula:

DISCOM TUFI SHOULD YOU RECEIVE THE WARNING OF FARELY [sic] CONTINUOUS EARTH TREMOURERS [sic] IT MAY BE ADVISABLE TO EVACUATE YOUR AREA ESPECIALLY THE AREA AROUND MT VICTORY ADVISE GOVSEC AND DISCOM LAE IF TREMOURS [sic] EXPERIENCED ADMINISTRATOR. (Administrator 1951).

Tuesday 23 January: Burying the Dead Begins

Official and volunteer members of the Red Cross Society's Division in Port Moresby, chaired by John H. Ahearn, had been having a busy past 24 hours—and on two main fronts. First, the stressed if not traumatised European evacuees from Popondetta were being looked after by the volunteers, coordinated by Mrs Reita M. Wardrop, general secretary of the local division. The evacuees were provided with clothing and toiletries from local stores, assisted in making contact with relatives in Australia and helped with making travel arrangements to addresses in Australia (Wardrop 1951b).

Second, the local Red Cross officials responded to the urgent need for additional supplies of blood plasma for the burn victims, and particularly for those casualties at Lae Hospital and at Popondetta where there were still injuries to be treated. The Red Cross officials in Port Moresby had contacted Dr Eric Shaw, director of the Queensland Red Cross Blood Transfusion Service in Brisbane, late on Monday afternoon (Wardrop 1951b; Cannon 1951). Shaw promptly made a call for blood donors, arranged for the urgent delivery of blood plasma from both Brisbane and Townsville to the Territory, and 'a dramatic dash was made by plane with 90 litres of serum [plasma] at 1.15 am today [Tuesday]', reported Red Cross headquarters in Melbourne in a press release (Australian Red Cross Society 1951). Fifty 'giving sets' (Wardrop 1951b, 2; Cannon 1951) were also provided. Gunther later wrote:

> Our technique at the Popondetta evacuation casualty station was to give plasma without thought to dressings then simply to dress them for their evacuation by air when their general condition allowed. Plasma was not then given en route but immediately to those requiring it at Lae or Port Moresby [hospitals] on admission.
>
> The total number of patients treated will never be known as reports went by the board as our and Mission casualty clearing stations met the first impact. Seventy burnt patients were evacuated by air to Lae and Port Moresby Hospitals with three deaths only. (Gunther 1951b, 1)

Dr Gunther also expressed his personal appreciation to Dr Shaw and the blood donors:

> You should not need to be told that your plasma was life saving … From our own stores we were able to use plasma on our arrival [Monday], then your supplies arrived as we ran out. This was a tremendous relief as we had had to start to ration by clinical selection, an extremely difficult responsibility in such a rush emergency.
>
> If there is any way you can publicly thank the people of Queensland for me who so quickly rallied to your call to meet our tragedy I would appreciate it … there need be no doubt their blood really saved lives as the result of one of the worst holocausts of our time. (Gunther 1951b, 1)

The number of injured was, in fact, relatively small compared to the much greater number of people killed by the eruption, and the medical team at Popondetta would have relatively little work to do after the first day or two and particularly after the injured requiring hospital attention had been flown out to Lae and Port Moresby. Further supplies of plasma were not needed, and some plasma was returned to Australia.

Tony Taylor undertook two aerial inspections from an Auster aircraft piloted by J. Arthur, director of the Department of Civil Aviation, on this Tuesday (Taylor 1951). They were accompanied by Fred Kleckham, who was included also in aerial inspections on the following day, because of his knowledge of the geography of the Lamington area. Taylor and aircraft pilots would subsequently make many potentially hazardous flights over the crater area, which were clearly necessary to observe any important changes to the state of the volcano, weather and visibility permitting. Later that day, Taylor collected volcanic samples from the Sangara–Higaturu area, which were shipped for scientific examination to his superior Dr N.H. 'Doc' Fisher, chief geologist of the Bureau of Mineral Resources, Geology and Geophysics (BMR) in Canberra. This was just the beginning of a scientific assessment of the eruptions by Taylor and colleagues that would last discontinuously for two years (Taylor 1958). Taylor would be assisted in fieldwork for much of this time by Leslie Topue, a Tolai man from East New Britain who was a volcanological assistant employed at the observatory in Rabaul. However, an urgent requirement for administration staff was not 'science' but, rather, access to Higaturu Station and Sangara Mission.

Duties this day were prioritised for the new relief and rescue workers. Ivan Champion directed Patrol Officer Des Martin and a team of Papua New Guinean police early on Tuesday to clear the road into Higaturu to retrieve moneys and documents in the safe at administration headquarters using spare keys that had been brought over from Port Moresby. The sight of the volcanic destruction astounded and horrified these first people who tried to negotiate the side road that climbed through the devastated area southwards to Higaturu–Sangara from the arterial Popondetta–Kokoda road. The destruction seemed complete—as if a bomb had exploded, blasting everything away. Vegetation had been stripped, trees felled and remnant trunks split and abraded. Most buildings had been obliterated. Ash covered everything, creating a bleak and monotonous 'moonscape'. Most horrifying of all were the burnt human corpses, including hundreds littered along the access road itself, the fleeing people apparently having been felled as they attempted their escape (Figure 5.2). Martin and the police tried to move to one side the bodies that lay in the road, but the scale of the task, including burial of the already rapidly decomposing bodies, was overwhelming and the actual work seemingly futile. Martin reported the situation back to Ivan Champion and, years later, wrote:

> Thousands of rotting corpses were scattered throughout the [devastated] area mostly covered in ash. Many hundreds more were spread out along the road from Higaturu where they had been attending church services on the Sunday morning … Large numbers of the bodies had split open with intestines spilling out. The stench was appalling …
>
> Initially we tried to shovel bodies off the road into drainage ditches with four of us working together using shovels to do so. The masses of bodies along the road actually made it difficult to move around without stepping on one. In those days the native police had bare feet and what with ruptured bodies and exuding body fluids the police were slipping and sliding about … In retrospect it really was the stuff of nightmares. (Martin 2013, 44)

Figure 5.2. Casualties on the Higaturu access road
Casualties on the Higaturu access road are seen in this photograph taken on Tuesday 23 January, two days after the catastrophic Sunday eruption (Taylor 1958, fig. 76). Photograph supplied courtesy of Geoscience Australia (negative number M/1745).

Two other senior administration officers who had arrived at Popondetta were Acting Government Secretary Claude Champion, brother of Ivan and Allan, and Acting Assistant District Officer D. Clifton-Bassett (Murray Administrator 1951k). They led a party of police, labourers and others on foot by the road across the Ambogo River into both Higaturu Station and Sangara Mission. The visit was a short one, however, for fear of further volcanic eruptions taking place. Champion, on the following day, 24 January, and after his return to Port Moresby, dictated a moving report that was telephoned through to Canberra that afternoon:

> After reaching Higaturu we made a detailed survey, [but] were unable to move collapsed buildings. Several Europeans and natives were found in vicinity of the District Commissioner's residence—highly decomposed condition. It was difficult to distinguish between Europeans and natives as most of the clothing was apparently blown off. Without question, we have definitely identified C. Cowley who was sitting in his land rover. Mr. Williams, Works and Housing, Mr. Cook, Works and Housing, a European woman not yet identified but believed to be Mrs. Lock … Three other European males not yet identified were also found. One is believed to be [Erl] Cowley, another Stewart or Humphries. Dr and Mrs Martin and child were found near jeep apparently endeavouring to escape from their house. Works and Housing jeep was found suspended ten feet from the ground on a tree stump. (C. Champion 1951, 1; see Figure 5.3)

Figure 5.3. Devastated area at Higaturu including destroyed jeeps
Two destroyed jeeps at Higaturu are seen in the devastated area of Mount Lamington (Taylor 1958, fig. 69). The pyroclastic flow ran from left to right. Leslie Topue is in the centre of the photograph. Photograph supplied courtesy of Geoscience Australia (negative number GB/1060).

Claude Champion concluded from the disposition of the bodies at Higaturu that people must have had a few minutes of warning as most in the vicinity of the district commissioner's residence seemed to have been trying to escape northwards down towards the Ambogo River. A survey of the damaged buildings was made, most of which had been flattened. They were unable in the time available to lift the ruins to determine whether there were any bodies underneath them. Champion noted, however, that there was no 'stench' near the buildings. He estimated, further, that '400 natives perished at Higaturu Station alone', and that all 'Europeans and natives found on Higaturu Station were buried' (C. Champion 1951, 1).

What the Champion party saw at Sangara Mission was no less distressing:

> The road was strewn with dead natives. In Reverend Taylor's house which was still standing we found one of their children aged 4 or 5. The Taylor child was easily recognisable and was not burned at all. About 200 yards further through the Mission Station the body of Miss De Bibra who was fully clothed even to shoes was

found. She was apparently killed by blast as she did not appear otherwise injured and was not burned. Those bodies were buried at Sangara. (Champion. C. 1951, 1)

They next made a search of the mission's coffee plantations, which was where Reverend Taylor, before he died overnight at Popondetta, had said he had left his wife and two children hiding behind a tree stump. Many bodies were found in this area but identifying the victims was difficult:

> We then passed through Sangara Village … Dead natives were strewn everywhere … The whole area was a scene of utter desolation and it would be impossible for any one to still be alive in the area covered by the party. It is intended to clear the road leading to [Higaturu] to enable trucks to get by with large search parties in an endeavour to find more bodies …
>
> The burial on the roadside is a major task as we saw approximately 400 on the roadway to [Higaturu] … There are at least 9 villages whose inhabitants were completely obliterated and many more dead from burns. It will be some time before a reasonably accurate death toll can be given. At the moment it is estimated that there are 4000 dead and injured. The biggest proportion being dead. (C. Champion 1951, 1–2)

Claude Champion's official field party had demonstrated clearly the scale of the disaster management tasks ahead. Champion's figure of 4,000 dead and injured would later be used commonly in newspapers and reports as the actual death toll for the Lamington disaster, and this statistic became well distributed before a more accurate, but less publicised, estimate could be made when opportunity allowed in later weeks.

Anglicans Reverend W.E. Moren and Paul Rautamara flew to Popondetta on 23 January from Lae. They accompanied the Champion party into Higaturu Station and Sangara Mission, and undertook Christian burial services there (Murray Administrator 1951b; Strong 1951; Rautamara 1951). Reverend Moren thought that other Anglican priests in the area may not have been able to attend to such services as quickly as he could by flying in from Lae, but he found that Reverend John Anderson had already arrived in the disaster area. Moren returned to Lae on a flight that same day. Peter Rautamara described finding and burying recognisable bodies at Higaturu and Sangara Mission, including those of his brother Reverend John Rautamaru and family members:

> About 12 yards along the path that leads from the mission house to the vestry I found Mona, John's wife, and Cecil Marua's wife, Maud. Alongside the rubber trees nearby my brother John's life had ended. Dulcie, his daughter, lay at his head and I was glad that I was there to represent the Anglican mission as a witness. Weeping I took a spade and buried the bodies and Fr. Moren said the prayers (Rautamara 1951, 9)

Many hundreds of corpses had to be buried before the tropical climate caused any further deterioration of the cadavers thus creating a health risk, and to avoid as much as possible the scavenging of bodies by pigs, dogs and poultry. Identifying the European victims from their remains was also important, but difficult, for the administration so that the Australian Government in Canberra and the victim's next of kin could be advised. That same attention was not, and could not, be given to the thousands of dead Papuans. Champion had already alluded to difficulties in body identification, especially where clothes had been blown off, and the skin colour of the burnt corpses could not always be determined. Taylor (1958, 49) thought this 'may have been partly due to an intense post-mortem lividity which is characteristic of deaths from asphyxia'.

Judge Phillips flew out of Popondetta on Tuesday morning and returned to Port Moresby. Professional volcanological advice was now being given directly to the administrator in the Lamington area by volcanologist Tony Taylor, but the deputy administrator, in a telegram to Canberra that evening, offered some further volcanological opinion and observations on the basis of his Rabaul volcano experience in 1937. He noted first that the:

> Great field of pumice [on the slopes] was scored very freely by what seemed to be many water courses possibly made by heavy rain or by sudden cloud burst due to condensation of vapour column as happened in Rabaul in 1937… [and, second, that] … the pumice that had banked up around the core of the volcano … might tend to act as a stopper which volcano forces may yet attempt to remove. (Phillips Deputy Administrator 1951, 4–5)

The *kiap* at Kokoda, Acting Assistant District Officer 'Bunny' Yeoman, first visited the disaster area on this Tuesday when there was 'No disturbance of Lamington apparent' (Yeoman 1951, 2). Mrs Searle was surprised to see Yeoman when he arrived at Waseta:

> Why had Bunny walked here NOW, for what reason? Bunny had come to take us OUT of the area, and up to Kokoda. From the beginning I had felt his unease at coming into an area where everywhere was thick with volcanic ash and debris. (Searle 1995, 248)

Mrs Searle and the three children packed their bags for their hike with Yeoman and a line of carriers to the Kumusi River, crossing it at Wairopi by the narrow, timber-floored swinging foot bridge, and up to the government rest house where they stayed the night. Yeoman was anxious to start again in the morning, however, so the group was up by 5.00 am and they resumed their relentless trek to Kokoda. Eventually, they met a truck coming down the road, which turned around and took them all back to Kokoda. Mrs Searle's husband, Clen, stayed behind at Waseta and Awala to assist with rescue and response efforts. Anthropologist Marie Reay left Waseta later than the Searle–Yeoman group, but she too had reached Kokoda by Wednesday (Anonymous 1951a). The European women and children all flew to Port Moresby on the Thursday, where Mary Rose was finally reunited with her anxious parents (Searle 1995). These arrivals at Jacksons Airstrip were filmed, and the Searles and Marie Reay were shown in a newsreel entitled 'New Guinea: The Haunted Mountain in Eruption' (*Gaumont British News* 1951).

Wednesday 24 January: Media, Support from Australia and Ecumenism

Claude Champion returned to Port Moresby on 24 January. His emotional breakdown was witnessed at Jacksons Airfield and later reported in newspapers, but Champion soon focused on providing a dictated report that was sent to the Department of External Territories in Canberra by radiophone (C. Champion 1951). Press journalists and photographers from Australia had arrived in Port Moresby and Lae from Tuesday onwards 'in greater numbers than at any time since the war', the first representatives being from the Brisbane *Courier Mail* (*South Pacific Post* 1951c, 3). Reporters from the Sydney *Daily Telegraph*, however, were quick to charter an aircraft on Wednesday and were able to return photographs to Sydney in time for publication on Thursday. Other journalists arrived from Manus Island where they had been covering war crime trials. Most of the journalists made their headquarters in Lae where they had easier access to the disaster area at Mount Lamington.

An informed Australian Government back in Canberra had already been active in arranging to send two Dakota C47 aircraft from the Royal Australian Air Force (RAAF) to the Territory in support of the relief effort by air (Bullard 2017; see also Sinclair 1986). Dakotas were the main transport aircraft for the RAAF during World War II (WWII). They had a payload of 3,400 kilograms and a capacity for airdropping supplies and so were well suited to the task of supplying the growing refugee camp at Wairopi where there was no nearby airstrip. The first Dakota had departed from Australia on the previous day, 23 January, carrying dropping-parachutes, water containers and blood plasma provided by the Australian Red Cross (Bullard 2017). The second aircraft left the next day. These departures were the beginning of what would become weeks of similar RAAF support for the administration and Lamington evacuees (Figure 5.4). Qantas aircraft also participated in dropping operations (e.g. Civil Aviation 1951). The Australian Red Cross, both in Port Moresby and in Australia, played an important backup role to the administration during the relief phase at Mount Lamington but much less so in the disaster area itself (Wardrop 1951b; Ahearn 1951a, 1951b; Australian Red Cross Society 1951; *South Pacific Post* 1951d; Bullard 2017).

Administrator Murray that evening sent a comprehensive telegram from Popondetta to the minister in Canberra reporting on events and progress (Murray Administrator 1951c). He had visited Higaturu Station himself during the day, together with Dr Gunther and Ivan Champion, and thought that as many as 700 bodies had been buried that day (Murray Administrator 1951k). Normal burials were not feasible in the conditions they faced and bodies were 'being interred by heaping pumice over them … The dead must be interred where they lie … Stoic fortitude patience and smiles of the treated dying will live in memory' (Murray Administrator 1951c, 1–2). Body identification remained a problem. Murray was complimentary of all those who were involved with the relief effort, mentioning notably that the missionaries had done 'more than their best'. Eight bulldozers and a tractor had been flown in to improve the airstrip at Popondetta.

Figure 5.4. Dakota crew preparing to airdrop supplies
A Dakota crew prepares to airdrop supplies for evacuees in the Lamington disaster area. The photographer is unknown, but the photograph appeared on the front page of a Brisbane newspaper on Thursday 25 January 1951 (*Courier Mail* 1951). This digital copy was provided courtesy of the Kleckham family.

Murray also reported that the whole disaster area had been closed to all except officials and permit carriers, and indeed no further administration parties entered the Higaturu area for another week (Murray Administrator 1951k). This prohibition, however, did not come into effect until two general burial services had been held, overlooking the now devastated Sangara Mission Station and Higaturu Government Station. The first ceremony was led by the Anglican Reverend Anderson and supported by Roman Catholic Father Justin Lockie who had flown in from Lae (Justin 1951; Henderson 2001, 2007). The administrator read a lesson from the Bible. The second service was a requiem mass led by Father Justin who made use of the bonnet of a jeep (Figure 5.5) and who was assisted by Reverend Anderson (Justin 1951). The administrator reported Father Justin's own words that 'calamity leads us … to realise our oneness' (Murray Administrator 1951c, 2). Sister Henderson recalled the service as 'a wonderful ecumenical moment' (Henderson 2001, 6).

Figure 5.5. Requiem mass held by Father Justin on bonnet of jeep
The requiem mass took place on 24 January 1951 at the edge of the devastated area. Senior administration officers are, from left to right: Ivan Champion, carrying a hat in his hands; Administrator J.K. Murray wearing sunglasses; Dr John Gunther; and the uniformed J.S. Grimshaw, commissioner of police. Patrol Officer Des Martin is in the centre-rear (behind the unidentified European clasping his hands in front) wearing a surgical mask around his neck. Martin had just returned from work in the nearby devastated area and had doused the surgical mask with disinfectant to cope better with the smell of putrefying bodies. His photograph was published in the *Sphere* magazine of 10 February 1951. The photographer is unknown. This digital copy was provided by D. Martin.

The acting government secretary in Port Moresby, Lonergan, telephoned the Department of External Territories in Canberra at 10.00 pm, and the conversation was typed for the record (Anonymous 1951a). Lonergan covered several topics, including the limited success in identifying European bodies, although the body of Erl Cowley, son of the district commissioner, had been found. He noted the successful airlifts that had taken place but also that the arrival of so many aircraft at Popondetta out of Lae had held up aircraft leaving Port Moresby. Nevertheless, the delivered cargo included two jeeps, two lighting sets, fuel for motor vehicles, spares and food stuffs. He said that Mrs Searle, her two children, Mary Rose Henderson and Marie Reay would be flown to Port Moresby the next morning.

The deputy administrator, Judge Phillips, then came on the telephone to advise that a journalist in Port Moresby was pressing for information to be sent to Australia about the Lamington eruption along the lines that 'the Government had not done enough to foresee this disaster and take steps. Apparently they based this on talk of women who got out from Higaturu one of whom [gave] a talk over 9 PA [the local radio station] the other night' (Anonymous 1951a, 1). Phillips stated that he had agreed to give a press conference on the matter the following day. Further, he had completed that day a formal report for the attention, in due course, of the administrator (see Phillips Deputy Administrator 1951). This report was dispatched to Canberra the following day together with a covering letter from the acting government secretary. The radio broadcasting woman was identified in the letter as Mrs Gwilt whose comments were reported as having been 'rather hysterical'. Mrs Gwilt had said also that there had been earth tremors in the area for six weeks prior to the catastrophic eruption, which 'was certainly news to us as there had been no report from Cec. Cowley of this and I very much doubt that the statement is a rational one' (Acting Government Secretary 1951, 1).

Meanwhile, an issue of a different kind was brewing for Tony Taylor back at Mount Lamington. He had been informed by administration officers in the field that 'further activity was imminent', although the reasons for this volcanic forecast were not recorded (Taylor 1951, 2). An eruption, nevertheless, did take place at 3.00 am the next day, and Taylor immediately advised Ivan Champion that field parties should not enter the area throughout the coming Thursday.

Thursday 25 January: New Eruption, Bishop Strong and Prohibitions

Mr Lonergan telephoned Canberra in the morning advising the Department of External Territories about the new eruptive activity, together with the related news from Lae that the Department of Civil Aviation had prohibited all aircraft approaching within 50 miles of Mount Lamington (Anonymous 1951b). Aircraft heading for Popondetta, however, could do so by approaching from the north-east over the sea. Lonergan also said that more European bodies had been found, that 520 other bodies had been buried and that:

> Accommodation at Popondetta for Europeans is strained to the utmost, and sight-seers are not permitted to enter … We have allowed press to go in up to the present and we will as far as possible continue to do this. (Anonymous 1951b, 1)

Dr Gunther had said there was now ample medical aid and that offers from organisations such as the Red Cross were not required at present. The number of evacuees at the Wairopi camp was now about 2,500.

Concerns had emerged that Popondetta, which so far had escaped the worst of the eruption, might not itself be invulnerable to future volcanic activity and that an alternative wartime airstrip may be required. Colonel Murray told news media in Port Moresby that:

> We are planning a main operational base at Embi, only 18 miles from Mount Lamington. This will be an ideal spot, as the airstrip there can take big transport planes even in bad weather. With a heavy fall of rain, Popondetta would be out of operation for anything but small aircraft, but it could still be used as an advance base for small planes. (*South Pacific Post* 1951b, 1)

Embi Lakes are near Inonda where there were evacuees. Tony Taylor—after an aerial inspection of the Lamington crater in the morning—flew over Embi Lakes, which he determined were not directly of volcanic origin and were therefore not a potential threat (Taylor 1951). Four Douglas C-54 'Skymaster' aircraft were able to land at Embi, and both Popondetta and Embi were able to be used during the relief and recovery efforts in the days and weeks ahead.

This Thursday was when Bishop of New Guinea Philip Strong first arrived at Popondetta after sailing from Dogurua to Cape Killerton on the mission boat *St George* (Strong 1951, 1981). Strong would stay for 10 days and witness firsthand the volcanic devastation in the area, including the destruction of Sangara Mission where there had been so many deaths of the members and missionaries of his own Anglican diocese. The blow must have been severe, coming after the tragedy of the wartime murders and martyrdom of the Anglican missionaries that had resulted from his decision not to evacuate in advance of the Japanese invasion.

Bishop Strong had noted the following in his diary for Sunday 21 January—that is, before he heard about the terrible effects of the catastrophic eruption that day:

> I was oppressed throughout the day with a deep sense of gloom, fears and evil forebodings. Spent most of the morning wrestling in my chapel. Have seldom experienced anything so intense or so terrifying. Felt utterly that I had failed and all kinds of terrible possibilities seemed to brood up before me … awful depression. (Strong 1981, 212)

The editor of Strong's published diaries noted that they, as a whole:

> Make a powerful cumulative impact as they portray in some detail the slow and agonizing process of adapting to the consequences of a belief that missionaries should stay where they were. In short, the 'Call', as he perceived it, had to be worked out regardless of military strategy or the fortunes of great-power politics. (Wetherell, quoted in Strong 1981, x)

On 25 January, the bishop visited great crowds of evacuated people milling around at Cape Killerton, speaking and praying with them, and trying to offer comfort. Reverend John Anderson then took him to Popondetta where he stayed in the house where Dennis Taylor had died. He noted for this day some talk that Popondetta, although still safe, may have to be evacuated and that the administration was considering establishment of a new camp at Embi.

Another telephone call took place between Port Moresby and Canberra that evening, at 9.10 pm (Anonymous 1951c). Lonergan informed Halligan that the road into Higaturu had still not been fully cleared and that Tony Taylor had advised against the entry of burial parties because of concerns about the possible impact of new eruptions at the volcano. Taylor's senior at the BMR in Canberra, Dr N.H. Fisher, an ex-volcanologist with Rabaul experience, had enquired through the Department of External Territories about the work being done by Taylor and had offered to visit the Lamington area himself. The administrator, who, on this day, was back in Port Moresby, said that he was very satisfied with, and confident about, Taylor's ability. However, he would be pleased to have Dr Fisher visit the Territory because 'the Lamington experience requires examination of the Kokopo-Rapopo site having regard to Toma Mount Varzin' (Anonymous 1951c, 1). Murray was here referring to his involvement in the ongoing issue in East New Britain of transferring the functions of the volcanically vulnerable town of Rabaul to the Kokopo area, and to the fact that Mount Varzin, which is very close to Toma, but less so to Kokopo, was an apparently extinct volcano.

Lonergan also advised Halligan that a press conference had taken place that afternoon in Port Moresby. This meeting with the press involved the administrator, his deputy, Judge Phillips, and the government secretary. Judge Phillips had read out his report concerning his knowledge of the lead-up to disaster at Mount Lamington. The conference was said by Lonergan to have been 'very amicable and very successful' (Anonymous 1951c, 1). However, questions about the role of the government and of Phillips himself would grow in the days ahead. The members of the press clearly suspected there was an important story to be followed up after the public remarks that had been made by Mrs Gwilt and the other European women.

Friday 26 January: Criticisms and Thoughts about Rabaul

Details of the relief work undertaken in the Lamington disaster area since Monday dominated the front page of the *South Pacific Post* (1951b) on this Friday, appearing under the headline 'Plan Ready for Any New Emergency in Our Worst Disaster'. An appreciation was also published of the now deceased District Commissioner Cecil Cowley, which had been written by Sergeant-Major Guise of the Royal Papuan Constabulary who had served under Cowley in 1947. A photograph of the previous Thursday's eruption taken by the late Kevin Woiwod was also published, together with a caption saying that the image had appeared already in national newspapers throughout Australia.

This Friday's issue of the *South Pacific Post* also contained a letter from E.L. Hand who was highly critical of the reception given to the Popondetta evacuees on Monday 22 January by Port Moresby residents. Hand suggested that, in future, St John's Ambulance staff should form a welcoming committee, thus criticising the Australian Red Cross who, in fact, had provided considerable assistance in Port Moresby. This criticism of the Australian Red Cross was strongly rebutted the following week in a letter signed by eight of the evacuees who warmly praised the Red Cross for their work—namely, Heather Gwilt, Marie Reay, Mary Henderson, Marjorie Kleckham, Pat Searle, J. Boyd and Connie Morris, as well as Maggie Rae whose name should not be confused with that of anthropologist Marie Reay (*South Pacific Post* 1951c, 8). Further, a Brisbane-based letter writer in the same issue also stressed the role of the Red Cross in both Brisbane and Port Moresby in coordinating the provision of blood plasma. Finally, the *South Pacific Post* itself combated the implied criticism in an extended article entitled 'Red Cross Was Ready for Action' (*South Pacific Post* 1951d, 8; see also correspondence on files of the Australian Red Cross Society 1951).

Taylor at Lamington saw marked changes to the crater area as a result of a morning aerial inspection on this Friday (Taylor 1951). He had been tracing previous changes over the past few days, which would become even more marked over the coming weekend and into the following week. Taylor attempted to reach Isivita villages on foot to check seismic activity there, but failed owing to mudflows in the Ambogo River. Seismic data were recorded by him 'by improvised methods' throughout the night at Sangara Plantation, but there is no record of exactly what those methods were (Taylor 1951, 2). Taylor had no seismograph at this time, but he had a particular interest in observing whether some kinds of seismic signal preceded identifiable types of eruptive activity. Other people who were there would relate, and not apocryphally, how Taylor would lie on the floor flat on his back to best 'feel' ground shakes, and to observe the seismically induced ripples on the surface of a glass of water (e.g. Blaikie 2006).

Steve Lonergan in Port Moresby and Reg Halligan in Canberra had a further telephone conversation on what was the last day of the public service working week in both capitals. Halligan referred to an article in the *Canberra Times* that morning containing information that was said to have come from Port Moresby:

> Authorities have again refused to issue the names of the European dead found today [25 January]. They are having difficulty in identifying such bodies and will leave it to Canberra to announce the names after next of kin have been notified. (Anonymous 1951d)

The newspaper headline read '34 Europeans dead—20 bodies recovered'. The two bureaucrats then compared their respective lists of European casualties and concluded that 11 of 14 bodies had been identified, meaning that, at this particular time, as many as 24 out of a total of 35 were still unaccounted for. Identifying the dead and informing next of kin would continue for many months, as would any final estimation of the very many more Papuans who had lost their lives.

Mr Lonergan also reported that Assistant District Officer Holmes had inspected 15 villages south of Inonda down the eastern side of Mount Lamington. Among these would have been the two Anglican mission stations of Sewa and Sehaparete that Margaret de Bibra mentioned in her letter of 21 January (Figure 4.6). Sehaparete Mission was within the zone of complete destruction. Nearby Sewa was beyond it and had escaped the pyroclastic flows. About 100 survivors were evacuated from affected villages, but there were many more fatalities. Ivan Champion had reported that 'Holmes did [a] magnificent job and buried several hundred dead he found' (Anonymous 1951d, 2). A base would be established at Embi and three aircraft were flying to Popondetta and Embi that morning. Two RAAF aircraft were still in use, and the population at Wairopi had grown to 3,500. Lonergan also wrote to Champion saying that he:

> Should give consideration to relieving the pressure on some of your chaps, even if only temporarily, and I do suggest that as soon as possible you should yourself come to Moresby for 24 hours to be spent in bed. Good luck to you, you are doing a grand job. (Lonergan 1951b)

The administrator considered that, as a result of the Lamington disaster, the move from Rabaul must be regarded as an urgent matter. Dr Fisher had advised that a Lamington-type eruption was unlikely at Rabaul, but there was no need for concern about the Toma–Mount Varzin area as the active volcanoes were all inside the caldera harbour at Rabaul (Territories 1951).

Dr John Gunther, director of public health, was back in Port Moresby on Friday 26 January where he wrote a comprehensive account of his visit. He noted the health challenges ahead, and pointedly placed the Orokaiva catastrophe, whose effects he had witnessed, in its double-impact, historical context:

> Our problem remains to protect from epidemic disease some 8,000 people who are refugees from their homes and who in the short space of eight years have now twice seen their villages destroyed [—i.e.] by the explosion of war and the explosion of Nature. (Gunther 1951b, 5)

The two 'explosions' were also in the context of adaptation to almost 50 years of Australian colonialism, during which time traditional ways had had to change and adapt to, and equilibrate with, the ways of an outside world that clearly would not be disappearing any time soon.

Saturday 27 January: Aerial Inspections and 'Secondary' Explosions

Taylor made three flights in a Dragon aircraft on 27 January to check on the crater again, but also to investigate reports of new eruptive vents having formed on the mountain. Such a report had been received the previous day and the alleged vent had been examined from the air. Taylor concluded, however, that these 'vents' were 'secondary ash bed phenomenon' (Taylor 1951, 2). Hot, wet masses of recently deposited ash were exploding as a result of internal water vapour pressure building up and then being released explosively, giving the impression of a new vent. Taylor also noted a 'very encouraging correlation of seismic activity and eruption [was] established by observations at Popondetta during the night' (2).

Bishop Strong said mass in his house that day, John Anderson having prepared the altar, and attendance of the service included Rodd Hart and some local people (Strong 1981). Strong marvelled that Rodd and Madeleine Hart's lives had been spared owing to them being at Jegarata on their honeymoon rather than at Sangara Mission. He also wrote a confidential letter to the administrator, but its contents are not included in the published version of his diaries.

Sunday 28 January: One Week Later

Tony Taylor undertook another aerial inspection in the morning. He noted later that:

> Vigorous activity had begun at 0600 hours and continued until heavy cloud prevented further observations. At 1100 hours the Administrator and a party entered the area with the intention of proceeding to Higaturu. His Honour and party were advised against proceeding further. (Taylor 1951, 2)

Patrol Officer Bob Blaikie was at Popondetta later that morning when:

> A ragged, dirty and quite exhausted Bill Schleusener staggered into our forward base. He had walked alone for a week searching for and burying the dead and assisting the living … Dr Svirklys [Sverklys] quickly had Bill on to the operating table as it was feared that his lungs were clogged with pumice dust and ash … [Pilot John

> Arthur, together with Tony Taylor on board, and after returning to Popondetta from the aerial inspection,] flew his aircraft extremely low over the house revving his engine up and down warning us of a further eruption … At just after midday Mt Lamington again erupted with multiple explosive outbursts … Then suddenly, like Lazarus arising from the dead, Bill leapt up from the operating table shouting something to the effect that 'It nearly got me the first time but it won't get me again'. (Blaikie 2006, 38)

Schleusener raced outside but was persuaded to return by Patrol Officer Blaikie. Events of a quite different kind meanwhile were taking place that day at Gona.

First, Bishop Strong celebrated the morning service in the Holy Cross Church at Gona: 'A great mass of people present. Quite a thousand, overflowing the church and joining in the service from outside' (Strong 1981, 214–15). Then, in the afternoon, and to Strong's 'surprise and joy', Bishop David Hand arrived. Hand had heard about the eruption and disaster while in Australia, and had been asked by Strong to return, as he explained in a mission publication:

> I am going back in response to a message from my superior officer, Bishop Philip Strong. I am not sorry that this is the order, because knowing that district as I do and being the only European who knows the language and the native people of that district, I feel that I may have something to offer in assistance in the rehabilitation and helping of these sadly smitten people. (Hand 1951, 21)

Hand's arrival was a 'great relief' to Strong who eventually handed over to him mission responsibilities in the disaster area after a stay of 10 days so that he could return to duties at Dogura and elsewhere in the diocese (Strong 1951, 50).

Strong (1981) wrote in his diary for this day words that would be shared later with Anglicans in Australia through a national Anglican publication (Strong 1951). The bishop provided a mystical and religious response to what he had been experiencing in the Lamington disaster area:

> God has taken into the eternal sphere of His Kingdom not only the members of His Church at Sangara, but their priests, their missionaries and their teachers as well … We must not grieve for the dead. They are in God's keeping. Indeed we can rejoice for them and give thanks, for with very many of them their call came to them on the LORD'S OWN DAY [Sunday] … What a blessed

viaticum! [i.e. the Holy Eucharist offered as last rites before death] … and as we remember the suddenness of the call that came to so many of our dear ones that Sunday morning, we must let the volcano be a Voice calling us to live our lives day by day so near to God that we may be ever ready to meet Him beyond the veil of death. (Strong 1951, 50)

The role of God—in particular his wrath—in explaining the cause of the disaster would be taken up by others who were less celebratory of the spiritual meaning of the eruption and its effects on the lives of so many people.

Monday 29 January: Re-establishing Mission Work

Bishop Strong heard that the administrator, Colonel Murray, was planning to enter the Sangara Mission area on Monday 29 January. The bishop joined Murray in the hope of being able to find the bodies of Mrs Taylor and her children; to identify and give Christian burial to the bodies of mission teachers, if they could be found; and to retrieve any station records. The group reached as far as Sangara Rubber Plantation and some of the devastated villages where there was a:

> Terrible sight indeed with dead bodies still lying about. Complete and utter desolation. Not a speck of green or a blade of grass anywhere … The Administrator said that no scene that he had witnessed in either of the two wars was so terrible. (Strong 1981, 215)

The group could see across to the Sangara Mission Station, but Tony Taylor had come along with the party and he turned them back saying 'he could not permit anyone to go in, as he considered another explosion might be imminent' (Strong 1951, 49).

Bishop Strong and Colonel Murray that afternoon travelled down to the north coast to visit the evacuees at Cape Killerton as the administrator was anxious to see the situation there for himself. They later sailed round to Gona on the mission boat *St George* and both knelt by the side of the grave of Reverend Dennis Taylor who had been buried at the foot of the mission cross, which still bore the marks of Japanese bullet impacts (Murray Administrator 1951d; Strong 1951; Tomkins and Hughes 1969;

Strong 1981). Mission losses, both Papuan and European, were great: Dennis Taylor and all of his family, many hundreds of baptised church members, the Reverend John Rautamara, 18 Papuan teachers who were at Miss de Bibra's training course and Miss Peggy De Bibra.

The bishop had already spoken to the administrator and had received his agreement about the opening of mission schools at Wairopi, which was now the largest of the evacuation camps, holding about 4,000 people. Ivan Champion had suggested that the mission's existing outstation of Eiwo, which was close to Wairopi, would be the best place for schools, and the Harts had expressed their willingness to go there (Strong 1951, 1981). They, together with Albert Rarika, George Ambo and other mission teachers, all of whom had survived the tragedy, flew out of Popondetta to Kokoda and hence to Wairopi and Eiwa, joining Father Porter in this restoration of the mission's work in the area. The bishop visited them all during the week before his departure, noting that 1,000 people had gathered for Evensong in the open air on the night he was there.

Colonel Murray in the evening sent another telegram to the Department of External Territories reporting on the day's events (Murray Administrator 1951d). He added that the road into Higaturu still had to be cleared, but that surviving government documents, as well as some private belongings, had been retrieved from what remained of the government station. Vaccinations against whooping cough were progressing well among the refugees in the camps. The challenge of water supply was being handled resolutely, but there were still problems of hygiene and sanitation. He advised, too, that the evacuation camp at Oro Bay was much better than the one at Cape Killerton, which he would be closing (Murray Administrator 1951d). One disadvantage of Cape Killerton was that it backed on to swamps, so diseases such as malaria were a threat. Further, the mountain Orokaiva in these camps were now in 'enemy' Yega territory, were apprehensive about the sea and had regard to the threat of tsunamis.

A canteen run by the Red Cross in Port Moresby began operating at Jacksons Airstrip on this day 'to provide morning and afternoon tea and lunch for the crews of relief planes, ground staff and members of the Administration, particularly Native Services' (Rooney 1951, 1; see also Wardrop 1951b; Australian Red Cross Society 1951). This service was provided until Thursday 15 February, but was not required at weekends. 'Biscuits, cheese, fruit honey and jam were placed on the tables before morning tea for it was found that some members of the crew preferred these things before undertaking a flight', reported organiser Petrea Rooney (1951, 1).

Tuesday 30 January: Changing Responsibilities and Research Directions

The volcano was more active in the morning of 30 January, starting at 5.00 am, although debris fallout appeared to be confined to the general area of the crater, reported the administrator at 8.00 am (Murray Administrator 1951e). Colonel Murray also advised that he had asked Tony Taylor to report directly to the Department of External Territories in Canberra rather than through him.

The administration in Port Moresby at 9.45 am sent the department an update about the ongoing volcanic activity, adding that 20 days of supplies would be delivered at Wairopi by RAAF airdrop on the following day, Wednesday (Administration 1951b). They mentioned too that anthropologist Marie Reay would be relocating her research work to New Ireland. She did not return to the Northern Division.

A report dated 29 January appeared in an Australian newspaper on 30 January stating that the looting of European houses had been taking place at Higaturu, which was within the area still regarded as volcanically dangerous (*Sun* 1951). Police had been 'risking their lives rounding up looters'. However, further looting does not seem to have been a problem in the disaster area.

Wednesday 31 January: Rehabilitation and Instrumental Monitoring

By the end of January, serious attention was being paid by senior administration officers to a reorganisation of the Northern Division and to rehabilitation of people displaced by the eruption of 21 January. These officers included the government secretary and director of the Department of Agriculture, Stock and Fisheries (DASF) (Dwyer 1951)—both in Port Moresby—and Ivan Champion at Popondetta (Rich 1951). The challenges were listed in a memorandum, apparently from the government secretary to the administrator, highlighting:

> Preparation of a plan with consideration of a number of major points particularly decisions as to a new HQ for the Division; appointment of a District Commissioner; compensation; repatriation of time expired labourers; acquisition of land for resettlement purposes; establishment of an administrative rehabilitation group;

production of foodstuffs; transportation; possibly resubdivision of the Division; establishment of a special subdivision to include selected resettlement areas the administration of which would be a dual concern of the HQs of the Administration and the District Commissioner selected to control the Northern Division. The tasks would be primarily for the Department of District Services and Native Affairs but in these it would be assisted by specialist officers of the Departments of Health[,] Agriculture, Lands and Education. (Memorandum 1951)

On 31 January, Administrator Colonel Murray, together with Dr Gunther and Ivan Champion, again visited Higaturu, the third occasion on which senior administration staff had been able to do so (Murray Administrator 1951k). Access to Sangara Mission, however, remained problematic, and the three men would not visit the Higaturu area again together until 15 February. Floods and mudflows down the Ambogo River were becoming hazardous (Taylor 1958).

Dr N.H. 'Doc' Fisher, Taylor's superior, arrived at Popondetta on this day, and a seismograph was on its way from the BMR in Melbourne (Taylor 1951). Visual observations of the crater continued but all operations over the next few days were concentrated on the erection of housing and the installation of power for the seismograph at Sangara Rubber Plantation. The seismograph began recording good data at the observation post on 8 February (Taylor 1958). Fisher stayed in the Lamington and Rabaul areas for two weeks, helping to take some of the workload off Taylor, engaging in important discussions with the administrator and participating in volcanological fieldwork (Figure 5.6).

Tony Taylor up to this time had had to work without any supporting volcano-monitoring instruments, such as a seismograph, in a situation in which, originally, he also knew nothing about the geology of Lamington volcano and, therefore, its past eruptive behaviour. Nevertheless, he had, by this time, gained the confidence and respect of the administrator and others, as well as the authority to control the movements of burial parties and others into what he decided were vulnerable areas at high-risk times. His numerous aerial inspections in aircraft flown by adventurous pilots to, and over, the active crater were no less striking. Indeed, observations from aeroplanes using binoculars and a camera probably provided his greatest opportunity for making volcanological advances during these early days, combined with intuition and a framework of professional volcanological knowledge.

Figure 5.6. Dr Fisher and Leslie Topue during fieldwork in the disaster area

Dr N.H. Fisher (right) and field assistant Leslie Topue are here photographed undertaking fieldwork in the Lamington disaster area in early February 1951. Fisher appears to be thinking about collecting a rock sample with his small geological hammer from the large lava block under his left foot. Photograph supplied courtesy of Geoscience Australia (negative number GB/3236).

Taylor for over a week had been tracking the changes to the crater floor at Lamington as a result of his aerial inspections (Taylor 1951). Explosive eruptions on Thursday 25 January had created a smooth conical depression in the previously debris-filled crater, but within 24 hours uplift of the crater floor had created a shallow basin and new vents and, by 30 January, the uplifted floor was almost flat (Taylor 1958). Bulging started to produce large curved and smaller concentric cracks on the last day of January. Uplift and bulging were evidently being caused by a new body of active magma rising beneath the crater floor. This might be one of the reasons why Taylor had been so cautious about letting people into the area he had declared prohibited, because the new magma, once it broke through, conceivably might produce further devastating explosive eruptions. However, and as Taylor soon recognised, the features that he had been witnessing signalled the birth of a new lava dome on Lamington volcano in which magma of high viscosity—that is, low fluidity—remains plastic in the volcano conduit but then solidifies rapidly after the lava emerges onto the surface. Dome growth would escalate in the first week of February and from this time on it would be a defining characteristic of the Lamington eruption (Figures 5.7–5.8). This growth, however, would be interrupted and become complicated for another two months by repeated explosive eruptions from vents in the crater, some of which at times partly destroyed the developing dome (Taylor 1958).

Figure 5.7. Aerial photograph of Lamington from the north on 8 February 1951

The devastated area dominates the foreground of this photograph and extends back to the breached crater of the volcano where the early stages of growth of the active, vapour-emitting lava dome can be seen. Visible dome growth was especially rapid between 2 and 9 February. The dark areas on the right are mudflows of originally hot ash on the north-east flanks of the volcano in tributaries of the Ambogo River. Old lava domes form the rugged summit of the mountain. The photographer was probably G.A.M. Taylor (1958, fig. 118). Photograph supplied courtesy of Geoscience Australia (negative number GA/9938).

Figure 5.8. Taylor and Crellin approaching the active crater on 11 February 1951
Volcanologist Tony Taylor (in front) and Patrol Officer Bill Crellin are walking across recent pyroclastic flow deposits on a visit to the youthful lava dome crater near the head of the avalanche valley on 11 February 1951 (Taylor 1958, fig. 49). This photograph was taken by Dr Fisher. Some explosive activity is taking place on the south side of the dome, which is relatively small at this time (see, however, Figure 7.6). Photograph supplied courtesy of Geoscience Australia (negative number GB/3012).

Newspapers and the Phillips Controversy

'Doc' Fisher later wrote that the Lamington eruption of 1951:

> Catapulted Taylor, normally one of the most reserved and retiring of men, into public prominence and provided the opportunity to put into effect the studies of the effects of volcanic eruptions of various types that he had been assiduously pursuing. (Fisher 1976, x)

Taylor's name soon appeared in newspapers and magazines as news of the Lamington disaster came to the attention of the news media and radio broadcasters, particularly in Australia. The names of other previously unknown Europeans appeared in the newspapers too, especially those of the dead whose bodies had been identified quickly and their next of kin informed. Also prominent were the names of evacuees met by the news media at Jacksons Airstrip in Port Moresby on their arrival from Popondetta.

News from Port Moresby was transferred to Australia quickly by radiogram and telephone, and press releases were provided by the Australian Government out of Canberra. There was a demand for photographs of the Higaturu–Sangara and Lamington area both before and after the eruption of 21 January, and especially of the eruption and volcano themselves (Figures 5.9–5.10). Captain Jacobson's aerial shots, for example, were popular. Comparisons were made between the catastrophic eruption cloud and the shape and 'blast' effects of the atomic bomb clouds of 1945, together with those of the atmospheric tests of nuclear bombs being undertaken at Bikini Atoll by the Americans. Rough sketch maps were published for the benefit of the many readers who would have had little idea of the locations of places such as Mount Lamington, Higaturu and Popondetta. Headlines were justifiably dramatic. These newspaper reports were the start of an accumulation of information about Lamington volcano and its 1951 eruption that would continue for many more decades as books, scientific papers, letters, opinion pieces, anniversary articles, memoirs and diaries became available.

The news media, therefore, played a vital role in the initial reporting on the disaster, although, as might be expected, quality varied and errors crept into some published articles—to the annoyance of those who had survived and knew otherwise. For example, early reporting in the February issue of the regional magazine *Pacific Islands Monthly* contained criticism about the lack of early warning of the catastrophic eruption, which drew the attention of the Department of External Territories in Canberra and of the administration in Port Moresby (e.g. Murray 1951a). Nevertheless, the administrator himself, in a reflective mood, wrote: 'One of my abiding memories is that of the courtesy and restraint of the journalists … in this scene of disaster unparalleled in Australian history' (Murray 1968, 21). Colonel Murray also added his support to the Australian Broadcasting Commission (ABC) in Port Moresby following a protest letter that had been sent to the radio broadcaster by Bishop Strong. Words used in an ABC broadcast gave the false impression, to Bishop Strong at least, that Reverend Taylor had left his wife and children in order to get help. The manager for the ABC in Port Moresby, Glenister, discussed the matter at length with both Colonel Murray and Dr John Gunther. They concluded that the words did not 'brand' Reverend Taylor in a negative way, and the matter seems to have drawn to a close after Glenister wrote to both Bishop Strong and then to Ivan Champion (Glenister 1951).

The role of the news media, however, was not restricted to basic reporting but increasingly also to asking questions. How could so many people be killed by a mountain that was not even known to be a volcano? Was anyone responsible? Was there any truth in the words of the angry European women who arrived in Port Moresby in the days after the disaster had taken place?

A statement urging the establishment of a public inquiry into the lead-up to the Lamington disaster was published in the *South Pacific Post*, a weekly Port Moresby newspaper, on 2 February 1951 (Figure 5.9c(ii)). It was felt that the inquiry should be 'headed by an impartial and competent authority, such as Justice Gore, giving such committee the widest possible terms of reference for their investigation of the disaster' (*South Pacific Post* 1951c). Six questions were asked:

1. Had any action been taken before the first eruption to advise the Government Vulcanologist, G.A.M. Taylor, that earth tremors were being felt around Higaturu?
2. Had any members of the Higaturu–Sangara community, before the disastrous eruption, communicated their personal views and fears to any member of the Administration?
3. Did any of the native population who had previously had experience of volcanoes communicate their opinions and then flee the district?
4. What prevented the vulcanologist from arriving at the scene until 4,000 people had been wiped out?
5. What were the factors that led Mr Justice Phillips into making a decision not to evacuate Higaturu?
6. Was the Administration aware that for many weeks before the eruption earth tremors were continually being experienced in the area? (*South Pacific Post* 1951c)

Figure 5.9a. Headline cuttings representing only a small number of the many articles that were published on the Lamington disaster in different Australian and Port Moresby newspapers

i. *Sunday Sun* and *Guardian* (Sydney), Sunday 28 January 1951, 3. This photograph of the 'cauliflower'-shaped eruption cloud was taken by Captain Arthur Jacobson on 21 January shortly before the collapse of the cloud, as seen in Figure 4.5.

ii. *Herald* (Melbourne), Monday 22 January 1951, 1. Note that this article was published in an Australia newspaper only one day after the catastrophic eruption on 21 January 1951.

iii. *Sun* (Sydney), Tuesday 23 January 1951, 1. The statistic of '4000 casualties' represents only the very first estimate from the devastated area.

5. THE NEXT 10 DAYS

3,000 KILLED IN ERUPTION
33 Missing Whites Believed Dead

Reports received in Canberra last night stated that more than 3,000 natives are believed to have died in the eruption from Mt. Lamington (Papua) on Sunday.

The reports said that the 33 missing Europeans must be presumed dead.

All injured Europeans have been removed from the devastated area which has been closed by proclamation.

The bodies of most of the European victims have been buried where found, after identification when possible.

Burned and maimed natives are being brought to hospital by their tribesmen on improvised stretchers. Doctors and nurses are working at full pressure and have appealed to the mainland for blood supplies. (See Page 6.)

All aircraft in New Guinea have been commandeered to run a shuttle service between Lae and Popondetta to carry food, water, medical supplies and comforts and to evacuate the injured and refugees.

TERRIFIED NATIVES FLEE

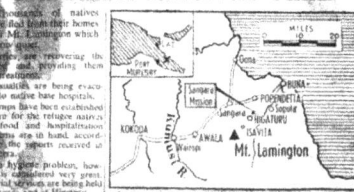

i

THE NEWS

Europeans' Bodies Found
S.A. FAMILY OF FOUR MISSING
Grim story of N.G. eruption

iii

IEW GUINEA DISASTER
Havoc Likened to Atom Blast

Reports filtering through to the Department of External Territories, Canberra, list 33 Europeans, mostly Australians, missing and fears for their safety mount every hour.

Air circuits of the volcano have shown 20 villages badly damaged and no sign of life.

Latest reports state the disturbance is abating and it is believed that the major eruption in the mountain has burnt itself out.

One report from the Director of Public Health in New Guinea (Dr. Gunther) quotes him as likening the devastation about Lamington as similar to that caused by the atomic bomb.

The report states trees have been blown to the ground, uprooted and stripped of foliage, while native villages are blasted with roofs torn off and houses completely demolished.

All the trees were blown to the ground in one direction—sloping away from Lamington—an indication of the intensity of the blast.

Plasma, food, clothing and medical assistance are being rushed to the stricken area.

the 20 wrecked villages about the base of the mountain.

Following on his flight he issued orders for parties to go out and bury the dead and survey the damage.

A continuous airlift is being maintained with Popondetta, the last link with the devastated area. Planes are constantly leaving Lae airstrip with supplies.

A terrific rainstorm swept Moresby yesterday moved away and may be travelling towards the volcano area, although pilots reported flying conditions between Lae and Popondetta as good.

Dr. Gunther, who was at Aiwala, near Lamington, said damage there was slight and all Europeans were safe.

He said he was making arrangements to have 1000 natives in the area evacuated.

ii

Missing Man Took This Picture

This dramatic picture of Mount Lamington's first eruption last Thursday was taken by young Works and Housing employee Kevin Woiwood, who is now listed among the missing. Woiwood's picture appeared in national newspapers throughout Australia. As far as is known it is the only photograph of the original eruption.

iv

Figure 5.9b. Four additional newspaper headlines

i. *Sydney Morning Herald*, Wednesday 24 January 1951, 1. The estimate of '3000 killed' is very close to the final death toll calculated weeks later.

ii. *Bendigo Advertiser*, Wednesday 24 January 1951, 2. Claimed similarities between the volcanic eruption of 21 January and atomic bomb explosions or 'blasts' was a common misconception in the early days of the relief and recovery phase.

iii *News* (Adelaide), Wednesday 24 January 1951, 1. Some emphasis is given to South Australian losses in this Adelaide newspaper.

iv. *South Pacific Post* (Port Moresby), Friday 26 January 1951, 1. Kevin Woiwod took this photograph from Higaturu of the eruption cloud at Mount Lamington on Thursday 17 January 1951, just three days before he was killed by the catastrophic eruption of Sunday 21 January.

Figure 5.9c. Four more newspaper headlines

i. *Sun News-Pictorial* (Melbourne), Tuesday 30 January 1951, 9. Looting at Higaturu is headlined in this article.

ii. *South Pacific Post* (Port Moresby), Friday 2 February 1951, 1. The need for an inquiry into the Lamington disaster was highlighted on the front page of this newspaper published in Port Moresby.

iii. *Age* (Melbourne), Thursday 1 February 1951, 4. Volcanologist John Best is quoted — perhaps misquoted and out of context — as saying in Lae on Wednesday 31 January that the worst of the eruptions at Mount Lamington was over and that the volcano 'may never erupt seriously again'.

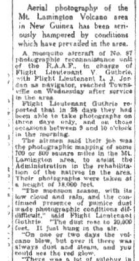

iv. *North Queensland Register* (Townsville), Saturday 3 March 1951, 15. Two RAAF 'Mosquito' aircrew undertaking the aerial photography survey of Mount Lamington are photographed for this article in which attention is drawn to the poor visibility that was hindering the aerial surveying of the Lamington area.

Minister for the Department of External Territories Percy Spender and his advisers in Canberra had already heard about the rising public and media disquiet and that same day, 2 February, they released a long statement for the press defending the actions of Judge Phillips and the administration in Port Moresby. 'We can all be wise after the event', said Spender, ending his press release with:

> The whole of the facts and attendant circumstances relating to the eruption will, of course, be carefully scrutinised so as to learn from them all lessons that may be learned. I do not, however, see any grounds whatever for any public enquiry. Generally I think the Administration has done a very good job and would personally like to pay a public tribute to the zeal and devotion displayed not only by it but by many others, in dealing with this awful and devastating disaster. (Spender 1951a, 3)

Much of the ministers' statement was published in the February issue of *Pacific Islands Monthly* in an article entitled 'Why No Official Warning? Demand for Inquiry about Lamington Disaster'. It contained the following statement:

> The local newspaper, *South Pacific Post*, has soberly but strongly voiced the people's demand for an inquiry. 'What is the use of maintaining a vulcanological service in the Territory if no attempt is made to study volcanoes outside of Rabaul?' sums up the viewpoint of the ordinary man. (*Pacific Islands Monthly* 1951c, 10)

The administration, as noted by the minister, had indeed undertaken outstanding relief work in the aftermath of the disaster. Further, there was recognition not only of this achievement but also of some opposition from the general public to the idea of an inquiry, if published letters by W. Kienzle (*South Pacific Post* 1951d) and T.W. Upson (*South Pacific Post* 1951e) are representative. No official inquiry took place, but questions continued to be asked concerning events *before* the catastrophic eruption of 21 January. Judge Phillips was still under scrutiny and was anxious to defend himself. On 3 February 1951 he wrote a detailed, 10-page memorandum, which included three appendices, to the Administrator Colonel Murray (Deputy Administrator 1951; see also Phillips 1951b). This report was forwarded to the minister in Canberra. Spender and his advisers were not totally convinced, however, and the minister responded on 13 February as follows:

> I desire to have followed up why no action appears to have been taken when Mr Cowley at least suggested that 'someone should go in and take a look' (18.1.51). Was Judge Phillips visit at all connected with this[?] I am not completely satisfied on this aspect particularly in view of [the] fact that Cowley clearly expected a vulcanologist to arrive. (Spender 1951b)

Judge Phillips in his response of 27 February to this ministerial instruction said that he had no knowledge of the radio call from Cowley when he made the 'entirely spontaneous' decision on Thursday 18 January to fly to Higaturu (Phillips 1951c, 1). Perhaps the minister or his advisers could have explored further whether Judge Phillips, because of his previous experience with volcanic eruptions at Rabaul in 1937, thought that he was adequately qualified to deal with the reports from Higaturu of the volcanic eruptions at Lamington. Why did he not delegate the task to the administration's own volcanologist in Rabaul? However, in reality, this would have made little difference, as Tony Taylor would have had to travel to Popondetta, at the very earliest, on Friday 19 January—the day he said he heard about the Lamington unrest—assuming that a flight from Rabaul, and a connecting flight to Popondetta, had been available. On arrival at Popondetta, Taylor would have had insufficient time to make any sort of reasonable evidence-based forecast of the terrible events that followed the next morning of Sunday 21 January. Indeed, he likely would have been killed himself had he decided to base himself at Higaturu and to undertake observational fieldwork on the volcano.

Judge Phillips, in his reply of 27 February, also reported on what more he had found out about the radio-telephone conversation between Cowley in Higaturu and Samson in Port Moresby on Thursday 18 January—that is, the exchange that had been so difficult to understand because of the radio static apparently being caused by the volcanic activity at Lamington. Sansom, on 29 January, had handed Deputy Administrator Phillips a memorandum stating: 1) that a 24-hour emergency radio call arrangement had been put in place at that time; and 2) that 'Mr Cowley stated that he did not consider there was any cause for alarm, but that in the event that the situation changed, he would immediately forward advice through the emergency communication' (Phillips 1951c, 2). However, Phillips was also advised by the government secretary's office on 1 February that Jefford, who had monitored and assisted at the radio-telephone call on 18 January, reported that Cowley had indeed said 'that someone should go in and have a look' (2).

Figure 5.10. Photograph of Lamington in full eruption

This dramatic and probably trimmed photograph of Mount Lamington in eruption was published in sepia on the large-format front cover of the *Illustrated London News* on Saturday 24 February 1951. The dense, wide eruption column appears ready to collapse and so form pyroclastic flows. This volcanic activity is dated Saturday 18 February and is described in the caption of the published photograph as the 'second eruption'. This is somewhat misleading as other significant explosive eruptions took place between 21 January and 18 February (see Taylor 1958). The name of the photographer is unknown, as is the precise time of day that the photograph was taken. Taylor (1958) did not use this photograph in his BMR Bulletin. Note that 18 February is only six days before the date of publication of the magazine in London, meaning that the photograph must have been transported expressly by air from Papua to the British capital.

Three particular points can be made with regard to the available documentation: 1) administration officers more senior than Samson and Jefford were evidently not informed of Cowley's request for assistance on 18 January; 2) there is no specific mention in any of the correspondence, even in Judge Phillips' detailed reports, of the need for the Territory's own government volcanologist in Rabaul to be advised of the Lamington volcanic activity, even though the administrator himself, Colonel Murray, would be in Rabaul the next day; 3) there appears to have been no dire urgency or any official formality in the request made by Cowley, even though he clearly expected a volcanologist to arrive at Popondetta airstrip on Friday 19 January.

There is also a suspicion that the poor communications between Port Moresby and Rabaul may have been influenced in part by a residual polarisation of loyalties between matters 'Papuan' and matters 'New Guinean' when the two territories were separate entities. Murray, however, who was in Rabaul anyway, would not have been impressed if this indeed had been the case. Why did Phillips not contact Murray by radio-telephone and why was the district commissioner in Rabaul, Keith McCarthy, evidently reluctant to let Tony Taylor leave for Lamington when he first heard about the volcanic unrest, if the later account of events by John Best is true?

One additional point can be offered with regard to the decision not to evacuate made on 18 January by Judge Phillips and Reverend Dennis Taylor—and secondarily by their subordinates Cowley and Reverend Porter: the contrast between the reactions and responses of European men and women. The men seem to have adhered to the principal of staying calm and not appearing fearful in the face of danger, bringing to mind the British wartime expression 'keep calm and carry on', which carries a hint of fatalism and is not necessarily the best advice when facing an unknown, yet escalating, volcanic threat. An antithetic slogan is 'don't wait for what happens next'. The European women were justifiably frightened by the volcanic displays at Mount Lamington and what they might portend, but their human responses both before and after the disaster were treated, by at least some of their male counterparts, as emotional and irrational. These times, one is obliged to note, were dominated by masculinity— an admiration of male self-reliance and probably (and understandably) male militaristic sentiments left over from the war and from ANGAU (i.e. Australian New Guinea Administrative Unit) times.

6

BEGINNING DISASTER RECOVERY

Geoscience Support at Lamington and Rabaul

The administration in Port Moresby and the Department of External Territories in Canberra in February had been managing the media fallout relating to the proposal for a public inquiry on what led to the disaster. Meanwhile, on Sunday 4 February, Judge Phillips, who was at the centre of the dispute, reported to the administrator that he had been assisting lawyers at the government secretary's office to finalise a 'volcanic and seismic disturbances' ordinance that would cover the official relief effort and state of emergency at Lamington, to be renewed on a month-by-month basis (Phillips 1951b; Crown Law Officer 1951). Phillips added that the acting government secretary himself, Steve Lonergan, and his assistant, had 'worked incessantly and unsparingly' and that, on the previous day, Lonergan 'looked on the verge of collapse' (Phillips 1951b, 1).

The first 10 days of the relief phase at Lamington had been implemented rapidly and can be judged to have been a significant success. The administrator in Popondetta, however, was still focusing his immediate attention on continuing effective relief effort in the disaster area, and February thus became a month of many multifaceted and interrelated activities for him and his staff. February also represents the start of a transition from the 'relief' phase of the post-disaster period into a much longer and more difficult 'recovery' phase. Several of the main tasks facing the administration at this time can be identified from messages sent by

Colonel Murray from both Popondetta and Port Moresby to Canberra between 3 and 28 February (Murray Administrator 1951f–k). The first of these tasks was the challenge of continuing scientific observations and instrumental monitoring of the still active and threatening volcano as a basis for early warning of future eruptions.

Volcanologist Tony Taylor was required to stay on at Lamington to continue the volcano monitoring, thus beginning his nearly two years of study, broken at times by other commitments elsewhere in the Territory. He was supported in his work by other scientists seconded from the Bureau of Mineral Resources, Geology and Geophysics (BMR) in Canberra. Paramount in the early days was the support provided by Dr N.H. 'Doc' Fisher, chief government geologist, who had come to the disaster area carrying the benefit of his prewar experience in volcanological work in the Territory of New Guinea and especially at Rabaul in 1937–42. His seniority and experience were invaluable and timely as he was able to engage in discussions with Colonel Murray not only about the situation at Lamington, but also about the volcanic threats elsewhere in the Territory of Papua and New Guinea, including Rabaul.

Other BMR scientists who came to Lamington were seismologist W.J. 'Bill' Langron and geologist John G. Best. Bill Langron contributed greatly to the scientific and technical work through long hours of duty in collecting much of the instrumental data that was recorded on the seismograph (Taylor 1958). John Best came early but stayed only briefly as he was required to travel on to Rabaul to continue, in Taylor's absence, the running of the government's volcanological observatory and to deal with eruptions taking place elsewhere in the Territory. Best had the frightening experience on Wednesday 7 February of sinking 'up to his neck' in quicksand while crossing one of the flooded rivers, probably the Ambogo, but being pulled out by accompanying patrol officers using his camera strap (Littler 2005, 69).

Administrator Murray and Dr Fisher went to Embi airstrip on the morning of Saturday 3 February to meet the crew of a Royal Australian Air Force (RAAF) 'Mosquito' aircraft equipped for aerial photography (Murray Administrator 1951f). The visit had been arranged by the Department of External Territories in Canberra and would include not only the aerial photographic survey of the disaster area, but also the aerial spreading of DDT for health purposes (see also Bullard 2017). Aerial photographs of the Lamington area were needed to map the extent of the disaster and changes in topography and infrastructure. Murray and Fisher discussed their requirements with the two flight-lieutenants in charge, but the subsequent flights were hampered by the weather and dust-laden atmosphere. Flight-Lieutenant Guthrie reported that in:

> [Twenty-eight] days they had been able to take photographs on three days only, and on those occasions between 9 and 10 o-clock in the morning … The monsoon season, with its low cloud and rain, and the continued presence of pumice dust made photographic conditions difficult. (*North Queensland Register* 1951, 15; see also Figure 5.9c(iv))

Doc Fisher also had the opportunity of following up on the concerns of 22 January that Mount Victory might break out in eruptive activity in a similar way to Lamington. He undertook an aerial inspection of Victory volcano, south of the government station at Tufi, but reported 'no change from its usual condition' (Murray Administrator 1951f, 2). In a magazine article published in June 1951, Fisher later described Victory as 'a rugged, partly eroded and heavily timbered cone … There are no recorded eruptions [sic]', and said that an estimated eruption type at the volcano was 'probably mild explosive' (Fisher 1951, 38, 40). This description is a reflection of what little was known about Victory volcano and its threats at that time, although Fisher did point out that thermal activity was still taking place in its summit crater and that there was a considerable coastal population just to the east near Wanigela.

Colonel Murray had yet another active volcano, Rabaul, on his mind—in addition to Victory and to the immediate problem of Lamington volcano and its ongoing eruptive activity. Doc Fisher was on hand, so the administrator could now discuss with him the issue of relocating the town of Rabaul in East New Britain to a volcanically safer place. Rabaul town had been destroyed by the end of the war by the Allied bombing of the then Japanese-held town, meaning there was now an opportunity for rebuilding it somewhere else. Gradually, however, Rabaul town had come to be reoccupied in the few years after war's end, particularly by local businesses that had had property there before the Japanese invasion. The proximity of the Rabaul wharfs and deep anchorage in the harbour were also clear advantages for trade. Murray in January 1951 was under pressure to allow this growth to continue, given especially that the volcanological observatory was being re-established for eruption early warning. In the wake of the Lamington eruption of 21 January, the issue was highlighted in an editorial in the *South Pacific Post* of Friday 26 January:

> The time for argument and indecision is long passed [sic]. The matter is no longer a question of comfort or discomfort, financial gain or loss. The people of Rabaul must be removed from the possibility of a repetition of the Higaturu horror … The important and glaring necessity is to get the place moved and get it moved quickly. If the Administration wants to clutter up its routine activities with red tape then it can do so. But red tape where human life is endangered cannot be tolerated. (*South Pacific Post* 1951b, 8)

Was there indeed any immediate risk that Rabaul, like Lamington, might break out in catastrophic eruption at any time? Murray favoured the Kokopo area to the south of Rabaul as an alternative town site, but Fisher preferred the Tavui area to the north. Doc Fisher flew to Rabaul and, on his return through Port Moresby, was able to reassure the administrator that there was 'no evidence whatever of impending [eruptive] activity for some considerable time and that in any case the present station he has at Rapindik [near Tavurvur volcano] can give two days notice of major eruption' (Murray Administrator 1951i, 1; see also *South Pacific Post* 1951e).

All of this information was sent by Colonel Murray to the minister through the Department of External Territories in Canberra on Wednesday 14 February—the day that Fisher returned to Australia—together with an opinion 'that without compulsion [it] would be unlikely that majority of total nonnative [sic] population would move out of Rabaul township' (Murray Administrator 1951i, 1). Public safety concerns in Rabaul, however, evidently were becoming prioritised by the experience of the Lamington disaster as District Commissioner J.K. McCarthy cancelled a Rabaul evacuation plan dated 1950 and introduced a new one on 15 February 1951 (McCarthy 1951a). The administration even arranged for a representative party of Rabaul residents to visit the Lamington area for two days, leaving Rabaul on 12 May (*South Pacific Post* 1951f) and—as stated in the caption on the front cover of the July issue of the *Pacific Islands Monthly*—'apparently with the idea of impressing upon them what a volcano can do' (Figure 6.1). Nevertheless, the rebuilding of Rabaul township continued on its existing site and was undertaken officially following government approval by the Australian Cabinet in Canberra in June 1952 (Territories 1952).

Figure 6.1. Rabaul residents visiting Lamington area in mid-1951
A group of Rabaul residents poses in front of Lamington volcano in the second week of May 1951. A similar photograph to this one was published on the front cover of the July issue of *Pacific Islands Monthly* where the caption includes the statement that: 'On their return to Rabaul all were of the opinion that the sooner that volcano-encircled town was moved to a safer spot the happier they would be'. Photograph supplied courtesy of Geoscience Australia (negative number M/2438-3-1).

Doc Fisher, before his departure from the Territory, gave Colonel Murray a list of 22 volcanoes in the Territory that required instrumental monitoring. He also advised the administrator that Popondetta was 'safe for all time' from volcanic eruptions and was therefore a suitable place for new headquarters for the Northern Division (Murray Administrator 1951i, 1). Colonel Murray advised Canberra that the administration, therefore, would be using Popondetta as temporary headquarters until a final decision on a permanent base could be made.

Development of Evacuation Centres

Wairopi

The Wairopi evacuation camp had been established in the first few days after the eruption on the western side of the Kumusi River, on level grassy ground and on the main road connecting Kokoda and Popondetta. Kokoda airstrip was not far off. The Kumusi could be crossed by a suspension foot bridge ('wire rope') high above the fluctuating water levels of the river, and hence by the road west to Kokoda. The camp itself seemed to be in a relatively safe place well west of the ongoing eruptive activity at Lamington volcano, but the flat ground was the flood plain of the large Kumusi River and the camp was set between it and the nearby Oiva stream. Water in the Kumusi was suitable for general washing and cleaning and in the Oiva for drinking (Administrator, quoted in *South Pacific Post* 1951d).

Overall responsibility for managing the large evacuation camp at Wairopi belonged to Assistant District Officer F.P.C. 'Fred' Kaad, a former Australian New Guinea Administrative Unit officer, assisted by administration patrol officers such as Geoff Littler. Kaad and his staff had to oversee many different aspects of temporary life at the Wairopi camp, but the overall aim was to determine, finally, how best the evacuees could be settled on a more permanent basis in a safe place acceptable to the displaced communities themselves. Patrol Officer Henry or 'Harry' Plant came to the area and used his anthropological training to identify and map the lands owned by different groups of mountain Orokaiva as a basis for resettlement plans (Plant 1951). Other patrol officers, such as Bob Blaikie and Des Martin, were carrying out duties elsewhere, including helping with burial parties. Their work was exhausting, seemingly unrelenting and emotionally demanding, and they were transferred out of the disaster area within two or three weeks of arrival for recovery elsewhere. They never returned to the Lamington area and, later in life, stated openly that they had, in different degrees, suffered post-traumatic stress disorder (Blaikie 2005–12; Martin 2007–15).

The number of evacuees at Wairopi increased steadily in the hours and then days and weeks after the eruption of 21 January—from a few hundred up to as many as 4,000, or even more. The number was this large for two main reasons: first, because many evacuees on Sunday 21 January were already migrating there along the road away from the devastated western slopes of the volcano; and, second, because many refugees in other parts of the Northern Division were encouraged by the administration to move there to centralise the disaster recovery work.

Figure 6.2. Wairopi and pedestrian bridge over the Kumusi River
Wairopi and the pedestrian bridge across the Kumusi River are seen in this aerial photograph supplied by the Kleckham family. The Kumusi River is in full flow, but not carrying any obvious floating debris. Scores of people are assembled in front of the large building near the bridge, possibly for a church service. The date of the photograph is unknown but it could have been one of the Sundays earlier in January 1951. Mr Kleckham, an amateur photographer, is known to have taken an aerial trip earlier in January.

The unsuitable evacuation settlement at swampy Cape Killerton was soon abandoned, and Sangara and Isivita evacuees were shifted along the coast to Eroro and Oro Bay, respectively. Colonel Murray visited the area and noted in his telegram of 3 February to Canberra that progress had been made at Oro and that the Anglican mission in the area, based at Eroro, was helping with accommodation and hospitalisation of the evacuees and was boosting morale. Bishop Strong was reported by the administrator as saying that 'organisation at Wairope [Wairopi] evacuees camp wonderful and Kaad doing excellent work' (Murray Administrator 1951f, 2).

The mountain Orokaiva refugees at the coast were in foreign Yega territory. They were also fearful of the sea and the prospect of tsunamis, and wanted to move back inland to higher ground. This was only one of the challenges that John R. Foldi had to deal with at the Oro Bay refugee camp. Foldi was district commissioner at Samarai and he came to Oro Bay to provide the emergency leadership needed by the administration. He was accompanied by his wife, Sister Vera Foldi, who provided invaluable medical support for the refugees in the camp (e.g. Kettle 1979).

Wairopi was not too far from the former, now destroyed villages of the mountain Orokaiva. Most of the evacuees were from the nearby Waseta–Isivita–Awala area. Others were those few Sangara people who were fortunate enough to have survived the eruption of 21 January, having been outside of what would become the devastated area. There were, however, some non-Orokaiva evacuees, notably the Koiari-speaking and much less populous Omie people from villages on the south-western flank of the mountain (Modjeska 2009, 2012, 2017). Taylor's mapped limits of 'complete devastation' and 'heat effect and partial destruction' caused by the pyroclastic flows extends down the south-western and south-eastern flanks of the volcano to the Mamama River, so the Omie suffered in the disaster too (Figure 4.6). In contrast, the Managalasi people further to the west and south-west appear to have escaped the deadly effects of the eruption. They may have self-evacuated from their threatened villages and gardens during the days of the ashfalls that preceded the eruption of 21 January.

Medical staff in the Northern Division had been dealing with an outbreak of whooping cough before the eruption and now there were the increased risks of other transmittable diseases in the disaster relief area, such as dysentery, typhoid, tuberculosis and pneumonia. Mosquitoes and the ever-present malaria also had to be taken into account. Effective and urgent health services, including extensive programs of immunisation, were therefore required for the evacuees at Wairopi where a tent community was growing (Gunther 1951a, 1951–52; Best 1951; Kettle 1979). Refugee malnutrition was another potential problem and attention was given to the growing of vegetables, supervised by an onsite agricultural officer, and obtaining them from local villages. Medical equipment was flown in to Kokoda and then transported by road to Wairopi. Other supplies including rice and tinned meat continued to be dropped by parachute. The RAAF 'Mosquito' crew also completed their aerial spraying of DDT in the area (Murray Administrator 1951f; *North Queensland Register* 1951; Bullard 2017).

Dr Kenneth Pike was put in charge of health services in the Northern Division as the replacement to Dr Pal Martin who had perished at Higaturu in the eruption of 21 January. Lon Tomlinson, an experienced administration medical assistant, was appointed officer-in-charge and responsible for the difficult health challenges at Wairopi. Sister Pat Durdin shifted from Popondetta to the camp on Friday 26 January to assist Tomlinson with the medical work, joining other mission staff who were living in tents (Kettle 1979). The numerous Papuan evacuees were having to adapt to a new, post-catastrophe life in temporary accommodation, and this included having to cope with the grief of losing so many family and friends and having no access to their traditional lands. Decades later, in 2007, Sister Durdin recalled her impressions of the people in the evacuation camps at both Wairopi and Popondetta:

> We would hear the traditional wailing and expression of grief at night. But we could not but be impressed by the overall attitude of acceptance, and readiness to respond to the immediate demands of the situation; and to express even at that stage their desire to return to their own villages and rebuild their lives. That was their overwhelming urge—to get back to their own land, though for many months it was not possible, until the area had been declared safe by the government authorities. (Durdin 2007, 1)

Other European observers noted that the Orokaiva at this time had a strong sense of independence, alertness, self-reliance and dignity (Keesing 1952). Visitors also observed that the refugees showed restraint and an imperturbability at meeting unexpected events. The Orokaiva, however, also could be vocally assertive if not excitable in some conversations. These characteristics were tested to the full in the weeks and months ahead in the large, crowded refugee camps. The Orokaiva of 1951 were, after all, the descendants of warriors who had resisted the invading colonists in battle.

Camp hygiene, supplies of clean water and disease prevention were demanding particular attention at Wairopi, as they had from the beginning, and despite the natural resilience of the evacuees. Dr Gunther on the evening of 29 January in Port Moresby had telephoned Sister Edna Gilbert, a nurse undertaking infant welfare work in the capital. Sister Gilbert was asked to fly to Kokoda the next morning, and then travel by road to Wairopi, taking with her supplies of powdered milk and vitamins for babies. She also brought 'a gavage tube and funnel lest there be any premature babies following the shock of the eruption' (Kettle 1979, 140). Lon Tomlinson was greatly relieved to have the help of Sister Gilbert who was placed in charge of the care of all pregnant women and all children under five years of age. Tomlinson himself focused on hygiene and battling the threat of dysentery and other infectious diseases. An education officer, Percy Jensen, was brought in to set up schools for both child and adult education. The concentration of so many local people in one place was an excellent opportunity for the administration to demonstrate and teach a range of subjects, perhaps most notably and immediately the principles of sanitation and hygiene that could be applied later to normal village life.

The administrator in early February recognised that mudflows were rapidly silting the river channels on and around Mount Lamington, concluding that there was a risk of flooding (Taylor 1958). He was concerned particularly about the potential vulnerability of the Wairopi camp on the bank of the Kumusi River. An aerial inspection of the headwaters of the Kumusi and its large catchment area was, therefore, carried out on 8 February. The main tributary, the Mamama River, was receiving heavy loads of fragmental debris from the denuded southern slopes of the volcano, and logs brought down from the destroyed forest appeared to be blocking narrow parts of the valley. Staff at the Wairopi camp were alerted. Refugees at Wairopi, however, according to one journalist, had been expressing their own concerns about the camp's safety, presumably because of their knowledge of riverine flood hazards:

> Then, for no apparent reason, the natives of Wairope began to talk of moving out. They seemed frightened of 'big trouble'. When those in charge explained that they were out of range of any possible future blast from Lamington they were not comforted. The natives said they must get away from the river. (Best 1951, 20)

Figure 6.3. Flooding of Kumusi at Wairopi refugee camp
Part of the tented refugee camp at Wairopi is seen in this aerial view taken on 19 February 1951. The photograph was published by Taylor (1958, fig. 104; compare with Figure 6.2) and was accompanied by the following caption: 'Flooding of Kumusi River and undermining of Wairopi Evacuation Camp. The large building on the left of the bridge remnant has partly collapsed'. Photograph supplied courtesy of Geoscience Australia (negative number GB/1893).

The Kumusi River flooded that afternoon, 8 February, but subsided rapidly (Taylor 1958). Further flooding by 19 February, however, caused the river to break its eastern banks and erode the camp site on the opposite side (Figure 6.3). The camp would have to be abandoned and relocated somewhere safer, despite all the gruelling work and achievement at Wairopi during the previous few weeks. New staff had arrived at Wairopi by this time including medical assistant Albert 'Bert' Speer who was just in time to help with the arduous transfer (Figure 6.4). The new evacuation site was at Ilimo, 6.5 kilometres along the road west of Wairopi and closer to the Kokoda Airstrip. Ilimo, however, was further away from the traditional homelands of the refugees and more distant from the still temporary but developing provincial headquarters at Popondetta.

Ilimo

Shifting the entire Wairopi camp and its occupants to Ilimo was hardly a straightforward task (Best 1951; Kettle 1979). About 2,000 people were transferred to local villages. Most of the remaining 2,000 evacuees walked to Ilimo along the road from Wairopi, but the old and ill were carried by two jeeps shuttling between the camps. In the first three days, the new camp was soaked by torrential downpours, slowing down building construction and increasing the dangers of disease. The old Wairopi camp was flooded and became submerged completely, as were the gardens of Ajeka village on the low, opposite, eastern side of the Kumusi River. The village itself also suffered from ash falls, but the higher gardens behind the village survived and the Ajeka people expressed a desire to reoccupy the site. A patrol officer at Ilimo, possibly I.W. Wiseman, wrote on 23 February that:

> It is a grand site for a settlement standing as it does on good high ground and with ample acreage for possible expansion. In the days ahead, when the Kumusi River returns to its normal course the river flats, where the gardens previously were, should prove excellent land for all kind of cultivation. (Patrol Officer 1951, 1)

The Ajeka people clearly were quite accepting of future flood risk on the banks of the Kumusi.

Figure 6.4. Bert Speer photograph of evacuation of Wairopi camp
Sister Gilbert in the front seat and Sister Pat Durdin behind her are here seen departing from the abandoned Wairopi camp, escorting infants in the trailer behind the left-hand-drive jeep, to Ilimo camp (Speer 2005, photograph no. 29). Courtesy of the National Library of Australia.

The Ilimo camp eventually began to take form during the remainder of February. Bush-material houses for the evacuees were constructed and arranged in regimented straight lines, and support buildings were built, including a temporary hospital that attracted villagers from the surrounding areas. Ilimo was not a 'tent town' like Wairopi but, rather, a large, temporary and changing 'village' of houses built by the refugees themselves and by local villagers. The number of refugees at Ilimo was increased when the 'Isivita' people at Oro Bay were relocated there, transported in small groups by launch to Cape Killerton, truck to Popondetta, small aircraft to Kokoda, and from there to Ilimo on foot (Keesing 1952). The Sangara refugees at Eroro, in contrast, took a much less circuitous route when they were transported to the Popondetta camp and nearby areas closer to their homes.

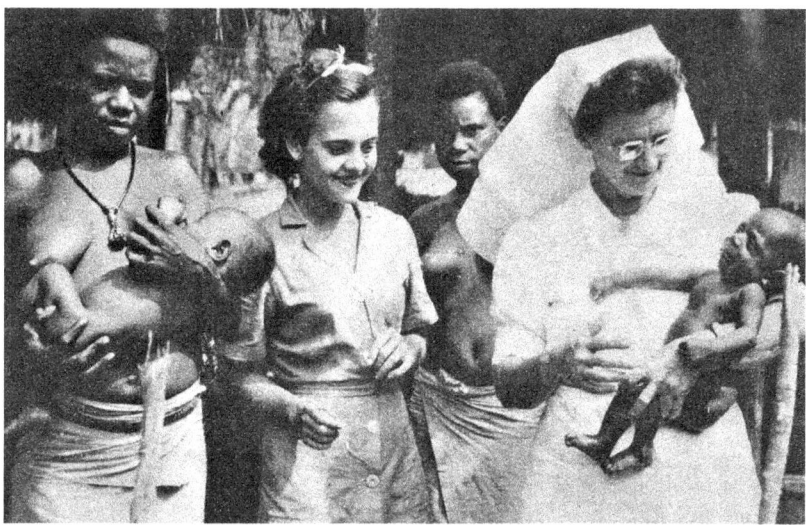

Figure 6.5. Twin babies at Ilimo refugee camp
Twin babies and their mother are here photographed at Ilimo evacuation camp, together with infant welfare officers Sister Edna Gilbert on the right and Ivane Champion in the centre (Best 1951, 21). It may well have been a celebratory moment for them, judging by the expressions on the faces of the two European women. The two Papuan women seem more curious about the camera, however. Reproduced with the permission of Bauer Media Pty Ltd.

Health, education and local agricultural developments continued as priorities at Ilimo as they had been at Wairopi, but all this work was still against the established backdrop of how the evacuees could be resettled on a more permanent basis, once the eruptive activity at Lamington volcano had ceased. Lon Tomlinson worked heroically at achieving an epidemic-free environment:

> Before the month ended Tomlinson had given 3840 whooping-cough injections and 3150 [for] typhoid. He started vitamin courses for the hundreds of under-nourished children, distributed malaria preventives, treated thousands of tropical ulcers and eye infections … In the first week Tomlinson got a total of 10 hours sleep—but he got the epidemics under control. (Best 1951, 20)

Sister Gilbert was similarly busy with the refugee infants. She was joined by 20-year-old Miss Ivane Champion, daughter of Ivan Champion, who had been flown in urgently to assist Sister Gilbert, even though still only partly trained in infant welfare. Both women never worked less than 15-hour days. Both also appeared, together with a Papuan mother who had given birth to twins, in a photograph that was published in the widely read *Australian Women's Weekly* (Figure 6.5).

Staff and the refugees at Ilimo still relied largely on parachute drops for food made by both the RAAF and Qantas, but officers of the Department of Agriculture—first W. 'Bill' Conroy, then Malcolm McIndoe and Alan Boag—became busy with teams of men clearing forest and undergrowth and planting rice, sweet potatoes and peanuts (Kettle 1979). Agricultural officer Fred Kleckham was originally assigned to rice-growing work at Wairopi but he was injured in a road accident on the way to the camp. Kleckham had to be flown out to Port Moresby for X-ray examination and Conroy took over the farming work at Wairopi (e.g. *South Pacific Post* 1951c). This important agricultural work was an opportunity to teach the principles of agricultural mass production and the cooperative farming of food. Meanwhile, the parachute drops were greatly appreciated by the hard-working administration officers on the ground at Ilimo, who, for amusement, would assess the cargo-dropping skills of the different aircraft crews. They reached the general conclusion that Qantas pilots were more successful than the postwar pilots of the RAAF (Littler 2005).

Life in the large, cramped camp at Ilimo cannot have been easy for the thousands of refugees who were more used to community life in their widespread hamlets and nearby gardens. This was despite the close attention and support being provided by dedicated administration staff. The administration sought to counter the potential problem of boredom among the male refugees, in particular, by keeping them busy up to a point with tasks such as construction, clearing land, gardening and hygiene. The refugees in the camps could hardly be accused of being 'mollycoddled', as one anonymous letter writer claimed (Old Planter 1951). It was, however, still a time of dislocation, uncertainty, worry and tension for the encamped refugees (Belshaw 1951b; Keesing 1952). Tempers could flare excitedly, quarrels and fights could break out, blood could be spilt, and women could be assaulted by fractious, frustrated husbands. The large squads of native police led to friction, sometimes over women, and sometimes through a general resentment of being ordered about. Sharing common latrines was something new and stressful for some of the refugees. Some believed that the changed circumstances might permit sorcerers to take advantage.

Albert Maclaren Ririka, who had escaped the eruption through being at Isivita rather than at Sangara Mission, came to the Ilimo camp as a schoolteacher. While there he composed two songs or laments, one of which was later included in a songbook distributed to primary schools in Papua (Figure 6.6). The English translations of four verses selected from the two songs are reproduced as follows:

6. BEGINNING DISASTER RECOVERY

We were at Sangara
Gathered together
With all our brothers
Living together

The mountain was made by Thee
It was not seen by us before;
Lord, when it appeared
We were wounded.

In the land of Sangara
Are the bodies of our brothers
As though they were sleeping
But we will see them again in the end.

The evening was bright
On the hills of Ilimo
But our thoughts
Are always with our brothers. (Hand 2002, 65–66)

Ewa ge language,
Popondetta,
Northern Province.

NANGO EINDA SANGARA DA
(LAMINGTON LAMENT)

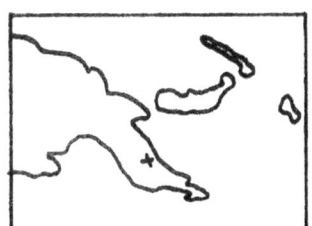

Figure 6.6. Lamington lament words and music in Balob songbook

This detail includes the first bars of the song or lament written originally by Albert Ririka in 1951 and presented later in an educational songbook in a local language (Balob Teachers' College 1976, 13). Reproduced courtesy of the editor and compiler of the songbook, C.K. Thorp.

Visits to Higaturu and Andemba

Health staff were hard at work in the refugee camps coping with medical issues. They included Medical Assistant Bert Speer who also travelled widely through the area, undertaking vaccinations and general health work (Speer 2007, 2005–14). At times, his activities away from the camps entailed him entering the devastated area where the horror of the disaster was still to be seen weeks after the catastrophic eruption of 21 January, as Speer described in his diary:

> Monday 26 February 1951: Today I awoke with a stinking cold in the nose and head. However flew over to Embi and checked the stores over there and then returned home to Popondetta in time to go up to Higaturu—This was one of the worst areas of devastation I have ever seen! Everything totally destroyed for miles around, the station just tossed and turned around and dead bodies everywhere. Natives poor souls who never had a chance. Dr Pike and I salvaged—in pouring rain about £100 worth of instruments here. I was interested in records but none found as it was too wet, I didn't disturb more than I could help. It was a peculiar feeling to be there amongst the rotting dead with an active volcano at one side and all around teeming rain—it seemed to spell disaster itself. I hope I never see a similar sight again. The flies were active in all the bodies and in the heat I should imagine the stench would be terrific. God help them and rest their souls. It makes one wonder just what is found in life here. People strive to build something beautiful and then all is wiped off the earth.

> Wednesday 14 March: Today, up at 7 A.M. … Then after tea with Tony Taylor and Jim Robinson and Peter (the cop) procured some rations and then Jim took me off to Andemba village and the coffee plantation on the banks of the Ambogin [Ambogo] River. Here [north of Higaturu] the river is just a hot ash bed with smoke and fumes arising. But oh the destruction of it all and the loneliness. A trade store with its poor dead—guardian just a skeleton now! Then the village in all stages of destruction, with its corpses and blowflies everywhere, and across the hot and desolate river all that remains of poor twisted Higaturu with its D.O.'s house and the Mission house standing shaken and sentinel against the desolation. A site to ever remember. This was a station, here lived people and here they died, the black with the white and none to tell the difference, now or ever. God rest their poor souls. At the top of it all stands the smoking burning volcano a mass of hot and burning hill, that in its wrath has spilled out over the land

it [over]looks … Tony [Taylor] seems to think all will be OK to go into Higaturu now, but is cautious! (Speer 2007; text lightly edited by author)

Dr Pike had a strong interest in butterflies, and Speer told of them both entering the devastated area in search of the large, brilliantly coloured Blue Emperor butterfly (Speer 2007, 7). They found the butterflies flitting among the death and destruction, attracted by the decaying cadavers. This association of butterflies and death is part of ancient mythology, commonly attracting meanings of spirituality and representing symbols of human rebirth (e.g. McPhedran 2002), not that Speer alluded to this directly.

Restarting the Plantation Economy

Re-establishing village life in the Lamington area was one priority for the administrator and his administration. Another was restarting the economy of the Northern Division, based on plantation productivity. Colonel Murray informed Canberra on Saturday 3 February that the Territory's director of agriculture, R.E.P. Dwyer, was assessing the extent of damage and that Dwyer and Dr Fisher were discussing when the plantations might recommence their activities (Murray Administrator 1951f). The administrator, just three days later, informed the Department of External Territories that the two scientists had advised 'plantation personnel may return' (Murray Administrator 1951g, 1; see also Administration 1951d).

Director Dwyer reported that crop damage in the main Sangara Rubber Plantation did not exceed 4 per cent on average, and that damage to the rubber trees at Awala Plantation ranged from 3 to 18 per cent. The young rubber on the Sangara subsidiary plantation at Widjo, however, had suffered complete destruction. Further, rubber-tapping panels would need much clearing before tapping could be restarted. Awala cocoa had been damaged. The highest rate was estimated at six trees per acre, but damage to young cocoa was less. Damage to village taro and sweet potato gardens in the area between Sangara and Awala was minor, and the greatest damage was on a ridge at Agenahambo. Dwyer had been working since the previous Saturday and fuller checks would be undertaken in the days ahead. Assessment of damage to plantation buildings had not yet been completed, but the administration had made arrangements with the director of the Department of Works and Housing to make available an officer who would assess damage to both privately or company-owned buildings in the large area originally closed within a 16-mile radius from the crater (Administration 1951d). Native-owned buildings would be assessed by the Department of District Services and Native Affairs.

The Hendersons, then, would return to re-establish Sangara Plantation. They would also host the Sangara Observation Post on the edge of their property near the western bank of the Ambogo River. Volcanologist Tony Taylor used the Sangara Observation Post as his base and wrote later of his:

> Deep appreciation of the unfailing kindness, patience, and truly gracious hospitality of Mr and Mrs T.G. Henderson, who, at Sangara Plantation, had the doubtful privilege of accommodating for almost two years seemingly obsessed addicts to a scientific cause. (Taylor 1958, 12)

However, in early February 1951, the Ambogo River itself was still presenting problems for the administration.

Improved Access to the Disaster Area

Administration officers in the second week after the eruption of 21 January were still trying to find a trafficable way across the Ambogo River into Higaturu and hence to Sangara Mission. Colonel Murray noted on 3 February that he was considering the erection of a 'flying fox' across the river. He noted also that there were risks to villages on the lower parts of the rivers well beyond the eruption area owing to the immense quantities of material being transported and fanning out where the river gradient lessened (Murray Administrator 1951f).

Active mudflows down the numerous stream valleys on the denuded northern flanks of Lamington in February 1951 were a consequence of the huge abundances of loose, fragmental materials recently deposited there by the eruption, and their movement triggered by periods of ongoing monsoonal rainfall. The run-off 'became great rumbling torrents of viscous mud and assorted debris which periodically descended the water courses, cutting communications, scouring out the valleys, and depositing enormous quantities of material on the lower country' (Taylor 1958, 56).

The Ambogo River drained from the active summit crater down across the loose volcanic debris of the bare devastated area. The river became notable for its mudflows, particularly downstream at Double Crossing where the road to Popondetta was repeatedly destroyed, starting on Friday 26 January, and then had to be reopened. Larger, later mudflows would reach full flood in a matter of minutes, some looking like 'a conveyor belt loaded with logs … their movement was silent apart from the rumbling impact of large boulders, semi-buoyant in the dense stream … [They left behind] hot quagmires which were impassable until they cooled and set' (Taylor 1958, 56)—quagmires and quicksands that BMR geologist John Best may have experienced firsthand.

At other times, loud roars from more mobile mudflows upstream in the Ambogo River were so loud at the Sangara Observation Post that local people became alarmed, and ground vibrations were recorded as distinctive 'grass'-like patterns on the seismograms. The Ambogo mudflow discharges were preventing easy access to Sangara Mission, the administration advising Canberra on Tuesday 6 February that the normal Higaturu road was impassable owing to mud deposition and a deepened channel. Colonel Murray, Dr Gunther and others, however, had negotiated the Ambogo River at another place and had got through to Sangara Mission on a more direct track on the previous morning. They said they planned to make the track southwards to Higaturu 'jeepable' that afternoon (Administration 1951c). The administrator and his group saw about 150 still unburied bodies at Sombo village and reported that most of the contents of the still-standing mission house were salvageable.

Another significant decision announced by Colonel Murray on 3 February, and one that also dealt with access, was a reduction of the radius of the prohibited area from 16 miles (about 26 kilometres) to 10 miles (about 16 kilometres) (Murray Administrator 1951f; see also I.F. Champion 1951b). This was to allow greater ease of access—including by local people to their former villages and gardens—to the annular zone now created between the two concentric circles. Ivan Champion estimated that about 3,000 people out of a total of about 6,000 refugees thus were able to return to their homes or to lands near them, particularly the 'Isivita' people who earlier had refused the offer of lands near Kokoda well to the west of their homelands (I.F. Champion 1951b). Yet, the reduced size of the prohibited area was still large. It easily covered the devastated area mapped by Taylor who still had ongoing concerns about future eruptions and the mudflow and run-off problem. The reduction, nevertheless, meant that places like

Popondetta, the two airstrips and the Wairopi evacuation camp now lay outside the prohibited area. At about this time, and for the government secretary's consideration, Champion also set out the advantages and disadvantages of three possible sites for new divisional headquarters—Oro Bay, Popondetta and some Crown land in the Ambogo River area (I.F. Champion 1951b).

A further reduction of the prohibited area to 8 miles radius was later recommended by Dr Fisher, which would mean that the Sangara and Awala plantations, the Sangara Observation Post and all of the Wairopi–Popondetta road would also be outside the prohibited area, and an even greater area could be made available for visits to the western slopes by villagers (Murray Administrator 1951i). There is no evidence that the perimeters of either of these large, ideally circular, reduced areas were patrolled rigorously given their great lengths. A day-to-day pragmatism would have had to govern the decisions that were made. Further, on 3 February, Colonel Murray had announced that a siren warning system had been proposed, that villagers who wanted to enter the annular zone were to be informed of the warning system, and that warnings would be based on the volcanologists' decisions (Murray Administrator 1951f). However, a suitable, long-range siren could not be found in Australia.

Compensation and the Disaster Relief Fund

The administrator informed the minister in Canberra by telegram on Thursday 8 February that the Territory's Executive Council on the previous day had endorsed a proposal to establish a 'Mount Lamington Disaster Relief Fund' (Murray Administrator 1951h), although arguably, given the timing, it should have been called a 'recovery fund'. The fund's committee of nine consisted of prominent Territory citizens from businesses, charities, banks and the Department of Finance, and would be chaired by Justice Ralph Gore. The proposal had already received publicity during the previous week in the *South Pacific Post*, which, on 2 February ran the front-page headline: 'Administrator Launches Relief Fund for Lamington Victims' (*South Pacific Post* 1951c). The idea seemed reasonable and appropriate, but the Executive Committee was careful in its formal comment, as relayed to the minister in the administrator's telegram:

> FUND WILL BE ADMINISTERED FOR BENEFIT OF ALL WHO SUFFERED IN DISASTER WITH PROPER ALLOCATION TO GREATEST NEED BUT WITH RELATION TO COMMITMENTS OF ADMINISTRATION SO THAT SPHERE OF ACTION OF ONE WILL NOT UNNECESSARILY INTRUDE ON PROVINCE OF THE OTHER. (Murray Administrator 1951h)

Thousands of Papuans had been killed and there were additional thousands who had lost their villages, gardens, families and clan members. A fair and equitable allocation of money from the disaster fund clearly was not going to be an easy process for Judge Gore and his committee members. The administration already had provided, and would continue to provide, substantial relief support for the refugees in the evacuation camps, so would these people be given additional monetary support and, if so, how much? Many of those killed, both European and Melanesian, worked for the administration, meaning that formal provision of compensation to their next of kin was a probable government obligation. However, the deadly eruption took place on a Sunday—a day normally used for recreation and churchgoing, so were the administration people 'on duty' or not? If not, what were the implications? Would the families of senior, European officers of the administration at Higaturu receive the same treatment as those for deceased members of, say, the 'native' constabulary? Further, would Europeans in practice be treated preferentially, in spite of the fund being 'administered for the benefit of all', as Judge Gore had said (Murray Administrator 1951h, 1)? Some of the European dead had not yet been found and identified, and contacting their next of kin was not a straightforward process and would, and indeed did, inevitably lead to delays.

These administrative difficulties would face the relief fund, the administration and the Department of External Territories in the weeks and months ahead. Meanwhile, however, the front-page headline for the *South Pacific Post* of Friday 9 February read: 'Lamington Relief Fund Gets Fine Start: Hallstrom Gives £1,000' (*South Pacific Post* 1951d). Hallstrom was the founder of a livestock and fauna trust in the Territory, as well as chairman of the Taronga Park Zoo in Sydney. The famous Australian artist William Dobell donated one of his landscapes for auction as a contribution to the fund (*South Pacific Post* 1951e). Further, the Cadbury chocolate company agreed for Urquhart to donate the 16 guineas (£16 16s) he had received from those newspapers who had published his aerial photographs of the eruption cloud taken on the morning of 21 January (Urquhart 1951). Donations were made by other public companies and by the European community and Australian Red Cross (Ahearn 1951c). 'Native peoples' and 'Chinese people' also contributed generously, including local people of the Talasea area on the north coast of New Britain who even offered land to the displaced Orokaiva (McCarthy 1951b).

A fund total of £20,593 8s 3d was available for distribution when the Mount Lamington Disaster Relief Fund members met on 17 August 1951 (Chairman 1951): £10,000 would be distributed to nine children, four widows and three dependent mothers of Europeans killed in the eruption; another £10,000 would be given to the administration for onward distribution to surviving natives affected by the eruption. The balance would be kept for any further applications for assistance.

Final Death Toll Estimates and Defending the First Responders

Counting the dead had not been possible during the rescue and early recovery phases of the disaster. The total of 4,000 casualties suggested by Claude Champion as early as Tuesday 23 January was clearly a rough estimate, and burying the numerous dead in the days and weeks following could hardly be accompanied by the rigorous collection of accurate mortality statistics. However, the figure of 4,000 was used commonly in newspaper reports and, on occasion, as the full death toll figure rather than as a provisional casualty total that included the still-living injured. D.S. Wylie, managing director of Sangara Rubber Plantations, said at a lunch held on 21 February at the influential businessmen's 'Millions Club' in Sydney that the 'estimate of 4,000 dead is far too low' and that probably 8,000 people had lost their lives at Lamington (*Sydney Morning Herald* 1951, 7). The article was transcribed and placed on the files of the Department of External Territories in Canberra (Anonymous 1951e). The administrator on the following day in Port Moresby informed the department that a check of government records had been made and had revealed that a total of 3,466 local people—a surprisingly precise figure— had been killed or were missing. Further, Ivan Champion in Popondetta had advised that a figure in excess of 3,500 was extremely unlikely (Murray Administrator 1951j).

A 'final' figure of 2,907 Papuan dead resulted from a comprehensive investigation of local community losses made between 28 August and 2 October 1951 by administration officer R.M. Claridge (1951b; Elliott-Smith 1951a). This total was regarded as closer to the true death toll than 3,500 because of a duplication of numbers: the number of local workers killed in the eruption had also been included in the separate figures for villages. The administrator informed the Department of External Territories in Canberra of the result, adding that 'probably we will never get an actual death roll of this disaster and we must accept this report as final' (Murray 1951c, 1). The total of 35 Europeans dead and missing— the 'missing' now all presumed dead—had been determined in the first week following the eruption of 21 January, so the full, 'final' total was 2,942. However, most commentators simply refer to the total as 'almost 3,000' (e.g. Taylor 1958). Most of this total consists of people from the Sangara 'tribe', representing, according to one calculation, perhaps 94 per cent of the total Sangara population before the eruption engulfed them (Schwimmer 1969).

Another problem regarding finding the dead had to be addressed by the administrator as a result of media reports. This was in relation to a recording made by mission mechanic Rodd Hart on 25 January that was broadcast by the Australian Broadcasting Commission. The following statements were made: 'Elliott kept running amongst the bodies and kicked them to see if they were alive' and 'Blue Morris went to the lip of the crater' (Murray Administrator 1951k, 1). An Australian resident wrote to the minister of external territories on 31 January 1951 asking why a stethoscope or microphone could not have been used by the rescue party to determine death rather than 'kicking' bodies (Ferrier 1951). The writer also drew attention to media statements that the bodies of Europeans were being set aside for later exhumation and thus were being given burial preference over the Papuan dead.

The administrator was strong in his response and defence of Rodd Hart and the Andemba rescue party of Sunday 21 January (Murray Administrator 1951k). Colonel Murray pointed out that: 1) Hart, at the time of the recording, 'was under mental and emotional strain and perhaps did not realize fully what he was saying'; 2) Blue Morris had not gone to the lip of the crater; 3) 'Mr Kleckham stated that he did not see Elliott or anyone else kick bodies, but it is possible that the feet were used to roll some bodies over for further examination'; 4) no doctors, stethoscopes or microphone had been available to the rescue party; and

5) no preferential treatment was given to European bodies, although the administrator did not refer to the point that European bodes would be disinterred later. Colonel Murray stressed that:

> All the Europeans [in the rescue party] highly praised the work done by native Elliott during this rescue work and it is a pity that they have been subjected to ridicule instead of being highly commended for their bravery in carrying out rescue work in the highly dangerous area of ANDEMBA. (Murray Administrator 1951k, 1)

7
VOLCANOLOGICAL ANALYSIS AND NEW ERUPTIONS

Studying the Area of Total Devastation

The administrator in February was hard at work coping with the many diverse aspects of the disaster recovery phase at Lamington. Volcanologist Tony Taylor, meanwhile, was concentrating on scientific investigations aimed at trying to understand the geophysical conditions that led not only to the catastrophic eruptions of 21 January and their effects, but also to the ongoing eruptions at Lamington volcano.

Plants and fungi were active in re-establishing and colouring their presence on the mountain and its surrounds, as if they were in recovery mode too, and the early regrowth of tropical vegetation was of interest to agriculturalists and plant pathologists. In particular, the fact that many cultivated plants, especially root crops in destroyed gardens, were beginning to sprout luxuriantly green among the dull, grey ash meant that supplies of taro, yams, sweet potatoes and bananas could be gathered as supplements to the emergency supplies being provided by air and from newly planted gardens (Figure 7.1). The fresh ash seems to have formed a compost from the buried vegetation, which may have been enriched by potassic and phosphoric salts from the volcanic ash itself (Taylor 1958). Presumably too there was less competition from the slower-growing plants in the area.

Figure 7.1. Taylor and assistant undertaking fieldwork near shooting taro
Taylor and an unknown assistant are here photographed in the devastated area and tree blow-down zone of Mount Lamington. Note the shooting of taro plants to the right of the jeep. The lava dome at the rear of the photograph is growing and is emitting strong amounts of vapour. The precise date of the photograph is unknown. Photograph supplied courtesy of Geoscience Australia (negative number M/1733-3).

The first type of vegetation to be seen in the disaster area by Taylor and by agricultural officer Fred Kleckham was a bright orange-yellow fungus of the genus *Neurospora* (Burges and Chalmers 1952; Taylor 1958). The fungus appeared only three days after the main eruption of 21 January and after light rain had moistened the ash substrate. It was seen in patches and it disappeared gradually over the following six weeks. Very little of it appeared after subsequent eruptions, although small patches were noted on logs that had been buried by the pyroclastic flows. The species of the *Neurospora* was never determined, but the most likely contenders were either *N. crassa* or *N. intermedia* (Perkins, Turner and Barry 1976; Shaw 1980–82; Shaw 1982). Such precise taxonomic discrimination was not of immediate interest to volcanology and disaster relief. *Neurospora* species, however, require heat-shock to germinate and bloom in places such as bakeries or after grass and forest fires. The fungus, therefore, was of interest in providing some indication of the temperatures of emplacement of the pyroclastic flows. A temperature of 60°C lasting for an hour was one early published estimate for germination (Burges and Chalmers 1952).

Hundreds of people had been severely burned and killed in the Higaturu–Sangara area, yet volcanic temperatures at Higaturu were not sufficiently high that wood was ignited or charred (Taylor 1958). A reel of cotton and a leather drive belt of a sewing machine in one remaining house were unaffected by the heat, and there had been a softening and collapse of a plastic lamp shade above the sewing machine. Further, an unopened bottle of ether in the ruins of the hospital had not blown its cork, and an analysis of penicillin found in the hospital corresponded to temperatures of 145°C or more applied for 1 or 1.5 minutes. The most probable temperature and duration, concluded Taylor, was 200°C for 1 or 1.5 minutes. The two violins used by Mrs Cowley and daughter Pam at the district commissioner's house at Higaturu had not been burnt in these temperatures. Both instruments were retrieved and later sent by the administrator through the Australian Red Cross to Mrs Cowley in Sydney, but repairing them and recovering their tone seemed unlikely (Franceschi Cowley 1951; Wardrop 1951a). Judge Phillips bought Pam a new violin—a thoughtful gesture that, perhaps, was tinged with some guilt (Virtue 2018).

Figure 7.2. The Hendersons at a charred tree trunk
Toby and Hendy Henderson of Sangara Rubber Plantation are seen here at a charred tree trunk in the blow-down zone 'about two miles from the crater' (Taylor 1958, fig. 72). Higher-temperature charring of vegetation like this was absent further downslope in the Higaturu–Sangara area. The date of the photograph is unknown, but grasses have grown in what formerly had been the devastated area meaning the photograph may have been taken well after the last of the major explosive eruptions in March 1951. Photograph supplied courtesy of Geoscience Australia (negative number GB/2479).

Higher temperatures elsewhere in the zone of complete destruction were deduced from the distribution of charred trees, but they had 'characteristically erratic distributions that were not easy to explain', wrote Taylor (1958, 45). The charred tree trunk seen in Figure 7.2, for example, was only about 3 kilometres from the crater, so wood charring might be expected, but not all such trees were similarly affected. The conclusion reached for the charred trees was that the pyroclastic flow was so dense that it not only retained a high temperature but also caused the visible abrasion of the land surface, something not seen in areas of non-charred trees.

The speed and force of the laterally moving, ground-hugging, pyroclastic flows at Higaturu were other properties that received scientific attention. One early conclusion was that people at Higaturu may have seen the deadly pyroclastic flow coming towards them down from the mountain and that they may have had some time, perhaps just a few minutes, in which to attempt an escape. This was concluded, subjectively, from the disposition of bodies that seemed to correspond to people trying to evacuate from Higaturu (e.g. C. Champion 1951). This means, in turn, and if correct, that they died not from the near-instantaneous, lateral, atmospheric pressure wave or 'blast' that results from large explosions, such as an atomic bomb. Nevertheless, the force that created the physical damage to buildings at Higaturu and Sangara Mission was substantial. The new mission house was the only building that was practically undamaged by the pyroclastic flow at Sangara, and only one house at Higaturu remained reasonably intact. This was the:

> U-shaped residence of the District Commissioner … [which] was pushed fifteen feet northwards and damaged on the southern side by flying debris. Most of the other buildings at the government station were carried away and in most cases only floors remained. A group of three steel Sydney-Williams huts on the eastern side of the parade ground was badly damaged and had partly collapsed; on the opposite side of the parade ground the superstructure of the District Office was swept away completely. (Taylor 1958, 40)

Estimating what the speed and force of the cloud or flow may have been was not straightforward. A great deal of attention was spent later by specialists in attempting to determine the velocity and force from an inspection of a steel flagpole in the ruins of the Higaturu hospital where the otherwise straight pole had been bent conspicuously in two places. The pole was eroded on one side so the cloud consisted not just of air but also contained volcanic ash, and so was denser and more forceful than air alone. Further, the double bend in the hospital flagpole could be taken as evidence that velocities in the horizontally moving cloud were vertically stratified, and the fact that a jeep could be flung up into a tree probably meant that there were vortices in the cloud as well (Figure 7.3). Larger materials such as corrugated iron and wooden planks had been picked up and flung against other objects creating additional force and damage in some places. An overall conclusion, however, was that 'damage at Higaturu conformed well with hurricane-force winds, that is, with velocities of the order of 75 miles per hour' (Taylor 1958, 43).

Figure 7.3. Destroyed and stranded jeeps at Higaturu
This is a close-up of the destroyed and stranded jeeps at Higaturu seen also in Figure 5.3. Photograph supplied courtesy of Geoscience Australia (negative number GA/9830).

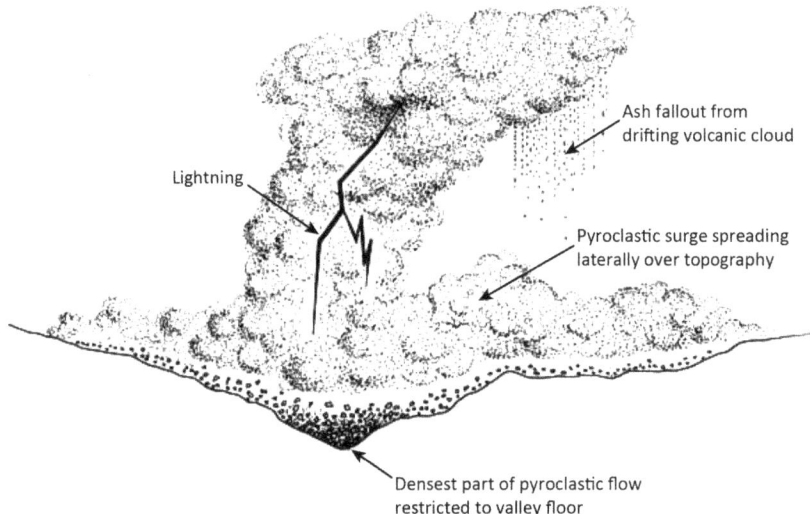

Figure 7.4. Three parts of a pyroclastic flow

Three different parts of a pyroclastic flow, or nuée ardente, being emplaced during an explosive eruption are shown in this diagram, which is based in part on Taylor's landmark study of the 1951 eruption at Mount Lamington (amended after Francis 1993, fig. 12.9): 1) a basal, dense part of the flow that is restricted to valley floors (open-circle pattern); 2) the less dense 'ash cloud hurricane' above it that spreads laterally across topography; and 3) ash falling from a cloud that has risen thermally from the underlying hot parts of the pyroclastic flow and that, in this sketch, discharges lightning. The reader must imagine facing into the direct path of the fast-encroaching flow.

Taylor introduced to volcanology the name 'ash hurricane' for this part of a pyroclastic flow, thus avoiding such potentially misleading terms as 'lateral blast' caused by an atmospheric wave of highly compressed air spreading outwards from an explosion. This ash hurricane component was in contrast to the lower, denser and hotter part of the pyroclastic flow that tended to follow valley floors gravitationally (Figure 7.4). Taylor (1958, 51) simply referred to this lower part as 'ash flow' and described its movement as 'ponderous'.

The exact cause of the human deaths in the ash hurricane at Mount Lamington could not be clarified by autopsy because cadaveric 'putrefaction was too advanced when the medical services were free from their urgent obligations to the living', wrote Taylor (1958, 49). The deaths, however, appeared to have essentially the same cause as those deduced at Mont Pelée and St Vincent in 1902, and through post-mortem examination of bodies after house fires. Respiratory systems probably suffered rapid damage through ingestion of hot, ash-laden air causing internal swelling, exfoliation and haemorrhaging. A form of asphyxia was also suggested by the difficulty rescuers had in distinguishing European from Papuan bodies because of the intense post-mortem lividity caused by blood migrating to the extremes of the body. Rigidity or cadaveric spasm was also noted, some corpses 'frozen' in sitting or kneeling positions a result of heat stiffening of muscles. Few people seem to have been killed by flying objects or crushed by falling buildings or trees, and no dismemberments were observed at Lamington, such as were common at Mont Pelée.

Taylor, as a result of his fieldwork in the devastated area at Higaturu–Sangara concluded, importantly, that the kind of lateral, atmospheric pressure wave or 'blast' that can result from bomb explosions had not taken place at Lamington, in contrast to some of the views expressed in newspapers and magazines at the time. The damage had been done by the 'ash hurricane'. This term, however, did not become used widely in the later volcanological literature. The preferred term today is 'pyroclastic surge'.

The origin of the new U-shaped crater was not addressed fully by Taylor, although he concluded that it had not been produced by an outward 'blast' as was commonly supposed by more casual observers of the effects of the Lamington eruption. Further, and notably, he retained the name 'avalanche valley' that he had used in interpreting the 1947 aerial photographs of the pre-1951 crater on Lamington. This implies that Taylor may have thought the new crater had formed through disintegration and avalanching of the crater wall. Debris-avalanche deposits formed in 1951 were identified many years later at Lamington, providing evidence for a lateral collapse origin for the U-shaped crater, much like the one at Galunggung volcano (Figure 3.10) rather than by outwards blast (Belousov et al. 2011a, 2011b; Hoblitt 1982).

Monitoring the Ongoing Explosive Eruptions

Tony Taylor was busy throughout February observing the volcano from the air (Figure 7.5) and during visits to the crater area (Figure 7.6). Not surprisingly, he was particularly concerned with the ongoing activity taking place at the summit crater, as this had been the source of the catastrophic eruptions of 21 January and was the most likely place where large eruptions might take place again. Taylor classified all of the observed crater activity of January–March 1951 into eight different types, plotting these systematically and individually in detailed time series charts, starting with the first emissions of vapour on 15 January and ending on 7 March (Taylor 1958, line figs 11–18). These valuable charts also include detailed plots of the number of earthquakes recorded on the Sangara seismograph from 8 February onwards, together with the 'height' of the earthquake vibrations on seismograms—that is, 'earthquake amplitude'—and shown in relation particularly to explosive eruptions.

Taylor gave particular attention to what he termed 'shallow-pocket' explosions, a term derived from the work of American volcanologist F.A. Perret during eruptions at Mont Pelée volcano in 1929–32 (Perret 1937). The shallow-pocket explosions are of interest in that they provide an indication of what happened on the morning of 21 January on a much larger scale, and how the pyroclastic flows, or *nuées ardentes*, were formed at Lamington. Explosions of notable shallow-pocket type took place on 5, 11 and 24 February 1951 (Figures 7.5–7.6). Taylor described their development as follows:

> Successive explosions fountained rapidly and extensively from many parts of the crater floor and filled the crater bowl with a massive convoluted cloud of fragmental lava and gas. The cloud usually showed little tendency to rise. The heavy, yet buoyant, mass seemed to behave as a layered hydrostatic column raised in the bowl of the crater. The heavier fractions poured out through the low gaps in the crater wall; the lighter fractions poured over the crater rim. (Taylor 1958, 32)

The whole bowl of the crater on 5 February 'filled with a huge seething cloud of ash' (Taylor 1958, 33). A pyroclastic flow moved down the avalanche valley and part of the cloud spilled over the western rim as seen in Figure 7.5. The whole cloud, however, soon lost 'its close-knit compactness and became diffuse' (33). Thus, pyroclastic flows can emerge gravitationally from the base of quite low eruption clouds, which nevertheless must be dense with ash and not yet forceful enough to be thrust high into the atmosphere.

Figure 7.5. Shallow-pocket eruption from Popondetta airstrip
A shallow-pocket eruption is seen in the right-hand background in this view southwards from Popondetta airstrip on 5 February 1951 (this detail was used by Taylor 1958, in his fig. 30). The low cloud on the right shown by the arrow is from a small pyroclastic flow running west of the crater. The aircraft is a De Havilland Dragon (Sinclair 1986), one of the aircraft that Tony Taylor, in the foreground, used for aerial inspections. Photograph supplied courtesy of Geoscience Australia (negative number GB/2770).

Administration officers were attuned to the results of the observational work being undertaken by volcanologist Taylor on these new explosive eruptions. They were aware that Taylor had remained vigilant and was concerned about the destructive impact of the ongoing eruptions, and indeed about the possibility of still larger eruptions taking place. Ivan Champion responded to this uncertainty by releasing a circular, dated 23 February, for the attention of all personnel in the area under control of the Administration Field Group. The threat of escalating volcanic activity clearly was still on the minds of the administration because Champion's circular was entitled 'Evacuation Instructions in Event of Second Major Eruption' (I.F. Champion 1951a).

Figure 7.6. Shallow-pocket eruption on 11 February 1951
A rising ash column from a shallow-pocket explosion was photographed on 11 February 1951 (Taylor 1958, similar to his fig. 51). Small pyroclastic flows (*nuées ardentes*) are issuing northwards from the base of the cloud, out through the avalanche valley where Taylor and others had been working in the morning (see in Figure 5.8). Photograph supplied courtesy of Geoscience Australia (negative number M/1770-16).

A large explosive eruption of a quite different kind to the February ones took place on 3–5 March 1951. It was the largest since the two major eruptions of 21 January and would not be exceeded by any of the explosions that took place afterwards. The March eruption is also illustrative of the 'ash densification' phenomena that characterised the massive eruption cloud of 21 January 1951. In practice, the early March eruption marked the end of the more dangerous phase of the 1951 eruption as a whole and thus the beginning of serious discussions on how the displaced Orokaiva could best be resettled in areas away from settlements that were devastated in January.

Tony Taylor informed the administration in Port Moresby, and hence the Department of Territories in Canberra, on Saturday 3 March that the new eruption had started at about midnight (Administration 1951e) and that pyroclastic flows had been emitted at about 6.00 am on Monday 5 March (Administration 1951f). Taylor was at the Sangara Observation Post and so was able to witness the 5 March eruption and its effects in some detail, as illustrated in the following extracts:

> At 0558 hours a small earthquake was felt at Sangara Observation Post and a moment later a brilliant display of stellar and chain lightning drew attention to the fact that an eruption had begun. A nuée [pyroclastic flow] covered all the upper slopes and a vertical column ascended, to expand prodigiously above the volcano. A few minutes later the column was short and thick with massive lateral extensions at its base and summit. The whole column appeared to thicken as the gas clouds billowed up from the laterally moving material … and it soon became evident that the main nuée was flowing down the avalanche valley on to the north-eastern slopes … Two streams then broke away from the main nuée and began flowing north in the direction of the Observation Post … the larger one … followed the valley of the Ambogo River. The realization that the main body of the nuée ardente was being strictly controlled by topography was the only reassuring point in an alarming situation. The main north-easterly body of the nuée appeared to have already exceeded the limits of the earlier devastation [of 21 January] and the eruption showed still no signs of abating. The northerly component, in the Ambogo valley, appeared to be advancing at a rate of 30 miles per hour … and the lubricant gases from this river of fragmental lava boiled up in turbulent convolutions to form a great wall which marked the course of the river valley. (Taylor 1958, 36, as shown in Figure 7.7)

Figure 7.7. Pyroclastic flow of 5 March 1951 in Ambogo River valley
A pyroclastic flow moves down the Ambogo River valley on 5 March 1951 and passes close to the observation post at Sangara Plantation (Taylor 1958, fig. 42). Photograph supplied courtesy of Geoscience Australia (negative number GA/8197).

The pyroclastic flow curved past the observation post about 700 metres to its west and continued down the Ambogo River beyond the former area of devastation. 'The main north-easterly body of the nuée' mentioned by Taylor ran down the Bangula River, also beyond the devastated area, and almost reached Jegarata (Figure 4.6). Taylor, on the morning of 5 March, advised the administration in Port Moresby that the pyroclastic flows as a whole had covered little more than half the area of the original devastated area and that no damage outside of the restricted area was expected in the event of a further eruption (Administration 1951f). No mention was made of any 'ash hurricane' effects. A change in wind direction, however, meant that 'heavy pumice dust' was falling on both Popondetta and Embi where both airstrips were closed. There would be a threat of mudflows once heavy rains took place.

Administrator Colonel Murray and Director of Public Health Dr Gunther were able to fly into Embi on a Royal Australian Air Force (RAAF) Dakota later that morning when visibility had cleared to assess the situation for themselves. They reported that fine volcanic ash covered the area all the way to the coast, including the evacuation camp at Oro Bay (Phillips Deputy 1951). The administrator recorded in an evening message from Popondetta to the Department of External Territories in Canberra that the local people at Oro Bay, Eroro Anglican mission, Embi and Dobudura were all upset by the eruption (Murray Administrator 1951l). Refugees at the coast, however, had been calmed and settled by the European staff of the mission and administration, including Mr and Mrs Foldi, Dr Biggs and Father Anderson. The eruption had also upset the 600 refugees at Popondetta. However, Ilimo camp and the Kumusi area had been little affected by the eruption. The administrator gave praise to all involved, including wireless-communication staff, the RAAF and airline services.

Cadet Patrol Officer R.M. Claridge was at Awala Plantation on 5 March, writing a comprehensive and informative report on the status of resettlement camps along the Wairope–Sangara road (Claridge 1951a). The people living in nine camps along that sector of the road already had identified escape routes and they had evacuated quickly and in an orderly fashion, northwards towards distant Togahau when the larger eruption took place that morning. Claridge reported that the water supply in the nine camps was satisfactory, but there were ongoing hygiene problems, as some latrines had not been dug deep enough and some people were 'still using the roadway and near-by bush for defecating' (Claridge 1951a, 2). Three people had died in the camps over the last two weeks—one old man and two children, one from pneumonia. Food requirements were being met satisfactorily by existing supplies from old village gardens, but taro had been rotting, caused either by poor air circulation in which the taro had been covered by ash—called 'dry rot'—or by 'damp rot' in which volcanic acid was absorbed by the plants. New village housing was being planned, including schools and teaching coordinated by the Anglican mission. There had been a breakdown in a double telephone line between Awala and Sangara but this was being fixed.

The following day, 6 March, Acting Government Secretary Steve Lonergan signed-off on a list of European 'dead and missing' (Lonergan 1951b). The bodies of only 16 of the 35 dead had been identified by this time, more than six weeks after the catastrophic eruption, but the full names of all the adults, and those of some of the children, were given together with the names and addresses of next of kin, mainly in Australia.

A heavy electrical storm took place in the Lamington area on 23 March leading, wrote Taylor in a telegram to Port Moresby on 24 March, to a 'spectacular [secondary] eruption in hot ash beds and river valleys'. He noted, too, that 'the effect at Sangara was similar to a major eruption[,] the area being blacked out for three hours by dust clouds' (quoted in Murray Administrator 1951m). A large, hot mudflow had moved down the Ambogo River valley temporarily destroying communication with Popondetta and flooding a village. District Services officers were again able to calm the Orokaiva people in the Sangara area.

All of Taylor's considerations about the nature of the explosive eruptions at Lamington, from 21 January to 23 March, led him to reflect that:

> In some respects the Peléan type volcano resembles a normal explosive volcano that has degenerated into a low-pressure activity while still retaining the power of voluminous discharge … In the course of an eruptive cycle, however, the volcano occasionally 'reverts to type', producing normal vertical explosions, included among which may be vulcanian outbursts of great violence. The largest, purely vulcanian outburst from Lamington occurred at 2045 hours on 21st January 1951, ten hours after the catastrophic eruption. (Taylor 1958, 35)

This is volcanologically important in the taxonomy of volcanic eruptions and is one of several reasons why '*peléean*' is no longer used widely for volcanoes that simply produce pyroclastic flows as a biproduct. The basic explosive eruption type at Mount Lamington was 'vulcanian', a term used commonly for many eruptions worldwide including elsewhere in Papua New Guinea. *Nueés ardentes* are often a secondary product of vulcanian explosions, but commonly their lethal nature attracts more attention than do the primary eruptions that generate them (e.g. Francis 1993). Similarly, the name *nuées ardentes* is no longer fashionable taxonomically because pyroclastic flows can be of different types and not restricted to the kind of pyroclastic flows witnessed at Mont Pelée in 1902. Nevertheless, most of the *nuées* at Mont Pelée in 1902 appear to have been what Lacroix himself referred to as '*nuees ardentes d'explosions vulcaniennes*' rather than the less common 'directed'—perhaps meaning lateral blast—type that he referred to as '*nuées peléeans d'explosions dirigées*' (Lacroix 1904; Francis 1993). Volcanological taxonomy was not, however, foremost in the minds of the administration officers who were managing the practical aspects of the recovery phase of the Lamington disaster.

Four Other Aspects of the Eruption

Dome growth

The dominant type of eruptive activity in the summit crater after 5 March was not explosive activity, but rather the long-term growth of the lava dome that had been partly destroyed by the large eruption of 5 March. This new phase of dome growth lasted throughout 1951 up to January 1952, the dome eventually filling much of the crater and reaching a height greater than that of the crater rim. Taylor monitored and reported on this dome growth in some detail and with reference not only to ongoing earthquake activity but also to measurements of ground tilting using a single-component, spirit level tiltmeter at the Sangara Observation Post. These were, however, far from ideal geodetic conditions for a single, basic, one-component instrument located more than 12 kilometres from the crater. While the results conformed to changes in eruptive activity, they had to be interpreted in the context of crustal movements also being caused by the gravitational influences of the sun and moon, and by changes in temperature, air-pressure and rainfall.

A period of particularly rapid growth of the lava dome took place between 3 and 9 February when the top surface of the dome rose at a rate of 100 feet, or 30 metres, each day. Taylor noted that this rate was probably the highest on record for dome uplift anywhere up to that time. Rapid growth also continued after the 5 March explosive eruption, but was spasmodic from mid-May to mid-August, after which the dome crumbled, producing flank avalanches (Figure 7.8). Then a new phase of growth took place at the end of October, culminating when a summit spine of lava reached a terminal height of more than 1,900 feet (580 metres). The volume or mass of the lava dome continued to grow throughout 1952, even though its height diminished a little, and the final shape looked like a truncated elliptical cone having a height of about 1,850 feet (565 metres) above the crater floor (Figures 7.9–7.10).

Figure 7.8. Avalanche on northern side of lava dome
An avalanche is seen descending from the new northern part of the lava dome in August 1951 (Taylor 1958, fig. 136). The camera was tilted when this photograph was taken. Photograph supplied courtesy of Geoscience Australia (negative number GA/9889).

Figure 7.9. Fully grown lava dome in Lamington avalanche amphitheatre
The lava dome appears to be fully grown in this photograph, exceeding the heights of the surrounding residual peaks. Its height is given as 1,679 metres above sea level on a Royal Australian Survey Corps topographic map published in 1974. The date of the photograph, which was provided by Albert Speer, is unknown but likely was late 1951 or early 1952, judging by the direction of the winds of the 'north-west' monsoonal season. The lava dome is still hot and water vapour emissions are prominent. There is a slight greening of valley walls and slopes, and there are no obvious new deposits such as pyroclastic flows or mudflows.

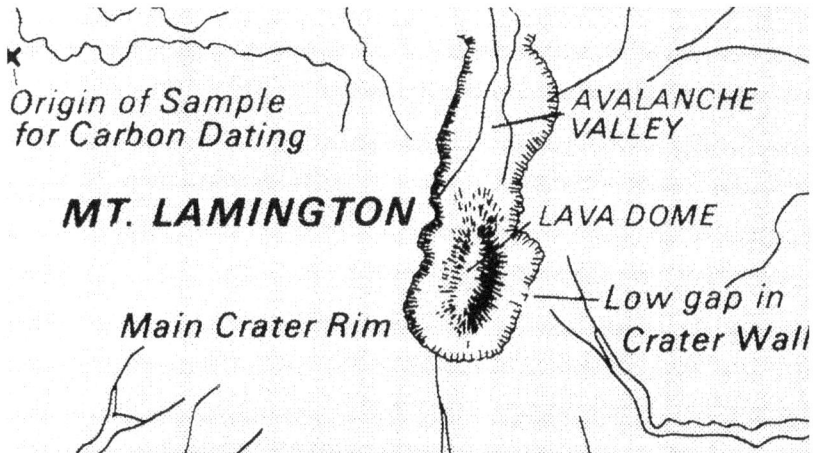

Figure 7.10. Sketch map of summit dome and avalanche amphitheatre
The shape of the avalanche amphitheatre and lava dome at the summit area of Mount Lamington is shown diagrammatically in this detail from the map by Taylor (1958, fig. 52). The dome is elliptical in plan, measuring 3,300 x 2,100 feet (Taylor 1958, 58). Note also that the western side of the avalanche amphitheatre is much straighter than the eastern side, possibly because it is controlled by a geological fault. The cross in the top left-hand corner refers to collection point for the radiocarbon sample in the Embogo Valley that yielded a radiocarbon age of 13,000±500 years (Taylor 1958, 17).

Earth tides

Taylor had a particular interest in studying the possible gravitational influence of the sun and moon on the eruptive activity at Lamington—what he referred to as 'luni-solar influences'. He thought that the gravitational pull of the sun and moon at critical times of the year had an eruption-triggering effect, particularly during the early, highly explosive phase of the 1951 eruption. Most of the large explosions, including those of 21 January and 5 March, he pointed out, took place around the spring tide periods of full and new moon, and the three explosive eruptions on 18, 22 and 24 February were grouped about the time of the full moon on 21 February.

The influence of earth tides on volcanic activity is a contentious subject among volcanologists but was a theme that Taylor and colleagues also pursued strongly in later years in the Territory. Volcanoes, at the very least, have to be ready or, as it were, 'primed' for eruption if the slight changes in the forces of earth tides are to have any effect. The earth tide effect may be more noticeable at volcanoes in equatorial zones, such as at Lamington.

Tectonic stress release and eruption time clusters

Another topic pursued resolutely by Taylor was the influence of periods of regional, tectonic earthquakes on phases of eruption at active volcanoes in the Papua and New Guinea region. This idea was examined at a time well before the theory of plate tectonics had emerged and when mapping the positions of many tectonic earthquakes was made difficult by a deficiency of data caused by the small number of seismological stations in the region. Nevertheless, Taylor suggested that the release of stress from tectonic earthquakes could be sufficient to trigger eruptions across a volcanic region at more than one volcano.

Taylor pointed out that the Lamington eruptive activity of 1951–52 was part of a time cluster of eruptions that ranged up to 1954 at volcanoes that included Long, Tuluman and Langila, as well as at Bagana—starting in 1950—during what he called a 'seismic fever' (Taylor 1958, 86–87). Activity at an unnamed submarine volcano near Karkar Island in 1951 can also be included in this range, as well as eruptions at Manam and Bam volcanoes where the range is extended up to 1957.

Eruption periodicity

Finally, Taylor was also interested in how often major eruptions take place at Mount Lamington. The 1951 eruption was clearly the only one known historically and there was no unambiguous evidence of eruptions having been witnessed by the Orokaiva before colonisation. Eruption periodicity was not easy for Taylor to establish through comprehensive geological studies over a wide area given the priority of monitoring the ongoing eruption. However, he pointed out that a radiocarbon sample from an old deposit in the Embogo Valley within the devastated area yielded a radiocarbon age of $13,000 \pm 500$ years (Taylor 1958, 17; see also Figure 7.10). This is not necessarily the age of the previous major eruption at Lamington but may be indicative of long periods between successive eruptions.

Reconstructing the Catastrophic Eruption of 21 January

An attempt, then, can be made to summarise what happened volcanologically on 21 January 1951 using Taylor's conclusions and by incorporating the results of more modern field studies at Lamington and at volcanoes such as Bezymianny, Russia, in 1957; Mount Helens, United States, in 1980; and Soufrière Hill, Montserrat, in 1997 (Belousov et al. 2011a, 2011b; Hoblitt 1982). Such an attempt is based on the premise that the whole eruptive period at Lamington conforms to that of a series of vulcanian eruptions, including the formation of pyroclastic flows and the long-term growth of a lava dome. Vulcanian eruptions commonly take place at so-called 'andesitic', circum-Pacific volcanoes where 'andesite'— named after the Andes—is a rock name for lavas generally rich in large crystals such as those found at Mount Lamington. The name 'vulcanian', however, derives from Vulcan Island in the Mediterranean, named after the Roman god of fire.

Vulcanian magmas are, in general terms, hot, gas rich and 'viscous', and they fragment intensely where gas is emitted explosively from a volcanic vent. The explosions produce dust, ash, loose crystals, pumice and lava fragments that range from pea-size pieces to blocks a few metres in width. Vulcanian eruptions also form so-called 'breadcrust bombs' in which the glassy rind or crust of a chilled but still molten lava fragment is split open by the swelling interior of the lava as gas bubbles increase in size. The dense, hot, volcanic clouds of enduring vulcanian eruptions rise in thermally driven columns up to heights up to 20 kilometres, although generally they are much lower and shorter lived. The columns once formed can rise quite noiselessly, even eerily.

First, then, in this interpretation: hot, gas-rich magma is emplaced beneath Mount Lamington at an unknown time in a reservoir of still unknown depth, size and shape. The magma is buoyant and begins rising through a conduit directly beneath the floor of the old crater, or debris-avalanche amphitheatre, that faces northwards towards Higaturu and Sangara. Ascent of the subterranean magma causes cracking of rocks and local felt earthquakes take place that became most noticeable on Monday 15 January, but may well have taken place also in previous days if not weeks.

The magma in the conduit comes close to the surface, heats the crater floor and causes emission of the first vapour clouds from vents in the crater, as well as causing small landslides that represent the first evidence during the volcanic unrest of instability in the walls of the old crater. Rocks in the steep walls of the old crater may have been weathered and weakened by tropical downpours since the previous eruption, possibly centuries or millennia earlier.

The first explosive eruptions take place, possibly including the breaking and expulsion of conduit-wall rocks as the magma clears a passage for the fresh magma that follows. Gases dissolved in the magma come out of solution, creating bubbles as well as the powerful disruption of the magma itself. These produce the first ash in rising eruption columns of 'vulcanian' type that are blown by low-level north-west winds away from Higaturu–Sangara (Figure 7.11a; see also Figure 4.4, left). Earth tremors continue. These initial eruptions are well established by Thursday 18 January and continue in the days ahead. They may have caused further widening of the conduit, as well as additional weakening of the crater walls and further landslides.

The eruption starts becoming climactic at 10.40 am on Sunday 21 January when major vulcanian explosive eruptions form a rapidly ascending cloud that conceals the summit area of the volcano and lofts ash high into the upper atmosphere initially forming a 'cauliflower'-shaped eruption cloud (Figures 5.9a(i) and 7.11b). This spectacular event is soon accompanied, however, by the catastrophic disintegration and collapse of crater-wall rocks, and the formation of rock avalanches that are discharged gravitationally northwards out of the crater area and onto the upper, northern flanks of Mount Lamington. The height of the entire volcano is reduced by several hundred metres. Further, the 'breached crater' is greatly enlarged forming a 1.2-kilometre-wide, amphitheatre-shaped crater that, like the earlier one, opens to the north and that, together with the avalanche valley, is about 3.5 kilometres long. These events were unlikely to have been observed, however, because of the ash cloud concealing them, but the proposed results of this catastrophic collapse are not unlike those mapped at Galunggung volcano in Indonesia (Figure 3.10).

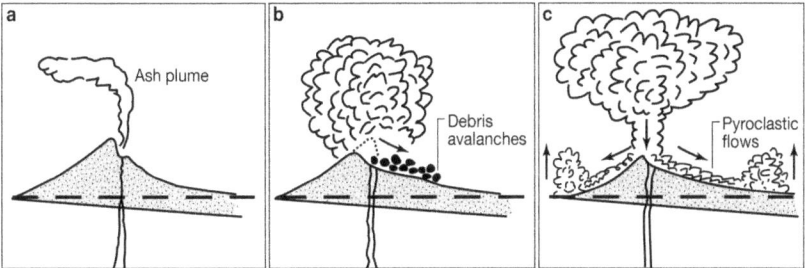

Figure 7.11. Three-part evolution of catastrophic eruption of 21 January 1951

This is a highly diagrammatic sequence, a to c, of the events at Mount Lamington leading up to the catastrophic eruption of 21 January 1951. The diagrams are not to scale but the sections are shown roughly on the same south–north (left–right) orientation. Features are exaggerated, including the sloping basement on which the asymmetric volcano may have been built. 'Phoenix' clouds are seen (c) rising only from the extremities of the pyroclastic flows, as shown by the arrows pointing upwards.

The removal of so much rock from the summit of the volcano, and the ongoing widening of the conduit by the violent explosive eruptions, leads to a massive disgorgement of vesiculating magma forming ash clouds that rise into the ever-growing eruption column (Figure 7.11c). So much pyroclastic material is ejected, however, that the lower parts of the ash column become heavy through ash densification and the column begins to collapse gravitationally, crashing down to the land surface around the entire volcano. Voluminous hot pyroclastic flows move rapidly and radially down the flanks in all directions but especially on the northern flank where the new north-facing amphitheatre helps to guide the deadly flows, or *nuées ardentes*, in that direction towards settlements. The 'ash hurricane' component of these northerly flows destroys Higaturu–Sangara, and deposition from the flows covers much of the debris-avalanche material just deposited by the preceding crater-wall collapses.

Eruptions from the volcano decline after these overlapping and catastrophic events on the morning of 21 January, but there was still gas-rich magma 'brewing' beneath the volcano. This would reach the surface by the evening of 21 January, nine or 10 hours later, and produce the second major eruption of the day. The darkness of night prevented good observations being made, but the evening eruption appears to have been 'pure' vulcanian—that is, a highly explosive and high rising eruption that did not yield the heavy, laterally extensive, and disastrous discharges of pyroclastic flows experienced in the morning. The evening eruption was certainly powerful, however, and the apparent absence of pyroclastic flows may mean that the newly created configuration of crater and conduit allowed the free, upward discharge of ash such that much less densification and column collapse took place.

Smaller vulcanian eruptions continued through February into March, some producing pyroclastic flows closer to the new amphitheatre and overlapping with the period of initial lava dome growth, but the last significant one was that of 5 March. Thereafter, the eruption at Lamington was characterised mainly by the slow and ongoing development of the summit lava dome, long-term cooling and a gradual decline in the emission of vapour and residual volcanic gases.

PART 3. AFTER THE DISASTER

The past is never fully gone. It is absorbed into the present and the future. It stays to shape what we are and what we do.

— William P. Deane (1996, 1)

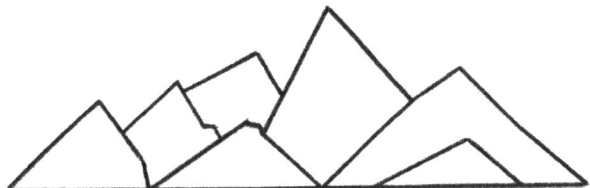

8
RESETTLEMENT, MYTHS AND MEMORIALISATION

Shifting to Saiho

Administration plans for resettling the displaced Orokaiva advanced during March–April following what appeared to have been the last of the large explosive eruptions on 5 March. This did not mean that the area of total devastation would be redeveloped—far from it. Neither the administration nor the Anglican Church favoured the rebuilding of either Higaturu Government Station or Sangara Mission in what had been demonstrated very clearly as sites that were too hazardous for reoccupation. Many of the surviving refugees felt similarly.

Development of new villages and support facilities along the Waseta–Popondetta road was favoured by the administration, although they were aware that they could be accused of taking advantage of the disaster to promulgate a government policy that had been favoured for years. Small settlements or hamlets of less than a hundred people distributed over a wide area may have allowed ready access of the Orokaiva to nearby traditional lands, and separated them from enemies, but in the context of improved postwar community development and the efficient provision of health, educational, agricultural and administrative services, larger centres were needed. A further advantage of developing villages and facilities along the Waseta–Popondetta road was that the road itself could continue to be a 'lifeline' in the event of future volcanic eruptions.

Mr Fred Kaad and his staff at Ilimo were heavily involved in the planning for the resettlement work, in association with administration officers in Port Moresby. So too was Sydney Elliott-Smith who was sworn in as acting district commissioner of the Northern Division on 12 March 1951, thus occupying the position left vacant by the death of Cecil Cowley at Higaturu (e.g. *Pacific Islands Monthly* 1951d). Colonel Elliott-Smith had had former work experience in the Northern Division. He was a Territorian 'old hand', his career extending back to 1928 when he came to Papua as a patrol officer (Sinclair 1981). Elliott-Smith had resigned a position in Western Australia to assist with the Lamington recovery. He had primary responsibility in the division for the resettlement work but he had to work with departmental heads based in Port Moresby—notably for health, district services and agriculture—as well as the administrator, his deputy and Bishop David Hand who had his own ideas about resettlement. There were some strong personalities at work and, inevitably, there were at times disagreements if not conflicts.

Elliott-Smith and his staff worked out of Popondetta, which was becoming accepted as the most likely new divisional headquarters, but accommodation was crude and temporary. There was still an emergency medical hospital at Popondetta. All of the officers of the administration were under some pressure to advance the closure of the camps and to resettle the Orokaiva. The costs of continuing to supply and run the camps were growing significantly, although so too was the disaster relief fund (e.g. *Pacific Islands Monthly* 1951d). Further, the Orokaiva themselves were anxious to leave the camps and to restart and redefine their lives in times that had changed from their prewar environment. The disaster and the rapid response of the administration to their needs had brought some benefits in this regard.

Two overseas visitors assisted the administration with their resettlement planning. They were anthropologists Felix M. Keesing and Cyril S. Belshaw. Their investigations were undertaken at different times of the resettlement period and, to a large extent, their findings complemented those already accomplished by Patrol Officer Harry Plant (Plant 1951). The administration here was following in the tradition of using the expertise of academic anthropologists in the application of development policy and, more particularly in this case, post-disaster resettlement.

Keesing was a professor in anthropology at Stanford University in California, the senior United States commissioner on the South Pacific Commission and an authority on Pacific 'races' (*Pacific Islands Monthly*

1951d). However, unlike Belshaw, he had no previous work experience in Papua. Keesing visited the Lamington area in the latter part of March and early April, inspecting the camps and engaging in discussions with administration officials and camp refugees (Keesing 1952). Cyril Belshaw was an anthropological researcher at The Australian National University in Canberra. He visited the area from 25 April to 5 May, providing professional opinions that added further to those of Keesing and Plant (Belshaw 1951a–c). These contributions, together with other reports, provide a valuable historical record of the resettlement phase at Lamington at a time when administration staff were heavily involved in the practical work of trying to implement the resettlement. Anthropologist Marie Reay might well have contributed significantly too, but her experience of the eruption and disaster had been traumatic. Reay never returned to the area to complete her research, but she did publish an informative paper on the social anthropology of the Orokaiva based on the earlier work of F.E. Williams (Reay 1953).

A principal aim in constructing the new villages was to encourage the development of larger communities of up to about 400, such as existed already at Kokoda and at the coast. The 'Kokoda'-model villages consisted of straight lines of bush-material houses along three sides of an open, grassed, rectangular area for community use. Refugees at the Ilimo camp, for example, were now familiar with this tidy-line arrangement favoured by the administration. They went along with the plan, particularly when they were informed that access to their traditional lands away from the devastated area would not be restricted, and when roads were constructed at right angles to the main Waseta–Popondetta road to assist access. Men left the camps first to start building the new villages under the guidance of administration patrol officers who had to be careful not to be too controlling and prescriptive. Leaving wives and children back in the camps must have been somewhat motivational for the Papuan men in completing the building as effectively and rapidly as possible.

Another important aspect of the resettlement of the populous Wasita–Isivita–Awala area was the provision of new and appropriate health services along the main road. Constructing a hospital close to the western flank of Mount Lamington, where many of the refugees had resided before the January eruption, was also necessary. The hospital site favoured by Dr Gunther was near Awala Plantation at Saiho where a government station had been established. Saiho was much closer to the soon-to-be densely populated area than Popondetta. However, there was a considerable distance between Saiho and Popondetta and its airstrip, from which supplies would have to be transported by road—at times across flooding creeks such as the irrepressibly threatening Ambogo River.

Shifting the temporary health centre at Ilimo to Saiho and moving the hundreds of refugees to their new villages on the Waseta–Popondetta road was no easy task. The refugees already had to move first to Wairopi, and then on to Ilimo after the Kumusi flooding, and now they—plus those shifted to Ilimo from Oro Bay—were having to move yet again. They had to retrace their steps in April–May eastwards to the Kumusi River where there was now no footbridge across the river, and then on to Saiho and the new villages. The European women of the Ilimo medical staff who were accompanying patients were all carried across the Kumusi:

> But the patrol officer carrying Ivane Champion slipped and both ended up in the river. From there it was an hour's walk to the Embara river but first all the breast milk had to be expressed and the premature babies fed. From the Embara river they were ferried by jeep to the new site at Saiho.
>
> The move to Saiho [however] was made before anything there had been established, so it was back to primitive life in a tent and cooking over an open fire in the rain. It was the wet season and as no drains had been dug, they had to work in gum boots. The nurses' tent leaked and the tent used as a milk room collapsed on top of everything. The women and small children, who had already suffered greatly, were to suffer more during the time their new and permanent village was being built. (Kettle 1979, 143)

The closure of the three remaining evacuation camps was well underway by 15 May and the numbers were looking much better: only 530 people still at Ilimo, 227 at Popondetta and 127 at Inonda (Official Secretary 1951). However, 4,503 people who had been rehabilitated to the new villages were still being rationed, as were a further 775 people living in villages but who were not refugees. The Oro Bay and Eroro camps had already been closed by this time. Ilimo camp officially closed on 1 June (Elliott-Smith 1951b; see also *Pacific Islands Monthly* 1951e).

The site of the hospital built at the Saiho Government Station had been selected by Dr Gunther, director of health, but the hospital itself was designed by the deputy-director, Dr Harold Gilbey-Brown (Kettle 1979). The design was unusual but effective for a Territory hospital, consisting of 11 long wards, each 20 metres long and 6.5 metres wide, that radiated from a central office hub like the blades of a windmill. Staff could see along the corridors of each ward and monitor any human activity between them. The hospital was built of native bush materials and so had a limited life, although it did last into the 1960s (e.g. Radford 2012). Other challenges included reassuring mothers in the hospital when they panicked during frequent electrical storms that these were not from the volcano breaking out into eruption again. Medical Assistant Bert Speer helped establish the hospital and he stayed on as part of the new staff. Friendships were established between administration and medical staff that would last lifetimes. There was romance too: Sister Win Swift and agricultural officer Alan Boag later married, as did Harry Plant and Ivane Champion.

Bishop Hand, the Wrath of God and Myths

Another high-profile person during the resettlement period at Lamington was Bishop David Hand who, on his return from Australia, had been given the task of rebuilding the work of the Anglican mission in the area. Hand had come back to a devastated mission network after the destruction of Sangara Mission and the Martyrs Secondary School. He had lost many friends and colleagues, both European and Orokaiva, as a result of the eruption, including Reverend Dennis Taylor and his family, Reverend John Rautamara, Miss Margaret de Bibra to whom he had almost proposed marriage, plus many Orokaiva people who had been baptised into the Christian faith. How he coped with this grief is unknown, but certainly he applied himself to the task of rebuilding the mission with great energy and serious determination. Sister Nancy White suffered personal losses too. Like the bishop, she had been in Australia at the time of the 21 January disaster, and she returned to help the mission's rebuilding (White 1991). Veteran missionary Reverend Romney Gill also arrived, from England, at about the same time, returning to his former mission station on the Mambare River so as to contribute what he could to repairing the decimated diocese (Garland 2000).

Bishop Hand worked with administration officers in the resettlement efforts along and adjacent to the Wasita–Popondetta road, but he had an agenda informed by the needs of the Anglican mission and by a strong confidence in the value of his past experience through working with the Orokaiva and mission parishioners. His pastoral duties involved visiting settlements of all kinds in a jeep or on foot. These visits were aimed at re-establishing some sort of community life, and providing 'for the Church's continuing ministry of word and sacrament and to re-activate primary schools and establish new ones' (Hand 2002, 63). Martyrs Memorial School would be rebuilt, but not at Sangara, and St James' Church, formerly at Sangara, would have to be replaced and relocated.

There had been competition between the administration and mission, particularly concerning educational and agricultural development, that extended back well before World War II (WWII). This adversarial situation continued during the tense atmosphere of the disaster resettlement period. Bishop Hand had his own ideas about how resettlement should proceed, even arguing that the new administration headquarters should be built at Kirewo, or Girua, over towards the Sambogo River that emerges from the Hydrographers Range. The supply and quality of water there were much better than at Popondetta, and there was even some hydro-electric potential (Hand 2002). Tensions between administration and mission authorities rippled like an undercurrent for weeks, but serious conflict emerged in July, long after the resettlement had started and particularly after the government office and hospital had been built by the administration at Saiho.

Fred Kaad, who was now acting assistant district officer at Saiho, reported on 24 July to District Commissioner Elliott-Smith in Popondetta that Bishop Hand had visited Saiho on 4 July and, 'during the course of the conversation, said that the Administration had taken the Church's land' (Kaad 1951, 1). The situation became worse when local hospital staff at Saiho reported that the bishop had said the hospital would be destroyed because the land belonged to God and not to the administration. Dr Gillbee Brown reported that the bishop had ordered young nurses-in-training at Saiho to return to the mission school, even though they were over 14 years of age and entitled to training and employment (Gillbee Brown 1951, 1). Further, the district commissioner reported to Dr Gunther that the bishop had directly approached junior administration officers in a 'surreptitious attempt at an eventual "smear" campaign … [and that these] attempts were being made to encourage some junior officers to make hasty, rash statements which could be turned against them' (Gunther 1951c, 1). Dr Gunther characterised the bishop's style of Christianity as 'militant'.

8. RESETTLEMENT, MYTHS AND MEMORIALISATION

Figure 8.1. David Hand and Sydney Elliott-Smith at Saiho hospital
District Commissioner Elliott-Smith, right, and Bishop Hand are seen here in discussion in front of the newly completed hospital at Saiho with some assembled hospital staff (Speer 2005, photograph no. 53).

The rumours about Bishop Hand became extraordinary when he was accused of *causing* the disastrous eruption of 21 January and the deaths of thousands. These arose—as Hand himself wrote later—'from a sort of Old Testament type interpretation of the eruption as punishment which I arranged with God for the people's disobedience to God's word!' (Hand 2002, 59). Fear of the white man's Old Testament God, Jehovah, is something that had been noticed elsewhere in the New Guinea area as far back as the late nineteenth century—at Chads Bay by MacGregor in 1888 (Wetherell 1977) and in the Torres Strait Islands (Haddon 1901)— so its appearance after the Lamington disaster of 1951, perhaps, is not so surprising. It cannot, however, have been pleasing for the Christian missionaries who were promoting a god of love and forgiveness based on the life of Jesus Christ rather than a god of retribution, Jehovah. Who started the rumours, who contributed to their growth and whether there were people—European or Papuan—who manipulated and took advantage of the rift between the administration and mission is unknown. However, the bishop, in his memoirs, stated that the accusations have 'hurt me more than anything else I have ever experienced' (Hand 2002, 59).

Anthropologist Marie Reay referred briefly to the 'wrath of god' explanation in her diary entry of Friday 19 January, and the stories were prevalent when both anthropologists Felix Keesing and Cyril Belshaw undertook their separate investigations (Reay 1951; Belshaw 1951a–c; Keesing 1952). More importantly, however, both Belshaw and Keesing related the 'wrath of God' stories to a strong sense of wrongdoing, sinfulness, insecurity and guilt among the camp refugees. The Orokaiva believed they had not supported the mission and administration sufficiently in their work before the eruption; had not built new churches, as requested by the bishop; and/or had not helped the Allies enough during WWII. The disaster was thus, in their minds, a punishment for that non-cooperation. Keesing noted, however, that:

> Officials who know the Orokaiva considered that these feelings undoubtedly helped to foster the extraordinary degree of cooperation and orderliness in situations where large numbers of people were necessarily herded together and shifted around without benefit of the traditional niceties and proprieties. (Keesing 1952, 18)

There is a hint of fatalism in the 'wrath of God' stories told by the Orokaiva—'a resignation to one's fate', as encapsulated in the words of another researcher writing more generally about disasters and preliterate societies globally:

> When catastrophe is thought to be engendered primarily by spiritual forces, man can himself do little to alter the course of events apart from recourse to religious and/or magical practices … Add to this the meagreness of technological know-how of the sort that would be useful in disaster rehabilitation and we see that mute acceptance of one's lot is the logical result. (Sjoberg 1962, 363)

The veteran missionary Reverend Romney Gill, ever the pragmatist, was scathing of the Orokaiva 'wrath of God' explanations, and of fatalism, when he stressed the need for people to exercise personal responsibility by using their own human attributes:

> I always feel we are inclined to bow too much in reverent resignation to the 'Divine Ordering'. My Hat! I can imagine the Lord God Almighty exclaiming to many new arrivals 'on the other side', 'Now what has brought _you_ here before your time? I never called you away. If only you people would use the brains and develop more of the skill which is potentially yours, yes the BRAINS I have endowed you with'. (Garland 2000, 384, original emphasis)

This, in the context of the Lamington disaster, can be regarded as good disaster prevention advice that could have been applied without discrimination to both Europeans and Papuans in the Territory. The Orokaiva, in any case, were now more motivated to do things differently in a more informed postwar world as they moved forward with their 'new day' or *iji eha*. Perhaps, too, there began some thinking about the nature of volcanoes and their activity. That thinking did not seem to be prevalent at all in the refugee camps such as Ilimo, according to Belshaw, but the education officer there, Percy Jensen, was apparently considering including volcanoes as a topic in school classes. 'It should be a simple matter to make visual aid charts taken from elementary geography textbooks, possibly with the vulcanologist's assistance', wrote Belshaw (1951a, 8).

Cyril Belshaw, in 'Social Consequences of the Mount Lamington Eruption', reproduced, but did not comment on, a myth that he said had been included in a patrol report written by Atkinson in 1948. In fact, the report was written by Patrol Officer H.M. Corderoy, who was based at Higaturu, following a patrol he had made to the Isivita area between 2 April and 1 May:

> Long ago a man, a woman and a dog went up into the area which was then flat land with no hills. The man wished to have intercourse with the woman and she consented, thereby doing wrong. They did not return to the village but lived in the area. The people did not see them again but periodically used to ask how they were by shouting into the bush. First they learnt that the dog had died, then the woman, then the man (the man's spirit told them the last fact). The hills appeared, and it was always cold and wet on top. It is not good for the people to go into the area. (Corderoy 1948, 10; see also Belshaw 1951b, 252)

This version of the legend is similar to the one recorded in Mrs Amalya Cowley's radiogram of 19 January 1951. Her version can be recast as follows:

> The legend concerns a man called Sumbirita. He is also known as Kamikari which means 'shut in', apparently referring to the imprisonment of his sweetheart Subitita on the mountain. But a dog, presumably Sumbirita's, finds an entrance to a bowl near the summit. Sumbirita has sex with Subitita against her wishes. The mountain in anger closes the entrance with stones, and the bowl slowly rises. The dog looks for the possibility of escape but is thrown over the side of the bowl and is crushed to death.

> The trapped Subitita dies a lingering death. Neighbours later visit the mountain and call out to Sumbirita and Subitita seeking an explanation. Sumbirita admits responsibility and his guilt. They call again a month later but there is no answer. (Correspondent 1951)

Bishop Hand also referred briefly to two versions of the same legend that he had heard before the 1951 eruption: the woman in one was the man's wife, whereas the man in the other committed adultery with a woman stolen from another man (Hand 2002). Hand concluded, unequivocally, that both versions referred to earlier volcanic activity at Mount Lamington, which is consistent with the contents of the letter written by Mr O.T. Atkinson after the eruption of January 1951 (Atkinson 1951).

Should anything volcanological be inferred from any of these accounts, and is there anything that might be related to the geomorphological features of the volcano? The case for volcanic activity itself is very weak, but arguably the 'bowl' might refer to the old crater amphitheatre at the top of Lamington volcano. Further, could the mountain closing the 'entrance' with stones in anger, and the bowl slowly rising, refer to avalanches from the crater wall that then partly fill the crater? All such interpretations should be regarded sceptically, as these pre-1951 myths were designed as cultural stories rather than carriers of scientific information. The myths are, however, of considerable interest in that together they represent the starting point of yet more elaborations of the same legend that would be heard and recorded by Europeans in the years ahead. A feature of these later versions is the extensive use of the man's name of 'Sumbiripa', which was mentioned for the first time, as 'Sumbirita', in Mrs Cowley's version of the legend.

Administration and the Changing Political Scene in 1952

Percy Spender, Minister of External Territories, had had to deal with public criticism of the Territory administration following the Lamington disaster. This criticism had focused on Judge Phillips who, at the time of the 21 January eruption, had been acting administrator of the Australian trusteeship of the conjoined New Guinea and Papua territories. The Menzies Government in Canberra in mid-1951 underwent a Cabinet reshuffle and Spender was eventually replaced by Paul Hasluck who was sworn in on 11 May 1951 as minister of a new Department of Territories that now included the Northern Territory in Australia (Hasluck 1976; see also Downs 1980). Hasluck would remain in this ministerial position until 1963. Ministerial attention now focused on the Territory administrator, Colonel Murray.

Both ministers, Spender and Hasluck, were concerned about Murray's effectiveness and, particularly, his relationship with the central government and bureaucracy in Canberra. Hasluck admired 'this good and devoted man', noting that 'in the [Lamington] emergency Murray had shown up well. He had organised and directed the work of rescue and rehabilitation and had put in promptly all the required resources needed for the task' (Hasluck 1976, 15, 22). This conclusion can hardly be disputed, added to which is the fact that Murray and the administration in Port Moresby had kept Canberra well informed of post-disaster developments in the Lamington area. The minister, however, noted that in 1951 Murray, who was 62, was already 'a tired and disappointed man' (15), which perhaps is not surprising given the considerable challenges of postwar redevelopment and, now, his frontline leadership of the relief and recovery phases of the Lamington disaster. The basic problem for Hasluck, however, was that Murray was 'not only unskilled in the use of the tools of public administration and politics but did not know what some of the tools were' (51). Hasluck also detected in Murray a sense of disengagement from Canberra, an obsession about his own rank and status and aspirations that the role of administrator perhaps should be a vice-regal one. Hasluck expressed some amusement that Murray had designed for himself, and had had made in London, a uniform to be worn on formal occasions (see, for example, Figure 3.8).

Minister Hasluck visited the Territory, including the Lamington area, shortly after his appointment in mid-1951 when the future of Murray was still on his mind. He visited Saiho, met Tony Taylor and flew with the volcanologist in a Dragon-Rapide biplane to the Lamington crater, saw its large emissions of vapour and noted that 'a great rock the size of a house was slowly dislodged from the rim and tumbled and rolled in a ponderous way down into the mass of detritus on the hillside' (Hasluck 1976, 21). The walls of the new crater clearly were still unstable. Hasluck added that Taylor 'seemed to have developed a sort of affection for Mt Lamington. "She was a bit uneasy last night." "She seems to be settling down." "She's still got one or two bad symptoms"' (21). This volcanological experience for the new minister was, one imagines, just an interesting side-line to the greater problem of re-organising the administration of the whole territory.

Two positions of deputy administrator whose work would be more closely tied with Canberra's needs had been advertised in Spender's time. These were changed, however, into a new single position of assistant administrator. Donald M. Cleland was selected for the job after an appropriate selection procedure (Hasluck 1976). Cleland was a lawyer and ex-military, having been a brigadier and Australian New Guinea Administrative Unit (ANGAU) chief of staff during the war (Nelson 1993; see also Cleland 1984). He also had been director of the federal secretariat of the Liberal Party, helping organise an effective political campaign during the 1949 election. Brigadier Cleland would have to work with the administrator, Colonel Murray, as well as with the government in Canberra who had appointed him, and its bureaucracy.

The world was being dominated by the postwar politics of the Cold War, and there were anti-communist and anti-socialist sentiments both in the Menzies Government and within the Territory (e.g. *Pacific Islands Monthly* 1952). A Legislative Assembly was inaugurated in the Territory in 1951 (Downs 1980). It served like an embryonic but non-democratic 'parliament' and was dominated by white men. District Advisory Councils were appointed for the whole Territory, permitting devolution of greater power to the district commissioners. The Northern Division became the Northern District. An announcement appeared in the July issue of *Pacific Islands Monthly* that the new headquarters for the Northern Division would be at Popondetta, despite its poor climate and unattractive setting compared to the former, ill-fated, government station at Higaturu (*Pacific Islands Monthly* 1951f).

The United Nations (UN) sent several missions to the Territory, starting in 1950 and continuing into the 1970s (Downs 1980). These missions had a desire for global decolonisation and they reported on progress with the UN trusteeship being administered by Australia. Colonialism was being questioned elsewhere and there were signs of violent unrest in some colonies in Africa. An example is Kenya where the Mau Mau uprising or rebellion against the British colonial government began in 1952, lasting up to the time of Kenya's independence in 1963. It had its origins in the sense of deprivation felt by the Kikuyu who, like some Papua New Guineans, had lost much of their land to white settlers. There were some fears of similar unrest and even uprisings in the Territory, although these never eventuated to anywhere near the same extent as in Kenya and other colonies of the former British Empire. There were certainly no signs of such political uprisings among the Orokaiva in the Lamington area at this time.

The acting district commissioner at Popondetta, in his weekly summary for 20–26 May 1951, was highly complimentary of administration staff who had advanced the resettlement of the refugees, noting particularly the work being undertaken by Department of Health staff at Saiho (Elliott-Smith 1951b). There had been disagreements among senior administration staff about the merits of a quick return of the refugees to their traditional lands, and the returned people may not have been receiving the same close attention as in the camps, but 'they are immeasurably happier and I am glad of it, as should be the far seeing Administrator [Murray] and Director of District Services [Champion] who countenanced the plan' (Elliott-Smith 1951b, 1). Building of additional facilities was taking place at the new headquarters at Popondetta, including construction of police facilities under the direction of Sub-Inspector George Allen. Telephone lines to Awala and Saiho had been laid, and the power plant at Higaturu had been salvaged. Supplying distant Saiho was being carried out using 3-ton trucks, although flooding of the Ambogo River continued to be problematic. These achievements and several others were set out proudly by the acting district commissioner, leading to a suggestion that his weekly reports could now be replaced by monthly ones.

Another update was provided nine months later in a quarterly report for the Northern District:

> Little now remains of the Mt Lamington disaster, except the memory of those who died. The slopes of the mountain [are] again covered in luscious green growth, prodigious quantities of the most extraordinary examples of native food [are] being taken from the area by the people … the situation is normal, the task is complete. (Elliott-Smith 1952, 1–2)

Admiring words about the Orokaiva were included as advice for future administering officers:

> The background of the Orokaiva, as with all independent spirited people has been a tragic one and should be taken into very clear account before passing judgement—I who have served them in so many categories and studied them closely for so long know full well the service or otherwise they may one day be able to render the Crown. (Elliott-Smith 1952, 1)

A visit had been paid to what was called the 'Sangara settlement'—presumably at Irihambo—where about 400 survivors who 'probably have suffered the most, both mentally and physically' had assembled. They offered generous gifts of food to the district commissioner, and a spokesman called Ojarembo said:

> Taubada, on this occasion we the Sangara people want this small offering to be a true gift without payment. It is little enough to tell you how much we the Sangara people think of what the white people have done for us during the past many months after the volcano blew up and we would like you to tell the Governor this for us. That is all. (Elliott-Smith 1952, 2)

In fact, the administration's post-disaster work was not so 'complete'. There was an admission that rehabilitation of administration affairs based at Popondetta was 'not so good' and that reconstruction programs had had only temporary results, as building materials were simply of perishable native materials. Further, the building of a memorial cemetery at Popondetta was still underway—under the unflagging direction of Police Sub-Inspector Allen. Bodies would have to be disinterred and reburied.

The Anglican mission had been achieving some success too. This was not reported by Elliott-Smith, although it was by Reverend Henry T.A. Kendall. Kendall and his wife Ray, a teacher, were in England when they heard about the Lamington disaster and they offered their services to the mission as replacements for the Taylor priest-and-teacher team killed by the eruption at Sangara Mission (Kendall 1988). The Kendalls arrived in Papua in April 1952, and Reverend Kendall was inducted as priest-in-charge of the Popondetta District in September. Kendall noted in his memoirs that Bishop David had set the Sangara people at Irihambo 'an exercise in occupational therapy: to build a church' (Kendall 1988, 145). The people insisted that they name their church 'St James', after the one destroyed at Sangara Mission, rather than 'Resurrection', the name preferred by the bishop. The 'Church of the Resurrection' was built in Popondetta where the mission had decided to locate its headquarters not far from those of the administration. Relationships between the administration and mission were clearly still not satisfactory, as Kendall tells the story of villagers, including mission men, attending a Christmas party and being arrested for trespassing on government land. The acting district commissioner later relented, although Kendall wrote pointedly about the incident and about the officer, who was not named, being 'a bit of a nark anyway' (Kendall 1988, 149). Elliott-Smith was 'on leave' by this time (Sinclair 1981, 100).

On 30 April 1952, the Canberra-based Australian Cabinet decided to terminate Colonel Murray's appointment as administrator of the Territory. His last day would be in two months time on 30 June (Hasluck 1976; Downs 1980). Murray, who was on holiday at the time in Queensland, was informed by a letter dated 2 May from Hasluck, and he returned to Port Moresby with his wife to begin packing and making their final departure. This was an understandably bitter time for Murray after all of his achievements as head of the Territory, but there were powerful political forces at work that were being driven for clearly articulated reasons. They could not be ignored. His departure was controversial, particularly when speculations were aired in the media that the plan was motivated by the Liberal Government who, all along, wanted to replace Murray with Liberal supporter Brigadier Cleland, the new assistant administrator. This was firmly denied by the minister (Hasluck 1976). Support for Murray and arguments against his dismissal came from many Christian missions and Bishop Phillip Strong, in particular, continued to be a loyal ally (Strong 1981). This, perhaps, is a somewhat odd situation, given that senior men lower in the hierarchies of both mission and government were so at odds with each other over the disaster recovery and resettlement plans at Lamington. Ward, the Labor minister who had appointed Murray in the first place, also came to Murray's defence.

Judge Ralph Gore, president of the Mount Lamington Disaster Relief Fund, wrote to the new acting administrator on 23 July 1952 informing him that the fund committee had had its final meeting on 18 July (Gore 1952). He included a report in which he stressed the generosity of the wide range of people who had contributed to the fund that had reached a grand total of £21,300. Most funds had been allocated for the benefit of European dependents and the creation of trusts in the case of orphans, and an amount of £8,000 had been allocated for 'native relief in kind', which was furnished to individuals through the district commissioner (Gore 1952, 2). The dependents of 11 administration employees who had been killed at Higaturu had already been provided with support using the government compensation scheme, once agreement had been reached that the deceased were all actually on duty on the Sunday morning. The Department of the Government Secretary informed the Department of Treasury of the need to proceed with the compensation payments, enclosing a document that referred to the eruption as 'an Act of God, of which there was some slight warning' (Head 1951, 3). A problem that had arisen in relation to one particular employee was that he had two dependent families, one in Victoria and the other in India where a mother and two children were living at St Michael's Convent in Bangalore.

Memorialisation and Awards

A piece of administration business that would never be completed was the discovery and identification of the remains of all those people killed at Lamington, whether Papuan or European. How many of the dead Papuans were disinterred, identified and reburied in villages is unknown, but likely the number was very small, given the prohibitions on villagers entering the devastated area for body retrieval, the haste with which hundreds of bodies were buried where they were found, and the extreme difficulties in identifying individual people after burial and tropical decay. This, however, would not interfere with the preparation and then unveiling of a Mount Lamington Memorial Cemetery at Popondetta in late November 1952. None of the thousands of dead Orokaiva villagers were buried at the cemetery.

There had been discussions about using the parade ground at Higaturu as the site of a disaster memorial, but Colonel Murray on 19 September 1951 advised the department in Canberra that the administration would:

> Exhume, in January, 1952, all the European bodies at Higaturu and re-inter them in a prepared cemetery at Popondetta. It is likely that some of the missing persons will then be identified. You will be kept informed of all developments. (Murray 1951b, 1)

This wording is perhaps indicative that the memorial cemetery was intended only for identifiable Europeans, bearing in mind too that the Department of Territories as late as 10 November 1952 was still issuing the list of 'names of Europeans who were killed *or are still missing* as a result of the Mount Lamington eruption in January of last year' (Brack 1952, 1, emphasis added). One example of a deceased European administration officer whose body was not recovered was Dickie Humphries who, Pat Searle suggested, may not have been at Higaturu at the time of the eruption and may have been walking to Awala Plantation that morning for a lunch appointment at the plantation (Searle 1995). The overall

8. RESETTLEMENT, MYTHS AND MEMORIALISATION

impression from this is that the cemetery was intended to be one for white people only. The reburials at Popondetta, however, also included those of Papuan policemen.

The task of disinterment of the bodies at Higaturu and their reburial at Popondetta was undertaken by Sub-Inspector George B. Allen, members of the Royal Papuan and New Guinea Constabulary and prisoners. They were assisted at times by others, including Albert Speer who recalled some of the difficulties they encountered:

> We asked for coffins but were refused. We then asked for body bags, but the Government would not foot the bill for those either. We had to use mechanical post hole drills and put the bones of the bodies into sacks and bury them vertically. (Speer 2015, 109)

Sangara Mission staff killed in the eruption had already been buried at places other than Popondetta, so the disinterments at Higaturu probably were mainly, if not entirely, of people connected with the administration, and their relatives, rather than with the Anglican mission. Reverend Dennis Taylor had been interred at Gona, and Mrs Lesley Taylor, her four children and Margaret de Bibra had all been buried at the Martyrs' Cemetery at the now deserted Sangara Mission. Papuan priest Reverend John Rautamara, mission teachers and members of their families were also buried alongside the graves of the wartime martyrs at Sangara (e.g. White 1991). In practice, the memorial cemetery at Popondetta was, therefore, one for the colonial administration rather than simply a burial place for all those European victims who could be identified. Colonial discipline and organisation indeed were on full display at the opening of the cemetery on Monday 24 November 1952 (Australia Department of Territories 1953).

The memorial cemetery at Popondetta occupied a large, rectangular, park-like space and contained intersecting coral pathways (Figure 8.2). These formed a large white Christian cross within which a smaller central cross was constructed from raised garden beds bordered by stone. The distinctive design was visible for miles around when viewed from the air. An oblique aerial photograph of the memorial cemetery appeared in a small brochure produced as a program for the dedication ceremonies (Memorial Cemetery Popondetta 1952). The brochure included the statement that the 'beautiful little Memorial Cemetery at Popondetta is the last resting place of a number of residents of Higaturu and the surrounding country, who died as a result of the eruption'; exactly how many that 'number' represented was unstated. However, 34 small white crosses were erected in two parallel lines in the upper two quarters formed by the larger coral cross, each one representing the life of an individual lost in the disaster. Further, the following words formed part of an inscription on a general memorial plaque that was placed at the centre of the cemetery: 'To the memory of those who lost their lives in the eruption of Mt Lamington 21st January, 1951' (Memorial Cemetery Popondetta 1952, cover page). Some ambiguity about these arrangements remained, and questions would be asked later concerning which individuals made up the small number of people actually buried in the cemetery and which people comprised the much larger number of casualties who were being memorialised, but had not been buried there. Even the use and meaning of the word 'cemetery' was questioned.

Figure 8.2. Opening of the Mount Lamington Memorial Cemetery in 1952
Colonial authorities arranged for the ceremonial opening of the Mount Lamington Memorial Cemetery on 24 November 1952 and ensured that everyone knew their place in the official proceedings. The original single panoramic photograph taken from the 'Official Record of the Unveiling of the Mount Lamington Memorial' has been split here into two overlapping parts, the left half above, the right below (Australia Department of Territories 1953; this is the first of nine unnumbered plates from the official record in which the photography is attributed to Papuan Prints, Port Moresby).

The official party at the dedication was led by Minister for Territories Paul Hasluck and included Acting Administrator Cleland, Anglican Bishop Phillip Strong and Acting District Commissioner Elliott-Smith (Figure 8.3). Many European guests attended from Port Moresby and Australia, including three widows—Mrs M. Humphries, Mrs A.M. Cowley and Mrs D. Maher-Kelly. The graves of the victims were consecrated by Bishop Strong and Reverend Father Conlen from Port Moresby. Colonel J.K. Murray and Judge F.M. Phillips did not attend. About 1,500 'Papuans of the District, in ceremonial headdress and paint' (Australia Department of Territories 1953, 3) were arranged tidily on three sides of the cemetery—the straight lines of colonialism—while the Europeans were free to move around (Marsh 2005–06).

Figure 8.3. Paul Hasluck speaking at the opening of the memorial cemetery

Australian Minister for Territories Paul Hasluck is seen here addressing the gathering at the Mount Lamington Memorial Cemetery, Popondetta, on 24 November 1952, just before his unveiling of the memorial plaque. D.M. Cleland, acting administrator of the Territory, is second from the left and District Commissioner S. Elliott-Smith is third from the left (Australia Department of Territories 1953; this is the second of nine unnumbered plates; photograph attributed to Papuan Prints, Port Moresby).

The program for 24 November at Popondetta also included a ceremony for the investiture by the acting administrator of awards to five people (Figure 8.4). A total of 14 awards in recognition of services rendered following the eruption of Mount Lamington had been approved by Her Majesty, Queen Elizabeth II, who that year had taken the throne following the death of her father King George VI. The 14 awards were announced by the Central Chancery of Orders of Knighthood at St James's Palace, London, on 22 April 1952 and published in a supplement to the *London Gazette*. Tony Taylor was awarded the George Cross for 'conspicuous courage in the face of great danger' (*London Gazette* 1952, 2165). His Tolai volcanological assistant, Leslie Topue, received the British Empire Medal, and Bill Schleusener was awarded the George Medal. The other awardees—missionaries, pilots and administration staff—received either OBEs or MBEs. Colonel Murray did not receive an award that might have acknowledged his leadership as administrator during the difficult but successful relief and recovery phases of the Lamington disaster. This was something that surprised at least some people in administration circles, but one historian of the Trusteeship quoted a view from within the new Australian Government that 'the Administrator and his officers had been doing no more than their duty in the Lamington emergency' (Downs 1980, 83).

There is a sense in recalling the unveiling of the Mount Lamington Memorial and the investiture of awards for courageous people that the period of disaster response and resettlement had come to an end. Perhaps 1953 would bring a sense of fresh opportunity and a new start for the people of the Northern District, the administration and the Anglican mission? When, however, do the effects of a major disaster end? Grieving for personal loss continues, and ongoing trauma and disturbed memories persist, and there is an accepted need for communities to remember and commemorate disasters. This applies in the case of the Lamington disaster to both the Orokaiva and the Europeans. Memories are retained into old age, memoirs are written, articles published and stories are told to children.

Figure 8.4. Tony Taylor being presented with the George Cross
Acting Administrator Donald Cleland presents Tony Taylor with his George Cross medal at Popondetta on 24 November 1952. Four other people who were given their awards that day are sitting in the front row: Barbara Lane, Rodd Hart, Robert Porter and Leslie Topue. This photograph was supplied by Albert Speer. The remaining nine awardees had received their medals at an investiture held at Government House in Port Moresby on 25 October (Australia Department of Territories 1953).

After disasters such as at Mount Lamington, a persistent challenge for governing authorities, whether colonial or not, is to remember and learn from the achievements and failures of the experience. This certainly applied to the aftermath of the Lamington disaster, not only during the following 23 years of Australian colonialism, but also beyond 1975, the year of Papua New Guinea's independence. What lessons were learnt? What could be done better next time? Can prevention and preparedness plans be improved by disaster experiences from the past? What new disaster-risk reduction policies should be approved? Can the next catastrophic eruption at Lamington be predicted scientifically?

> **Awards for services following the Lamington disaster of 21 January 1951 (London Gazette, 1952)**
>
> **George Cross:**
> Mr G.A. Taylor, Government Volcanologist
>
> **OBE (Civil):**
> Mr T.J.S. Arthur, Regional Director, Department of Civil Aviation
> Miss P.M. Durdin, Anglican Missionary, Isivita, Papua
> Mr L.J. Hart, Anglican Missionary, Sangara, Papua
> Mr F.H.A. Kleckham, Agricultural Officer, Department of Agriculture, Stock and Fisheries
> Mrs Barbara Lane, Anglican Missionary, Isivita, Papua
> Reverend R.G. Porter, Anglican Missionary, Isivita, Papua
>
> **MBE (Civil):**
> Mr J.J. McKee, First Officer, Qantas Empire Airlines Ltd
> Mr J.R. Rose, Pilot, Qantas Empire Airlines Ltd
> Mr C.E. Searle, Planter, Awala, Papua
> Mr I.C. Taylor, First Officer, Qantas Empire Airlines Ltd
> Mr Tomnavadila Iabwau (Elliott Elijah), Native Co-operative Adviser, Department of District Services
>
> **George Medal:**
> Mr B. Schleusener, Sangara Rubber Plantations, Sangara, Papua
>
> **BEM (Civil):**
> Mr Leslie Topue, Assistant to the Government Volcanologist, Rabaul

Disaster Management Reviewed

Prevention and preparedness

The four vulnerability factors identified previously from the earlier review of the pre-1951 European history of the Lamington are as follows:

1. Too many people had settled on the rich volcanic soils of a volcanically hazardous place, although WWII may have temporarily reduced population growth.
2. Postwar colonial development in the area mainly for agricultural and missionary purposes represented investment of what was at least planned to be a growing economy.
3. There existed still the situation of a strong colonial power in charge of, and controlling, a largely preliterate people through the immediate triple presence of representatives of State, Church and the commercialised white planter community.

4. No one in January 1951 in the Lamington area itself appears to have had sufficient information and knowledge that Mount Lamington was a potentially active volcano, even though mysterious 'roars' had been heard on the mountain in the 1930s by missionaries; that a Dutch geologist in 1939 had specifically identified, although perhaps mistakenly, the volcano as an 'active' one; that a Higaturu-based patrol officer had identified a youthful volcanic crater on Lamington in 1948; and that youthful lava domes, coulées and a geothermal area were visible on aerial photographs taken in 1947. Even the Orokaiva seemed to have no knowledge of previous volcanic activity. As Keesing (1952, 16) concluded following his admittedly short visit: 'No tradition exists showing familiarity with vulcanism in the area, apart from one or two dubious hints in myth incident'.

This fourth point is perhaps the most crucial in reviewing the nature of the decision-making that took place in the week before the catastrophic eruption of 21 January 1951. Such a review can be made with regard to six questions that appeared on the front page of the *South Pacific Post* on 2 February 1951 (Figure 5.9c(ii)) and are as relevant today as they were 69 years ago.

1) 'Was the Administration aware that for many weeks before the eruption earth tremors were continually being experienced in the area?'

The answer to this first question is a qualified 'no', assuming that 'administration' refers to central headquarters in Port Moresby. Earth tremors may well have been experienced, however, by administration staff at Higaturu and particularly by people living closer to the volcano. Further, a technical question that arises necessarily is: what sort of 'earth tremors' were being considered? Were they earthquakes taking place beneath the volcano in which rising deep-seated magma breaks through surrounding rocks, or were they nearby earthquakes of tectonic origin that were not related directly to the volcano? A network of seismographs on the mountain could have answered these questions, but instrumental monitoring was unlikely to have been on the minds of administration officers in the weeks before the catastrophic eruption.

2) 'What were the factors that led Mr Justice Phillips into making a decision not to evacuate Higaturu?'

Judge F. 'Monte' Phillips, acting administrator, flew down to Higaturu on Friday 19 January out of personal interest and almost nonchalantly, bearing in mind that he also hired a second aircraft so that his wife could also witness the volcanic cloud emerging from Mount Lamington. His trip was not a formal or 'official' visit such as a trained government volcanologist might have been instructed to make. Phillips did not send a radiogram to the administrator, the district commissioner in East New Britain or the Rabaul Volcanological Observatory advising of his intentions, something that would have not only alerted the observatory to the volcanic unrest but also provided file-copy evidence that he was following an appropriate government protocol.

The volcanic cloud that Phillips saw from the air and at Popondetta airstrip on Friday 19 January was vapour-laden, although it did contain ash. It was rising slowly and non-threateningly and seemed like the later explosive eruptions the judge had witnessed himself at Vulcan and Tavurvur volcanoes at Rabaul in 1937. Volcanic pressure was being relieved quite satisfactorily, he thought. Phillips, in fact, had neither the knowledge nor the intuition to support an alternative opinion that the volcano was in the later stages of developing a major vulcanian eruption cloud that would become so ash laden and dense that it would collapse, forming widespread and deadly hot pyroclastic flows. At the airstrip, Judge Phillips provided his opinion to District Commissioner Cecil Cowley, who had no volcanological experience himself, and then flew back to Port Moresby with his wife for the weekend. Paul Quinlivan worked as a law assistant for Judge Phillips in Port Moresby and he later wrote a summary of Phillips's successful life of public service. Quinlivan (1988, 2) concluded that 'his advice, given two days before the Mount Lamington eruption, that the volcano posed no immediate danger, was misguided'. No records appear to exist of how Judge Phillips coped with his error and probable guilt in what otherwise had been an outstandingly successful career.

3) 'Had any action been taken before the first eruption to advise the Government Vulcanologist, Mr G.A. Taylor, that earth tremors were being felt around Higaturu?'; and
4) 'What prevented the vulcanologist from arriving at the scene until after 4000 [sic] people had been killed?'

Questions 3 and 4 can be addressed concurrently but not answered confidently. Taylor wrote that he heard about the Lamington eruptive activity by listening to a radio broadcast in Rabaul, East New Britain, on Friday 19 January. The fact that he did not write that this was the *first* time he had heard about the Lamington unrest is perhaps a simple and unintended omission on his part. It contrasts quite strongly, however, with the detailed summary of events provided by volcanologist J.G. Best who arrived in Rabaul after the disaster to run the volcanological observatory in Taylor's absence and for years thereafter, working closely with him on volcanological matters in the Territory. John Best stated, writing assertively but 37 years after the events, that Taylor was aware of the Lamington unrest from radio broadcasts as early as Monday 15 January (Best 1988). This assertion at face value is questionable as the early changes to the mountain on that day were perhaps not all that newsworthy, unless a European correspondent in the Higaturu–Sangara area was keeping the radio station informed of events from the first day of the week. This is nothing less than historical speculation, however. What is known is that the district commissioner's wife, Mrs Amalya Cowley, contacted the radio station on Friday 19 January after Judge Phillips' peremptory departure from Popondetta.

Taylor was unable to reach Popondetta before Sunday 21 January because of a delay in decision-making by the district commissioner in Rabaul, J.K. McCarthy, during the working week of 15–19 January—at least according to John Best (1988). Taylor would have had very little time in which to arrange immediate aircraft flights to Popondetta, if indeed, as he wrote himself, he did not hear about the volcanic eruptions at Lamington until Friday 19 January. District Commissioner Cecil Cowley at Higaturu had expected the arrival of a volcanologist on the Friday, as stated quite clearly by Judge Phillips himself. Taylor was able to join the same flight that was taking the administrator back to Port Moresby on the Monday morning, but that was far too late. A further point is that Taylor would have had very little time to make a proper assessment of the volcanic conditions on the mountain if he arrived at Popondetta as late as the

Friday or Saturday. Indeed, he would probably have been killed had he decided to use Higaturu as his base for fieldwork on the flanks of Mount Lamington to the south.

5) 'Had any members of the Higaturu–Sangara community, before the disastrous eruption, communicated their personal views and fears to any member of the Administration?'

The answer to this question is certainly 'yes' given the written records of the fear and concern expressed to Judge Phillips by Mrs Cowley and by other European women at the Popondetta airstrip. Evacuation was very much on Mrs Cowley's mind. She and daughter Pam stayed overnight at Sangara Rubber Plantation on Saturday 20 January partly because of this fear and uncertainty of what might happen. Cecil Cowley himself was concerned and certainly discussed the situation with administration officers by radio on Thursday 18 January, although the nature of the conversation, what was said and how it was said remain unclear because of the radio interference caused by the eruptions.

6) 'Did any of the native population who had previously had experience of volcanoes communicate their opinions and then flee the district?'

There are two parts to this question. First, the only certain evidence of local people having experienced previous volcanic eruptions, and having communicated this to Europeans, is the case of the young Tufi cook at Sangara Plantation who had witnessed the eruptive activity at Goropu volcano in 1943–44. Other examples told by local Orokaiva in the form of 'myths' are too uncertain to have had any concrete value by, say, the end of 1952, as are the speculations that some of them may have been aware through their ancestors of the eruptive activity at Victory volcano in the late nineteenth century.

The second part of the question, dealing with local people fleeing the district, is an important one in assessing the 'preparedness' phase of the disaster management spectrum at Mount Lamington. Villagers self-evacuated from their homes high on the north-western flanks of the mountain, but they went only as far as Isivita Mission, because of the supporting presence there of trusted European missionaries. Cadet Patrol Officer Athol J. Earl had written from Higaturu to his parents on Thursday 18 January that: 'The native[s] from all around here deserted with all their belongings, however, I notice they had started to come back tonight' (Earl 1951, 2).

Further, missionary Rodd Hart said afterwards in an exchange with Reverend Romney Gill that the Sangara people would have self-evacuated were it not for the European's decision to stay (Garland 2000). Many Orokaiva may have had a natural inclination to flee, bearing in mind their traditional, although not necessarily volcanic, fears of the mountain. The Europeans—both administration and mission—who were carrying and displaying superior technical and religious knowledge were not fleeing, so many Orokaiva must have felt that this was a good enough reason for them to remain where they were. The Orokaiva unfortunately suffered from a lack of information and knowledge, as did the Europeans on whom they depended. Colonial policies for disaster prevention and preparedness did not exist in the Lamington area before the catastrophic eruption of 21 January 1951.

Relief, recovery, and trauma

There is little doubt that the Territory administration undertook the relief and recovery phases of the Lamington disaster under difficult circumstances yet with remarkable success. A key element of the achievement was the strong leadership provided by people such as Colonel Murray, Dr Gunther, Ivan Champion and Fred Kaad. Many of these leaders had had wartime experience, including with ANGAU, and this organisational ability shone through during the military-like, rapid deployment of aircraft and resources to the stricken area. Even the potentially disastrous flooding of the Wairopi evacuation camp was dealt with effectively once the potential threat had been identified. Then there were those people whose 'backroom' coordination role in Port Moresby was just as important. Acting Government Secretary Steve Lonergan is an outstanding example, of whom Dr Gunther said on the occasion of Lonergan's retirement in 1959: 'In getting the tools and the needs of the field party to them Mr Lonergan probably contributed more than any one other individual towards that great achievement' (Legislative Council Debates 1959, 577). Another attribute of the administration was its openness to outside advice, such as that offered by anthropologists Keesing and Belshaw.

The administration and the Anglican mission also provided outstanding medical service. Burns were treated for those victims who were not evacuated, serious outbreaks of epidemics were controlled through inoculation programs, and treatment was provided for people who were scalded after venturing through the hot waters of streams draining off the volcano. The treatment of physical injuries was, therefore, done well in what were stressful circumstances. Post-recovery mental health issues were dealt with less obviously. Post-traumatic stress disorder was not an expression that was used in the early 1950s. Its partial equivalent, 'shell-shock', was seen by military authorities in the two world wars but not always sympathetically, particularly in World War I when some strong military men may have equated it with mental weakness. Post-traumatic stress disorder must be assumed to have been prevalent among both the Orokaiva and Europeans in the years after the 1951 eruption, at least based on a few known examples.

Keesing, in 'The Papuan Orokaiva vs Mt Lamington: Cultural Shock and its Aftermath', wrote that the Lamington disaster produced 'cultural trauma of the first magnitude'. He witnessed the overt emotional stress in the Ilimo camp and asked whether this type of response was something culturally innate or an effect of the constrained, controlled environment of the refugee camps plus grief and uncertainty about future. His concluding impression was that, 'subject to inevitable factors of shock and disorganization, the Orokaiva were culturally predisposed to respond to the traumatic experience here described with something approaching maximum adaptability' (Keesing 1952, 18). That broad, positive cultural response, however, almost certainly hid individual cases of trauma.

Struggles of coping with loss, grief and trauma continued long after the closure of the refugee camps. Mission teacher Mrs Ray Kendall referred to boys in her class who had been playing cricket in one of the villages that was destroyed by the eruption. They managed to escape, but in Mrs Kendall's class a year later:

> They were angry they were difficult (LOST—everything). I knew nothing about Helen Kubler Ross's stages of grief—I wouldn't let them talk about it because it upset them. If only I had known better. (Kendall 2006, 3; Kübler-Ross [1969])

Mrs Kendall also wrote about a local woman, Rebecca, whom she knew. Rebecca was down at a stream collecting water at the time of the eruption and she returned to find her husband and all six children dead. Rebecca committed suicide about a year later. The number of suicides among the Orokaiva that can be attributed to the disaster is unknown but should be born in mind in considering any final, exact, death toll.

The Anglican Church must have played an important role in its use of prayer, ceremonies and church building as a de facto 'grief counselling' service. The building of the new and impressive St James Church is an example of how 'therapy' (Kendall 1988) may have helped not only the surviving parishioners but also Bishop Hand—his authoritarian and combative conflicts with the administration being another possible example of grief-related anger and unresolved frustration. Other Europeans were notably affected by trauma and loss too. The example given of patrol officers Des Martin and Bob Blaikie and their exhausting and emotionally demanding work—and their transfer out of the disaster area—is but one (Blaikie 2007; Martin 2007–15, 2013). Two other cases relate to Marie Reay and Pam Virtue.

Marie Reay, after her evacuation from Wasita and aborted fieldwork in the Territory, suffered a nervous breakdown on her return to Sydney (Glick and Beckett 2005). Her former colleague at the Australian School of Pacific Administration, Australian lawyer and later judge Hal Wooten, recalled 'visiting her in hospital with other colleagues, when she did not recognise us' (Wooten quoted in Glick and Beckett 2005, 395). Dr Reay, however, did return to the Territory—in 1953, beginning new fieldwork and a long association with the peoples of the Highlands region (e.g. Reay 1992), but not to the Northern District.

A story of grief, trauma and some later catharsis is seen in the post-disaster lives of Amalya Cowley and daughter Pamela who returned to a new life in Sydney without husband and father Cecil and son and brother Erl. Amalya Cowley died in 1999 but her memoirs formed the basis of a book *The Volcano's Wife*, which was compiled and expanded by Pamela, now Mrs Virtue. Amalya Cowley began writing her memoirs in 1995 at the age of 90: 'she took out her trusty Remington typewriter, which had somehow survived being buried in volcanic ash, and began typing' (Cowley and Virtue 2015, 9). The book ends with descriptions of the emotional return in 2003 and 2004 of Pam and her late husband, Gerry, to Popondetta and the site of old Higaturu. They could not find the burial places of Cecil and Erl Cowley in the neglected and overgrown memorial cemetery as all of the white marker crosses had been removed from individual graves.

Tony Taylor's important account of the 1951 eruption was published in 1958. By this time, and after the award of his George Cross for courage, Taylor had been acclaimed publicly as a scientist hero, and his work had an international impact volcanologically. His account was very much a scientifically clinical report. Taylor acknowledged particularly the strong practical support provided to him by Colonel Murray, and also the help of His Honour Brigadier D.M. Cleland CBE. No mention was made of the Judge Phillips controversy, nor of the public comments surrounding Taylor's perceived late arrival from Rabaul to the disaster area. Dr N.H. Fisher wrote the foreword, extolling the value of Taylor's account and his talent in narrative writing, but also producing the following statement:

> Mt Lamington was not merely regarded as extinct—it was not even considered as a volcano at all. The presence of a crater had not been recognized—it had not been examined by a geologist—and, being completely open on the northern side, it appeared only as one of the heads of the stream system of the Ambogo river, which rises in a series of rugged hills. (Fisher in Taylor 1958, foreword)

9
LEAD-UP TO INDEPENDENCE

CSIRO on Mount Lamington

Jim Sinclair, a *kiap* who would later become well known as an author and historian of Papua New Guinea, went to the Northern District at the end of 1952 just before Christmas:

> Popondetta was not an impressive station … the crude emergency accommodation hastily constructed [after the 1951 disaster] … to house the great influx of relief workers still stood. A lot had been achieved, but much remained to be done. (Sinclair 1981, 100)

Compared with the old Higaturu, Popondetta was not nearly as attractive and inspiring a location (e.g. *Pacific Islands Monthly* 1951f), and persuading administration staff to occupy positions at Popondetta must have been inherently problematic. Further, staff of the Department of Agriculture, Stock and Fisheries were reported as having been withdrawn from the Northern District 'once the need for producing food for relief measure had passed … Interest waned and was reported to be "completely dead" in 1953' (Waddell and Krinks 1968, 16).

There is an impression here of post-disaster, administration fatigue—a vacuum, perhaps created in part by the departure of Murray, but probably more so by the lack of resources needed to make significant, ongoing improvements in the still isolated and recovering district in the early 1950s. Even the volcanologist Tony Taylor had departed after two years of fieldwork in the area. Taylor spent part of the next few years at the Bureau of Mineral Resources, Geology and Geophysics (BMR) headquarters in Canberra writing his major report on the 1951 eruption, but he maintained a strong commitment to work on other active volcanoes in the Territory. Volcanologist John Best continued running the volcanological observatory in Rabaul in Taylor's absence, and was heavily involved with Taylor and new recruit Max A. Reynolds in assessing several eruptions at other volcanoes during 1953–57, none of which, however, included Lamington. There would be, nevertheless, a considerable amount of further interest paid to Lamington volcano over the next 20 years—up to the time of self-government for Papua and New Guinea in 1973—and, further, to 1975 when Papua New Guinea achieved independence from Australian rule.

An announcement was published in the *Pacific Islands Monthly* of February 1953 advising that a team of government scientists from Australia would be starting a major land resources survey of the Territory, beginning in the Northern Division (*Pacific Islands Monthly* 1953a). The first study area, 'Buna–Kokoda', was the one that included Mount Lamington and its disaster area. The team was from the Land Resources and Regional Survey Section of the Australian Government's Commonwealth Scientific and Industrial Research Organisation (CSIRO), newly named in 1949. An advance team, led by Dr C.S. Christian, had visited the Territory in January 1953 and the field party itself arrived in early July (*Pacific Islands Monthly* 1953b). A request for CSIRO's involvement in survey work for postwar development purposes in the Territory can be traced back to Administrator Colonel J.K. Murray in 1947, as can the decision to start with the Mount Lamington area—Murray prioritised Mount Lamington in May 1951, shortly before his removal as administrator (McAlpine 2017; Keig et al. 2019). The Buna–Kokoda study was the first of 15 land resource surveys conducted by CSIRO in the Territory up to 1973. The Wanigela–Cape Vogel area immediately south-east of Mount Lamington was the second area to be studied.

The survey methodology adopted by CSIRO was innovative. It involved conducting integrated land resource surveys rapidly, and it adopted a multidisciplinary approach aimed at assessing land use potential for agricultural and other developmental purposes by using the skills of a range of scientists—mainly geomorphologists, pedologists, plant ecologists, botanists, foresters and climatologists (Christian 1958; Christian and Stewart 1964; Blake and Paijmans 1973; Keig et al. 2019; Bellamy 2019).

The survey teams used new, cloud-free aerial photography as a basis for the mapping, and they defined and mapped so-called 'land systems'—that is, areas or an area where there is a recurring pattern of 'land units', each with its own distinctive combination of topography, soil and vegetation. As many as 30 land systems were identified in the Buna–Kokoda area, for example.

The early CSIRO surveys undertaken in north-eastern Papua were not without difficulties. Postwar land survey techniques had been developed in the arid and semi-arid areas of northern Australia and adapting the methodologies in the early 1950s to the tropical climate, vegetation cover and mountainous terrains of Papua were challenging, and more so initially. Access was difficult and helicopter support was not used until later years. Another important limitation in the early years was the unsuitability over large areas of existing aerial photographic and topographic map coverage. New aerial photography had to be obtained. Additional challenges facing the two initial land surveys immediately following the 1951 Lamington eruption included the extensive ash cover on much of the landscape as well as the social impact of so many deaths. All of these challenges, and others, meant that the reports and coloured maps for the first two land survey sheets could not be published until 1964—that is, 10 years after completion of the surveys (Haantjens et al. [1964a] 2010a, [1964b] 2010b). Notable later successes, however, were also achieved by climatologists, including those from The Australian National University (ANU), in their provision of meteorological data compilations for the Territory and region—for example, for rainfall and wind (Brookfield and Hart 1966; Fitzpatrick, Hart and Brookfield 1966; McAlpine, Keig and Short 1975). These compilations were invaluable not only for the CSIRO land surveys themselves but also for later volcanological hazard assessments.

Several conclusions of volcanological and disaster management significance to the Lamington story can be highlighted from the final CSIRO report and maps for the Buna–Kokoda area. First, a clear age differentiation is made on the main accompanying map (Figure 9.1) between the young Lamington volcano in the west and the larger, but older Hydrographers Range in the east, unlike in previously published, coloured, geological maps up to this time (Figures 2.3 and 3.5).

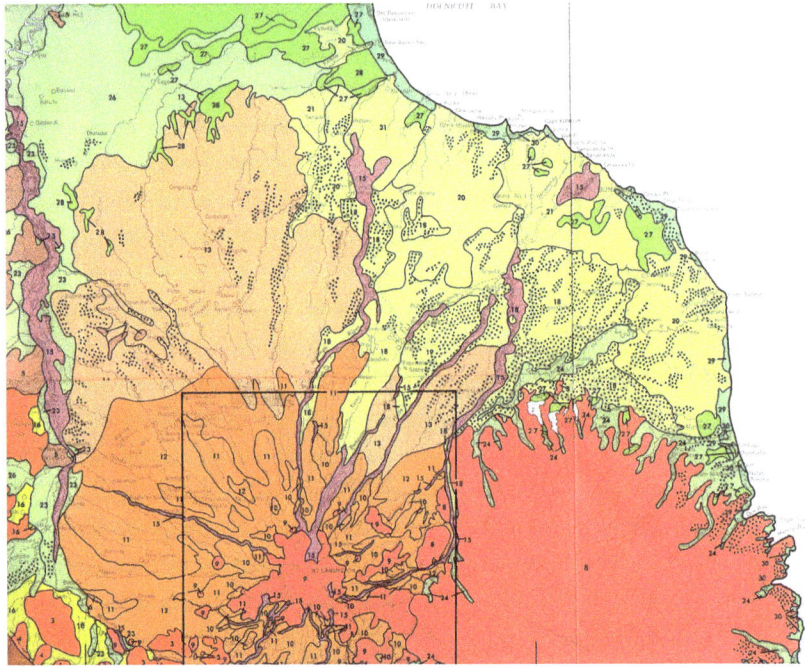

Figure 9.1. Part of the CSIRO land use map

The width of the outlined box from this map by Haantjens et al. ([1964a] 2010a) is equivalent to about 22 kilometres from east to west and refers to the enlarged map shown in Figure 9.2. The southern edge of the Lamington volcano is outside the southern limit of the Buna–Kokoda sheet area (see Ruxton et al. [1967] 2010, however, who map this southern area but at a larger scale). One of the land systems, called Oivi (number 3 in the south-west corner), consists of ultramafic and mafic rock, which are illustrative of the close proximity of the volcano to the Papuan Ultramafic Belt and Owen Stanley Range. Reproduced with the permission of CSIRO Publishing.

Second, as many as 11 different land systems are numbered for a smaller area encompassing Mount Lamington and within the box shown in Figure 9.1. One of these, number 15, is called the 'Ambogo' land system, which is readily seen on the map by the several narrow, irregular strips—coloured in mauve—like streams escaping from the summit area. These are particularly noticeable on the northern and north-eastern side of the mountain, including along the Ambogo River itself, almost reaching the coast. One patch is actually at the coast, near Buna. This land system is described as a 'complex' consisting of 1) slopes made up of mudflow and pyroclastic flow deposits including those of the 1951 eruption, 2) a piedmont and flood plain and 3) a volcanic outwash plain. Many of these deposits occupy pre-existing valleys that are dangerous because of the propensity of rapidly descending mudflows and pyroclastic flows to follow them, as experienced during 1951. The ridges or interfluves between the valleys, however, are not necessarily safer places during larger eruptions where widespread hot 'ash hurricane' may blanket much larger areas, as on 21 January 1951.

A third notable point is the mapping of numerous 'satellite', 'adventive' or 'parasitic' volcanic features on the western side of the mountain, as shown on a separate and more detailed map (Figure 9.2). Many of these minor features can be seen also on the oblique aerial photograph taken in 1947 (Figure 3.9). They are small, geologically youthful extrusions of lava that have formed domes and coulées, together with a few small cones probably made up of ash and other types of pyroclastic material. Note how many of these features are sited within a broad band running east-north-eastwards up the western flank of the volcano and encompassing the summit area, as shown by the two red dashed lines. This may define a zone of weakness on this part of the volcano where small eruptions can break out in different places, rather than from the summit crater alone. A rift-like zone of linear fractures can also be seen on the 1947 aerial photograph (Figure 3.9). Three adventive features on the lower south-eastern flank of the volcano, however, are not part of this zone. The geological history of the whole zone is unknown but these sites of satellite volcanic activity cannot yet be claimed to be major sites of explosive volcanism. They may, however, represent minor eruptive activity that is younger than the latest major explosive eruption at Lamington before 1951.

A fourth aspect of the CSIRO study of Mount Lamington is the determination of the times and rates at which different plant species recovered in the disaster area. This was potentially of more interest to volcanology in general, as it involved the dating of old areas of volcanic destruction where the precise age of the eruption may have been unknown (Taylor 1958). CSIRO plant ecologist B.W. Taylor gave particular attention to this aspect of the land use survey in 1953, visiting not only Lamington but also the previously devastated Papuan volcanoes of Mount Victory and Goropu volcano (Taylor 1957).

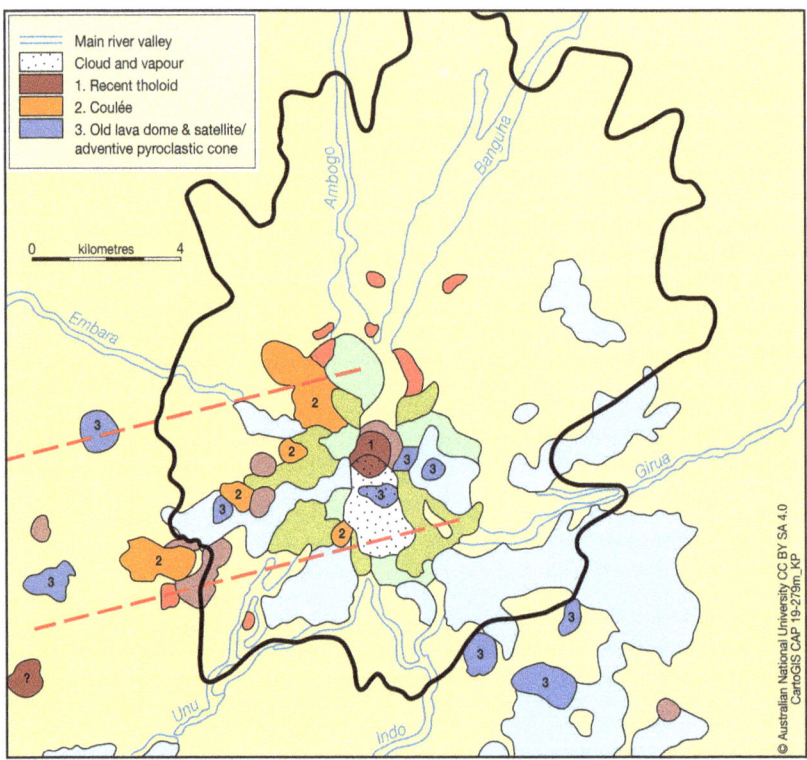

Figure 9.2. Land use 'units' in the Lamington area

Eleven different 'units' are distinguished in this map of the 'Lamington' land system (number 9) by Haantjens et al. ([1964a] 2010a), showing them in different colours and shades (compare with Figure 9.1). These were mapped relative to the limit of complete destruction of vegetation caused by the eruption of 21 January 1951 (the solid thick black line; after Taylor 1958). Numbers have been added to this adapted figure for only three of the 11 units as follows: 1) a 'recent tholoid' shown in red and referring to a) the central lava dome created within the summit crater in 1951–52 and including talus on its north-eastern side (the stippled area represents cloud and vapour from the still-hot tholoid seen on aerial photographs) and b) a 'recent tholoid' in the bottom left-hand corner that must be presumed to be older than the central 1951 lava dome; 2) coulées or thick, bulbous lava flows; 3) old lava domes and satellite/adventive pyroclastic cones. Note also that the feature in the bottom left-hand corner (see 1b above) is on fairly flat ground north-west of the Asopa airstrip and well away from the base of the Lamington cone. Compare this map with the digital elevation model image in Figure 10.1.

Finally, scientists from the CSIRO Cement and Ceramics Section in Melbourne tested the physical 'pozzolanic' qualities of ash samples from the 1951 eruption (Alexander and Vivian 1957). The scientists concluded that the ash could indeed be mixed satisfactorily with Portland cement in the production of concrete, perhaps for local use.

Ruxton on the Managalese Plateau

Another CSIRO land resource field team mapped the 'Safia–Pongani' sheet area south and south-east of Mount Lamington in 1963–64. Only the extreme southern tip of the Lamington cone itself is seen on this sheet area, but volcanic ashes from the volcano are found considerable distances south-east of the mountain. The ash cover 32 kilometres south-east from the Lamington crater is as much as 12 metres thick on the Safia–Pongani sheet (Ruxton 1966a). Such a thickness is an attraction to any geologist interested in reconstructing the life history of a volcano, and CSIRO geologist Bryan P. Ruxton took up the challenge, reporting widely on his findings (Ruxton 1966a, 1966b, 1988, 1999; Ruxton et al. [1967] 2010; Ruxton and McDougall 1967).

Ruxton was aware of the limitations of his published conclusions. First, the ash cover was not well exposed because of the extensive tropical vegetation. Many pits and auger holes had to be dug and sections along footpaths scraped away to reveal the ash layers, and only the upper sixth of the ash mantle was studied in detail anyway. The fine ash of the 1951 eruption was barely represented in Ruxton's study, much of it having drifted onto forest canopies and 'lost' in the underlying leaf litter of the forest floor. Ruxton also recognised that he was studying ash sequences on only one side of the volcano, and that sequences elsewhere, deposited by different winds, might be quite different. This is an important point as there is meteorological evidence from Port Moresby that winds higher than about 5,000 metres above sea level blow east to west all year round in Papua (Figure 9.3). This is in contrast to winds below 5,000 metres, which change from north-westerly during the 'wet' monsoonal season to south-easterly during the 'dry' season of south-east trade winds.

Ruxton (1966a) collected about 300 ash samples for later laboratory study of grain size and mineral content, but even these did not help greatly in distinguishing marked differences between the different ashes in any one section or between sections. Further, the ashes were weathered and coloured by oxidation of iron oxides in different degrees, inhibiting recognition of the deposits of individual eruptions. All of the ashes were of the air-fall type and none were recognised as having been deposited by pyroclastic flows. However, the presence of buried soil layers, signifying breaks in eruptive activity, were helpful, as were four radiocarbon dates on charred wood fragments.

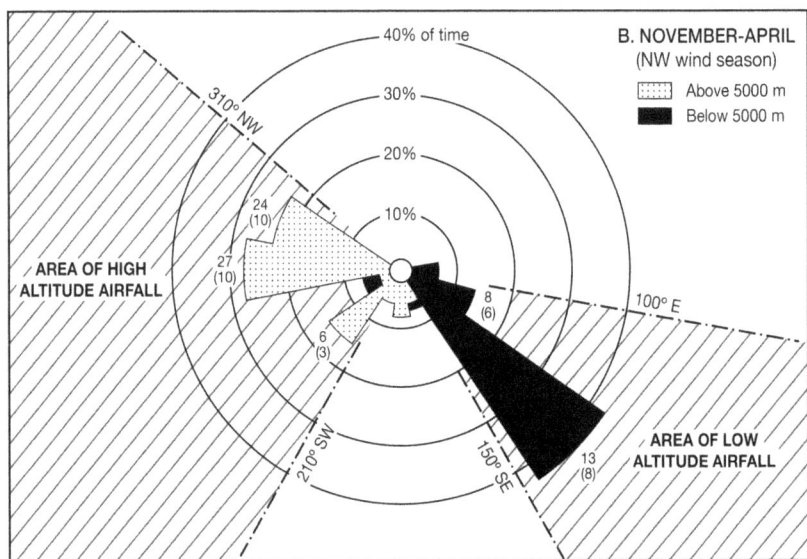

Figure 9.3. Wind directions at Port Moresby above and below 5,000 metres

Wind data for the north-west monsoonal season from November to April are shown in this 'rose' diagram by the stipple and solid patterns respectively (de Saint Ours 1988; only the lower part of his fig. 4 is shown here). The meteorological data used are from McAlpine, Keig and Short (1975), and the extent to which they can be applied in detail to Mount Lamington is uncertain. The length of each sector is proportional to the time that winds blow in the plotted direction during this period. The numbers given for each sector are the maximum wind velocities given in knots (about 2 kilometres per hour) and the average wind velocity is given inside brackets. The wide fan-shaped and crosshatched areas represent the expected dispersion of air-fall ash, as suggested by de Saint Ours (1988).

Ruxton, despite these limitations, cautiously concluded the following:

1. Mount Lamington may have been inactive for well over 1,000 years prior to the 1951 eruption. This conclusion was on the basis of the age—supported by radiocarbon dates—of the youngest studied ash layer, the Silimbu Ash, which had 23 centimetres of topsoil developed on it. The conclusion needs to be qualified, however, because Ruxton did not address the possibility of younger ages for smaller eruptions whose deposits are more difficult to recognise, including those from the minor, well-formed, satellite volcanoes on the western side of the Lamington cone (Figure 9.2).

2. Each of three 'depositional units' in the upper-ash cover probably had durations of about 4–5,500 years, and separated by about 1,000 years in inactivity.

3. The character of the upper-ash layers corresponded to 'a discontinuous pattern of eruptive activity … an alternation of series of closely spaced larger explosions and periods with much smaller explosions or quiescence' (Ruxton 1966a, 63).
4. The age of Mount Lamington as a whole is probably less than 110,000 years—most likely within the range of 80–100,000 years.
5. Explosive activity may have changed during evolution of the volcano as the result of a decrease in the proportion of eruptions producing ash fall deposits, together with a complementary increase in those producing pyroclastic flows. This conclusion, however, presupposes that ash falls from the distal parts of early pyroclastic flows are not represented in the sections studied by Ruxton.

Determining the 'periodicity' of catastrophic eruptions that produce deadly pyroclastic flows at Mount Lamington continues to be a major challenge for volcanologists today, and Ruxton's work still represents the only published attempt to find a practical answer that might be useful for disaster management purposes.

Ruxton in 1967 also visited an archaeological site at Kosipe about 140 kilometres west of Mount Lamington and 135 kilometres north of Port Moresby. The surface layers at the site were identified as weathered volcanic ash, four of which were the ash 'depositional units' that Ruxton had recognised and named previously on the Managalase Plateau south-east of Lamington (White, Crook and Ruxton 1970). The full sequence, however, could not be observed and there had been some observable local thickening and redistribution of the ash. Nothing further was concluded on the subject of eruption periodicity, but the work demonstrated the potential for integrated field studies of Lamington ash deposits in other parts of the area around the volcano. It also demonstrated how volcanic ash, if correctly identified as originating from Mount Lamington, could be deposited well to the west of the volcano from the high-level east to west winds even during the 'north-west' season of low-level winds (Figure 9.3).

The ashes of Mount Lamington were just one of the subjects of volcanological interest to Bryan Ruxton during the mapping of the Safia–Pongani area. Another was the nature of the youthfully volcanic Managalese Plateau to the south-east of Lamington where about 30 small volcanic centres were defined. One of these was Mount Manna, a small volcano that Ruxton suspected had produced ashes that had slightly 'contaminated' the Lamington ash cover he had been studying. Two other minor volcanic centres on the plateau were together near Kururi, close to Afore, where a small pyroclastic cone and nearby explosion crater were reported by Ruxton as having been 'active in village memory' (Ruxton 1966b, 351; Figure 9.4). The precise age of the eruptions is not known but the activity may have been between the two world wars, or possibly even roughly synchronous with the eruptive activity at Goropu volcano in 1943–44 (Ruxton 2007). Kururi's name, then, can be added to the list of volcanoes in Papua known to have been historically active up to 1951—Victory, Goropu, Lamington and Kururi.

Figure 9.4. Kururi cone on the Managalase Plateau

This grass-covered pyroclastic cone is at Kururi in the western part of the Managalase Plateau (rephotographed from Ruxton et al. [1967] 2010, plate 9, fig. 2). B.P. Ruxton and K. Paijmans dug an auger hole on the summit of the volcanic cone but found only basaltic scoriae and no appreciable soil, consistent with the volcano's youthfulness (Ruxton 2007). Reproduced with the permission of CSIRO Publishing.

More Colonial Research and Surveying

The second of the 15 map sheets to be surveyed by a CSIRO land resources team was the 'Wanigela–Cape Vogel' area south-east of Mount Lamington (Haantjens et al. [1964b] 2010b; Keig et al. 2019). This survey took place in 1954 but, again, the published report did not appear until 1964. The map's area includes both Victory and Goropu, or Waiowa, volcanoes. Plant ecologist B.W. Taylor was part of the CSIRO team and he reported on 'succession' vegetation on what he called the 'blast areas' of both volcanoes and of Mount Lamington (Taylor 1957, 1964).

Taylor (1957) concluded that as much as 400 square kilometres of vegetation had been destroyed on Victory by its late nineteenth-century eruption, an area twice the size of the area of total devastation on Lamington in 1951. Four 'land systems' were mapped on Victory, reflecting different zones of vegetation, but little attention could be paid to studying all of them, and no follow-up surveys were undertaken that might have provided a longer time series of vegetation changes. The western slopes of Mount Victory had been referred to by Captain Moresby in 1874 as 'open grassy and wooded slopes, which have all the appearance of English parkland' (Moresby 1876, 276). These were likely to have been areas burnt regularly by the Orokaiva who appear to have abandoned this practice post-eruption, after which the area became invaded by secondary forest growth.

Another Australian Government geoscience agency, the BMR, was also involved in systematic postwar mapping in eastern Papua. This survey work was part of a regional geological program aimed at covering the whole of the Territory at 1:250,000-scale as a basis for mineral and petroleum exploration and resource assessment (e.g. Wilkinson 1996). The geological results published for the area incorporating Lamington volcano were rather unusual in that the volcano was seen to have been built up on part of a massive slab of crustal and upper-mantle rocks that formerly had made up the deep floor of an ocean (Thompson and Fisher 1965). These rocks had been thrust up by powerful tectonic forces forming the so-called 'Papuan Ultramafic Belt' (PUB), which makes up the towering barrier of the Owen Stanley Range (Davies 1971). Small pieces of these distinctively dark PUB rocks could be seen in the light-coloured deposits and lava dome rocks produced by the Lamington eruption of 1951 (e.g. Taylor 1958). The PUB is known technically as an 'ophiolite' belt. It dips north-eastwards, possibly providing the sloping surface on which Lamington volcano was built later.

These broadscale geological or regional-tectonic relationships would form the basis for later discussions on why and how Lamington came to have grown at that particular place. In the meantime, one of the BMR geologists, Ian E.M. Smith, was taking a particular interest in all of the volcanic rocks, of different ages, in eastern Papua (e.g. Davies and Smith 1971). This included reporting separately on the volcanic geology of Mount Victory, results that complemented those obtained earlier by the CSIRO scientists (Smith 1969, 1981).

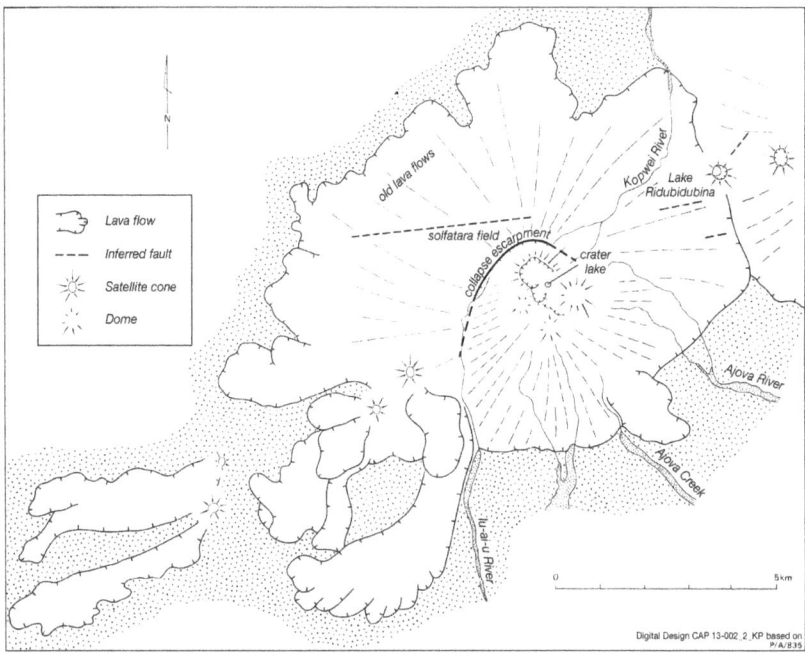

Figure 9.5. Volcanic features of Mount Victory
This map is based almost entirely on the map published by I.E.M. Smith (1981, adapted from his fig. 2).

Victory is a 1,925-metre-high, somewhat asymmetric, volcanic cone (Figure 9.5). In the late 1960s, its summit area was dominated by a small crater complex and three lava domes, together with some thermal activity. These volcanic features appeared to have been built against a larger, parabolic, south-east facing crater wall. Other lava domes on Victory were found to the south-west and north-east of the summit on a line that extended towards Mount Trafalgar. 'Thick fresh looking ash deposits' were found in river valleys to the north-west and south-east, possibly corresponding to the 'burning rivers' noted by local people at the time of the late nineteenth-century explosive eruption (Smith 1969, 11). Eruptive activity likely continued into the early twentieth century, possibly at a time when lava domes, or a dome, were being emplaced and causing night-time glows that—like natural lighthouses—were seen by people on passing ships. The south-east-facing crater wall could be that of a debris-avalanche escarpment. The 'Wanigela' and 'Kopwei' land systems on Victory were found to consist of outwash fans of volcanic sands and gravel, and were best developed on the south-eastern side of the mountain (see map in Haantjens et al. [1964b] 2010b). Therefore, collapses of the volcano may have taken place preferentially in the same direction, although debris-avalanche deposits had not been recognised.

There are some notable similarities between Lamington and Victory volcanoes, even though little is known about their respective eruptive histories. Both are high, asymmetric, volcanic cones that have breached 'crater' walls facing the sea, together with fans of volcanic debris deposited preferentially in the same direction. Both volcanoes have numerous small lava domes, many of which are possibly restricted to defined zones on each mountain. Both have had apparently similar historical eruptions and both retained thermal activity for many years after their latest eruptions. These last points are the reasons why Dr Fisher (1957) included Lamington and Victory in Part V of the *Catalogue of the Active Volcanoes of the World including Solfatara Fields* published by the International Volcanological Association in 1957.

There are differences, however, between the two volcanoes. Victory is much further from the Owen Stanley Range. It also has numerous old lava flows that are more clearly recognisable on aerial photographs than at Lamington (Figure 9.5). Further, Bryan Ruxton thought that Victory was 'a much less vigorous producer of ash fall layers than Lamington' (Ruxton 1966a, 61). This was on the basis of only thin ash layers being preserved on nearby Trafalgar volcano (after Haantjens et al. [1964b] 2010b). Further, Ruxton did not recognise ashes from Victory in the ash-cover sequence he studied south-east of Mount Lamington, although identifying them would have been difficult.

New geoscientific staff from Australia began work at the Rabaul Volcanological Observatory (RVO) during the early 1960s. A seismograph and two tiltmeters for earthquake and ground-tilt recording, respectively, were installed 14 kilometres from the summit of Mount Lamington by the RVO in December 1960 at the Martyrs' Memorial School, now rebuilt at Agenahambo on the main Popondetta road (McKee 1976). Fairly regular inspections of the volcano were carried out during these years—some routinely, others in response to reports of increased vapour emission from the dome or other changes. Avalanching, explosions and changes to the height and shape of the dome had been noticed since 1955, and temperatures of over 300°C could be measured in some places on the dome. No unusual evidence was found, however, that Lamington was about to produce another eruption of the type seen on 21 January 1951. The dome not unexpectedly was cooling and changing slowly. An oblique aerial colour photograph of the dome was taken in 1962 by a *National Geographic* magazine photographer (Scofield 1962). RVO staff could use this exceptionally well-positioned and clear photograph for comparative purposes during their inspections (Figure 9.6; McKee 1976).

Figure 9.6. Oblique aerial view of summit area of Lamington

The summit lava dome in the avalanche amphitheatre of Mount Lamington is seen clearly in this photograph taken from the south in 1962 (Scofield 1962). Mild vapour emission is taking place from the top of the dome where there are small lava spines. Vegetation is now extensive on the outer flanks of the volcano, but less so on the lava dome and amphitheatre walls. Ingleby (1966) provided a description of the Lamington area as it was in 1966.

Other research personnel arrived in Port Moresby from Australia in the early 1960s. They were from the Research School of Pacific Studies (RSPAS) at ANU in Canberra, and they established in 1961 a New Guinea Research Unit (NGRU) (May 2006). This was not the first time that ANU RSPAS researchers had shown an interest in the Territory. The university had been created as a postwar venture in 1946 and three professors in history, geography, economics and related subjects from RSPAS visited the Territory on a reconnaissance trip between 14 October and 10 November 1951 (Spate, Davidson and Firth 1952). The aim was to explore potential areas of research that might be of interest to RSPAS. The three academics did not visit the Northern District and the Lamington disaster received very little mention, although one of the authors briefly listed 11 research topics, the eleventh of which was entitled 'Changes in the settlement pattern in the Mount Lamington area' (Spate 1952, 12–13).

NGRU research staff were mainly economists, sociologists and anthropologists, and their interests focused on indigenous land use, land tenure and relationships to monetary concepts that might underpin an economic future for the Territory once colonialism had ended. Substantial attention was paid to the Orokaiva in the post-disaster Northern District where there was already a history of cooperative movements, cash cropping schemes and economic development that had been deeply influenced by World War II (WWII) and by the disastrous Lamington eruption. Many reports on the Orokaiva were published in the NGRU Bulletin series (e.g. Crocombe 1964; Howlett 1965; Rimoldi 1966; New Guinea Research Bulletin 1966; Waddell and Krinks 1968; see also Newton 1985) as well as in university theses and published in peer-reviewed journals.

The first multiracial House of Assembly, a first parliament of elected members, met in 1964 (Downs 1980). Other important developments in Port Moresby included the start, also in 1964, of an Administration College and, in 1965, the creation of the University of Papua New Guinea (UPNG) (Meek 1982). New educational and political opportunities were being provided from this time onwards for Papua New Guineans at both institutions (Nelson 1972). The Administration College seeded the political influence of a progressive 'Committee of Thirteen'—Papua New Guineans who publicly proposed early self-government. The group had started out informally as the 'Bully Beef Club' but it led to the creation of the *Pangu Pati* (Nelson 1982). The future inaugural prime minister, Michael Somare, was a member of the 'angry Thirteen', and so too was Trobriand Islander Elliot Elijah, the MBE awardee who had been recognised for his services during the initial disaster relief phase at Mount Lamington in 1951.

UPNG also fostered the intellectual development of post-Independence leaders. John Waiko, for example, a Binandere man from Orokaiva country, was one of the first graduates from the university. He later joined UPNG as a lecturer in history before entering national politics (e.g. Waiko 2003). Further, one of the first UPNG graduates in geology in 1977 was Benjamin Talai, a man from the Duke of York Islands east of Rabaul, who would later become the first Papua New Guinean to lead the RVO (Talai 2006).

Sumbiripa and Science

Revised mythologies

Important anthropological fieldwork of disaster management significance was undertaken among the mountain Orokaiva during the 1960s by Dutch-born Erik Schwimmer, an anthropologist based at the University of Oregon in the US. His fieldwork was part of a larger, international, comparative study being run by his university on cultural change and stability in communities displaced by disasters of one kind or another. Schwimmer's comprehensive and insightful publications represent an important benchmark study of the mountain Orokaiva 15 years after the 1951 eruption (Schwimmer 1969, 1973, 1977).

Schwimmer selected three villages for his study. First was Sivepe on the western slopes of the mountain about 11 kilometres from the summit. Its people had fled the eruption and been accommodated at Wairopi and Ilimo evacuation camps. A large Anglican mission complex was established after the eruption near Sivepe at Sasembata that included a school, church and hospital (see also Kettle 1979). The second study village was a 'control group' of people at Inonda who had neither evacuated nor been relocated as a result of the disaster. Both Sivepe and Inonda had been studied previously by land use researchers from the NGRU. The third village studied by Schwimmer was Hohorita, population 348, which was made up of survivors from the now decimated Sangara people. They had built a recovery village at Irihambo, but were ordered to leave it some years later because it was found to be situated on Crown land intended for the settlement of Australian ex-servicemen. Hohorito was established in 1957–59 on the main road north-west of the former Sangara Mission Station. This involved abandoning the fine church they had built after the eruption at Irihambo and rebuilding another, less-impressive one at Hohorita (e.g. Schwimmer 1969, 1977).

Schwimmer introduced his substantial report of 1969 with the following words:

> Mount Lamington has long had, to the Orokaiva people, a significance somewhat similar to that of Mount Olympos [sic] to the Ancient Greeks. It is the omphalos kosmou [centre of the cosmos] of Orokaiva myth: the origin of death, warfare, fire—and generally of all those cultural elements established by the transforming deities—are traced to the Mountain, while the division of the people into distinct language groups is likewise a primordial event that occurred on the Mountain. The departed spirits of the Orokaiva have their home there, headed by the first man to have suffered death, Sumbiripa, to whom all the activity of the Mountain is ascribed. Signs from Sumbiripa reach the living regularly, because at all times the Mountain has rumbled and sent forth tremors and smoke.
>
> These facts appear clearly from the cycle of myths, centred on the Mountain, collected by me in the vernacular in 1966–1967. The cycle is far too elaborate to be explained as a recent development. It might, however, be argued that before the disaster of 1951, the omphalos kosmou was located elsewhere and that it has since been 'relocated' to Mount Lamington. (Schwimmer 1969, 5)

Four versions of the Sumbiripa-Kanekari legend were collected by Schwimmer from different communities who, however, were telling their stories 15 years after the 1951 eruption rather than before it. 'Kanekari' in these stories now means the 'separation' of Sumbiripa rather than 'shut in' as in the version of the myth recorded by Amalya Cowley in January 1951. All four versions deal with Sumbiri and his wife Suja—these are Schwimmer's spellings of the names—hunting on the mountain for several weeks. The mountain, in three of the versions, begins to rise because Sumbiri, ignoring a taboo, had sex with his wife. Several crags formed on the angry mountain and the couple became isolated on one of them, from which they leapt into a 'crater' formed between the crags. Orokaiva historian Maclaren Hiari also recorded that 'Sumbiri'—without the suffix 'pa'—is the name of a tribal warrior from the Angereufu clan of the Songe tribe (Hiari 2013).

Figure 9.7. Drawings of the Sumbiripa myth by Maine Winny and Louise Bass

Post-1951 versions of the Sumbiripa myth are captured in these two drawings. The one on the left is by Maine Winny (Johnston 1995, 12). Sumbiripa and his wife Suja and their dog are trapped in a hole on the mountain. Attempts by villagers to rescue them, apparently using a line of cane, are frustrated by the hole becoming deeper as the mountain grows higher, and they perish. This version of the myth was told in some detail by Cedrick S. Mimari of Kendata Village in 1987, assisted by his nephew Winterford Poraripa (Johnston 1995). The drawing is reproduced here courtesy of the Johnston family, Melbourne. Villagers in the sketch on the right by Louise Bass are dropping food into the hole for the trapped Sumbiripa. This drawing accompanied a short version of the legend written in Orokaiva by Joel Oreba (1976, 5).

A version of the myth told at Hohorita, where Sangara survivors of the eruption now lived, deals primarily with a fight between a pig and a large dog, or dogs, during which the mountain became divided into different parts or peaks. The accompanying man and woman became separated on different peaks where they died of loneliness and despair. Schwimmer (1969) said that this version was 'the richest in mythological content' (6). It could also be said to have 'geological content', although the creation of crags, peaks and craters is not mentioned in versions of the legend told before 21 January 1951.

Pre-eruption mythology does seem to have evolved to something different and more substantial after the 1951 eruption. This is not all that surprising given, first, the massive damage, disruption and trauma imposed on Orokaiva communities; second, the need to explain the unexpected disaster with equally dramatic and meaningful stories; and third, the fact that any one story depends also on who is telling a particular version of it. By the 1960s, the name Sumbiripa was prominent in many different versions of the myth collected by different people at different times (e.g. Wodak 1969; Schwimmer 1969; Horne 1974a; Oreba 1976; Newton 1985; Johnston 1995; Radford 2012; Larsen 2017; see Figure 9.7). Further, by the mid-1960s, 'Sumbiripa' was the name being given locally to the mountain itself, in place of 'Lamington' (e.g. Radford 2012; see also Figure 9.8).

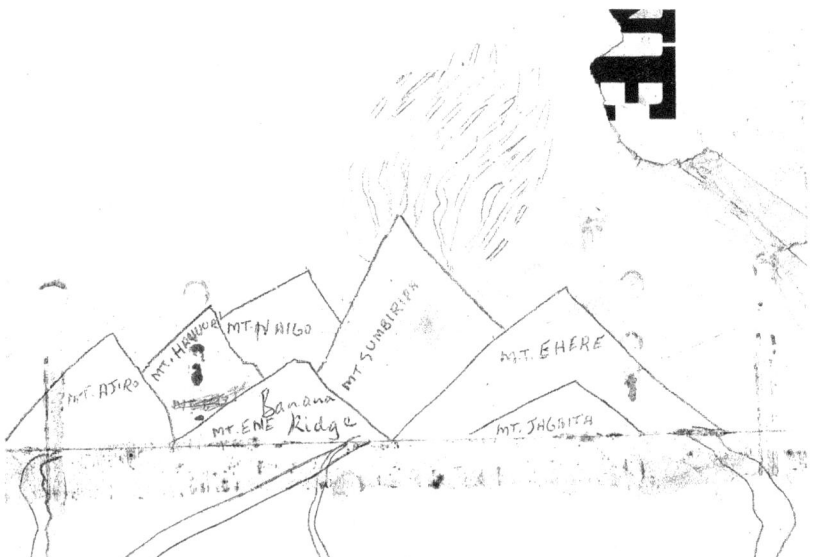

Figure 9.8. Local names for Lamington peaks drawn on old milk label
Water vapour is seen rising from the summit of Mount Sumbiripa, previously known as Mount Lamington. This sketch was drawn in 1969 on the label of a powdered milk container provided by an Orokaiva landowner called Barnabas who used only local names for the numerous peaks. The diagram was provided courtesy of Mr John R. Horne. Mr Horne himself later added the roads in the foreground and the name 'Banana Ridge'. The sketch of peaks used on the title pages of each of the four parts of this book is based on the drawing shown here.

The statement made by Schwimmer (1969, 5) that 'at all times the Mountain has rumbled and sent forth tremors and smoke' perhaps carries a hint that the Orokaiva had always known that Lamington, or Sumbiripa, was a 'volcano'. The word 'smoke' in this context could easily be equated with actual eruptive activity. Schwimmer could not confirm this, however, and later wrote that 'before 1951, Sumbiripa was not known by Orokaiva to have ever erupted' (Schwimmer 1977, 321). Extracting scientific interpretations from powerful and strongly told myths after disasters can be a fraught exercise, but one can conclude in the case of Mount Lamington that evidence of witnessed, undoubted, pre-1951 eruptive activity cannot be confidently obtained from the myths. Schwimmer himself was sensitive to such doubts when, in another context, he wrote that:

> The history of anthropology is a history of questions asked by westerners and related to western intellectual preoccupations. One might well argue that even those anthropologists who collect folk-explanations and folk-philosophies are pursuing western preoccupations, inasmuch as they write up their findings in the context of western scientific debate. (Schwimmer 1976, 34)

Does all of this mean that the mountain Orokaiva had no pre-1951 knowledge of what 'volcanic eruptions' were in a general sense and, perhaps, no specific word for them or for 'volcano'? Europeans were certainly aware that the Orokaiva treated the mountain with considerable respect and apprehension as the home of powerful spirits, as noted by Wilfred Beaver as early as 1913–14. The same local apprehension was also witnessed, for example, by the missionaries who climbed the mountain in the 1930s and heard 'roars' that, at the time, they could not explain. However, were the roars from the cascading waters of nearby torrents, or from more distant thunder storms, or from a small avalanche nearby, or from nearby earthquakes not related to the volcanic mountain? Before 1951, the latest major explosive eruption at Lamington may have been so long ago as to be 'lost' in cultural memory, but the same cannot be said necessarily about the smaller eruptions that are presumed to have created the geologically very youthful minor cones on the western flank of the mountain. These minor eruptions, speculatively, could have taken place within the last few centuries and, potentially, would be less vulnerable to cultural-memory loss.

The speculation by Schwimmer that 'the *omphalos kosmou* was located elsewhere and had since been "relocated" to Mount Lamington' is a tantalising one. Ruxton (1966a) concluded, tentatively, that Lamington may not have had a significant explosive eruption for about a thousand years before the one in 1951. To what extent, however, had stories about the powerful eruption at Mount Victory in the late nineteenth century infiltrated the cultural mores of the mountain Orokaiva in relation to their own stories about Mount Lamington and its 'roars'? Did some mountain Orokaiva see and hear the Victory eruption and pass the story on to descendants? The Baigona or Snake cargo cult of 1912 began at the summit of Victory volcano and news of the cult was known to have spread throughout much of Orokaiva country. To what extent also were similar stories about Victory distributed during the closely following and widespread Taro Cult (Figure 2.5). Did these stories carry with them accounts of the overwhelming fierceness of the devastating eruption at Mount Victory together with a derived understanding of 'the origin of death, warfare, [and] fire'? Further, had the reduction of conflicts between Orokaiva groups and the construction of the road between the coast and Kokoda across the slopes of Lamington—Monckton's 'Yodda Road' to the goldfields—brought about by the colonists provided greater opportunities for the sharing of information and stories across Orokaiva country?

The effects of the eruptions at Goropu in 1943–44 also must have been known quite widely by people in the Lamington area—and not just by Reverend Dennis Taylor and the concerned young Tufi cook at Sangara Plantation. People may have heard even about the minor volcanic eruptions at Kururi on the Managalase Plateau to the south.

Four explanations for the disaster

The dominant explanation for the 1951 eruption found by Schwimmer among the mountain Orokaiva was, not surprisingly, the anger of the mountain or of the mountain spirit Sumbiripa (Schwimmer 1969, 1977). The anger had been caused by loud noises—by disrespectful acts, such as grenades being thrown near the crater during the war and, after the war, Orokaiva, and especially the Sangara people, hunting on the mountain with newly acquired guns, thereby depleting the ready availability of meat.

A second version of this explanation noted by Schwimmer derives not from the mountain Orokaiva but from the coastal Yega people who were traditional enemies of the now decimated 'inlanders'. This information was contained in an undated, unpublished account written by Fred Kleckham probably shortly after the 1951 eruption. The Yega said that the anger of the mountain was being directed at the Europeans as payback for the hangings of the Orokaiva at Higaturu in 1943. The mountain Orokaiva do not seem to have been predisposed to such an explanation, as it does not explain why thousands of them also had to perish in the eruption as collateral damage. The Yega explanation may have resided somewhere within a cargo cult that was prevalent in 1951. The cult appears to have been politically benign—simply a magico-religious means of acquiring the same European knowledge that yielded wealth not yet possessed by the Yega (Schwimmer 1977). Revenge aimed against the Europeans and the tyranny of the hangings does not seem to have been an anti-colonial expression of the cult, although such a justification was warranted. A prophet at Buna also reported that before the eruption a coastal spirit had visited her and said that 'he was to be responsible for the eruption. He was ordered to come inland and blow up the mountain' (Opeba 1977, 228). A reason why the spirit had to undertake such drastic action does not accompany this very brief story.

A third explanation listed by Schwimmer is the now familiar one: that the wrath of the Christian but Jehovah-like God, rather than the anger of Sumbiripa, had caused the disaster because of transgressions by the Orokaiva. This was the dominant theme during the anthropological investigations undertaken in 1951 by Cyril Belshaw and Felix Keesing, neither of whom mention Sumbiripa by name in their separate reports. However, Christian Orokaiva interviewed by Schwimmer in 1966–67 were rejecting the wrath of God explanation as 'resting on a misunderstanding of the nature of God' (Schwimmer 1977, 317). The Anglican mission led by Bishop Hand and others must have made that point rather clearly following the 1951 disaster.

A general conclusion from Schwimmer's research was that the Orokaiva explanations, whether based on the anger of Sumbiripa, the Christian God or even the government, were consistent with a basic world view of the fundamental importance of exchange and reciprocity arrangements in all aspects of life (see also Schwimmer 1973). The Orokaiva would have believed that they had violated an agreement and, accordingly, that the volcanic disaster was a reciprocating punishment. Such a view is not all that dissimilar to Newton's Third Law of Motion: that for every action there is an equal and opposite reaction. Science, in fact, underpinned a fourth explanation for the disaster, but one that was held by only a minority of Orokaiva.

The fourth explanation is strictly geophysical: that volcanoes operate through natural laws that are quite unrelated to magical and religious beliefs. The Anglican mission itself put forward that scientific view after the 1951 eruption, which seems a rational and sensible step to take. However, according to Schwimmer, white planters and public servants claimed that the mission had been promulgating the false wrath of God explanation, and that now the mission was promoting the 'geophysical' explanation simply to counter that earlier criticism from the planters and public servants. In so doing, Schwimmer (1977, 319) concluded that the mission's critics were 'pursuing obscurantist and reprehensible power politics'.

Those Orokaiva who accepted the geophysical view, rather than a magical/religious one, now could regard themselves as modern people, members of a new elite, holding enlightened opinions that were the same as those of the knowledgeable Europeans. How many of these new elite Orokaiva asked why the all-knowing and powerful Europeans had not interpreted correctly the geophysical early warning signs of the catastrophic eruption? Were the Europeans at Higaturu Government Station and Sangara Mission at fault for not providing an early warning that might have saved thousands of Orokaiva lives? The second question is answered affirmatively today by the Orokaiva and some speak bitterly about the failure of the colonial administration to evacuate people (Stead 2018). Conversely, at least some Orokaiva have said that senior staff of both the administration at Higaturu and the local Anglican mission had recommended an evacuation (Didymus 1974; Cowley and Virtue 2015). Such disparate opinions are part of a more complex situation of remembrance and opinion that depend on context (Stead 2018).

Attributing the volcanic disaster to generally articulated 'geophysical' causes is acceptable in a modern, secular-rationalist society, but were those causes well understood and, more particularly, to what extent are those causes understood even today? Fundamental questions of causation needed to be explained. Why did Mount Lamington grow in that particular place? Where, how and when does the magma form deep in the earth beneath the volcano? Where is the magma stored, if it is 'stored' at all, and for how long before a major explosive eruption takes place? What are the factors that control the frequency, size and timing of major eruptions? Does installing volcano-monitoring equipment at Martyrs' School help answer the question of how the volcano operates as an integrated geophysical system? Remarkably, a geoscientific revolution was taking place in the late 1960s that carried at least some potential to answer some of these questions.

The BMR established a geophysical observatory in Port Moresby in 1957 as part of a broad network of earthquake and geomagnetic recording stations covering the Australian region (e.g. Denham 1969). Mapping the location of earthquakes taking place in the Territory had not been easy because of a deficiency of seismographs in the wider region, but this changed in 1964 when the World-Wide Standardized Seismograph Network (WWSSN) was established by the US. The WWSSN is used for the global monitoring of earthquakes and nuclear explosions. Improved earthquake mapping from numerous stations worldwide underpinned development of the revolutionary theory of plate tectonics that emerged in 1967–68 and whose impact became clearer during the early 1970s. The whole surface of the Earth is covered by tectonic 'plates'—some large, others small—that move relative to one another along linear, earthquake-defined boundaries. Explosive, andesitic volcanoes such as Mont Pelée in the Caribbean, Mount Fuji in Japan or Rhuapehu in New Zealand were shown to be near zones where two plates converge and where one of the plates is 'subducted' or underthrust beneath the other. The passage of a down-going plate into the Earth's upper mantle is tracked by increasingly deeper earthquakes. These were so-called 'Wadati-Benioff' earthquake zones, named after the seismologists who first identified them. Volcanoes that form above these down-going 'subducting slabs' typically produced magmas of andesitic composition, just like those of Lamington and Victory. The volcanoes related to any one subduction zone form long lines or 'arcs' parallel to the convergent plate boundary itself.

The Territory of Papua and New Guinea was demonstrated to have subduction zones, such as beneath New Britain and Bougainville Island. It also has numerous plate boundaries defining the margins of two major plates—named Pacific and Australian—as well as at least two minor, less well-defined plates sandwiched between them (e.g. Johnson and Molnar 1972). Both of the active volcanoes of Lamington and Victory are at the south-western margin of a 'Solomon Sea' plate where there is no active subduction (Figure 9.9). Rather, the earthquake zone here runs along or near the Owen Stanley Range including the large, near-vertical, Owen Stanley Fault and Timena Fault (Davies 1971). These and other vertical faults in the area were considered to represent evidence for pronounced uplift in geologically recent times, and to be associated with 'block-faulted' terrain such as Ruxton (1966a) had mapped in the Managalase area. Mount Lamington, therefore, was not conforming to the subduction zone model, meaning that generalisations about the behaviour of explosive volcanoes at subduction zones elsewhere could not necessarily be transferred to Lamington. Further, earthquakes may be felt, or heard, as roars in the vicinity of Mount Lamington that are of plate-tectonic rather than volcanic origin.

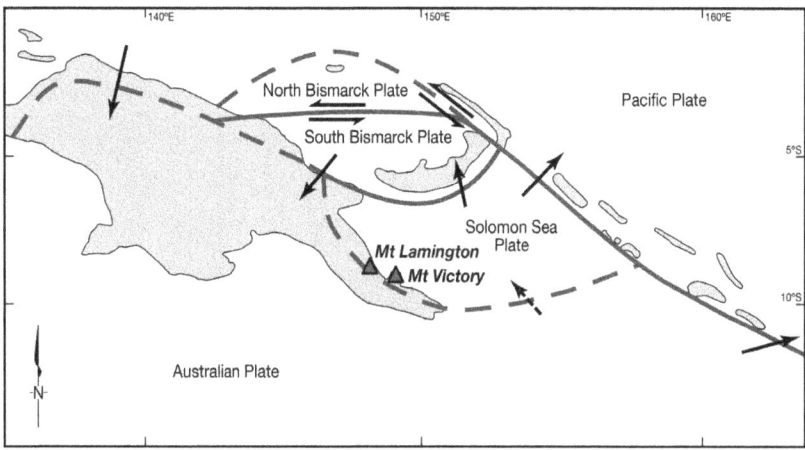

Figure 9.9. Plate boundaries in Papua New Guinea
The active volcanoes of Mount Lamington and Mount Victory are here plotted relative to the south-western margin of the minor Solomon Sea plate where no plate subduction is taking place currently (Johnson and Molnar 1972, adapted from fig. 2). This south-western margin is defined by uncommon tectonic earthquakes, many of which take place below the Owen Stanley Range. The short north-west pointing arrow to the east of Mount Victory refers to the same Solomon Sea plate boundary in the Woodlark Basin, which is where tectonic plates are moving apart from each other (see also, for example, Luyendyk, MacDonald and Bryan 1973). This version of plate boundary distribution in the Papua New Guinea region presented by Johnson and Molnar (1972) was the first of many to be published subsequently, not all of which, however, recognised the Owen Stanley Range as an active plate boundary.

Final Colonial Days

Inspections of the still-hot summit lava dome of Mount Lamington were undertaken by RVO volcanologists, and by others, in each of the years from 1970 to 1975 (McKee 1976). Some of these visits were in response to reports of increased volcanic activity at the volcano but all were identified as 'false alarms'. The temperatures of gas- and vapour-emitting areas known as fumaroles were measured fairly regularly, and condensates of gases were collected at times (Crick 1973). Permanent instrumental monitoring of Lamington volcano was enhanced in June 1970 when a seismograph and telemetry station were installed on the north-western flank of the volcano about 2 kilometres from the summit dome, thus permitting seismic signals to be transmitted by radio to a recorder in Popondetta (Figure 9.10).

Figure 9.10. Seismometer and radio link equipment on Lamington in 1972
The equipment on Mount Lamington is here being inspected by an RVO field team in 1972. The photograph was taken by J.E. Zwartko. Photograph supplied courtesy of Geoscience Australia (negative number GA/5957).

The Lamington/Popondetta recording station was used in 1973 during a major 'East Papua Crustal Survey' undertaken by seven, mainly Australian, geophysical agencies, including BMR and ANU. The joint team used a total of 42 recording stations in a broad belt across the entire Papuan Peninsula to determine the crustal structure beneath Mount Lamington (Finlayson et al. 1976). Numerous artificial explosions were fired from ships at sea to the north-east (in the Solomon Sea) and south-west (in the Coral Sea), and the seismic signals were recorded at the land-based stations. The broad structure of the PUB as an area of crustal thickening was confirmed, but the thickness of the crust beneath Lamington was found to be only 8 kilometres. Deeper structures, such as any seismically inactive subducted slabs, could not be determined by the survey.

Lamington was no longer in eruptive mode in the early 1970s, but other volcanoes in the Territory certainly were. Six volcanoes along the southern margin of the South Bismarck plate (Figure 9.9) were volcanically active during 1972–75 in a remarkable 'time cluster' of eruptions (Cooke et al. 1976). One of the six volcanoes was Manam Island, which broke out in eruption in May 1974 after a period of eight years of relative inactivity. Manam volcano always had been of strong professional interest to volcanologist Tony Taylor and, in 1972, he undertook a field inspection of the volcano. Tragically, Taylor died on the island on 19 August, apparently from a heart attack after returning from a climb towards the summit crater (Fisher 1976).

G.A.M. Taylor's unexpected death in 1972 represented the end of a pioneering, postwar period for volcanologists working in the Territory of Papua and New Guinea. The imminent and inevitable end of the longer era of Australian colonialism was also becoming more obvious to indigenous people throughout the Territory, as well as to the Australian Government and the United Nations (e.g. Downs 1980; Meek 1982; Nelson 1982; Denoon 2005). Local 'micro-national' or 'sub-national' political movements emerged in different parts of the Territory, some of them espousing elements of separatism and local independence. The vigorous Mataungan Association, for example, was created in the Rabaul area in 1969, its political aspirations publicised when, in 1971, the European district commissioner, Jack Emmanuel, was murdered during what may have been a quite local misunderstanding and altercation. Two other examples are the Napidakoe Navitu political group, which represented the future interests of people on Bougainville Island, and the Papua Basena party, which was led by Josephine Abaijah, a charismatic activist who campaigned for Papuan separatism. The whole Territory took a major step towards its new status of nation-state when, in 1972, a national coalition government was formed. Its chief minister was Michael Somare, leader of the clearly nationalistic Pangu Pati.

Nationalist rather than separatist sentiments were being expressed at this time in the Northern District. Paulus Arek, who was born in Wanigela, had been the headmaster at the Popondetta primary school and, in 1968, he nominated for the Ijivitari Open electorate (Langmore 1993). Arek won convincingly—and was re-elected in 1972. Arek had a forceful, outspoken and flamboyant personality, and was an ardent nationalist, serious-minded politician and trade unionist. He was sympathetic with the nationalistic views of the Pangu Pati but became a member of Julius Chan's People's Progress Party. Paulus Arek proposed in 1969 that an all-parties committee be established in Port Moresby to consider the constitutional development of a future self-governing country. The report of the 'Arek Select Committee' released in 1971 contained proposals for the structure of parliament and electorates as well as blueprints for self-government and independence (e.g. Langmore 1993; Denoon 2005).

The district commissioner of the Northern District at this time of political change was David R.M. Marsh. He had begun his service as the district commissioner in Popondetta in 1968 and had attended the opening of the Mount Lamington Memorial Cemetery in the town in 1952 (Marsh 2005–08). The significance and symbolism of the colonial memorial cemetery came under scrutiny during his time as district commissioner from aspiring leaders and other 'big men' in the Popondetta area. Marsh had to manage the situation as diplomatically as he could, not only on behalf of the administration, but also of the Australian Government, which was largely in favour of the resolute trend towards self-government and independence, more so after Gough Whitlam, leader of the Australian Labor Party, became prime minister in 1972.

None of the thousands of villagers killed by the Lamington eruption of 1951 were buried in the Mount Lamington Memorial Cemetery. Further, the burials there had been of bones disinterred by Sub-Inspector George Allen and then reburied at Popondetta in 1952, after a period in police storage. How were the remains identified? Some of the European bodies had never been found and the Anglican mission had buried its own European dead, so who was actually buried in the cemetery? The question was raised in Marsh's mind, and no doubt in others, of whether the park was, in fact, a memorial rather than a true 'cemetery'. Marsh made two decisions: first, to have the individual white crosses removed from the park; second, for the accompanying identification plaques at each of the former burial sites to be shifted to the centre of the park near the generic memorial plaque. These removals of personal identity would lead to unpleasant disputes several decades later, and to disaffection among those European relatives of the deceased who wanted to visit grave sites in what had become an unkempt and deteriorating park (Marsh 2005–08; Speer 2005–14).

Self-Government Day was declared on 1 December 1973. Arek had died of cancer on 22 November 1973, just eight days earlier. Independence Day was celebrated on 16 September 1975.

One final contribution from the Australian colonial period—one that has disaster management significance—is a topographic map entitled 'Popondetta' that was published by the Australian military in 1974 for general use (Royal Australian Survey Corps 1974). The map is at 1:100,000 scale and was produced from triangulation surveys and from aerial photographs flown in 1973, supplemented by track and village information taken from patrol reports up to 1973. The volcano is named Mount Lamington rather than Sumbiripa. The value of the map rests in providing a benchmark record of settlement and infrastructure in the Lamington area, defining the layout of the road and track system and so on as they were in 1974 at the end of Australian colonialism. The map can also be taken as marking the end of the disaster recovery phase of the 1951–52 eruption but only in the sense that recovery and resettlement gradually migrate into future development strategies informed by the experiences of the past.

The old sites of the Higaturu Government Station, Sangara Mission and nearby villages are not on the map. Isivita is not shown either, but a foot track runs from Kendata on the north-western flank of the mountain down to Sasembata Mission, and a road then runs through Sivepe to the main road at Waseta. The main road along the northern side of the mountain eastwards to Popondetta has a string of settlements, including two villages at Awala, together with nearby Saiho where the hospital had long since been closed. The road continues eastwards through Soroputa to a larger cluster of buildings at Agenahambo, which includes St Michaels Mission and Martyrs School, and then on to Koipa and Hohorita School near the western side of Ambogo River. The road turns abruptly northwards, avoiding a river 'double crossing' at that point, and splitting into different parts near plantation blocks at Sangara, one road swinging southwards past the old, now disused, wartime airstrip that had operated during the disaster relief phase in 1951. The main road then runs up into the town of Popondetta itself, which is 20 kilometres from the summit of Mount Lamington and is now by far the largest of all the settlements in the Lamington area. Roads head northwards to the coast, and one runs southwards through Jegarata before turning eastwards across the Girua River to Inonda and to Girua where a new domestic airport had been built. The road then runs past the Embi Lakes to the coast of Oro Bay.

The overall impression from the map is one of authorities and communities having learnt the lessons of the volcanic disaster of 1951. The northern, vegetated flanks of the mountain seem appropriately bare of settlement, despite the attraction of their volcanically rich soils. There are, however, minor signs of reoccupation beginning to take place. For example, Wijo Plantation, which was within the limit of total devastation in 1951, is shown on the 1974 map as growing rubber and cocoa, and tracks run upslope from it to a few houses on a creek draining from the higher parts of the volcano. Resettlement of parts of the devastated area had started already.

10

LIVING WITH MOUNT LAMINGTON IN POSTCOLONIAL TIMES

New Histories

The Orokaiva have had a remarkable history since white men first landed on their shores in 1874 asserting their authority and firing their guns. They faced the imposition of colonial control; the invasion of gold miners; deadly battles with white men; the establishment of a new religion, Christianity, in its Anglican form; the banning of cultural behaviours such as cannibalism and inter-tribal fighting; racial discrimination; appropriation of traditional lands for colonial purposes; learning to understand, speak and write the foreign language of English; a deadly world war in which Orokaiva men played an enforced role mainly as carriers of supplies and wounded Allied and Japanese soldiers; public hangings for betraying missionaries and others to occupying Japanese forces; and, finally, the return to Higaturu of Australian colonial rule after the war. Their adaptability to new, unstoppable, historical forces and to volcanic disaster stands out.

Australian colonialism continued for almost 25 years after the 1951 eruption at Mount Lamington and a considerable amount of attention was paid during this time to the nature of the volcano and to the economic development and safety of the people living on and near the mountain. Further, this attention carried momentum, meaning there was no decline after 1975 when Papua New Guinea became an independent country.

That year was also when primary responsibility for managing disaster-risk reduction strategies on Mount Lamington was inherited by the new sovereign nation-state.

New histories are being created today, both nationally and more locally in what is referred to widely and informally as Oro Province, the former 'Northern Division' of colonial times. Further, international volcanology has progressed steadily, providing information and ideas of value in assessing the nature of explosive volcanoes in general, and of Lamington volcano and its eruption of 1951. National and foreign socioeconomic researchers, disaster managers, anthropologists and historians also continue to maintain an interest in the Orokaiva and their volcanic country. An indication of this ongoing work is provided in Appendix B where a post-1975 time sequence of selected events and activities is provided. Four disaster management themes can be discussed in relation to this time series.

Forecasting the Next Eruption

When will the next eruption take place at Lamington volcano? Will it be any different from the catastrophic one that devastated the lives of the mountain Orokaiva in January 1951? How often do similarly large eruptions break out on the mountain?

The 1951 eruption at Mount Lamington was not necessarily the same as those that have happened in the more distant past or those that may take place in the future at the volcano. The 1951 eruption has been given a Volcanic Explosivity Index of 4 on a VEI scale of 0–8, and hopefully the next eruption will score less than 4 (Siebert, Simkin and Kimberley 2010; see 2010 in Appendix B). It could be larger, however, as anticipated in the volcanic-hazard maps produced by the Rabaul Volcanological Observatory (RVO) (de Saint Ours 1988). Three hazard zones for pyroclastic flows, mud flows and lava flows are identified by this mapping. The highest hazard area is a 5-kilometre-wide circular area around the summit. A second zone of potential 'flowage' threat consists of numerous radial ribbons extending down the river valleys and having considerable impact to the north, well away from the summit of the volcano. The third zone of potential threat is for widespread pyroclastic flows ranging 8–20 kilometres from the summit crater. These last two hazard zones are notable because they are larger than the devastated areas produced by the 1951 eruption, including in the Ambogo River valley. The two proposed zones also cut the Kokoda–Popondetta road in several places, and they reach Popondetta township itself. This is at variance with Dr Fisher's conclusion in 1951 that Popondetta was 'safe for all time' and, therefore, suitable for a divisional headquarters (Murray Administrator 1951i, 1). Thousands of people today live within the boundaries of the 8–20-kilometre pyroclastic flow zone proposed by de Saint Ours.

Mount Lamington is the kind of volcano that does not produce eruptions very often, at least in comparison to other volcanoes in Papua New Guinea such as Manam and Bagana. Its actual 'eruption periodicity' through time, however, is unknown because the record of historical eruptions is far too short and its longer eruption history is still poorly known. This means that forecasting the start time and duration of the next eruption is very uncertain indeed. The 1951 eruption and its volcanic deposits have received significant attention from investigating scientists in the field, but the best known source for the volcano's early geology is still the published work of Bryan Ruxton undertaken in the 1960s. Ruxton, however, was the first to emphasise the limitations of his fieldwork. His five principal conclusions still remain the basis for any further fieldwork on Lamington volcano (Ruxton 1966a). These conclusions included the fact that Mount Lamington may have been inactive for well over 1,000 years before the 1951 eruption; that the age of Mount Lamington as a whole is probably within the range of 80–100,000 years; and that explosive activity may have changed during evolution of the volcano as the result of a decrease in the proportion of eruptions producing ash fall deposits, together with a complementary increase in those producing pyroclastic flows.

Ruxton also concluded that each of three weathered 'depositional units' in the upper-ash cover of Mount Lamington probably had durations of about 4–5,500 years, separated by about 1,000 years of inactivity. How many separate eruptions are present in each of these units is unclear, but the 1,000-year timescales and intervals are roughly consistent with some global statistical data for volcanoes like Lamington that have produced VEI-4 eruptions. The intervals between 376 worldwide eruptions of VEI-4 magnitude at different volcanoes are mainly in the range 10 to 1,000 years, and the range 100 to 1,000 years has the highest percentage of eruptions of all five different interval categories (Siebert, Simkin and Kimberley 2010).

Fieldwork is not easy in the Mount Lamington area. Tropical vegetation covers most of the volcano and surrounding terrain, and access is poor or not possible in many parts of the area. Further, rocks and deposits are not well exposed in situ because the volcano is not deeply cut by erosion, except perhaps on the southern flank of the mountain. Deposits produced by the more distant fallout of ash from earlier eruptions are certainly present away from the volcano. However, as the Owen Stanley Range is extremely rugged, sequences may be incomplete because of erosion and any pyroclastic flow history is unlikely to be represented there. Nevertheless, research on the distal ash fall history is worth pursuing if resources could be found for a comprehensive field study even if this requires local drilling and helicopter support. An attempt to map ash layers near or alongside the maintained Kokoda Track is one possibility, given that recent geological work at pits dug for archaeological purposes at Myola Lakes revealed 2.5-metre layers of ash from Mount Lamington together with soil horizons (Davies 2017–18). The age at the bottom of the pits is about 35,000 years but the base of the sequence was not reached by the drilling. The area west of Mount Lamington is rather important in deducing the history and eruptive periodicity of the volcano as high-rising eruption clouds are likely to have deposited ash there at any time of the year because of the year-round high altitude east to west winds, unlike on the eastern side of the volcano (Figure 9.3).

A further aspect of the nature of the volcano that requires attention is research on the gravitational instability of Mount Lamington, bearing in mind the asymmetry of the volcano, the avalanche-amphitheatre shape of the 1951 crater, the presence of debris-avalanche deposits, and ongoing uplift and seismicity in the nearby Owen Stanley Range. Gravitational instability and downslope slippage along a sloping basement were measured recently on Etna volcano in Italy by means of a detailed geodetic survey (Murray et al. 2018). This survey, however, required deployment of numerous GPS receivers operating over an extended period—a field survey that would be expensive and difficult to undertake at Mount Lamington at the present time.

Instrumental Monitoring by the Rabaul Volcanological Observatory

The RVO continues its work as the national volcanological service in Papua New Guinea, much as it did in colonial times. Its broad aim and operational style are based on those of observatories that were built in Europe, and especially in Italy on Etna and Vesuvius, in the late nineteenth century and were introduced to the Territory of New Guinea from the Netherlands Indies after the 1937 eruptions at Rabaul.

The observatory's aim in the twenty-first century is defined in the first part of its mission statement: 'to study and monitor volcanoes in Papua New Guinea effectively so that early warnings of volcanic eruptions can be provided to authorities'. This is an aspirational statement that can be applied to most volcanological observatories worldwide. Well-equipped observatories in developed countries such as Japan, the US, Italy and Russia are in a strong position to provide an effective eruption early warning service, particularly on volcanoes where recent eruptions have been monitored and eruption precursors are known. Rabaul volcano is the best monitored volcano in Papua New Guinea, having received extra international development assistance resources in 1983–85 during an earthquake and ground-uplift crisis, and then after the disastrous eruptions of 1994.

The RVO and Papua New Guinea Government are generally limited by available resources in their selection of which, and how many, volcanoes can be monitored instrumentally at any one time. There have been attempts to rank and prioritise those volcanoes that carry what is thought to be the greatest risk, but the choice is difficult and omitting particular volcanoes can be shown, retrospectively, to have been risky when they break out in eruptive activity 'unannounced', as it were. There has been remarkable progress, however, in monitoring the state of terrestrial volcanoes from space using instruments carried on both orbital and geostationary satellites and the results being distributed globally through the internet. For example, the extent and volume of emissions of volcanic sulphur dioxide and water vapour from individual volcanoes can be mapped remotely by satellite. Further, the strides made in satellite-based geodetic monitoring have been outstanding. Detailed digital elevation models of changes for the whole of the surface of a volcano can be mapped by, for example, radar methods, and digital elevation model maps produced (see, for example, Wadge et al. 2018). Satellite monitoring of Lamington is likely to be an important methodology during any forthcoming volcanic crisis on the mountain (Figure 10.1).

Mount Lamington is only one of many active or otherwise youthful and, therefore, potentially active volcanoes in Papua New Guinea that could break out in eruption again causing loss of life and property. It is also one of several volcanoes where an attempt is being made by RVO to provide onsite instrumental monitoring to identify early warning signs of future eruptive activity. This investment, however, is costly and is not always sustainable. Volcano-monitoring equipment can deteriorate in the tropical climate, and it can be destroyed or damaged by lightning strikes, theft and vandalism. Further, single instruments such as those installed on Lamington are limited in what they can measure. A single seismometer on the volcano is useful but, ideally, a network of stations is required so that the place of origin of the earthquake can be calculated through triangulation, and any spatial and temporal trends of earthquake epicentres and depths calculated. Similarly, the overall geodetic pattern of ground-level changes on the volcano is best deduced by a network of instruments. Networks, however, are expensive to install and to maintain, especially where access to widely spaced stations is difficult, such as at Lamington.

The RVO headquarters are 675 kilometres from Lamington in a direct line across the Solomon Sea. This means that air travel costs from Rabaul via Port Moresby are expensive for professional volcanological support, on-sight inspection of the volcano, technical repairs, equipment transport and any additional helicopter requirements. Yet, the presence of a local 'volcano observer' at Popondetta equipped with high-frequency radio communications linked to RVO headquarters is advantageous, particularly if the observer responds well to training, stays in the position, gains experience, and secures the confidence of local people and the provincial authorities. The task of 'observing' a volcano such as Lamington that has had no eruptions in recent times can be unrewarding in some ways, yet stressful if the observer becomes the first point of contact when unsubstantiated rumours spread that the volcano is becoming active again and immediate professional advice is needed.

Figure 10.1. Digital elevation model for the Mount Lamington area

This is an example of a satellite-derived digital elevation model image of Mount Lamington today. It was produced by Dorothy D. Pion of the Papua New Guinea Mineral Resources Authority (MRA), Port Moresby, and was provided courtesy of the MRA and H.L. Davies (formerly of the University of Papua New Guinea). North is to the top and the distance across is about 18 kilometres. Note the clustering of lava domes and coulées on and around the mountain; an apparent linear fault running north-north-east on the western side of the 1951 summit dome, defining the north-western edge of the 'avalanche valley'; and the great expanse of the 'piedmont' area to the north towards the Solomon Sea (compare with Figures 9.1 and 9.2). The western end of the Hydrographers Range is seen in the bottom right-hand corner.

Lamington volcano has not been in eruption since 1951. This represents 69 years of subsequent volcanic inactivity, and the 1951 event being the only eruption in the last, say, 130 years since the mountain was recognised and named during William McGregor's colonial rule. Is instrumental monitoring worthwhile in the short term at Lamington in a situation in which intervals between eruptions may be measured in centuries or even millennia? This question is relevant especially in a situation in which other unmonitored volcanoes in Papua New Guinea may have a greater need at any particular time. A recent example is Kadovar Island, an instrumentally unmonitored volcano off the north-east coast of mainland New Guinea, whose previous eruptive activity may have been as long ago as 1,700 AD, but that broke out in eruption in January 2018 causing evacuation of the islanders to displaced persons camps (Global Volcanism Program 2018). Further, there is no instrumental monitoring on the near-neighbour of Lamington, the historically active volcano of Mount Victory, where there is a risk to local communities not only of future explosive eruptions but also possible collapse of the coastal cone and the generation of tsunamis that could have widespread effects along coastlines of the Solomon Sea.

Commemoration and Communication

Mount Lamington today is shrouded in green, as it was before the 1951 eruption. The colonial disaster can be recalled by only a very few survivors and eyewitnesses of the disaster who still live in Oro Province or in Australia, most of whom were children at the time of the eruption. However, the disaster has not been forgotten. Commemorating the tragedy has been a near constant feature of the 69 years since the catastrophe. Commemorations have been held in both Papua New Guinea and Australia, and commemorative articles have been published in newspapers and magazines, as well as in memoirs, completed at different times since 1951. Grief is still remembered and expressed, including at commemorations of 'Eruption Day' in Oro Province itself. These are, at times, attended by Australians who lost family members in the disaster. Retelling the myth about Sumbiripa and his wife Suja is another effective way of recalling the nature of the mountain and its potential danger.

Remembrance is a key part of the disaster management spectrum. Indeed, 'remembrance' should, perhaps, be regarded as a third 'r' to be added to the post-disaster phases of relief and recovery. How a disaster is remembered and revisited—either in speech, using the written word, or on film and video—is crucial to making a 'lessons learnt' link back to the two pre-disaster phases of prevention and preparedness. A community not forgetting, but rather learning from, disaster experience is a highly effective way of helping to reduce contemporary natural hazard risk, so that communities become more risk-resilient and self-reliant. The second part of the RVO's mission statement, therefore, is: 'To work in partnership with … authorities and … communities to promote awareness of volcanic hazards and risks so that the communities become self-reliant'. The RVO is a source of information about the nature of volcanoes, particularly those in Papua New Guinea, and this knowledge can be put to good use in community awareness-raising work organised in partnership with local communities, their schools and colleges, local and provincial government authorities, and national disaster management agencies.

Historical memory and disaster memorialisation also have potential economic advantages, as evidenced by the numerous war tourists who travel to commemorations at war cemeteries, memorials and battlefields throughout the world. This is a phenomenon referred to by some people as 'dark tourism' (e.g. Lennon and Foley 2000), but by others as exemplifying the economic use of history as a 'resource' (Stead 2018). The Kokoda Track is one such war-linked attraction in Papua New Guinea. Higaturu could attract tourism because of the volcanic destruction of the Australian government station there in 1951 and also because of the systematic and horrific hangings of Orokaiva by the Australian Army in 1943. It is, therefore, a potential destination for guided tours and trekkers travelling along the Kokoda Track. Construction of a new memorial, together with a museum and guesthouse, was proposed and promoted several years ago by Hohorita people (Saunders 2018–19). Forgetting past tragedies—that is, the Higaturu hangings and the 1951 volcanic disaster—is unlikely to take place soon in these circumstances. The Mount Lamington Memorial Cemetery in Popondetta is a colonial park that equally could attract foreign tourists on account of its troubled history, even if does not meet the full requirements of people in modern-day Oro Province in remembering properly the thousands of Orokaiva killed, and particularly those at Hohorita who are the descendants of the Sangara.

Contemporary remembering of the Mount Lamington disaster is ambivalent and ambiguous in its content and expression (Stead 2018). People today speak bitterly about the failure of the colonial administration to provide early warning of the eruption and to provide for an evacuation, but there is also a shared experience that connects villagers around Higaturu with the descendants of those Europeans who died in the eruption and, thus, a motivation to pursue opportunities that they hope might lead to enduring relationships with them, if not to economic opportunities. An example is the way in which Pamela Virtue and her late father, Cecil Cowley, were honoured by people during the Virtues' visits in 2003 and 2004, including some people saying that District Commissioner Cowley had, in fact, recommended an evacuation (Cowley and Virtue 2015; see also Didymus 1974). Another version of this story, however, includes Mrs Virtue being petitioned by villagers for money to fund the proposed memorial, and asserting that her father was responsible for the high death toll of Orokaiva people in 1951 (Stead 2018).

What is the Risk?

A community can be said to be 'at-risk' from a natural hazard, such as a volcanic eruption or cyclonic flooding, if the hazard is frequent and if it is likely to have high impact when eventually it does strike. There is no risk if people do not live or work in such hazardous zones, but this means that when they do, the risk is a combination both of 1) the magnitude and frequency of the hazard and 2) what might be lost as a result of the hazard impact. Crucial to risk assessment, then, is knowing something about 'exposure'—that is, the vulnerability of populations, their built environment, services, agricultural lands, road systems, effective means of escape, up-to-date disaster management plans and so forth.

Risk can be mapped and semi-quantified in areas where there is good spatial or mappable information on likely hazard impacts and what might be lost. Such information can be digitised and added to Geographic Information Systems (GIS) where any one point on the digital maps can be linked to databases or 'attribute' data on what is found at that point—how many people, how much investment, proximity and access to essential services and so on—in other words, what is 'at-risk'. GIS are used globally for a wide range of purposes, but the term 'risk-GIS' has been introduced specifically as a means of focusing on how these systems can be used in disaster management for assessing risk and so contribute to plans for disaster prevention and preparedness (e.g. Granger 2000). There is 'nothing more certain in the disaster management business than the fact that once a disaster starts to unfold, it is too late to start looking for the information needed to manage it' (Granger 2000, 20).

The extent to which such risk-GIS technology can be introduced in Oro Province, maintained, updated and staffed by people trained to use it is resource dependent. This digital approach was introduced in East New Britain Province in 2013 (Bear-Crozier et al. 2013), but its usefulness has yet to be assessed during the real-time situation of a new, developing volcanic disaster.

What then can be said about the volcanic risk at Lamington volcano today? There is little doubt that more is 'at-risk' in the area compared to conditions in 1975 when Australian colonialism ended. The area devastated in 1951 has been reoccupied in part. There are more people, larger villages, more essential services, greater investment, and there is an agricultural economy underpinned by a now well-established oil palm industry. Further, there are many places on and near the mountain where communities escaped and survived the worst of the 1951 disaster, but which today are in areas that potentially are exposed to future volcanic activity and have been mapped as being in the flowage-hazard zones of the volcano. The risk on this basis alone can be said to be increasing even though it has not yet been quantified.

The problem in assessing the risk at Mount Lamington is not so much dealing with the vulnerability or 'exposure' of the communities, but rather with the uncertainties surrounding the volcanic hazard itself. The risk is high in the Mount Lamington area if there is confidence or near certainty that another VEI-4, or higher, explosive eruption will take place over the next few years. Conversely, it is very low if the next major explosive eruption is centuries away, or if the next eruption will be a smaller one limited to, say, the western flank of the volcano like those that formed the numerous minor satellite volcanoes. What should be done in these circumstances?

Communities themselves need to continue maintaining vigilance. Felt earthquakes, bare patches in the summit area, landslides, unusual smells and, of course, 'roars from the mountain', are all potential signs of volcanic unrest at Mount Lamington that can be detected and reported by people living on and near the volcano. Even the unusual behaviour of animals near villages, as featured in *The Mountain*, a novel about the Omie people and based on actual reports, should not be ignored (Modjeska 2012, 2017). The seismometer, tiltmeter and high-frequency radio system deployed by the RVO are advisable as an adjunct to community observations, provided government resources can be found to continue sustaining the instrumentation and assuming that vandalism and theft of the equipment do not take place. However, communities relying primarily on these technologies for early warnings of eruptions—that is, ahead of their own 'frontline' detection of changes—is not as advisable as the communities themselves acting as triggers for rapid-response investigations by RVO staff, even though 'false alarms' can be expected. Self-reliance can be enhanced too by continuing hazard-awareness information visits by RVO staff and other disaster managers. Hazard and risk maps should be updated progressively and displayed in schools and community centres, for example. There is also today the communication power of the internet, mobile telephones and social media—twenty-first-century global technology that was barely imaginable in 1951.

The name 'Higaturu' is now set securely in history. It refers to the still-deserted place associated with the Australian administration's former Higaturu Government Station where the wartime hangings of Orokaiva took place and which was subsequently destroyed by a catastrophic volcanic eruption. The name intones anger. Thus, the Anglican leader at Popondetta, Reverend Bishop Lindsley Ihove, is reported as saying that the 'human ignorance' of the white colonial authorities 'made people die' (Stead 2018, 25). This can hardly be disputed, the ignorance being equated with a lack of both relevant information and adequate experience of what to expect.

There was no colonial knowledge at Higaturu in January 1951 that Mount Lamington was a potentially active volcano, although there were weak pre-1951 hints that it might be. Further, the indecisive, almost diffident way in which the early warning signs of a catastrophe were dealt with by colonial authorities, and the decision to delay making any announcement to evacuate, turned out to be ill-advised and incorrect. Vulnerability soon turns into disaster when the wrong human decisions are made on the basis of inadequate knowledge. However, the written records left by many people, which form the basis of this book, mean that lessons can be learnt and that future volcanic disasters at Mount Lamington can be mitigated, and even avoided.

REFERENCES

Acting Government Secretary. 1951. Copy of letter signed by L. Odgers to Mr J.R. [Reg] Halligan, 25 January 1951. National Archives of Australia, Canberra. Series A518 (A518/1), Control Symbol AV918/1 Part 2; Title: Papuan—Miscellaneous—Volcanic Eruption—Mt Lamington.

Administration. 1951a. International telegram from Port Moresby to the Department of External Territories, Canberra, Thursday 18 January at 1710 hours. National Archives of Australia, Canberra, Series A518 (A518/1), Control Symbol AV918/1 Part 1; Title: Papuan—Miscellaneous—Volcanic Eruption—Mount Lamington.

Administration. 1951b. International telegram from Port Moresby for Mr Halligan, Department of External Territories, Canberra, Tuesday 30 January at 0945 hours. National Archives of Australia, Canberra. Series A518 (A518/1), Control Symbol AV918/1 Part 2; Title: Papuan—Miscellaneous—Volcanic Eruption—Mt Lamington.

Administration. 1951c. International telegram from Port Moresby (Phillips) to secretary, Department of External Territories, Canberra, Tuesday 6 February at 1050 hours. National Archives of Australia, Canberra. Series A518 (A518/1), Control Symbol AV918/1 Part 2; Title: Papuan—Miscellaneous—Volcanic Eruption—Mt Lamington.

Administration. 1951d. International telegram from Port Moresby (Phillips) to secretary, Department of External Territories, Canberra, Tuesday 6 February at 1445 hours. National Archives of Australia, Canberra. Series A518 (A518/1), Control Symbol AV918/1 Part 2; Title: Papuan—Miscellaneous—Volcanic Eruption—Mt Lamington.

Administration. 1951e. International telegram from Port Moresby to the Department of External Territories, Canberra, Saturday 3 March 1951 at 1140 hours. National Archives of Australia, Canberra. Series A518 (A518/1), Control Symbol AV918/1 Part 3; Title: Papuan—Miscellaneous—Volcanic Eruption—Mt Lamington.

Administration. 1951f. International telegram from Port Moresby to the Department of External Territories, Canberra, Monday 5 March 1951 at 1125 hours. National Archives of Australia, Canberra. Series A518 (A518/1), Control Symbol AV918/1 Part 3; Title: Volcanic eruption—Mt Lamington.

Administrator. 1904–05. 'Administrator's Notes on Reports by Officers. Northern Division'. In *British New Guinea Annual Report for 1904–05*, 13–14. Melbourne: Government Printer.

Administrator. 1951. Radiogram to DISCOM Tufi, 22 January 1951, probably at 5.35 pm. Papua New Guinea National Archives, File 32/4/39/24 (SN 677, AN 247, Box 307).

AGS (Allied Geographical Section). 1942a. *Terrain Study. Allied Geographical Section, Southwest Pacific Area. No. 27 Buna*. [Brisbane]: Allied Geographical Section, Southwest Pacific Area.

AGS (Allied Geographical Section). 1942b. 'Buna (South East) Two Miles to One Inch'. In *Terrain Study. Allied Geographical Section, Southwest Pacific Area. No. 27 Buna,* Part 3, Map 2. [Brisbane]: Allied Geographical Section, Southwest Pacific Area.

Ahearn, J.H. 1951a. Letter, 26 January 1951, from the chairman of the Papua and New Guinea Division of the Australian Red Cross, Port Moresby, to Sir John Newman-Morris, chairman of the Australian Red Cross Society, Melbourne. Australian Red Cross Society, National Office, Correspondence Files, National Headquarters. University of Melbourne Archives, 2015.0033, Unit 188, Folder 10, Natural Disasters Mt Lamington 1951.

Ahearn. J.H. 1951b. *Australian Red Cross Society Papua & New Guinea Division, Annual Report 1950–1951*. Australian Red Cross Society, National Office, Correspondence Files, National Headquarters. University of Melbourne Archives, 2015.0033, Unit 188, Folder 10, Natural Disasters Mt Lamington 1951.

Ahearn, J.H. 1951c. 'Mount Lamington Disaster Relief Fund'. Memorandum, 24 April 1951, from acting deputy chairman to 12 individuals involved in the work of the fund committee. Papua New Guinea National Archives, File GH1-5-8 (1) (SN667, AN244, BN136).

Alexander, K.M. and H.E. Vivian. 1957. 'Pozzolanic Activity of Ash Produced by the Eruption of Mt Lamington, New Guinea'. *Nature* 172, 1002–03. doi.org/10.1038/1721002b0.

Anglo-Persian Oil Company. 1930. *The Oil Exploration Work in Papua and New Guinea Conducted by the Anglo-Persian Oil Company on Behalf of the Government of the Commonwealth of Australia 1920–29.* [London: Anglo-Persian Oil Company].

Anonymous. 1951a. Telephone conversation with the acting government secretary [S.E. Lonergan], Port Moresby, 24 January 1951, 10.00 pm. National Archives of Australia, Canberra. Series A518 (A518/1), Control Symbol AV918/1 Part 1; Title: Papuan—Miscellaneous—Volcanic Eruption—Mt Lamington.

Anonymous. 1951b. Telephone conversation between Mr Lonergan and Mr Archer, 25 January 1951, 9.30 am. The author of the typed record is presumably Mr Archer. National Archives of Australia, Canberra. Series A518 (A518/1), Control Symbol AV918/1 Part 1; Title: Papuan—Miscellaneous—Volcanic Eruption—Mt Lamington.

Anonymous. 1951c. Telephone conversation between Mr Halligan and Mr Lonergan, 25 January 1951, 9.10 pm. National Archives of Australia, Canberra. Series A518 (A518/1), Control Symbol AV918/1 Part 1; Title: Papuan—Miscellaneous—Volcanic Eruption—Mt Lamington.

Anonymous. 1951d. Record of telephone conversation between Mr Halligan and Mr Lonergan, 26 January 1951, 9.10 pm. National Archives of Australia, Canberra. Series A518 (A518/1), Control Symbol AV918/1 Part 1; Title: Papuan—Miscellaneous—Volcanic Eruption—Mt Lamington.

Anonymous. 1951e. Extract from *Sydney Morning Herald* (22 February 1951). Typed version on file. National Archives of Australia, Canberra. Series A518 (A518/1), Control Symbol AV918/1 Part 3; Title: Papuan—Miscellaneous—Volcanic Eruption—Mt Lamington.

Anonymous. 1951f. 'The Preacher on the Burning Mount'. *People*, 23 May, 17–19.

Anonymous. n.d. 'European Residents in Higaturu District at Time of Eruption'. Typescript. The most likely date for this listing is late January 1951. Ivan Champion Collection, Fryer Library, University of Queensland, St Lucia, UQFL137, Box 6.

ANU (The Australian National University), Department of Anthropology and Sociology. 1968. *An Ethnographic Bibliography of New Guinea.* 3 Vols. Canberra: The Australian National University Press.

Armit, W.E. 1900a. 'Report on the New Road from Tamata to the Yodda Valley, on the Yodda Goldfield, and on the Natives Inhabiting the Kumusi and Yodda Valleys'. In *Annual Report on British New Guinea 1899–1900*, appendix S, 96–98. Brisbane: Government Printer.

Armit, W.E. 1900b. Untitled reply to Administrator G.R. Le Hunte, 11 August 1900. In *Annual Report on British New Guinea 1899–1900*, appendix R, 95. Brisbane: Government Printer.

Atkinson, O.J. 1951. 'Mt Lamington Eruption'. Letter, 8 March 1951, to the Department of District Services and Native Affairs, Port Moresby, and forwarded to the government secretary and administrator by I.F. Champion, director, District Services and Native Affairs. Papua New Guinea National Archives, File 32/4/39 (SN 677, AN 247, Box 305).

Austen, L. 1951. 'A Legend of Mount Lamington. Old Men Tell of a Great Cataclysm'. *Courier Mail* (Brisbane), 23 January, 2.

Australia Department of Territories. 1953. 'Official Record of the Unveiling of the Mount Lamington Memorial Popondetta Cemetery, Papua'. Canberra.

Australian Red Cross Society. 1951. Press release, 23 January 1951. Australian Red Cross Society, National Office, Correspondence Files, National Headquarters. University of Melbourne Archives, 2015.0033, Unit 188, Folder 10, Natural Disasters Mt Lamington 1951.

Baker, G. 1946. 'Preliminary Note on Volcanic Eruptions in the Goropu Mountains, Southeastern Papua, During the Period December, 1943, to August, 1944'. *Journal of Geology* 54, 19–31. doi.org/10.1086/625315.

Balob Teachers' College. 1976. 'Nango einda Sangara da (Lamington Lament)'. In *Song Book, Balob Teachers' College, Lae, Papua New Guinea*, edited by Kay Thorp, 13. Madang, Papua New Guinea: Anglican Centre.

Bashkow, I. 2006. *The Meaning of Whitemen: Race and Modernity in the Orokaiva Cultural World*. Chicago: University of Chicago Press. doi.org/10.7208/chicago/9780226530062.001.0001.

Bear-Crozier, A., G. Davies, M.A. Dunford, H. Ghasemi, N. Horspool, M. Jakab, L. Metz, V. Miller, L. Power and D. Robinson. 2013. 'Integrating Hazard and Exposure for East New Britain'. *Geoscience Australia Professional Opinion* 2013/07.

Beaver, W.N. 1913–14. 'Kumusi Division'. In *Papua Annual Report, 1913–14*, 69–72. Melbourne: Government Printer.

Beaver, W.N. 1914–15. 'Kumusi Division'. In *Papua Annual Report, 1914–15*, 48–55. Melbourne: Government Printer.

Beaver, W.N. 1918–19. 'Notes on Homicidal Emblems among the Orokaiva of the Mambare and Kumusi Divisions'. In *Papua Annual Report, 1918–19*, 96–99. Melbourne: Government Printer.

Bellamy, J.A. 2019. 'Background Notes on the History of CSIRO Land Surveys in the Territory of Papua New Guinea'. Unpublished manuscript accompanying e-mail, 14 May 2019. R.W.J. Collections: Box 36A, Lamington Eruption 1951, General Correspondence, 2017–19, Folder 4, sleeves 41–42.

Belousov, A., M. Belousova, H. Pati and R. Hoblitt. 2011a. 'The January 21, 1951 Blast of Mount Lamington in Papua New Guinea: Sequence of Events and Characteristics of the Deposits'. *Transactions of the America Geophysical Union* 92, no. 52 (Fall Meeting): supplement and poster presentation.

Belousov, A., M. Belousova, H. Patia and R. Hoblitt. 2011b. 'In the Shoes of Tony Taylor: Results of Reinvestigation of the 1951 Eruption of Mount Lamington, Papua New Guinea'. Unpublished PowerPoint presentation at IUGG General Assembly, Melbourne (copy in author's possession).

Belshaw, C.S. 1951a. 'Settlement in the Mount Lamington Area'. Unpublished report to the Territory administration. Papua New Guinea National Archives, File FN1-5-8 (SN 677, AN 244, Box 163).

Belshaw, C.S. 1951b. 'Social Consequences of the Mount Lamington Eruption'. *Oceania* 21 (4): 241–52. doi.org/10.1002/j.1834-4461.1951.tb00175.x.

Belshaw, C.S. 1951c. 'Mount Lamington: Re-Settling the Victims'. *Corona*, December, 467–70.

Benson, J. 1949a. 'Co-operatives in Papua'. *ABM Review*, 1 May, 69.

Benson, J. 1949b. 'New Guinea Mission (Papua): Christian Village Co-operatives, Part I'. *ABM Review*, 1 August, 116–17.

Benson, J. 1949c. 'Diocese of New Guinea: The Bishop of New Guinea Blessing Christian Village Co-operatives, Part II'. *ABM Review*, 1 September, 135–37.

Benson, J. 1955. 'The Bapa Saga and the Brothers Ambo' [Part 1 and Part 2]. *Anglican* (Sydney), 4 March, no. 134, 6, and 11 March, no. 135, 8.

Best, B. 1951. 'After the Volcano'. *Australian Women's Weekly*, 2 June, 20–21.

Best, J.G. 1988. Copy of unpublished letter to Senator Peter Cook, minister for resources and energy, Canberra, including two appendices dated 1 November 1988. Appendix A is entitled 'A Chronology of Events as They Involved G.A.M. Taylor, Volcanologist, Territory of Papua and New Guinea, during the Period January 15–21 1951'. R.W.J. Collections: Box 7B: G.A.M. Taylor Documents 1967–2014, Folder 4, sleeve 94.

Blaikie, R.W. 2005–12. Unpublished correspondence with author. R.W.J. Collections: Box 33A, Lamington Eruption 1951: Correspondence and Memoirs, A–G, Folder 3.

Blaikie, R.W. 2006. 'Bill Schleusener and the Mt Lamington Eruption'. *PNGAA Una Voce*, June, no. 2, 38–39.

Blaikie, R.W. 2007. 'Mt Lamington: Involvement in the Disaster (Second Account)'. Unpublished typescript. R.W.J. Collections: Box 33A, Lamington Eruption 1951, Correspondence and Memoirs A–G, Folder 3, sleeve 27.

Blake, D.H. and K. Paijmans. 1973. 'Reconnaissance Mapping of Land Resources in Papua New Guinea'. *Australian Geographical Studies* 11 (2): 201–10. doi.org/10.1111/j.1467-8470.1973.tb00150.x.

Brack, J. 1952. Letter, 10 November 1952, from assistant secretary, Department of Territories, Canberra, to Mrs W.J. Gale of Donnybrook, Western Australia. National Archives of Australia, Series A518 (A518/1), Control Symbol AV918/1B; Title: Volcanic Eruption—Mt Lamington—Next of Kin Victims.

Brookfield, H.C. and D. Hart. 1966. *Rainfall in the Tropical Southwest Pacific*. Canberra: Department of Geography, Research School of Pacific Studies [contributions to this publication have different paginations].

Bullard, S. 2017. *In Their Time of Need: Australian Overseas Emergency Relief Operations 1918–2000*. Vol. 4, Official History of Australian Peacekeeping, Humanitarian and Post-Cold War Operations. Melbourne: Cambridge University Press. doi.org/10.1017/9781108225441.

Burges, A. and B. Chalmers. 1952. 'Neurospora following a Volcanic Eruption'. *Nature* 170 (4324): 459–60. doi.org/10.1038/170459b0.

Cannon, J.H. 1951. 'Volcanic Disaster—Papua/ New Guinea'. Letter, 30 January 1951, from the (presumed) chairman of the Queensland Red Cross Division, Brisbane, to Sir John Newman-Morris, chairman of the Australian Red Cross Society, Melbourne. Australian Red Cross Society, National Office, Correspondence Files, National Headquarters. University of Melbourne Archives, 2015.0033, Unit 188, Folder 10, Natural Disasters Mt Lamington 1951.

Chairman. 1951. 'Mount Lamington Disaster Relief Fund'. Minutes of committee meeting held Friday 17 August 1951 at 8.45 am. Typescript. Ivan Champion Collection, Fryer Library, University of Queensland, St Lucia, UQFL137, Box 1.

Chalmers, J. 1887. 'Mr Chalmers' Narrative'. In *Picturesque New Guinea with An Historical Introduction and Supplementary Chapters on the Manners and Customs of the Papuans*, by Lindt, J.W., 95–103. London: Longmans, Green and Co.

Champion, A. 1950 [sic]. Two photographs held in the Ivan Champion Collection, Fryer Library, University of Queensland, St Lucia, UQFL137, Box 7.

Champion, C. 1951. Telephone message from government secretary, Port Moresby, 24 January 1951, 1.10 pm. National Archives of Australia, Canberra. Series A518 (A518/1), Control Symbol AV918/1 Part 1; Title: Papuan—Miscellaneous—Volcanic Eruption—Mt Lamington.

Champion, I. 1951. 'Authorisation to Officers in Support of the Work of the Administration Field Group'. Memoranda, 22 and 24 January 1951. Ivan Champion Collection, Fryer Library, University of Queensland, St Lucia, UQFL137, Box 6.

Champion, I.F. 1932. *Across New Guinea from the Fly to the Sepik*. London: Constable & Co.

Champion, I.F. 1951a. 'Evacuation Instructions in Event of a Second Major Eruption'. Circular instruction to all personnel in area under control of Administration Field Group, dated 23 February 1951. Ivan Champion Collection, Fryer Library, University of Queensland, St Lucia, UQFL137, Box 6.

Champion, I.F. 1951b. 'Re-Establishment of Disturbed Communities Mt Lamington Area'. Memorandum, 13 February 1951, to the government secretary, Port Moresby. Ivan Champion Collection, Fryer Library, University of Queensland, St Lucia, UQFL137, Box 6.

Chignell, A.K. 1911. *An Outpost in Papua*. London: Smith, Elder & Co.

Chignell, A.K. 1913. *Twenty-One Years in Papua: A History of the English Church Mission in New Guinea (1891–1912)*. London: A.R. Mowbray.

Chinnery, E.W.P. and W.N. Beaver. 1914–15a. 'Movements of the Tribes of the Mambare Division, Together with Migration Chart'. In *Papua Annual Report, 1914–15*, appendix 2, 158–61. Melbourne: Government Printer.

Chinnery, E.W.P. and W.N. Beaver. 1914–15b. 'Comparative Dialects of the Northern Districts of Papua with Language Chart'. In *Papua Annual Report, 1914–15*, appendix 3, 161–67. Melbourne: Government Printer.

Chinnery, E.W.P. and A.C. Haddon. 1917. 'Five New Religious Cults in British New Guinea'. *Hibbert Journal* 15, no. 3 (April): 448–63.

Christian, C.S. 1958. 'The Concept of Land Units and Land Systems'. *Proceedings of the 9th Pacific Science Congress* 20, 74–81. Batavia-Bandoeng: The Association.

Christian, C. S. and G. A. Stewart. 1964. 'Methodology of Integrated Surveys'. Conference on Principles and Methods of Integrating Aerial Studies of Natural Resources for Potential Development Toulouse, 21–25 September 1964, UNESCO, Paris. Accessed 21 September 2019, unesdoc.unesco.org/ark:/48223/pf0000153986?posInSet=7&queryId=N-EXPLORE-af60a2e7-24fa-475f-a1a9-12cbf6658365.

Chynoweth, N. n.d. 'A Virtual Martyr: A Brief Outline of the Story of James Benson, Priest of Gona, PNG'. Unfinished manuscript. Diocese of Canberra and Goulburn. Copy provided to the author by J. James.

Civil Aviation. 1951. 'Civil DC3 Aircraft Sorties to Popendetta [sic] from 21 January 1951 to 19 February 1951'. Papua New Guinea National Archives, File 1-5-8/35 (SN 677, AN 244, Box 163).

Claridge, R.M. 1951a. 'Report on Resettlement Camps Along the Sangara–Wairope Road'. Memorandum, 5 March 1951, to the director, District Services and Native Affairs, Port Moresby. Ivan Champion Collection, Fryer Library, University of Queensland, St Lucia, UQFL137, Box 6.

Claridge, R.M. 1951b. 'Special Report'. Memorandum, 2 October 1951, from Cadet Patrol Officer Claridge at Popondetta to district commissioner of the Northern Division. Papua New Guinea National Archives, File 45/9/3/65 (SN677, AN247, BN364).

Cleland, R. 1984. *Pathways to Independence: Story of Official and Family Life in Papua New Guinea from 1951 to 1975*. Singapore: Rachel Cleland.

Cooke, R.J., C.O. McKee, V.F. Dent and D.A. Wallace. 1976. 'Striking Sequence of Volcanic Eruptions in the Bismarck Volcanic Arc'. In *Volcanism in Australasia: A Collection of Papers in Honour of the Late G.A.M. Taylor*, edited by R.W. Johnson, 149–72. Amsterdam: G.C. Elsevier.

Corderoy, H.M. 1948. 'Legend of Mount Lamington'. Single paragraph on page 10 of a report on a patrol to the Isivita area, Northern Division, 2 April to 1 May 1948. Patrol report no. 7 of 1947/48 to the district officer at Higaturu, 4 May 1948. Digitised copy available online from the Library of the University of California at San Diego.

Correspondent [Cowley]. 1951. Copy of press message sent from Higaturu on the afternoon of 19 January 1951. Copy of radiogram presented as appendix B in Deputy Administrator 1951.

Courier Mail (Brisbane). 1951. 'Help Arrives for Papua Volcano Victims', 25 January, 1.

Cowley, A. 1953. 'The Last Five Days of Higaturu as I Remember Them'. Unpublished report sent to G.A.M. Taylor, 24 October 1953. R.W.J. Collections: Box 7A, G.A.M. Taylor Documents 1950–63, Folder 1, sleeves 39–40.

Cowley, A. and P. Virtue. 2015. *The Volcano's Wife: The Great Untold Story*. Calwell, ACT: Inspiring Publishers.

Crane, T. 1971. 'The Dead Were Everywhere, Burnt by Ash'. *Post Courier*, 21 January, 5.

Crick, I.H. 1973. 'Gas Condensate Collection Program—Progress Report October, 1973'. *Geological Survey of Papua New Guinea* 73 (19).

Crocombe, R.G. 1964. *Communal Cash Cropping among the Orokaiva*. New Guinea Research Bulletin 4. Canberra: New Guinea Research Unit, The Australian National University.

Crown Law Officer. 1951. 'Volcanic and Seismic Disturbances Ordinance 1951'. Memorandum to the government secretary, 31 May 1951. Papua New Guinea National Archives, File 1/3/9 (SN667, AN247, BN191).

Cunningham, J. 1974. 'Russian Scholarships for Aborigines'. *Sydney Morning Herald*, 20 July, 5.

Curson, P. and K. McCracken. 2019. 'The Nation's Worst Health Disaster Sailed in as the Great War Drew to a Close'. *Weekend Australian* (Inquirer), 12–13 January 2019, 19.

Dakeyne, R.B. 1966. 'Cooperatives at Yega'. *New Guinea Research Bulletin* 13, 5378.

David, T.W.E. 1950. *The Geology of the Commonwealth of Australia*. London: Edward Arnold.

Davies, H.L. 1971. *Peridotite-Gabbro-Basalt Complex in Eastern Papua: An Overthrust Plate of Oceanic Mantle and Crust*. Bureau of Mineral Resources Bulletin 128. Canberra: Department of National Development, Bureau of Mineral Resources, Geology and Geophysics.

Davies, H.L. 1987. 'Evan Richard Stanley, 1885–1924: Pioneer Geologist in Papua New Guinea'. *BMR Journal of Australian Geology and Geophysics* 10, 153–77.

Davies, H.L. 2017–18. Correspondence with author. R.W.J. Collections 36: Continuing Correspondence 2017–18, 16 November 2017, 23 January 2018.

Davies, H.L. and I.E. Smith. 1971. 'Geology of Eastern Papua'. *Bulletin of the Geological Society of America* 82 (12): 3299–312. doi.org/10.1130/0016-7606(1971)82[3299:goep]2.0.co;2.

Dawson, L.S. and Officers of the HMS Basilisk. 1886. *Cape Nelson to Hercules Bay. British New Guinea—NE Coast.* Published at the Admiralty 9th July 1896 under the superintendence of Captain W.J.L. Wharton, RN, FRS, Hydrographer (magnetic variation used as in 1919).

de Saint Ours, P. 1988. 'Potential Volcanic Hazards from Mt Lamington, Northern Province, Papua New Guinea'. *Geological Survey of Papua New Guinea* 86 (12).

Deane, W.[P.] 1996. *Some Signposts from Daguragu.* Canberra: Council for Aboriginal Reconciliation, Commonwealth of Australia.

Denham, D. 1969. 'Distribution of Earthquakes in the New Guinea—Solomon Islands Region'. *Journal of Geophysical Research* 74, 4239–99. doi.org/10.1029/jb074i017p04290.

Denoon, D. 2005. *A Trial Separation: Australia and the Decolonisation of Papua New Guinea.* Canberra: Pandanus Books. doi.org/10.22459/ts.05.2012.

Deputy Administrator. 1951. 'Mount Lamington Eruption'. Unpublished memorandum signed by Judge Phillips to His Honour the Administrator, Port Moresby, 3 February 1951. National Archives of Australia, Canberra. Series A518 (A518/1), Control Symbol AV918/1 Part 3, Volcanic Eruption—Mt Lamington.

Dexter, D. 1961. *The New Guinea Offensives.* Australia in the War of 1939–1945: Series 1, Army, vol. 6. Canberra: Australian War Memorial.

Didymus, H. trans. 1974. 'The Disasterous [sic] Catastrophe That Shook My Land and My People: "The Eruption of Mt Lamington" (Northern District)'. *PNG Public Works Department Magazine*, March, 5–7.

Downs, I. 1980. *The Australian Trusteeship: Papua New Guinea 1945–75.* Canberra: Australian Department of Home Affairs.

Durdin, P. 2007. Letter to author, 2 March 2007. R.W.J. Collections: Box 33A, Lamington Eruption 1951, Correspondence and Memoirs, Folder 4, sleeve 46.

Duyker, E. and M. Duyker, eds and trans. 2001. *Bruny D'Entrecasteaux: Voyage to Australia and the Pacific, 1791–1793*. Carlton South: Melbourne University Press.

Dwyer, R.E.P. 1951. 'Mt Lamington Eruption: Activities and Interests of the Department of Agriculture, Stock and Fisheries'. Memorandum, 30 January 1951, to government secretary, Port Moresby. Typescript. Ivan Champion Collection, Fryer Library, University of Queensland, St Lucia, UQFL137, Box 4.

Earl, A.J. 1951. Handwritten letter to 'Mum and Dad', written 18 January 1951 from the District Office at Higaturu. R.W.J. Collections: Box 33A, Lamington Eruption 1951, Correspondence and Memoirs, Folder 6, sleeve 52.

Elliott-Smith. S. 1951a. 'Mt Lamington Eruption Special Report by Mr R.M. Claridge Covering Death Roll and Surviving Dependents—All Areas'. Letter, 19 October 1951, to director, District Services and Native Affairs, Port Moresby. National Archives of Australia, Canberra. Series A518 (A518/1), Control Symbol AV918/1 Part 3; Title: Papuan—Miscellaneous—Volcanic Eruption—Mt Lamington.

Elliott-Smith, S. 1951b. Weekly summary, 20–26 May 1951, from acting district commissioner, Northern Division, Popondetta, to director, District Services and Native Affairs, Port Moresby. Papua New Guinea National Archives, File FN35/7/22 (SN 677, AN 247, Box 319).

Elliott-Smith, S. 1952. 'Quarterly report 31st March, 1952: Northern District. Mt Lamington Disaster—Rehabilitation'. Papua New Guinea National Archives, File FN35/7/22 (SN 677, AN 247, Box 319).

Escher, B.G. 1925. 'L'éboulement Préhistorique de Tasikmalaya et le Vulcan Galoungoung (Java)'. *Leidsche Geologische Mededeelingen* 1, 8–21.

Farquharson, J. 2002. 'Images from a Fascinating Life'. *Canberra Times* (*Panorama Magazine*), 27 July, 17.

Ferrier, P. 1951. Letter to minister for external territories, 31 January 1951. National Archives of Australia, Canberra. Series A518 (A518/1), Control Symbol AV918/1 Part 3; Title: Papuan—Miscellaneous—Volcanic Eruption—Mt Lamington.

Finlayson, D.M., B.J. Drummond, C.D.N. Collins and J.B. Connelly. 1976. 'Crustal Structure Under the Mount Lamington Region of Papua New Guinea'. In *Volcanism in Australasia: A Collection of Papers in Honour of the Late G.A.M. Taylor*, edited by R.W. Johnson, 259–74. Amsterdam: G.C. Elsevier.

Finsch. O. 1888. *Samoafahrten. Reisen in Kaiser Wilhelms-Land und Englisch Neu-Guinea in den Jahren 1884 u. 1885 an Bord des deutschen Dampfers Samoa*. Leipzig: Ferdinand Hirt & Sohn.

Fisher, N.H. 1939a. *Geology and Vulcanology of Blanche Bay, and the Surrounding Area, New Britain*. Territory of New Guinea Geological Bulletin 1. Canberra: Government Printer.

Fisher, N.H. 1939b. *Report on the Volcanoes of the Territory of New Guinea*. Territory of New Guinea Geological Bulletin 2. Canberra: Government Printer.

Fisher, N.H. 1940. 'Note on the Vulcanological Observatory at Rabaul'. *Bulletin Volcanologique* 6, 185–87. doi.org/10.1007/bf02994879.

Fisher, N.H. 1951. 'Volcanic Centres of New Guinea'. *Walkabout* 17 (6): 35–40.

Fisher, N.H. 1957. *Catalogue of the Active Volcanoes of the World including Solfatara Fields, Part V (Melanesia)*. Napoli: International Volcanological Association.

Fisher, N.H. 1976. 'Memorial—G.A.M. Taylor'. In *Volcanism in Australasia: A Collection of Papers in Honour of the Late G.A.M. Taylor*, edited by R.W. Johnson, ix–xiv. Amsterdam: Elsevier.

Fitzpatrick, E.A., D. Hart and H.C. Brookfield. 1966. 'Rainfall Seasonality in the Tropical Southwest Pacific'. *Erdkunde* 20, 181–94. doi.org/10.3112/erdkunde.1966.03.02.

Fitzsimons, P. 2004. *Kokoda*. Sydney: Hodder Headline Group.

Fortune, K. 1998. 'Introduction'. In *Malaguna Road: The Papua New Guinea Diaries of Sarah Chinnery*, by S. Chinnery, edited by K. Fortune, 1–6. Canberra: National Library of Australia.

Francis, P. 1993. *Volcanoes: A Planetary Perspective*. Oxford: Oxford University Press.

Franceschi Cowley, A. 1951. Letter from Mrs Amalya Cowley, Sydney, to Administrator Colonel Murray, Port Moresby. Papua New Guinea National Archives, File FN1-5-8(1) (SN 677, AN 244, Box 163).

Freycinet, L.C. de S. 1811. 'General Map of New Holland'. Paris. Copies held by the National Library of Australia, Canberra.

Gailey, H.A. 2000. *MacArthur Strikes Back: Decision at Buna, New Guinea 1942*. Novata, CA: Presidio Press.

Garland, C. 2000. *Romney Gill, Missionary 'Genius' and Craftsman*. Leicester: Christians Aware.

Garnaut, R. 2009. 'Foreword'. In *Not a Poor Man's Field: The New Guinea Goldfields to 1941: An Australian Colonial History*, by M. Waterhouse, 4–5. Braddon, ACT: Halstead Press.

Gaumont British News. 1951. 'New Guinea: The Haunted Mountain in Eruption'. Accessed 11 September 2019, www.britishpathe.com/video/VLVAW9G2W 2X17BLQMTIXG74Y5P1Y-PAPUA-NEW-GUINEA-VOLCANOES-MOUNT-LAMINGTON-ERUPTS/query/New+Guinea.

Gillbee Brown, H. 1951. Confidential memorandum to the director of public health, Port Moresby, 23 July 1951. Papua New Guinea National Archives, FN 47-19 (SN677, AN 405, Box 887).

Glaessner, M.F. 1950. 'Geotectonic Position of New Guinea'. *Bulletin of the American Association of Petroleum Geologists* 34 (5): 856–81. doi.org/10.1306/ 3D933F59-16B1-11D7-8645000102C1865D.

Glenister, R.C. 1951. Letter, 5 February 1951, to I.F. Champion from the manager of the Australian Broadcasting Commission in Papua and New Guinea. Ivan Champion Collection, Fryer Library, University of Queensland, St Lucia, UQFL137, Box 6.

Glick, P.B. and J. Beckett. 2005. 'Marie Reay, 1922–2004'. *Australian Journal of Anthropology* 16, 394–96. doi.org/10.1111/j.1835-9310.2005.tb00319.x.

Global Volcanism Program. 2018. 'Kadovar'. Online reports of volcanic activity in 2018. Accessed 21 September 2019, volcano.si.edu/volcano.cfm?vn=251002.

Godbold, K.E. 2010. 'Didiman: Australian Agricultural Extension Officers in the Territory of Papua and New Guinea, 1945–1975'. PhD thesis, Queensland University of Technology.

Golson, J., T. Denham, P. Hughes, P. Swadling and J. Muke, eds. 2017. *Ten Thousand Years of Cultivation at Kuk Swamp in the Highlands of Papua New Guinea*. Terra Australis 46. Canberra: ANU Press. doi.org/10.22459/ ta46.07.2017.

Goodman, J. 2005. *The Rattlesnake: A Voyage of Discovery to the Coral Sea*. London: Faber and Faber.

Gordon, D.C. 1951. *The Australian Frontier in New Guinea 1870–1885*. New York: Columbia University Press. doi.org/10.1017/s0003055400293970.

Gore, R.T. 1952. Letter, 23 July 1952, to His Honour the Acting Administrator, including a three-page report entitled 'Mount Lamington Disaster Relief Fund'. Papua New Guinea National Archives FN 1/8/1/61 (SN677, AN 244, Box 205).

Grahamslaw, T. 1971a. 'When Undisciplined, Poorly Led Troops Looted Port Moresby'. *Pacific Islands Monthly* 42 (3): 77–79 and 133–43.

Grahamslaw, T. 1971b. 'Missionaries Slaughtered in Grim Advance on Moresby'. *Pacific Islands Monthly* 42 (4): 71–75 and 117–23.

Grahamslaw, T. 1971c. 'Grim Retribution for Papuans Who Backed the Losing Side'. *Pacific Islands Monthly* 42 (5): 41–45 and 105–18.

Granger, K. 2000. 'An Information Infrastructure for Disaster Management in Pacific Islands'. *Australian Journal of Emergency Management*, Autumn, 20–32.

Grant, L. 2014. *Australian Soldiers in Asia-Pacific in World War II*. Sydney: NewSouth Publishing.

Gunther, J.T. 1951a. 'The Mount Lamington Volcanic Eruption'. Unpublished report, 29 January 1951. Sir John Gunther: files on health and related matters in Papua New Guinea 1947–1981. Pacific Manuscripts Bureau, File JG/5.

Gunther, J.T. 1951b. Copy of letter (typed 6 April 1951) from Dr Gunther, director of public health, Papua-New Guinea, to Dr Shaw, director of Queensland Red Cross blood transfusion service. Australian Red Cross Society, National Office, Correspondence Files, National Headquarters. University of Melbourne Archives, 2015.0033, Unit 188, Folder 10, Natural Disasters Mt Lamington 1951.

Gunther, J.T. 1951c. Confidential letter to Administrator Colonel J.K. Murray, 30 July 1951. Papua New Guinea National Archives, FN 1/8/1/61 (SN677, AN 244, Box 205).

Gunther, J.T. 1951–52. Untitled report. In *Territory of Papua Annual Report*, 35–36. Canberra: Parliament of the Commonwealth of Australia.

Gwilt, J.R. 1951. 'Lamington Disaster Sunday January 21st, 1951'. Copy of unpublished typescript. R.W.J. Collections: Box 7A, G.A.M. Taylor Documents 1950–1963, Folder 1, sleeves 8–11.

Haantjens, H.A., E.A. Fitzpatrick, B.W. Taylor and J.C. Saunders. (1964b) 2010b. 'No. 12 General Report on Lands of the Wanigela–Cape Vogel Area, Territory of Papua and New Guinea'. *Land Research Surveys* 1. Accessed 21 September 2019, www.publish.csiro.au/CR/LRS12.

Haantjens, H.A., S.J. Paterson, B.W. Taylor, R.O. Slatyer, G.A. Stewart and P. Green. (1964a) 2010a. 'No 10 General Report on Lands of the Buna–Kokoda Area, Territory of Papua and New Guinea'. *Land Research Surveys* 1. Accessed 21 September 2019, www.publish.csiro.au/CR/LRS10.

Haddon, A.D. 1901. *Head-Hunters: Black, White, and Brown*. London: Methuen.

Hall, G.M. 1995. *Love, War, and the 96th Engineers (Colored): The World War II New Guinea Diaries of Captain Hyman Samuelson*. Urbana: University of Illinois Press.

Hall, T. 1981. *New Guinea 1942–44*. Sydney: Methuen Australia.

Ham, P. 2004. *Kokoda*. Pymble: Harper Collins.

Hand, D. 1951. 'Stop Press: New Guinea Tragedy'. *ABM Review* 39 (1): 21.

Hand, D. 2002. *Modawa: Papua New Guinea and Me 1946–2002*. Port Moresby: SalPress.

Hart, R. 1953. 'At Jegarata'. Unpublished, undated and annotated typescript (first draft written by G.A. Taylor following an interview) together with covering letter from Taylor, 14 January 1953. R.W.J. Collections: Box 7A, G.A.M. Taylor Documents 1950–63, Folder 1, sleeve 37.

Hasluck, P. 1976. *A Time for Building: Australian Administration in Papua and New Guinea 1951–1963*. Melbourne: Melbourne University Press.

Head, E.A.F. 1951. 'Mt Lamington Eruption 21st January, 1951. Administration Employees' Compensation Ordinance 1949'. Memorandum, 13 September 1951, including a separate three-page minute dated 11 September 1951. Papua New Guinea National Archives FN 45/9/3/60 (SN677, AN 247, Box 364).

Henderson, J. 2001. 'Recollections of Mount Lamington'. Apostrophe (Vicarage at St Peter's Church, Eastern Hill, Melbourne, Information Sheet) 49, 4–9.

Henderson, J. 2007. Unpublished correspondence with author. R.W.J. Collections: Box 33B, Lamington Eruption 1951, Correspondence and Memoirs, H–Mars, Folder 10, sleeves 13–16.

Henderson, T.G. 1951. Unpublished, undated account of the pre-climax conditions at Lamington. R.W.J. Collections: Box 7A, G.A.M. Taylor Documents, 1950–1963, Folder 1, sleeve 22.

Henry, L.M. 1951. 'Work of Qantas in Emergency'. *South Pacific Post*, 2 February, 9.

Hiari, M. 2013. Letter to author, 19 February 2013. R.W.J. Collections: Box 33B, Lamington Eruption 1951, Correspondence and Memoirs, H–Mars, Folder 11, sleeve 20.

Hiery, H.J. 1995. *The Neglected War: The German South Pacific and the Influence of World War I*. Honolulu: University of Hawaii Press.

Hoblitt, R.P. 1982. 'Reconnaissance of the Area Devastated by the January 21, 1951 Eruption of Mount Lamington, Papua: August 10–18, 1982'. Unpublished administrative report, United States Geological Survey.

Horne, J.R. 1974a. 'Of Myths and Things'. Unpublished manuscript. R.W.J. Collections: Box 31A, John R. Horne Manuscripts and Correspondence 1973–2016, Folder 1, sleeves 2–4.

Horne, J.R. 1974b. 'The Late Nineteenth Century Eruption of Mt Victory'. Unpublished manuscript. R.W.J. Collections, Box 31A, John R. Horne Manuscripts and Correspondence 1973–2016, sleeve 13.

Horne, J.R. 1976. 'The Urquhart Photographs of the Mount Lamington eruption'. Unpublished manuscript. R.W.J. Collections: Box 31A, John R. Horne Manuscripts and Correspondence 1973–2016, Folder 1, sleeve 11.

Horne, J.R. 2017. Collection of articles and unpublished correspondence (mainly from the mid-1970s) on aspects of the Christian Co-operative Movement. R.W.J. Collections: Box 31B, John R. Horne Manuscripts and Correspondence 2017–18, Folders 2 and 3.

Howlett, D.R. 1965. *The European Land Settlement Scheme at Popondetta*. New Guinea Research Unit Bulletin 6. Canberra: New Guinea Research Unit, The Australian National University.

Hunt, B. 2017. *Australia's Northern Shield? Papua New Guinea and the Defence of Australia since 1880*. Clayton: Monash University Publishing.

Ingleby, I. 1966. 'Mount Lamington Fifteen Years Later'. *Australian External Territories* 6 (6), 28–34.

Inglis, A. 1974. *The White Women's Protection Ordinance: Sexual Anxiety and Politics in Papua*. London: Sussex University Press.

James, I. 1951. 'Mount Lamington Volcano: Last Days of Higaturu: Australians Unaware of Impending Disaster'. Typed extract from *Bairnsdale Advertiser*. R.W.J. Collections: Box 7A, G.A.M. Taylor Documents, Folder 1, sleeves 2 and 13.

Johnson, R.W. 2013. *Fire Mountains of the Islands: A History of Volcanic Eruptions and Disaster Management in Papua New Guinea and the Solomon Islands*. Canberra: ANU Press. doi.org/10.22459/fmi.12.2013.

Johnson, R.W. and N.A. Threlfall. 1985. *Volcano Town: The 1937–43 Rabaul Eruptions*. Bathurst: Robert Brown.

Johnson, T. and P. Molnar. 1972. 'Focal Mechanisms and Plate Tectonics of the Southwest Pacific'. *Journal of Geophysical Research* 77, 5000–32. doi.org/10.1029/jb077i026p05000.

Johnston, E. 1995. *Dodoima: Tales of Oro*. Auckland: Pasifika Press.

Johnston, E. 2003. *Bishop George: Man of Two Worlds*. Point Lonsdale, Vic.: E. Johnston.

Joyce, R.B. 1971. *Sir William MacGregor*. Melbourne: Oxford University Press.

Joyce, R.B. 1983. 'Lamington, Second Baron (1860–1940)'. *Australian Dictionary of Biography*. Vol. 9. Carlton: Melbourne University Press. adb.anu.edu.au/biography/lamington-second-baron-7018/text.

Justin (O.F.M.), Father. 1951. 'I Was at Mt Lamington'. *Crusader*, March, 7–8 and 12.

Kaad, F. P. 1951. 'Missions'. Two memoranda to the district commissioner, Northern Division, Popondetta, 23 and 24 July 1951. Papua New Guinea National Archives FN 47-19 (SN677, AN 405, Box 887).

Keesing, F.M. 1952. 'The Papuan Orokaiva vs Mt Lamington: Cultural Shock and its Aftermath'. *Human Organisation* 11 (1): 16–22. doi.org/10.17730/humo.11.1.kw0lj9064kv864jq.

Keig, G., R.L. Hide, S.M. Cuddy, H. Buettikofer, J.A. Bellamy, P. Bleeker, D. Freyne and J. McAlpine. 2019. 'CSIRO and Land Research in Papua New Guinea 1950–2000: Part 1: Pre-Independence'. *Historical Records of Australian Science* 30, 83–99. doi.org/10.1071/hr18019.

Kendall, H.T.A. 1988. *Not Forever in Green Pastures: The Personal Memoirs of the Rt. Revd H.T.A. Kendall, M.A.* Townsville: Diocese of North Queensland.

Kendall, R. 2006. Unpublished, untitled handwritten account. R.W.J. Collections: Box 33C: Lamington Eruption 1951, Correspondence and Memoirs, Mart–Z, Folder 23, sleeve 71.

Kettle, E.S. 1979. *That They Might Live*. Sydney: F.P. Leonard.

Kienzle, R. 2013. *The Architect of Kokoda: Bert Kienzle—the Man Who Made the Kokoda Trail*. Sydney: Hachette Australia.

Kienzle, W. 1951. Unpublished letter from Yodda Valley to Mr Taylor, 23 February 1951. R.W.J. Collections: Box 7A, G.A.M. Taylor Documents 1950–1963, Folder 1, sleeve 33.

Kleckham, M.S. 2003. 'Eruption of Mount Lamington, PNG, on 21 January 1951'. *PNGAA Una Voce* 2 (June): 11–15.

Kleckham, M.S. 2010. 'Eruption of Mount Lamington, PNG, on 21 January 1951'. *PNGAA Una Voce* 4 (December): 45–49.

Kokoda Initiative. 2015. *Voices from the War—Papua New Guinean Stories of the Kokoda Campaign, World War Two*. [Canberra]: Kokoda Initiative.

Kübler-Ross, E. [1969]. *On Death and Dying: What the Dying Have to Teach Doctors, Nurses, Clergy & Their Own Families*. New York: McMillan. doi.org/10.4324/9780203889657.

Lacroix, A. 1904. *La Montagne Pelée et ses Éruptions*. Paris: Masson et Cie.

Langmore, D. 1993. 'Arek, Paulus (1929–1973).' *Australian Dictionary of Biography*. Vol. 13. Melbourne: Melbourne University Press. adb.anu.edu.au/biography/arek-paulus-9378/text16475.

Langmore, D.L. 1974. *Tamate a King: James Chalmers in New Guinea 1877–1901*. Carlton: Melbourne University Press.

Langmore, D.L. 1989. *Missionary Lives: Papua, 1874–1914*. Honloulu: University of Hawaii Press.

Larsen, B. 2017. Unpublished correspondence with author, 10 November 2017. Lamington Eruption 1951: R.W.J. Collections: Box 36B, Lamington Eruption 1951, General Correspondence 2017–2019, J–Z, Folder 7, sleeves 18–19.

Larsen, M. 1984. 'Orokaiva-English Dictionary. Summer School of Linguistics, Ukarumpa, Papua New Guinea'. Unpublished txt-format version provided to author by Dr Malcolm Ross, The Australian National University, in 2019.

Lashmar, [L.]. 1935. 'News from Hostel Students'. *ABM Review*, 1 August, 91.

Le Hunte, G.R. 1900. 'Memorandum for Mr Armit, Resident Magistrate, Northern Division'. In *Annual Report on British New Guinea 1899–1900*, appendix R, 94–95. Brisbane: Government Printer.

Legge, J.D. 1956. *Australian Colonial Policy: A Survey of Native Administration and European Development in Papua*. Sydney: Angus & Robertson.

Legislative Council Debates. 1959. 'Retirement of Mr S.A. Lonergan'. *Territory of Papua and New Guinea Legislative Council* 4 no. 5 (23 March): 576–79.

Lennon, J. and M. Foley. 2000. *Dark Tourism: The Attraction of Death and Disaster*. London: Continuum.

Littler, G. 2005. Unpublished correspondence with author. R.W.J. Collections: Box 33B, Lamington Eruption 1951: Correspondence and Memoirs, H–Mars, Folder 16, sleeves 68–72.

London Gazette. 1952. 'Supplement', 22 April, 2165–66.

Lonergan, S. 1951a. Letter, 26 January 1951, to Ivan Champion from S.E. Lonergan, acting government secretary in Port Moresby. Ivan Champion Collection, Fryer Library, University of Queensland, St Lucia, UQFL137, Box 6.

Lonergan, S.A. 1951b. 'Mount Lamington Eruption, Northern Division—21.1.51'. List of dead and missing as at 6 March 1951. Typescript. Ivan Champion Collection, Fryer Library, University of Queensland, St Lucia, UQFL137, Box 6.

Long, G. 1973. *The Final Campaigns*. Australia in the War of 1939–1945: Series 1, Army, vol. 7. Canberra: Australian War Memorial.

Lutton, N. 1978. 'C.A.W. Monckton: Reprobate Magistrate'. In *Papua New Guinea Portraits: The Expatriate Experience*, edited by J. Griffith, 48–74. Canberra: Australian National University Press.

Luyendyk, B.P., K.C. MacDonald and W.B. Bryan. 1973. 'Rifting History of the Woodlark Basin in the Southwest Pacific'. *Bulletin of the Geological Society of America* 84, 1125–34. doi.org/10.1130/0016-7606(1973)84%3C1125:rhot wb%3E2.0.co;2.

Lyng, J. 1919. *Our New Possession*. Melbourne: Melbourne Publishing Company.

MacGregor, W.R. 1890. 'Despatch Reporting Inspection of the North-East Coast of the Possession'. In A*nnual Report on British New Guinea 1890–91*, appendix D, despatch no. 100 (16 September 1890), 10–18. Brisbane: Government Printer.

MacGregor, W.R. 1893. 'Despatch Reporting Inspection of the North-East Coast of the Possession'. In A*nnual Report on British New Guinea 1893–94*, appendix A, despatch no. 58 (24 October 1893), 1–8. Brisbane: Government Printer.

MacGregor, W.R. 1894. 'Despatch Reporting Visit of Inspection to the North-East Coast'. In A*nnual Report on British New Guinea 1893–94*, appendix F, despatch no. 19 (30 April 1894), 30–37. Brisbane: Government Printer.

MacGregor, W.R. 1895. 'Despatch Reporting Expedition Undertaken to Affect the Ascent of the Musa River'. In *Annual Report on British New Guinea 1895–96*, appendix E, despatch no. 60 (31 October 1895), 22–28. Brisbane: Government Printer.

MacGregor, W.R. 1898a. 'Services Rendered by Wesleyan Mission'. In *Annual Report on British New Guinea 1897–98*, Section 49, xxx–xxi. Brisbane: Government Printer.

MacGregor, W.R. 1898b. 'Visit of Lord Lamington and Sir H.M. Nelson'. In *Annual Report on British New Guinea 1897–98*, Section 22, xvii. Brisbane: Government Printer.

Mackenzie, S.S. 1987. *The Australians at Rabaul*. St Lucia: University of Queensland Press.

Mair, L.P. 1948. *Australia in New Guinea*. London: Christophers.

Maitland, A.G. 1892a. 'Geological Observations in British New Guinea in 1891'. In *Annual Report on British New Guinea 1891–92*, appendix M, 53–85. Brisbane: Government Printer.

Maitland, A.G. 1892b. *Geological Observations in British New Guinea in 1891*. Queensland Geological Survey Publication 85. Brisbane: J.C. Beal, Government Printer.

Manley, E. 1951. 'Mt Lamington Disaster: Elsie Manley's Experience'. Two-part article. *Albany Advertiser*, 6 March, 3, and 8 March, 5.

Marsh, D.R. 1944. 'Separate Report on Volcanic Disturbances Inland Collingwood Bay Tufi District'. National Archives of Australia, Canberra, Series A518/1, Item 432711, Folios 56–59.

Marsh, D.R. 2005–08. Unpublished correspondence with author. R.W.J. Collection no. 33B: Lamington Eruption 1951: Correspondence and Memoirs, H–Mars, Folder 17.

Martin, [J.]D. 2013. 'Mount Lamington'. *PNGAA Una Voce* 2 (June): 42–45.

Martin, J.D. 2007–15. Unpublished correspondence with author. R.W.J. Collections: Box 33C, Lamington Eruption 1951, Correspondence and Memoirs, Mart–Z, Folder 18.

May, R.J. 2006. 'Northern Exposure: The New Guinea Research Unit'. In *The Coombs: A House of Memories*, edited by B.V. Lal and A. Ley, 95–100. Canberra: Research School of Pacific and Asian Studies, The Australian National University.

Mayo, L. 1974. *Bloody Buna*. New York: DoubleDay.

McAlpine, G. 2017. 'CSIRO Surveys in PNG in the 1950s etc'. E-mails between Gael McAlpine, Ken Granger, Robin Hide and author in April 2017. R.W.J. Collections: Box 36B, Lamington Eruption 1951, General Correspondence, 2017–19, Folder 4, sleeves 34–37.

McAlpine, J.R., G. Keig and K. Short. 1975. Climatic Tables for Papua New Guinea. *Division of Land Use Research Technical Paper* 37. Melbourne: CSIRO.

McCarthy, D. 1959. *Southwest Pacific Area—First Year: Kokoda to Wau*. Australia in the War of 1939–1945: Series 1, Army, vol. 5: Canberra: Australian War Memorial.

McCarthy, J.K. 1951a. 'Appreciation and Plan—Volcanic Eruption, Rabaul'. Papua New Guinea National Archives, File GH1-5-7 (SN677, AN244, BN163).

McCarthy, J.K. 1951b. 'Higaturu Relief Fund and Land Settlement'. Memorandum, 7 February 1951, to director, District Services and Native Affairs, Port Moresby, from the district commissioner of the New Britain District. Papua New Guinea National Archives, File 1/8/1/61 (SN667, AN244, BN205).

McCarthy, J.K. 1971a. 'Warning Flags Were Flying in Rabaul but Nobody Took Heed'. *Post Courier* (Port Moresby), 19 July, 5.

McCarthy, J.K. 1971b. 'When Matupit Blew, it Was Time to Go'. *Post Courier* (Port Moresby) 20 July, 5.

McElhanon, K. and C.L. Voorhoeve. 1970. *The Trans–New Guinea Phylum: Explorations in Deep-Level Genetic Relationships*. Canberra: Linguistic Circle of Canberra.

McKee, C.O. 1976. 'Investigations at Mount Lamington 1960–75'. *Geological Survey of Papua New Guinea* 76 (21).

McPhedran, C. 2002. *White Butterflies*. Sydney: University of New South Wales Press.

Meek, V.L. 1982. *The University of Papua New Guinea: A Case Study in the Sociology of Higher Education*. St Lucia: University of Queensland Press.

Memorandum. 1951. 'Re-Organisation of Northern Division: Rehabilitation Resulting from Volcanic Disturbance of 21st January, 1951'. Copy of anonymous typescript, 31 January 1951, probably by the government secretary to Ivan Champion. Ivan Champion Collection, Fryer Library, University of Queensland, St Lucia, UQFL137, Box 4.

Memorial Cemetery Popondetta. 1952. 'Dedication Ceremonies 24th November, 1952'. Brochure. Ivan Champion Collection, Fryer Library, University of Queensland, St Lucia, UQFL137, Box 6.

Miles, J. 1956. 'Native Commercial Agriculture in Papua'. *South Pacific* 9 (2): 318–29.

Milner, S. 1957. *Victory in Papua*. United States Army in World War II: The War in the Pacific. Washington DC: Office of the Chief of Military History.

Modjeska, D. 2009. 'Fabric of Wisdom: The Context of Omie Nioge'. In *Wisdom of the Mountain: Art of the Omie*, by Sana Balai, 21–30. Melbourne: National Gallery of Victoria.

Modjeska, D. 2012. *The Mountain*. Sydney: Vintage, Random Press.

Modjeska, D. 2017. Unpublished correspondence with author dealing with anthropological work with the Omie people. R.W.J. Collections: Box 36B, Lamington Eruption 1951, General Correspondence 2017–19, J–K, Folder 7, sleeves 23–24.

Monckton, C.A.W. 1905. 'Resident Magistrate's Report—Northern Division'. In *Annual Report on British New Guinea 1899–1900*, appendix G, 33–38. Brisbane: Government Printer.

Monckton, C.A.W. 1921. *Some Experiences of a New Guinea Resident Magistrate*. London: John Lane the Bodley Head.

Monckton, C.A.W. 1922. *Last Days in New Guinea Being Further Experience of a New Guinea Resident Magistrate*. London: John Lane the Bodley Head Ltd.

Monckton, C.A.W. 1934. *New Guinea Recollections*. London: John Lane the Bodley Head Ltd.

Montgomery, J.N., M.F. Glaessner and N. Osbourne. 1950. 'Outline of the Geology of Australian New Guinea'. In T*he Geology of the Commonwealth of Australia*, vol. 1, by T.W.E. David, edited by W.R. Browne, 662–85. London: E. Arnold.

Montgomery, J.N., N. Osbourne and M.F. Glaessner. 1944. *Explanatory Notes to Accompany a Geological Sketch Map of Eastern New Guinea*. Melbourne: Australian Military Forces.

Moresby, J. 1876. *Discoveries and Surveys in New Guinea and the D'Entrecasteaux Islands. A Cruise in Polynesia and Visits to the Pearl-Shelling Stations in Torres Straits of HMS Basilisk*. London: John Murray.

Moreton, M.H. 1894. 'Enclosure to Despatch No. 19 [by W.R. MacGregor]'. In *Annual Report on British New Guinea 1893–94*, appendix A, 37. Brisbane: Government Printer.

Morris, G. 1951. Untitled, unpublished report, 31 January 1951, to government secretary, sent through the director of District Services and Native Affairs, Port Moresby. Papua New Guinea National Archives, File CA32/4/39/24 (SN677, AN247, BN307).

Moss, T., 2017. *Guarding the Periphery: The Australian Army in Papua New Guinea, 1951–75*. Cambridge: Cambridge University Press. doi.org/10.1017/9781108182638.

Murphy, J.J. 1951. 'Mt Lamington Volcano Ascent'. Memorandum to officer-in-charge, Administration Field Group, Popondetta, 8 February 1951, from acting assistant district officer, sub-district office, Aitape. R.W.J. Collections: Box 7A, G.A.M. Taylor Documents, sleeve 13.

Murray Administrator. 1951a. International telegram from Popondetta to Department of External Territories, Canberra, Monday 22 January at 11.45 pm. National Archives of Australia, Canberra. Series A518 (A518/1), Control Symbol AV918/1 Part 1; Title: Papuan—Miscellaneous—Volcanic Eruption—Mt Lamington.

Murray Administrator. 1951b. International telegram from Popondetta to Department of External Territories, Canberra, Tuesday 23 January at 1730 hours. National Archives of Australia, Canberra. Series A518 (A518/1), Control Symbol AV918/1 Part 1; Title: Papuan—Miscellaneous—Volcanic Eruption—Mt Lamington.

Murray Administrator. 1951c. International telegram from Popondetta for the minister, Department of External Territories, Canberra, Wednesday 24 January, at 8.30 pm. National Archives of Australia, Canberra. Series A518 (A518/1), Control Symbol AV918/1 Part 1; Title: Papuan—Miscellaneous—Volcanic Eruption—Mt Lamington.

Murray Administrator. 1951d. International telegram from Popondetta to the Department of External Territories, Canberra, Monday 29 January, at 0800 hours. National Archives of Australia, Canberra. Series A518 (A518/1), Control Symbol AV918/1 Part 2; Title: Papuan—Miscellaneous—Volcanic Eruption—Mt Lamington.

Murray Administrator. 1951e. International telegram from Popondetta for the minister, Department of External Territories, Canberra, Monday 29 January, at 2058 hours. National Archives of Australia, Canberra. Series A518 (A518/1), Control Symbol AV918/1 Part 2; Title: Papuan—Miscellaneous—Volcanic Eruption—Mt Lamington.

Murray Administrator. 1951f. International telegram from Popondetta to the Department of External Territories, Canberra, Saturday 3 February at 1500 hours. National Archives of Australia, Canberra. Series A518 (A518/1), Control Symbol AV918/1 Part 2; Title: Papuan—Miscellaneous—Volcanic Eruption—Mt Lamington.

Murray Administrator. 1951g. International telegram from Popondetta to the Department of External Territories, Canberra, Tuesday 6 February at 0920 hours. National Archives of Australia, Canberra. Series A518 (A518/1), Control Symbol AV918/1 Part 2; Title: Papuan—Miscellaneous—Volcanic Eruption—Mt Lamington.

Murray Administrator. 1951h. International telegram from Popondetta for the minister, Department of External Territories, Canberra, Thursday 8 February at 1235 hours. National Archives of Australia, Canberra. Series A518 (A518/1), Control Symbol AV918/1 Part 3; Title: Papuan—Miscellaneous—Volcanic Eruption—Mt Lamington.

Murray Administrator. 1951i. Typescript of international telegram from Popondetta for the minister, Department of External Territories, Canberra, Wednesday 14 February at 1410 hours. National Archives of Australia, Canberra. Series A518 (A518/1), Control Symbol AV918/1 Part 3; Title: Papuan—Miscellaneous—Volcanic Eruption—Mt Lamington.

Murray Administrator. 1951j. International telegram from Port Moresby to the Department of External Territories, Canberra, Friday 23 February at 1155 hours. National Archives of Australia, Canberra. Series A518 (A518/1), Control Symbol AV918/1 Part 3; Title: Papuan—Miscellaneous—Volcanic Eruption—Mt Lamington.

Murray Administrator. 1951k. 'Mount Lamington Eruption: Rescue Parties'. Letter to the secretary, Department of External Territories, Canberra, Wednesday 28 February 1951. National Archives of Australia, Canberra. Series A518 (A518/1), Control Symbol AV918/1 Part 3; Title: Papuan—Miscellaneous—Volcanic Eruption—Mt Lamington.

Murray Administrator. 1951l. International telegram from Port Moresby to the Department of External Territories, Canberra, Monday 5 March at 2100 hours. National Archives of Australia, Canberra. Series A518 (A518/1), Control Symbol AV918/1 Part 3; Title: Volcanic Eruption—Mt Lamington.

Murray Administrator. 1951m. International telegram from Port Moresby to the Department of External Territories, Canberra, Sunday 25 March at 1015 hours. National Archives of Australia, Canberra. Series A518 (A518/1), Control Symbol AV918/1 Part 3; Title: Volcanic Eruption—Mt Lamington.

Murray, J.B., B. van Wyk de Vries, A. Pitty, P. Sargent and L. Wooller. 2018. 'Gravitational Sliding of the Mt Etna Massif Along a Sloping Basement'. *Bulletin of Volcanology* 80 (40). doi.org/10.1007/s00445-018-1209-1.

Murray, J.H.P. 1912. *Papua or British New Guinea*. London: Fisher Unwin.

Murray, J.K. 1951a. 'Reports: Mount Lamington Eruption'. Memorandum, 31 March 1951, to the secretary of the Department of External Territories, Canberra. Papua New Guinea National Archives, File CA32/4/39/24 (SN677, AN247, BN 307).

Murray, J.K. 1951b. 'Victims: Mount Lamington Disaster'. Letter, 19 September 1951, to the secretary, Department of External Territories. Papua New Guinea National Archives FN 32/4/39 (SN 677, AN 247, Box 305).

Murray, J.K. 1951c. 'Mount Lamington Disaster Death Roll (Native)—List of Surviving Dependents'. Letter, 29 October 1951, to the secretary, Department of External Territories, Canberra. National Archives of Australia, Canberra. Series A518 (A518/1), Control Symbol AV918/1H; Title: Papuan—Volcanic Eruption—Mt Lamington—Death Roll, Native.

Murray, J.K. 1968. 'In Retrospect: 1945–1952'. Unpublished paper prepared on the occasion of the Second Waigani Seminar, Port Moresby. Typescript held in the Ivan Champion Collection, Fryer Library, University of Queensland, St Lucia, UQFL137, Box 5.

NAA (National Archives of Australia). 1943–45. 'Vulcanology and Volcanoes—Papua and New Guinea—Volcanic Eruption Goropu Papua 1948'. Series A518, Control Symbol E317/3/1, Item 432711.

Narakobi, B. 1980. *The Melanesian Way*. Port Moresby: Institute of Papua New Guinea Studies.

Nelson, H. 1972. *Papua New Guinea: Black Unity or Black Chaos*. Ringwood, Vic.: Penguin Books.

Nelson, H.N. 1976. *Black, White and Gold: Goldmining in Papua New Guinea 1878–1930*. Canberra: Australian National University Press. doi.org/10.22459/bwg.07.2016.

Nelson, H. 1978. 'The Swinging Index: Capital Punishment and British and Australian Administrations in Papua and New Guinea, 1888–1945'. *Journal of Pacific History* 13, 130–52. doi.org/10.1080/00223347808572351.

Nelson, H. 1982. *Taim Bilong Masta: The Australian Involvement with Papua New Guinea*. Sydney: Australian Broadcasting Commission.

Nelson, H.N. 1986. 'Murray, Sir John Hubert Plunkett (1861–1940)'. *Australian Dictionary of Biography*. Vol. 10. Carlton: Melbourne University Press. adb.anu.edu.au/biography/murray-sir-john-hubert-plunkett-7711/text13505.

Nelson, H.N. 1993. 'Cleland, Sir Donald Mackinnon (Don) (1901–1975)'. *Australian Dictionary of Biography*. Vol. 13. Melbourne: Melbourne University Press. adb.anu.edu.au/biography/cleland-sir-donald-mackinnon-don-9762.

New Guinea Research Bulletin. 1966. 'Orokaiva Papers: Miscellaneous Papers on the Orokaiva of North East Papua'. *NGRU Bulletin* 13.

New Guinea. 1945. *Laws of Territory of New Guinea, 1945–1949*. [Canberra]: Administration of the Territory of Papua-New Guinea.

Newton, J. 1985. *Orokaiva Production and Change*. Pacific Research Monograph 11. Canberra: Development Studies Centre, The Australian National University.

Nicholas, Justice [H.G.]. 1940. 'Sir Hubert Murray, KCMG'. *Australian Quarterly* 12 (2): 5–8. doi.org/10.2307/20630836.

North Queensland Register. 1951. 'Photographing Mt Lamington Area'. 3 March, 15.

Official Secretary. 1951. Memorandum to the administrator, 8 June 1951. Papua New Guinea National Archives, File FN1-5-8 (SN 677, AN 244, Box 163).

Old Planter. 1951. 'Are Lamington Refugees Being Mollycoddled?' *Pacific Islands Monthly* 21 (8): 102.

Opeba, W.J. 1977. 'The Peroveta of Buna'. In *The Prophets of Melanesia*, edited by G.W. Trompf, 212–37. Port Moresby: Institute of Papua New Guinea Studies.

Opeba, W.J. 1987. 'Melanesian Cult Movements as Traditional Religious and Ritual Responses to Change'. In *The Gospel Is Not Western: Black Theologies from the Southwest Pacific*, edited by G.W. Trompf, 49–66. New York: Orbis Books.

Oreba, J. 1976. 'Sumbiripa ta Hihi'. In *Joel ta Hihi Book*, by Joel Oreba, edited by B. Larsen, L.M. Gagari and L.V. Sareki. Ukarumpa, Papua New Guinea: Summer Institute of Linguistics.

Osmond, M., A. Pawley and M.A. Ross. 2007. 'The Landscape'. In *The Lexicon of Proto Oceanic: The Culture and Environment of Ancestral Oceanic Society*. Vol. 2: The Physical Environment, edited by M.A. Ross, A. Pawley and M. Osmond, 35–89. Pacific Linguistics 545. Canberra: Pacific Linguistics, The Australian National University. doi.org/10.22459/lpo.03.2007.

Pacific Islands Monthly. 1951a. 'Vale, "Dicky" Humphries: Well-Known Papuan Official Lost in Volcanic Disaster', February, no. 22 (2): 13.

Pacific Islands Monthly. 1951b. 'Operation Volcano', March, no. 22 (8): 35.

Pacific Islands Monthly. 1951c. 'Why No Official Warning? Demand for Inquiry about Lamington Disaster', no. 21 (7): 10.

Pacific Islands Monthly. 1951d. 'High Cost of Mt Lamington Eruption and Relief Fund Mounts', April, no. 21 (9): 31.

Pacific Islands Monthly. 1951e. 'Rehabilitation of Lamington Evacuees. Ilimo Camp Now Closed', June, no. 21 (11): 27.

Pacific Islands Monthly. 1951f. 'Headquarters to Replace Higaturu', July, no. 21 (12): 29.

Pacific Islands Monthly. 1952. 'NG's Irresponsible Critics: Red Crocodile Tears Over Natives', November, no. 23 (4): 14.

Pacific Islands Monthly. 1953a. 'Blue-Print for Future of N-Guinea'. February, no. 23 (7): 21.

Pacific Islands Monthly. 1953b. 'CSIRO Regional Survey Party', July, no. 23 (12): 35.

Palmer, H.E. 1992. 'Missionaries Murdered in WWII'. *Sydney Morning Herald*, 22 May, 12.

Papua. 1945a. *Laws of the Territory of Papua 1888–1945*. [Canberra]: Administration of the Territory of Papua-New Guinea.

Papua. 1945b. 'Natives' to 'Wills and Intestacy'. In *Laws of the Territory of Papua 1888–1945*, vol. 4, 3287–4422. [Canberra]: Administration of the Territory of Papua-New Guinea.

Papuan Courier. 1940. 'Sudden death of Sir Hubert Murray, KCMG. A Great Man's Burial'. 1 March 1940, 7.

Patience, Sister (P. Durdin). 2001. 'Recollections of Mount Lamington'. *Apostrophe* (Vicarage at St Peter's Church, Eastern Hill, Melbourne, Information Sheet) 49, 1–3.

Patrol Officer. 1951. 'Inspection—Ajeka Village'. Memorandum, 23 February 1951, from patrol officer at Ilimo to the officer-in-charge at Ilimo. The signature on the memorandum is indecipherable but may be that of I.W. Wiseman. Ivan Champion Collection, Fryer Library, University of Queensland, St Lucia, UQFL137, Box 6.

Paul, R. 1989. *Retreat from Kokoda: The Australian Campaign in New Guinea 1942*. Port Melbourne: Mandarin Australia.

Pawley, A. 2005. 'The Chequered Career of the Trans New Guinea Hypothesis: Recent Research and its Implications'. In *Papuan Pasts: Cultural, Linguistic and Biological Histories of Papuan-Speaking Peoples*, edited by A. Pawley, R. Attenborough, J. Golson and R. Hide, 67–107. Canberra: Pacific Linguistics, The Australian National University.

Pawley, A., R. Attenborough, J. Golson and R. Hide, eds. 2005. *Papuan Pasts: Cultural, Linguistic and Biological Histories of Papuan-Speaking Peoples*. Canberra: Pacific Linguistics, The Australian National University.

Pawley, A. and H. Hammarström. 2018. 'The Trans New Guinea Family'. In *The Languages and Linguistics of the New Guinea Area: A Comprehensive Guide*, edited by B. Palmer, 21–196. Berlin: de Gruyter Mouton. doi.org/10.1515/9783110295252-002.

Perkins, D.D., B.C. Turner and E.G. Barry. 1976. 'Strains of Neurospora Collected from Nature'. *Evolution* 30 (2): 281–313. doi.org/10.1111/j.1558-5646.1976.tb00910.x.

Perret, F.A. 1937. *The Eruption of Mt Pelée: 1929–1932*. Washington, DC: Carnegie Institute of Washington.

Phillips Deputy Administrator. 1951. International telegram from Port Moresby to Department of External Territories, Canberra, Tuesday 23 January, 2110 hours. National Archives of Australia, Canberra. Series A518 (A518/1), Control Symbol AV918/1 Part 1; Title: Papuan—Miscellaneous—Volcanic Eruption—Mt Lamington.

Phillips Deputy. 1951. International telegram from Port Moresby to the Department of External Territories, Canberra, Monday 5 March 1951 at 1400 hours. National Archives of Australia, Canberra. Series A518 (A518/1), Control Symbol AV918/1 Part 3; Title: Volcanic Eruption—Mt Lamington.

Phillips, F.B. 1951a. Copy of personal letter, 27 January 1951, from the deputy administrator to Air Marshal Williams, director general of the Department of Civil Aviation, regarding the work done by Mr Arthur, regional director, DCA. Papua New Guinea National Archives, File 32/4/39/24 (SN 677, AN 247, Box 307).

Phillips, F.B. 1951b. Letter, 4 February 1951, to His Honour the Administrator at Popondetta. Papua New Guinea National Archives, File GH1-5-7 (SN667, AN244, BN136).

Phillips, F.B. 1951c. Letter, 27 February 1951, from the Supreme Court, Port Moresby to His Honour the Administrator, Government House, Port Moresby. National Archives of Australia, Canberra. Series A518 (A518/1), Control Symbol AV918/1 Part 3; Title: Papuan—Miscellaneous—Volcanic Eruption—Mt Lamington.

Plant, H.T. 1951. 'Re-Establishment of the Isivita Villages'. Memorandum to the director, District Services and Native Affairs, Port Moresby, 24 March 1951. Manuscript copy lodged with the National Research Institute, Port Moresby.

Porter, R.G. 1951a. 'New Guinea: Eye-Witness Record'. *Australian Board of Missions Review* 34 (2): 24–27.

Porter, R.G. 1951b. 'Report on Incidents Concerning the Mount Lamington Eruption as Seen from Isivita'. R.W.J. Collections: Box 7A, G.A.M. Taylor Documents 1950–63, Folder 1, sleeve 23.

Porter, R.G. 1951c. 'New Guinea: A Mushroom Shape'. *The Living Church* 122 (16): 7–10.

Qantas. 1951. 'Operation Volcano'. *Qantas Empire Airways Staff Magazine*, March–May, 9–10 and 13.

Quinlivan, P.J. 1988. 'Phillips, Sir Frederick Beaumont (1890–1957)'. *Australian Dictionary of Biography*. Vol. 11. Melbourne: Melbourne University Press. adb.anu.edu.au/biography/phillips-sir-frederick-beaumont-8034.

Radford, A.J. 2012. *Singsings, Sutures & Sorcery: A 50 Year Experience in Papua New Guinea: A Dokta at Large in the Land of the Unexpected*. Preston: Mosaic Press.

Rautamara, P. 1951. 'The Higaturu Tragedy'. *Living Church* 122 (16): 9.

Reay, M. 1951. Diary entries for 16–19 January 1951. R.W.J. Collection 7: G.A.M. Taylor Documents, 1950–63, Folder 1, sleeve 4.

Reay, M. 1953. 'Social Control amongst the Orokaiva'. *Oceania* 24 (2): 110–18. doi.org/10.1002/j.1834-4461.1953.tb00594.x.

Reay, M. 1992. 'An Innocent in the Garden of Eden'. In *Ethnographic Presents: Pioneering Anthropologists in the Papua New Guinea Highlands*, edited by T.E. Hayes, 137–66. Berkeley: University of California Press. doi.org/10.1525/california/9780520077454.003.0005.

Redlich, P. 2012. *My Brother Vivian, and the Christian Martyrs of Papua New Guinea*. West Pennant Hills, NSW: Patrick Redlich.

Rich, M.C. 1951. 'Suggested Action in Relation to Re-Establishment in Devastated Areas of Northern Division'. Memorandum, 31 January 1951, to the administrator through the government secretary from the acting assistant director for the Department of District Services and Native Affairs. Typescript. Ivan Champion Collection, Fryer Library, University of Queensland, St Lucia, UQFL137, Box 6.

Rickwood, F. 1992. *The Kutubu Discovery: Papua New Guinea, its People, the Country and the Exploration and Discovery of Oil*. Glenroy, Vic.: Book Generation Pty Limited.

Rimoldi. M. 1966. *Land Tenure and Land Use among the Mount Lamington Orokaiva*. New Guinea Research Bulletin 11. Canberra: New Guinea Research Unit, The Australian National University.

Rooney, P. 1951. Memorandum to Mrs Wardrop, general secretary of the Red Cross Papua & New Guinea Division, Port Moresby. An annotation on the typescript reads: 'Under cover note dated 13/8/51'. Australian Red Cross Society, National Office, Correspondence Files, National Headquarters. University of Melbourne Archives, 2015.0033, Unit 188, Folder 10, Natural Disasters Mt Lamington 1951.

Ross, M. 2005. 'Pronouns as a Preliminary Diagnostic for Grouping Papuan Languages'. In *Papuan Pasts: Cultural, Linguistic and Biological Histories of Papuan-Speaking Peoples*, edited by A. Pawley, R. Attenborough, J. Golson and R. Hide, 15–65. Canberra: Pacific Linguistics, The Australian National University.

Royal Australian Survey Corps. 1974. 'Popondetta. 1:100,00 Scale Topographic Map 8580'. Produced under the direction of the Chief of the General Staff.

Ruxton, B.P. 1966a. 'Correlation and Stratigraphy of Dacitic Ash-Fall Layers in Northeastern Papua'. *Journal of the Geological Society of Australia* 13, 41–67. doi.org/10.1080/00167616608728605.

Ruxton, B.P. 1966b. 'A Late Pleistocene to Recent Rhyodacite-Trachybasalt-Basaltic Latite Association in North-East Papua'. *Bulletin Volcanologique* 29, 347–74. doi.org/10.1007/bf02597163.

Ruxton, B.P. 1988. 'Towards a Weathering Model of Mount Lamington Ash, Papua New Guinea'. *Earth-Science Reviews* 25, 387–97. doi.org/10.1016/0012-8252(88)90006-2.

Ruxton, B.P. 1999. 'The Managalase Volcanic Field and Associated Mineral Occurrences, Papua New Guinea'. In *Proceedings of the 1999 PacRim Congresses*, 335–40. Carlton, Vic.: Australasian Institute of Mining and Metallurgy.

Ruxton, B.P. 2007. 'Kururi Volcano: A Note on its Historical Activity'. Unpublished note by author based on interviews with Bryan Ruxton in 2006–07. R.W.J. Collections: Box 36A, Lamington Eruption 1951, General Correspondence, 2017–19, Folder 4, sleeve 43.

Ruxton, B.P., H.A. Haantjens, K. Paijmans and J.C. Saunders. (1967) 2010. 'Lands of the Safia–Pongani area, Territory of Papua and New Guinea'. Land Research Surveys 17. Accessed 21 September 2019, www.publish.csiro.au/CR/LRS17.

Ruxton, B.P. and I. McDougall. 1967. 'Denudation Rates in Northeast Papua from Potassium-Argon Dating of Lavas'. *American Journal of Science* 265: 545–61. doi.org/10.2475/ajs.265.7.545.

Ryan, P. 1968. 'The Australian New Guinea Administrative Unit'. Second Waigani Seminar, University of Papua New Guinea, Port Moresby, 30 May to 5 June 1968.

Ryan, P. 1973. 'The ANGAU Contribution'. In *Readings in New Guinea History*, edited by B. Jinks, P. Biskup and H. Nelson, 315–17. Sydney: Angus and Robertson.

Saunders, S.J. 2018–19. Unpublished correspondence with author dealing with Higaturu memorial notice board. R.W.J. Collections: Box 36B, Lamington Eruption 1951, General Correspondence 2017–19, J–K, Folder 8, sleeves 33–34.

Schleusener, W. 1951. Typescript of letter to his parents from the Cocoa Area, Sangara Rubber Plantation, on 21 January 1951. Slightly edited version reproduced by J.L. Searle (1995, 241–43). Undated copy in R.W.J. Collection 33C, sleeves 64–65.

Schwimmer, E. 1969. *Cultural Consequences of a Volcanic Eruption Experienced by the Mount Lamington Orokaiva*. Eugene, Oregon: Department of Anthropology.

Schwimmer, E. 1973. *Exchange in the Social Structure of the Orokaiva: Traditional and Emergent Ideologies in the Northern Division of Papua*. New York: St Martin's Press.

Schwimmer, E. 1976. 'Introduction'. In *'The Vailala Madness' and Other Essays*, edited by Francis Edgar Williams, 11–47. London: Hurst & Company. doi.org/10.1525/ae.1978.5.2.02a00170.

Schwimmer, E.G. 1977. 'What Did the Eruption Mean?' In *Exiles and Migrants in Oceania*, edited by M.D Lieber, 296–341 Honolulu: University Press of Hawaii. doi.org/10.2307/j.ctv9zckrr.17.

Scofield, J. 1962. 'Mount Lamington Still Smolders 11 Years after Blowing its Top'. Photograph reproduced in 'Netherlands New Guinea: Bone of Contention in the South Pacific'. *National Geographic* 121 (5): 628–29.

Searle, C.E. 1936. 'Mountains, Mist and Mud: A 300 Mile Trek in Papua'. *Radiogram* 3 (14): 28–30.

Searle, J.L. 1995. 'Memini … (I remember)'. Unpublished memoirs. National Library of Australia, MS 9425. See also R.W.J. Collections: Box 33C, Lamington Eruption 1951, Correspondence and Memoirs, Mart–Z, Folder 23, sleeve 61, for a copy of Part 9 of the memoirs entitled 'Volcanic Eruption—1951'.

Searle, P. n.d. 'Description of his Father's Wartime Activities around Kokoda by Peter Searle'. Accessed 11 September 2019, www.thestiks.com.au/Gallery pages/PageAwala.htm.

Shaw, D.E. 1980–82. Unpublished correspondence with author. R.W.J. Collections: Box 33C, Lamington Eruption 1951, Correspondence and Memoirs, Mart–Z, Folder 24.

Shaw, D.E. 1982. 'Ecology of Fungi in New Guinea'. In *Biogeography and Ecology of New Guinea*, edited by J.L. Gressit, 475–96. Dordrecht: Springer Netherlands. doi.org/10.1007/978-94-009-8632-9_20.

Siebert, L. 1984. 'Large Volcanic Debris Avalanches: Characteristics of Source Areas, Deposits, and Associated Eruptions'. *Journal of Volcanology and Geothermal Research* 22, 163–97. doi.org/10.1016/0377-0273(84)90002-7.

Siebert, L., T. Simkin and P. Kimberley. 2010. *Volcanoes of the World*, 3rd ed. Washington, DC: Smithsonian Institution and University of California Press.

Simkin, T. and L. Siebert. 1994. *Volcanoes of the World*, 2nd ed. Washington DC: Smithsonian Institution.

Sinclair, J. 1978. *Wings of Gold: How the Aeroplane Developed New Guinea*. Bathurst: Robert Brown.

Sinclair, J. 1981. *Kiap: Australia's Patrol Officers in Papua New Guinea*. Sydney: Pacific Publications.

Sinclair, J. 1986. *Balus: The Aeroplane in Papua New Guinea*. Vol. 1, The Early Years. Bathurst: Robert Brown & Associates.

Sinclair, J. 1988. *Last Frontiers: The Explorations of Ivan Champion*. Broadbeach Waters, Qld: Pacific Press.

Sjoberg, G. 1962. 'Disasters and Social Change'. In *Man and Society in Disaster*, edited by G. W. Baker and D.W. Chapman, 356–84. New York: Basic Books.

Sligo, G. 2013. *The Backroom Boys: Alfred Conlon and Army's Directorate of Research and Civil Affairs, 1942–46*. Newport, NSW: Big Sky Publishing.

Smith, I.E. 1969. 'Notes on the volcanoes of Mount Bagana and Mount Victory, Territory of Papua New Guinea'. *Bureau of Mineral Resources Record* 12.

Smith, I.E.M. 1981. 'Young Volcanoes in Eastern Papua'. In *Cooke-Ravian Volume of Volcanological Papers*, edited by R.W. Johnson, R.W., 257–65. Port Moresby: Department of Minerals and Energy.

South Pacific Post. 1951a. Articles in the issue of Friday 19 January. 'Mt Lamington Erupts' (p. 1). 'Administrator on Tour' (p. 2).

South Pacific Post. 1951b. Articles in the issue of Friday 26 January. 'Plan Ready for Any New Emergency in Our Worst Disaster' (pp. 1–2). 'Tribute of a Native' (p. 1). 'Missing Man Took This Picture' (p. 1). 'Casualty List' (p. 4). 'Natives Have Burns Treated' (p. 4). 'Unheeded Warning!' (p. 8). 'The Legend of Mount Lamington' (p. 8; by L. Austen). 'Letters to the Editor': 'Reception of Survivors' (by E.L. Hand) (p. 9). 'Australia Volcano Proof' (p. 10).

South Pacific Post. 1951c. Articles in the issue of Friday 2 February. 'Full Inquiry Is Essential' (p. 1). 'Administrator Launches Relief Fund for Lamington Victims' (p. 1). 'Map of Southeastern Papua' (p. 3). 'Big Team of Pressmen' (p. 3). 'Letters to the Editor': 'Criticism of Red Cross' (H. Gwilt and others), 'Plenty of Donors in Brisbane' ('H.B.'), 'Work of Qantas in Emergency (L.M. Henry) (p. 9).

South Pacific Post. 1951d. Articles in the issue of Friday 9 February. 'Lamington Relief Fund Gets Fine Start' (p. 1). 'Hallstrom Gives £1,000' (p. 1). 'No Need for Inquiry Says Spender' (p. 1). 'Photographs Needed' (p. 1). 'Judge Gore Launches Disaster Appeal' (p. 3). 'Donations Received' (p. 3). 'Appeal by Missions' (p. 3). 'The Last Poem of Victim [W.R. Humphries]' (p. 3). 'Red Cross Was Ready for Action' (p. 8). 'Letters To The Editor': 'Inquiry Not Supported' (W.A. Kienzle) (p. 9).

South Pacific Post. 1951e. Articles in the issue of Friday 16 February. 'Rabaul Volcanoes Unchanged' (p. 2). 'Dobell Landscape to Aid Fund' (p. 3). 'Donations Received' (p. 3). 'Letters to the Editor': 'The Lamington Disaster' (T.W. Upson) (p. 9).

South Pacific Post. 1951f. 'Rabaul Party to See Mt Lamington Area—Move By Administrator to Stress Horrors of Eruption', 11 May, p. 9.

Spate, O.K.H. 1952. 'Resources and Economic Potentialities'. Typescript. In Spate, Davidson and Firth 1952, Ivan Champion Collection, Fryer Library, University of Queensland, St Lucia, UQFL137, Box 4.

Spate, O.K.H., J.W. Davidson and R. Firth. 1952. 'Notes on New Guinea October–November 1951'. Typescripts of three separate reports by these authors, held in the Ivan Champion Collection, Fryer Library, University of Queensland, St Lucia, UQFL137, Box 4.

Speer, A. 2005. Album of 62 photographs. Collection of photographs and colour slides from the 1951 eruption of Mt Lamington Papua New Guinea/Albert Speer. National Library of Australia, Bibliographic ID 3511696.

Speer, A. 2005–14. Unpublished correspondence with author. R.W.J. Collections: Box 32, Albert Speer Correspondence on the Lamington Eruption 1951: 2005–14.

Speer, A. 2007. 'Bert (Albert) Speer MBE: Experiences at the Lamington Volcanic Disaster Area in 1951'. Unpublished manuscript. R.W.J. Collection: Box 32, Albert Speer Correspondence on the Lamington Eruption 1951, 2005–14, Folder 3, sleeve 42.

Speer, A. 2015. 'Albert Speer MBE'. In *The Volcano's Wife: The Great Untold Story*, by A. Cowley and P. Virtue, 105–09. Calwell, ACT: Inspiring Publishers.

Spender, P.C. 1951a. 'Statement by Minister for External Affairs and External Territories the Hon. P.C. Spender, Mount Lamington Eruption'. Reply to criticism of administration, 2 February 1951. National Archives of Australia, Canberra. Series A518 (A518/1), Control Symbol AV918/1 Part 2; Title: Papuan—Miscellaneous—Volcanic eruption—Mt Lamington.

Spender, P.C. 1951b. Handwritten note added to a memorandum entitled 'Mount Lamington Eruption: Criticism of Administration', 9 February 1951, from J.R. Halligan to the minister. National Archives of Australia, Canberra. Series A518 (A518/1), Control Symbol AV918/1 Part 2; Title: Papuan—Miscellaneous—Volcanic Eruption—Mt Lamington.

Stanley, E.R. 1918. 'Geological Expedition across the Owen Stanley Range'. In *Commonwealth of Australia Report for the Territory of Papua, 1917–18*, appendix D, 75–84 (map and cross section in appendix F). Melbourne: Government Printer.

Stanley, E.R. 1923. 'Report on the Salient Geological Features of the New Guinea Territory, Including Notes on Dialects and Ethnology'. In *Commonwealth of Australia Annual Report on Territory of New Guinea, 1921–22*, appendix B.

Stanley, E.R. 1924. *The Geology of Papua*. Melbourne: Government Printer.

Stead, V. 2018. 'History as Resource: Moral Reckoning with Place and with the Wartime Past in Oro Province, Papua New Guinea'. *Anthropological Forum* 28, 16–31. doi.org/10.1080/00664677.2018.1426439.

Stehn, Ch.E. and W.G. Woolnough. 1937. 'Report on Vulcanological and Seismological Investigations at Rabaul'. In *Commonwealth of Australia Parliamentary Paper 84 of 1937*, 149–58. Canberra: Government Printer.

Stephens, L.M. 1951. Untitled and incomplete report from Sangara, November 1951. R.W.J. Collections: Box 7A, G.A.M. Taylor Documents 1950–63, Folder 1, sleeve 13.

Stephens, L.M. 1953. 'The Mt Lamington Blast'. *Natural History* 62: 216–23.

Stone, P. 1995. *Hostages to Freedom—the Fall of Rabaul*. Yarrum, Vic.: Ocean Enterprises.

Strong, P. 1951. 'A Message to the Wider Church from the Bishop of New Guinea'. *Australian Board of Missions Review* 34 (3): 40–50.

Strong, P. 1981. *The New Guinea Diaries of Philip Strong 1936–1945*. Edited by D. Wetherell. South Melbourne: Macmillan.

Strong, W.M. 1916. 'Notes on the Northeastern Division of Papua'. *New Guinea. Geographical Journal* 48: 407–11, plus map following page 448. doi.org/10.2307/1779616.

Stuart, I. 1970. *Port Moresby Yesterday and Today*. Sydney: Pacific Publications.

Summerhayes, G.R., J.H. Field, B. Shaw and D. Gaffney. 2017. 'The Archaeology of Forest Exploitation and Change in the Tropics during the Pleistocene: The Case of Northern Sahul (Pleistocene New Guinea)'. *Quaternary International* 448, 14–30. doi.org/10.1016/j.quaint.2016.04.023.

Summerhayes, G.R., M. Leavesley, A. Fairbairn, H. Mandui, J. Field, A. Ford and R. Fullagar. 2010. 'Human Adaptation and Plant Use in Highland New Guinea 49,000 to 44,000 Years Ago'. *Science* 330 (6000): 78–81. doi.org/10.1126/science.1193130.

Sun (Melbourne). 1951. 'Police Round-Up on Volcano Slopes: Natives Break into Death Area, Loot Houses'. 30 January, 9.

Sydney Morning Herald. 1951. 'Volcano's Toll May Reach 8,000'. 22 February, 7.

Talai, B. 2006. 'Life History: Benjamin Patangala Talai & Rabaul Volcano Observatory'. Unpublished digital account provided to author. R.W.J. Collections: Box 25, RVO Staff Members and PNG Artists: Memoirs, Careers and Recollections, Folder 7.

Taylor, B.W. 1957. 'Plant Succession on Recent Volcanoes in Papua'. *Journal of Ecology* 45, 233–43. doi.org/10.2307/2257087.

Taylor, B.W. 1964. 'Vegetation of the Wanigela–Cape Vogel Area'. In Haantjens et al. (1964b) 2010b, 69–83.

Taylor, D. 1943. Untitled letter, 29 December [1943], to an unidentified recipient. Anglican Archives, New Guinea Collection, University of Papua New Guinea, Port Moresby. AA Box 57, File 7.

Taylor, G.A. 1951. 'Mount Lamington Eruption'. Report stating knowledge of the eruption up to 5 February 1951. Copy of unpublished typescript. R.W.J. Collections: Box 7A, G.A.M. Taylor Documents 1950–63, Folder 1, sleeves 35–36.

Taylor, G.A. 1956. 'Review of Volcanic Activity in the Territory of Papua-New Guinea, the Solomon and New Hebrides Islands'. *Bulletin Volcanologique* 18, 25–37. doi.org/10.1007/bf02596611.

Taylor, G.A.M. 1958. *The 1951 Eruption of Mount Lamington, Papua*. Bureau of Mineral Resources, Bulletin 38. Canberra: Commonwealth Government Printer.

Territories. 1951. Telegram, 26 January 1951, from the Department of External Territories, Canberra, to the administrator, Port Moresby, referring to the telephone conversation that morning between Mr Halligan and Mr Lonergan and dealing with advice from Dr Fisher (see Anonymous 1951d).

Territories. 1952. International telegram, 13 June 1952, to the administration in Port Moresby for the attention of the Cleland [Administrator D.M. Cleland] from Lambert [Secretary C.R. Lambert, Department of Territories] in Canberra. Papua New Guinea National Archives, File 44/4/4/4 (SN677, AN247, BN353).

Thompson, J.E. and N.H. Fisher. 1965. 'Mineral Deposits of New Guinea and Papua, and their Tectonic Setting'. Proceedings of the Eighth Commonwealth Mining and Metallurgical Congress Australia and New Zealand, Vol. 6—General, 115–48.

Tomkins, D. and B. Hughes. 1969. *The Road from Gona*. Sydney: Angus and Robertson.

Tomlin, J.W.S. 1951. *Awakening: A History of the New Guinea Mission*. London: New Guinea Mission, Fulham Palace.

Trompf, G.F., ed. 1977. *The Prophets of Melanesia*. Port Moresby: Institute of Papua New Guinea Studies.

Trompf, G.W., ed. 1987a. *The Gospel Is Not Western: Black Theologies from the Southwest Pacific*. New York: Orbis Books.

Trompf, G.W. 1987b. 'Geographical, Historical, and Intellectual Perspective'. In *The Gospel Is Not Western: Black Theologies from the Southwest Pacific*, edited by G.W. Trompf, 3–15. New York: Orbis Books.

Trompf, G.W. 2006. *Religions of Melanesia: A Bibliographic Survey*. Westport Connecticut and London: Praeger.

Urquhart, C.H. 1951. Letter, 28 March 1951, to Colonel J.K. Murray. Papua New Guinea National Archives, File GH1-5-8 (1) (SN667, AN244, BN136).

van Bemmelen, R.W. 1939. 'The Geotectonic Structure of New Guinea'. *De Ingenieur in Nederlandshe-Indië* 6 (2): 17–27.

van Bemmelen, R.W. 1982. Letter from R.W. van Bemmelen to R.W.J., 3 March 1982, dealing with van Bemmelen's paper of 1939. Copy includes a handwritten note by N.H. Fisher responding to the letter. R.W.J. Collections: Box 10, N.H. Fisher Publications, Correspondence, and Photographs 1939–2007, Folder 4, sleeve 35.

Virtue, P., 2018. Unpublished correspondence with author dealing with experiences during and after Lamington eruption of 1951. R.W.J. Collections: Box 36B, Lamington Eruption 1951, General Correspondence 2017–19, J–Z, Folder 9, sleeves 45–52.

Waddell, E.W. and P.A. Krinks. 1968. *The Organisation of Production and Distribution among the Orokaiva*. New Guinea Research Bulletin 24. Canberra: New Guinea Research Unit, The Australian National University.

Wadge, G., B.T. McCormick Kilbride, M. Edmonds and R.W. Johnson. 2018. 'Persistent Growth of a Young Andesite Lava Cone: Bagana Volcano, Papua New Guinea'. *Journal of Volcanology and Geothermal Research* 356, 304–15. doi.org/10.1016/j.jvolgeores.2018.03.012.

Waiko, J.D. 2003. *Papua New Guinea: A History of Our Times*. Melbourne: Oxford University Press.

Wakefield, D.C. 1989. 'Dog-Pigs and Other People'. In *Studies in Component Analysis*, edited by K. Franklin, 65–71. Ukarumpa: Summer School of Linguistics.

Wardrop, R.M. 1951a. Letter, 12 February 1951, to Sir John Newman-Morris, chairman of the Australian Red Cross Society. Australian Red Cross Society, National Office, Correspondence Files, National Headquarters. University of Melbourne Archives, 2015.0033, Unit 188, Folder 10, Natural Disasters Mt Lamington 1951.

Wardrop, R.M. 1951b. Report of the Papua and New Guinea Division of the Australian Red Cross on the Mt Lamington disaster by the general secretary, Port Moresby. Typed version, 5 April 1951. Australian Red Cross Society, National Office, Correspondence Files, National Headquarters. University of Melbourne Archives, 2015.0033, Unit 188, Folder 10, Natural Disasters Mt Lamington 1951.

Waterhouse, M. 2010. *Not a Poor Man's Field: The New Guinea Goldfields to 1941: An Australian Colonial History*. Braddon, ACT: Halstead Press.

West, F.J. 1968. *Hubert Murray: The Australian Pro-Consul*. Melbourne: Oxford University Press.

Wetherell, D. 1977. *Reluctant Mission: The Anglican Church in Papua New Guinea 1891–1942*. St Lucia: University of Queensland Press.

Wetherell, D. 1996. *Charles Able and the Kwato Mission of Papua New Guinea 1891–1975*. Melbourne: Melbourne University Press.

White, J.P., K.A.W. Crook and B.P. Ruxton. 1970. 'Kosipe: A Late Pleistocene Site in the Papuan Highlands'. *Proceedings of the Prehistoric Society* 36, 152–70. doi.org/10.1017/s0079497x00013128.

White, N.H. 1991. *Sharing the Climb*. Melbourne: Oxford University Press.

Whittaker, J.L., N.G. Gash, J.F. Hookey and R.J. Lacey. 1975. *Documents and Readings in New Guinea History: Prehistory to 1889*. Milton, Qld: The Jacaranda Press.

Wigmore, L. 1957. *The Japanese Thrust. Australia in the War of 1939–1945*. Series 1: Army, vol. 4. Canberra: Australian War Memorial.

Wilkinson, R. 1996. *Rocks to Riches: The Story of Australia's National Geological Survey*. St Leonards, NSW: Allen & Unwin.

Williams, F.E. 1928. *Orokaiva Magic*. London: Oxford University Press.

Williams, F.E. 1930. *Orokaiva Society*. London: Oxford University Press.

Williams, F.E. 1976. *'The Vailala Madness' and Other Essays*. London: C. Hurst & Company. doi.org/10.1525/ae.1978.5.2.02a00170.

Williams, F.E. 2001. *An Anthropologist in Papua: The Photography of F.E. Williams, 1922–23*. Adelaide: Crawford House Publishing.

Wodak, J. 1969. Joanne Wodak Collection of Ombisusu Stories (Folklore) from Papua New Guinea. Thirteen digitised stories including no. 11, 'Why Mt Lamington Erupted' (told by Hijo); no. 13, 'Sumbiripa Imbari (Mt Lamington)' (told by Hambo). The Australian National University Archives, AU ANUA 597. Accessed 21 September 2019, archivescollection.anu.edu.au/index.php/joanne-wodak-collection-of-ombisusu-stories-from-papua-new-guinea.

Worsley, P. 1970. *The Trumpet Shall Sound: A Study of 'Cargo' Cults in Melanesia*. London: Grenada Publishing.

Wurm, S.A., C.L. Voorhoeve and K. McElhanon. 1975. 'The Trans New Guinea Phylum in General'. In *New Guinea Area Languages and Language Study*, edited by S.A. Wurm, 299–322. Vol. 1. Papuan Languages and the New Guinea Linguistic Scene. Canberra: Pacific Linguistics, The Australian National University.

Yeoman, S.H. 1951. 'Observations Made at Kokoda, of Mt Lamington Eruption'. Unpublished memorandum to the director, DDS-NA, Port Moresby. R.W.J. Collection 7, sleeves 31–31. PMB 1362/28.

Young, M.W. and J. Clark, eds. 2001. 'Introduction'. In *An Anthropologist in Papua: The Photography of F.E. Williams 1922–23*, by F.E. Williams, 1–62. Adelaide: Crawford House Publishing.

APPENDICES

APPENDIX A: CORRESPONDENCE AND REFERENCE COLLECTIONS

R.W.J. Collections

Correspondence

The correspondence used for this study has been placed in nine archival boxes, classified into separate numbered files by the person's name and inserted into numbered sleeves. There is substantial crossover between the correspondence of many of the listed people in the collections, and names in some instances have had to be combined in the listings given below. Some files contain material from people with whom I did not correspond directly—notably, John Gunther, J.K. Murray, Marie Reay, Nancy White and F.W. Williams. The archival boxes, which are referred to as the 'R.W.J. Collections' in the reference list at the end of the book, will be offered for donation to the National Library of Australia.

Collection 31A, B, C: John R. Horne: A) 1973–2016, B) 2017–18 and C) 2018–19.

Collection 32: Albert Speer Correspondence 2005–14.

Collection 33A, A–G:

1. Cyril S. Belshaw
2. Peter V. Best and Gerry Bellis
3. Robert W. Blaikie

4. Alan Boag
5. Patricia M. Durdin (Sister Patience)
6. Philippa Earl and Athol James
7. General correspondence: mostly single items mainly from several otherwise listed people
8. John T. Gunther

Collection 33B, H–Mars:

1. Maxwell R. Hays
2. Jean Henderson
3. Maclaren J. Hiari
4. Nancy E. Johnstone
5. Frederick P.C. Kaad
6. Marjorie Kleckham, Betty Forster, Fred Kleckham Jr, Connie Morris, and Grainger Morris
7. Muriel L. Larner
8. Geoff Littler
9. David R.M. Marsh

Collection 33C, Mart–Z:

1. Desmond J. Martin
2. Harry T. and Ivane Plant
3. Betty and Robert G. Porter and Elsie Manley
4. Paul J. Quinlivan
5. Marie Reay and several others who corresponded on her life: Paula Brown Glick, Geoffrey Gray, Robin Hide, Francesca Merlan, May Stinear, Karina Taylor, Judith Wilson and Michael Young
6. Rhonwen Searle, Ray Kendall and Mary Rose Hermansen
7. Dorothy E. Shaw
8. Pamela Virtue
9. Nancy H. White
10. Bernard Woiwod and Kathleen Hirst

APPENDIX A

Collection 36A: General Correspondence 2017–19, A–I:
Italicised names refer to composite collections of correspondence

- Bryant Allen—see Robin Hide
- ANU General (including PAMBU)—also Nancy White
- Ira Bashkow
- Jenny Bellamy—see Ken Granger
- Alexander Belousov
- Ivan F. Champion
- Brian Cook—see Robyn Kienzle
- Hugh L. Davies
- Betty Forster—see Fred Kleckham Junior
- *Ken Granger*—also Jenny Bellamy, Mike Lean, Gael McAlpine, Bryan Ruxton and Kay Thorp
- Jason Gwilt
- Jan Hasselberg—see Robin Hide and Michael Young
- *Robin Hide*—also Bryant Allen, Jan Hasselberg, Sharryl Ivahupa, J.K. Murray and G.W. Trompf
- Sharryl Ivahupa—see Robin Hide

Collection 36B: General Correspondence, J–Y:

- Karl James
- *Johnston family (Elin)*—also Peter Milburn
- *Robyn Kienzle*—also Brian Cook
- *Fred Kleckham Junior*—also Betty Forster
- Bud and Marlys Larsen
- Mike Lean—see Ken Granger
- Gael McAlpine—see Ken Granger
- Peter Milburn—see Johnston family
- Drusilla Modjeska
- J.K. Murray—see Robin Hide
- Janice Newton
- Bryan Ruxton—see Ken Granger
- Steve Saunders
- Peter and Rhonwen Searle

- Victoria Stead
- Kay Thorp—see Ken Granger
- G.W. Trompf—see Robin Hide
- Pamela Virtue
- Nancy White—see ANU General
- F.E. Williams—see Michael Young
- *Michael Young*—also Jan Hasselberg and F.E. Williams

Other material

Collection 7: G.A.M. Taylor Documents A: 1950–63 and G.A.M. Taylor Documents B: 1967–2014. This collection has already been donated to, and accepted by, the National Library of Australia. Its contents have also been digitised for the RVO-IMS, and many of them have been microfilmed by PAMBU-ANU.

The following four collections will be offered to the National Library of Australia:

- Collection 25: RVO Staff Members and PNG Artists: Memoirs, Careers and Recollections.
- Collection 29: National Archives of Papua New Guinea: Notes and Copies of Folios on TPNG Files.
- Collection 34: Reports and Selected Folios of National Archives of Australia Files.
- Collection 35: Photographs and CD-ROMs/DVDs relating to the Lamington eruption of 1951.

APPENDIX B: A POSTCOLONIAL TIME SERIES

What follows is representative of the kind of ongoing interest shown in Mount Lamington and the mountain Orokaiva in some of the years following the independence of Papua New Guinea in 1975. The list is by no means complete, or even comprehensive, but it may serve as a starting point for any subsequent history, similar to this one, that may be written following the next volcanic eruption at Mount Lamington.

1980: An explosive volcanic eruption at Mount St Helens, Washington State, US, on 18 May 1980 had both similarities and differences to the one at Mount Lamington in 1951. A mass of magma—termed a 'cryptodome'—located just beneath the summit of Mount St Helens pushed out the northern flank of the volcano, causing gravitational collapse of the flank and creating a large debris avalanche (e.g. *Nature* 1980). This was followed by a 'lateral blast' similar to the 'ash hurricane' pyroclastic flow at Mount Lamington. The Mount St Helens eruption was studied in great detail by many scientists leading to a vast number of publications on the 1980 volcanic activity and its effects (see, for example, *Science* 1983). Some of these scientists later visited Mount Lamington to make comparisons between the two volcanoes.

Nature. 1980. 'Mount St Helens' Eruption. Summary Papers on Seismology, Volcanology, and Effects on Climate', no. 285 (5766): 529–35. doi.org/10.1038/285529a0.

Science. 1983. [Nine papers]. 30 September, no. 221 (4618): 1369–97.

1981: The Orokaiva historian, Maclaren Hiari of Popondetta—then a journalist with the Papua New Guinea Office of Information—published an article on the 1951 Lamington disaster on the occasion of the 30th anniversary of the eruption (Hiari 1981).

Hiari, M. 1981. 'Lamington'. *Paradise* (Air Niugini in-flight magazine), January, no. 27, 5–8.

1982: Fieldwork was undertaken at Mount Lamington by Richard Hoblitt, a volcanologist from the United States Geological Survey (USGS), and by staff from the Rabaul Volcanological Observatory, to 1) compare the products of the eruption at Lamington in 1951 with those at Mt St Helens in 1980, 2) assess the potential volcanic hazards at the volcano and 3) inspect and take temperatures at the summit dome (Hoblitt 1982; de Saint Ours 1988; see also Thompson 2000). Debris-avalanche deposits were identified and similarities drawn between the 1951 pyroclastic flow deposits at Lamington and the 'blast' deposit at Mount St Helens.

de Saint Ours, P. 1988. 'Potential Volcanic Hazards from Mt Lamington, Northern Province, Papua New Guinea'. *Geological Survey of Papua New Guinea* 86 (12).

Hoblitt, R.P. 1982. 'Reconnaissance of the Area Devastated by the January 21, 1951 Eruption of Mount Lamington, Papua: August 10–18, 1982'. Unpublished administrative report, United States Geological Survey.

Thompson, D. 2000. *Volcano Cowboys*. New York: St Martin's Press.

1982: The concept of a 'Volcanic Explosivity Index' or VEI was introduced as a way of measuring and comparing the size or 'bigness' of explosive eruptions worldwide (Newhall and Self 1982). VEIs range from 1 to 8, based incrementally on the volumes of material produced by eruptions, ranging from 'small' to 'very large'. The Lamington 1951 eruption, like that of Mont Pelée in 1902, has a VEI of 4 thus classifying as 'large' (Siebert, Simkin and Kimberley 2010). The 1951 eruption, however, is still significantly smaller than, say, that at Krakatau in 1883 (VEI-6) and smaller even than at Mount St Helens in 1980 (VEI-5).

Newhall, C.G. and S. Self. 1982. 'The Volcanic Explosivity Index (VEI): An Estimate of Explosive Magnitude for Historical Eruptions'. *Journal of Geophysical Research* 87 (C2): 1231–38. doi.org/10.1029/jc087ic02p01231.

Siebert, L., T. Simkin and P. Kimberley. 2010. *Volcanoes of the World*. Washington, DC: Smithsonian Institution.

1983: A second, redesigned edition of BMR Bulletin 38 on the 1951 Mount Lamington eruption (Taylor 1958) was published. The redesign, by Frank Roberts of BMR, included redrafting of diagrams—especially the bulky, fold-out, figures 11–19 of the first edition—and embedding the photographs and other illustrations in appropriate parts of the text, thus improving accessibility and readability of the account.

Taylor, G.A.M. 1983. *The 1951 Eruption of Mount Lamington, Papua*, 2nd ed. Bureau of Mineral Resources, Bulletin 38. Canberra: Australian Government Publishing Service.

1983: A detailed petrological study was conducted on rock samples collected in 1979 from the 1951 lava dome of Mount Lamington (Arculus et al. 1983). The analysed rocks had chemical compositions expected of an andesitic volcano related to plate subduction even though no Wadati-Benioff Zone is present beneath the volcano. The magmas, therefore, appear to have originated from parts of the Earth's upper mantle that had experienced subduction earlier in geological time (see also Johnson 1987a). A striking feature of the analysed samples is the presence of pieces of the crustal ophiolite through which the magmas had risen towards the surface.

Arculus, R.J., R.W. Johnson, B.W. Chappell, C.O. McKee and H. Sakai. 1983. Ophiolite-Contaminated Andesites, Trachybasalts, and Cognate Inclusions of Mount Lamington, Papua New Guinea: Anhydrite-Amphibole-Bearing Lavas and the 1951 Cumulodome'. *Journal of Volcanology and Geothermal Research* 18, 215–47. doi.org/10.1016/0377-0273(83)90010-0.

Johnson, R.W. 1987a. 'Delayed Partial Melting of Subduction-Modified Magma Sources in Western Melanesia: New Results from the Late Cainozoic'. *Pacific Rim Congress* 87, 211–14.

1984: A major, global review of the features and origin of large volcanic debris avalanches and related avalanche amphitheatres was published internationally, giving attention to well-known collapses such as those at Galunggung (see Figure 3.10), Bezymianny in 1956, Sheveluch in 1964 and Mount St Helens in 1980 (Siebert 1984). Avalanche amphitheatres are typically 1–3 kilometres in width but are larger in the direction of the collapse, as created at Mount Lamington in 1951.

Siebert, L. 1984. 'Large Volcanic Debris Avalanches: Characteristics of Source Areas, Deposits, and Associated Eruptions'. *Journal of Volcanology and Geothermal Research* 22, 163–97. doi.org/10.1016/0377-0273(84)90002-7.

1984: Two RVO volcanologists undertook a 'hazard-rating' assessment for 14 historically active and 22 'dormant' volcanoes in Papua New Guinea (Lowenstein and Talai 1984). Hazard scores were assigned to each volcano on the basis of past eruptive activity, the size of hazardous areas and the populations at-risk. Rabaul ranked as the most hazardous volcano and Lamington as the second most.

Lowenstein, P.L. and B. Talai. 1984. 'Volcanoes and Volcanic Hazards in Papua New Guinea'. *Geological Survey of Japan Report* 263, 315–31.

1985: A major report on the economic organisation of an Orokaiva village, Koropata 2, includes an extensive bibliography on Orokaiva history and related subjects (Newton 1985). Another version of the Sumbiripa myth was recorded during this research: Sumbiripa 'told his wife to take her tapa cloth off … When she did, he had intercourse with her and "kaboom", the mountain went up' (J. Newton, personal communication, 2017).

Newton, J. 1985. *Orokaiva Production and Change*. Pacific Research Monograph 11. Canberra: Development Studies Centre, The Australian National University.

1987: A review was undertaken of volcanoes in Papua New Guinea that retain evidence of gravitational collapses and the formation of avalanche amphitheatres and debris-avalanche deposits, including Lamington volcano (Johnson 1987b).

Johnson, R.W. 1987b. 'Large-Scale Volcanic Cone Collapse: The 1888 Slope Failure of Ritter Volcano, and Other Examples from Papua New Guinea'. *Bulletin of Volcanology* 49, 669–79. doi.org/10.1007/bf01080358.

1988: In retirement, volcanologist at the RVO after 21 January 1951, John Best, sent a formal letter to the minister in charge of the BMR, Canberra, concerning events at the RVO during the week of 15–20 January 1951. Best set out systematically the difficulties that his colleague and friend Tony Taylor had had, from Tuesday 16 January onwards, in persuading District Commissioner J.K. McCarthy to allow him to visit Lamington to assess the volcanic unrest being reported in radio broadcasts. Best wrote that 'the scientific-world, or more precisely part of it, has been duped by BMR, per medium of Bulletin 38, for 30 years. I have deliberately used "duped" because the deceptions incorporated in Bulletin 38 (in both editions) were devised by BMR staff' (Best 1988, 1). Best does not state who devised the deceptions and why.

APPENDIX B

Best, J.G. 1988. Copy of unpublished letter to Senator Peter Cook, minister for resources and energy, Canberra, including two appendices dated 1 November 1988. Appendix A is entitled 'A Chronology of Events as They Involved G.A.M. Taylor, Volcanologist, Territory of Papua and New Guinea, during the Period January 15–21 1951'. R.W.J. Collections: Box 7B: G.A.M. Taylor Documents 1967–2014, Folder 4, sleeve 94.

1988: This year was also marked by the release of an important hazard-assessment report on Mount Lamington. It was designed for use by provincial authorities in the Lamington area and was written by Patrice de Saint Ours, a volcanologist at the RVO. He described the nature of the hazards to be expected: earthquakes, volcanic gases, explosions, ashfalls, pyroclastic flows, mud flows, lava domes and flows, and flank eruptions (de Saint Ours 1988). Maps of areas most likely to be subjected to ashfalls, flowage hazards and flank eruptions are presented, and emergency management advice is provided for long-term development planning and for emergency planning and management.

de Saint Ours, P. 1988. 'Potential Volcanic Hazards from Mt Lamington, Northern Province, Papua New Guinea'. *Geological Survey of Papua New Guinea* 86 (12).

1991: Plans were made by the editorial committee of *Una Voce*, the journal of the Papua New Guinea Association of Australia, to prepare an account of the 1951 Lamington eruption on the occasion of the 40th anniversary of the disaster on 21 January 1991. Contributions were invited from readers, but publication did not take place because of conflicts with the information being provided (see the following issues of *Una Voce*: December 1990, page 18; March 1991, page 3; March 1992, page 25). These conflicts included, particularly, bitter differences of opinion expressed between former District Commissioner David Marsh and Police Superintendent George Allen over whether bodies were buried at the Mount Lamington Memorial Cemetery at Popondetta and thus whether the memorial park was a true cemetery (Marsh 2005–06; Speer 2005–14).

Marsh, D. 2005–06. Unpublished correspondence with author. R.W.J. Collections: Box 33B, Lamington Eruption 1951, Correspondence and Memoirs, H–Mars, Folder 17.

Speer, A. 2005–14. Unpublished correspondence with author. R.W.J. Collections: Box 32: Albert Speer Correspondence on the Lamington Eruption 1951.

1994: Eruptions at Tavurvur and Vulcan volcanoes in Rabaul Harbour in September devastated most of Rabaul town and much of the surrounding area. The need was identified for an upgrade of Papua New Guinea's national volcanological service, based at the RVO. The Australian Government provided 20 years of support, from 1995 to 2015, through its international development assistance program and by means of a scientific 'twinning' arrangement between the RVO and the Australian Geological Survey Organisation, formerly BMR, and now called Geoscience Australia, Canberra (Nancarrow and Johnson 2015). Five volcanoes were identified as 'high risk': Rabaul, Ulawun, Pago, Manam and Lamington. Seismometers and tiltmeters for monitoring eruption precursors were installed at each of these last four 'remote' volcanoes, including high-frequency radio links that permitted the transfer of early warning signals of potential eruptions to the recording room at RVO headquarters in Rabaul. Public awareness campaigns were also carried out among the at-risk communities at each volcano, including in Oro Province. Radio links were also provided for local volcano observers who could maintain regular, scheduled reporting to the RVO, including an observer at Popondetta for Lamington volcano.

Nancarrow, S.N. and R.W. Johnson. 2015. 'Rabaul Volcanological Observatory Twinning Program'. Unpublished project-completion report submitted to the Department of Foreign Affairs and Trade. Geoscience Australia, 9 December 2015.

1998: Ulawun volcano in New Britain was selected as an international 'Decade Volcano' as part of the UN-sponsored International Decade for Natural Disaster Reduction during the 1990s. The focus of a workshop held at Walindi, New Britain, in 1998 was on the gravitational collapse of volcanic cones (IAVCEI Workshop 1998). Ulawun was selected—rather than, say, Lamington—because of its considerable steepness, great height, ongoing eruptive activity and close proximity to a coastline (hence its tsunami-generating potential). The lessons learnt, however, are applicable to Mount Lamington.

IAVCEI Workshop. 1998. *Volcanic Cone Collapses and Tsunamis: Issues for Emergency Management in the Southwest Pacific Region.* Report of the Workshop on Ulawun Decade Volcano, Papua New Guinea. [Papua New Guinea]: International Association of Volcanology and Chemistry of the Earth's Interior.

2001: Explanatory notes for a new geological map of the Buna area including Mount Lamington were completed, although the map itself has still not been published (Davies and Williamson 2001). Several lineaments on the volcano are identified as radial faults, including part of the Ambogo River valley.

> Davies, H.L. and A.N. Williamson. 2001. 'Buna—1:250,000 Geological Series'. Explanatory notes to accompany Buna 1:250,000 geological map: Geological Survey of Papua New Guinea, Explanatory Notes SC/55-7. Port Moresby.

2001: Sixty-eight Australians attended a reunion at Palmwoods, inland from the Sunshine Coast of Queensland on 21 January 2001 to commemorate the 50th anniversary of the Lamington eruption (Boag 2001–05). The reunion, mainly of former administration staff and relatives, was organised by Alan Boag, his wife Win (née Swift) and Geoff Littler, all three of whom—together with three others attending the reunion—had been involved in shifting the evacuation camp at Ilimo back across the Kumusi River to Saiho in April–May 1951. Peter 'Fred' Kaad was also in attendance.

> Boag, A.D. 2001–14. Correspondence between Boag and author. R.W.J. Collections: Box 33A, Lamington Eruption 1951, Correspondence and Memoirs, A–G, Folder 4.

2002: Rumours and stories emerged in the Popondetta area in the first three weeks of April that possible volcanic activity was taking place at Mount Lamington (Itikarai and Bosco 2002). Fire, smoke, high temperatures and dead vegetation were reported from the summit area of the mountain, together with noises from the volcano. People visiting the summit lava dome reported becoming dizzy and their dogs fainting. Some schools in the area were closed as a precaution. RVO volcanologists investigated but found the reports to constitute a false alarm. Their report may represent the best documented example of a false alarm at Lamington volcano since 1951 and up to this time.

> Itikarai, I. and J. Bosco. 2002. 'Investigations at Lamington Volcano, Popondetta: 21st–25th April 2002'. Rabaul Volcanological Observatory, unpublished report.

2003: Mrs Pamela Virtue and her husband Gerry visited Popondetta in January. They located the neglected memorial cemetery and identified the brass plaques for the graves of Pamela's father, District Commissioner Cecil Cowley, and her brother Erl (Cowley and Virtue 2015). This was an emotional but eventually cathartic time for Mrs Virtue who had been very apprehensive about such a visit after 52 years of absence. Mrs Virtue was recognised and honoured by many local people and she and her husband attended a commemoration service in Popondetta on 'Eruption Day', 21 January. They met eruption survivors and encountered many expressions of ongoing local grief. They also attended a ceremony at Kiorata village, near what formerly had been Isivita, during which she was given a Papuan name, Ruja, and invited to return for Eruption Day the following year. Ruja—or Suja in other versions of the myth—is the wife of Sumbiripa, the local name for Mount Lamington.

Cowley, A. and P. Virtue. 2015. *The Volcano's Wife: The Great Untold Story*. Calwell, ACT: Inspiring Publishers.

2004: The Virtues returned to Oro Province for the fifty-third anniversary of the 1951 eruption, this time accompanied by their son, Mark, and by filmmaker Mike Dillon who made a documentary video of the visit (Cowley and Virtue 2015). A track through to deserted Higaturu had been prepared, where another emotional gathering took place in honour of Pamela née Cowley. Local people had decorated the site to represent the former graves of Cecil and Erl. The Eruption Day commemoration was held at Kiorata where the governor's representative told a version of the Sumbiripa and Ruja story in which 'Ruja was pregnant and she blew up, not Sumbiripa' (Cowley and Virtue 2015, 193).

Cowley, A. and P. Virtue. 2015. *The Volcano's Wife: The Great Untold Story*. Calwell, ACT: Inspiring Publishers.

2007: A four-person team from RVO and the Port Moresby Geophysical Observatory carried out a two-week volcanic-hazard awareness program in February among communities on the northern and western sides of Mount Lamington (Mulina, Baisa and Kuduon 2007). They gave PowerPoint talks, showed volcanic-hazard videos and distributed pamphlets, posters and copies of volcanic-hazard maps adapted from those prepared by de Saint Ours (1988). Villages within the defined hazard zones on Mount Lamington had been continuing to expand owing to population growth, meaning that volcanic risk was increasing again. Recommendations included establishment of a reliable high-frequency communication system and better use of the local radio station. The system of roads that link people in high-risk areas with the main, recently sealed, Kokoda–Popondetta road should be improved to enhance its use for evacuation routes. There was no road access to communities on the southern side of

Lamington. A hazard-awareness program was needed there, which should include communities on the eastern side as well. Any provincial evacuation plan should be tested by carrying out mock evacuations involving the communities themselves. Cyclone Guba produced severe damage across south-eastern Papua New Guinea in November, including Oro Province, and resulted in 149 fatalities.

de Saint Ours, P. 1988. 'Potential Volcanic Hazards from Mt Lamington, Northern Province, Papua New Guinea'. *Geological Survey of Papua New Guinea* 86 (12).

Mulina, K., L. Baisa and J. Kuduon. 2007. 'Community Awareness and Preparedness on Volcanic Hazards at Lamington Volcano, Oro Province'. Unpublished report, Rabaul Volcanological Observatory.

2007: A simple, disaster management methodology for comparing the four phases of prevention, preparedness, relief and recovery—actually at Lamington in 1951 and predictively in 2007—was devised and presented at an international volcanological conference in Japan (Johnson et al. 2007). Prevention and preparedness each scored higher in 2007 compared to 1951. Another conclusion was that the total score for prevention and preparedness in 2007 was still lower than that for relief and recovery (seven compared to 16). Further disaster-risk reduction work is required in the Lamington area, a situation that applies to most areas established as disaster prone throughout the world.

Johnson, R.W., K. Mulina, J. Kuduon, H. Patia and A. Simpson 2007. 'Comparative Assessment of Disaster Management Conditions at Lamington Volcano, Papua New Guinea in 1951 and 2007'. In *Abstracts Volume/Cities on Volcanoes 5 Conference, Shimabara, Japan, 19–23 November 2007*, 117. [Japan] : The Volcanological Society of Japan.

2009: An art exhibition of 34 works of barkcloth, or *nioge,* produced by Omie women who live high on the southern flank of Mount Lamington, was held at the National Gallery of Victory (NGV) in Melbourne. Earlier exhibitions of their work had taken place in Sydney in 2006 and 2009 and in Perth in 2007. A description of the cultural context of the Omie art was provided by author and historian Drusilla Modjeska in the catalogue for the NGV exhibition (Modjeska 2009). The spirit of Mount Lamington volcano is called 'Huvaemo' by the Omie, rather than Sumbiripa, the name given by the Orokaiva, their traditional enemies to the north.

The eruption of 1951 is accounted for by Huvaemo reacting angrily to the restless, wandering souls of the numerous soldiers killed during the World War II who had nowhere to rest (see also Modjeska 2012).

Modjeska, D. 2009. 'Fabric of Wisdom: The Context of Omie Nioge'. In *Wisdom of the Mountain: Art of the Omie*, by Sana Balai and Judith Ryan, 21–30. Melbourne: National Gallery of Victoria.

Modjeska, D. 2012. *The Mountain*. Sydney: Vintage, Random Press.

2010: A commemorative newspaper article was published, summarising the volcanic disaster of January 1951 (Hiari 2010). Attention was drawn again to the gruesome weeks of clearing up after the disaster and to the speed with which numerous burials had to be made for safety and health reasons. Some local people had been returning to live again in the former disaster area and had discovered skeletons in the ruins of the old Higaturu Government Station and the Sangara Mission.

Hiari, M. 2010. 'The Mount Lamington Tragedy Remembered'. *Sunday Chronicle*, 23 January. sundayfeatures.blogspot.com/2010/01/mt-lamington-tragedy-remembered.html (site discontinued). R.W.J. Collections: Box 33B, Lamington Eruption 1951, Correspondence and Memoirs, H–Mars, Folder 11, sleeve 22.

2010: RVO volcanologist Herman Patia attended a consultative stakeholders meeting of the Northern Province Restoration Authority in Oro (Patia 2010). Presentations were given by provincial and local government leaders on the considerable flood damage caused by Cyclone Guba in the province in 2007. Patia, in contrast, gave a presentation on planning for volcanic hazards in the event of a volcanic eruption at Mount Lamington, focusing on the disaster of 1951. He highlighted the volcanic-hazard awareness-raising visits that RVO had made to communities in the province in 2004 and 2007. Another community awareness visit would take place in November.

Patia, H. 2010. Unpublished correspondence between Herman Patia and author. R.W.J. Collections: Box 33B, Lamington Eruption 1951, Correspondence and Memoirs, H–Mars, Folder 11, sleeve 17.

2010: Two Russian volcanologists accompanied by RVO volcanologist Herman Patia undertook fieldwork at Mount Lamington (Belousov et al. 2011a, 2011b). Their aim was to restudy the volcanic deposits of the 1951 eruption and to make comparisons with other similar eruptions that had taken place at volcanoes such as Mount St Helens in 1980 and at the Kamchatkan volcanoes of Bezymianny in 1956 and Sheveluch in 1964. Results from the fieldwork complemented those obtained in 1982 by USGS volcanologist R.P. Hoblitt, and were presented jointly at two international conferences.

Belousov, A., M. Belousova, H. Patia and R. Hoblitt. 2011a. 'Deposits and Dynamics of the 1951 Pyroclastic Density Current of Mount Lamington, Papua New Guinea'. *Geophysical Research Abstracts* 13. European Geophysical Union General Assembly.

Belousov, A., M. Belousova, H. Patia and R. Hoblitt. 2011b. 'In the Shoes of Tony Taylor: Results of Reinvestigation of the 1951 Eruption of Mount Lamington, Papua New Guinea'. Unpublished PowerPoint presentation at IUGG General Assembly, Melbourne (copy in author's possession).

2011: Members of the family of Kevin Woiwod, who was killed in the 1951 eruption, visited Oro Province and attended the 60th anniversary of the Lamington disaster (Woiwod 2010–14). They were Kevin's brother, Bernard 'Bernie' Woiwod; his niece, Kathleen Hirst; and David Woiwod, Bernie's grandson and a television journalist. A documentary video of the visit, including interviews with survivors and eyewitnesses, was made by David Woiwod and cameraman Aiden Boem. The Mount Lamington Memorial Cemetery from colonial days in Popondetta was still in a neglected state in 2011 and Bernie Woiwod began efforts to have a new memorial built at Hohorita village in honour of all the victims of the eruption (Woiwod 2010–14; Woiwod 2014; McCullough, 2014–15).

McCullough, P. 2014–15. 'A Man on a Mission'. *Peninsula Essence* (Mornington Peninsula, Victoria) 15 (Summer): 72–75.

Woiwod, B. 2010–14. Unpublished correspondence between author and Bernie Woiwod and other family members. R.W.J. Collections: Box 33C, Lamington Eruption 1951, Correspondence and Memoirs, Mart–Z, Folder 27.

Woiwod, B. 2014. 'Do the Right Thing for Victims of Mt Lamington: A Proper Memorial Can Be Part of Kokoda Track Experience'. *National Weekender* (Port Moresby), 28 November, 4.

2012: An insightful novel about interracial relationships in Papua and New Guinea—love, work, motherhood, loss and so forth—was published to acclaim by literary reviewers in Australia. The story starts in the years just before Papua New Guinea self-government and takes place in and between Port Moresby and the Northern District (Modjeska 2012). The novel's title is *The Mountain* (the mountain is Huvaemo or Mount

Lamington) and the story focuses, in part, on the Omie people who live on the southern side of the volcano. The novel includes the story about the ghosts of numerous soldiers who had been killed during the war (see also Modjeska 2009). Their souls were wandering about lost and angry, having no-one to bury them, which upsets Huvaemo and results in the disastrous volcanic eruption of 1951. Further:

> Before the eruption, there had been signs that the mountain was angry. Cassowaries and bandicoots came into the village, wild boars came close to the houses. There were some great storms with lightning in the sky, and though the rain fell, the rivers ran dry, the water pulled back up into the mountain. When the water returned it was hot. (Modjeska 2012, 140)

Modjeska, D. 2009. 'Fabric of Wisdom: The Context of Omie *Nioge*'. In *Wisdom of the Mountain: Art of the Omie*, by Sana Balai and Judith Ryan, 21–30. Melbourne: National Gallery of Victoria.

Modjeska, D. 2012. *The Mountain*. Sydney: Vintage, Random Press.

2012: Mrs Pamela Virtue (née Cowley) drew attention in the magazine *Una Voce* to the neglected and overgrown state of the Mount Lamington Memorial Park at Popondetta in 2003, referring also to Bernie Woiwod's more recent visit to the cemetery (Virtue 2012). The poor condition of the park was in stark contrast to the 'immaculate condition' of the adjacent military Kokoda Memorial Park, which was being managed by the War Graves Commission based in Canberra. Both Mrs Virtue and Woiwod had contacted the Australian Government about the need for improved governmental maintenance of the Mount Lamington park but had received no positive responses. Mrs Virtue raised the possibility of her returning to Popondetta and having the bodies of her father and brother removed and reburied somewhere else where they could be given more appropriate respect.

Virtue, P. 2012. 'Popondetta Memorial Park to Mt Lamington Eruption'. *PNGAA Una Voce* 1 (March): 64.

2014: Staff from the RVO and the Volcanic Disaster Assistance Program (part of the USGS) participated in a joint workshop at RVO headquarters aimed at determining the relative threat levels of 52 Papua New Guinea volcanoes (RVO 2014). The methodologies and criteria used in the assessment were based on those devised by Ewert (2007). Rabaul volcano maintained the highest ranking, as determined previously by Lowenstein and Talai (1984). Lamington volcano, however, dropped to seventh position in the ranking but was grouped with nine other volcanoes in a 'high threat' group.

Ewert, J.W. 2007. 'System for Ranking Relative Threats of US Volcanoes'. *Natural Hazards Review* 8 (4):112–24.

Lowenstein, P.L. and B. Talai. 1984. 'Volcanoes and Volcanic Hazards in Papua New Guinea'. *Geological Survey of Japan Report* 263, 315–31.

RVO (Rabaul Volcanological Observatory). 2014. Nine unpublished lists, maps and guidelines resulting from the Papua New Guinea volcanoes threat-assessment workshop held in Rabaul, East New Britain.

2015: A book called *The Volcano's Wife* written jointly by the late Amalia (or Amalya) Cowley and her daughter Pamela Virtue was published privately (Cowley and Virtue 2015). The authors tell the dramatic story of the Cowley family, their involvement in the Lamington disaster of 1951 and the emotional difficulties faced by Mrs Virtue in having to cope with the deaths of her father and brother. This moving account has a cathartic finale, but the need to dispose of the trauma completely was not so easily dealt with. Mrs Virtue later took the advice of a sharma that she should give away her remaining copies of the book to take the 'weight' from her and so release the trauma. Mrs Virtue still, however, has the honorary but troubling title of Ruja—the 'Volcano's Wife'—to put behind her (Virtue 2018).

Cowley, A. and P. Virtue. 2015. *The Volcano's Wife: The Great Untold Story*. Calwell, ACT: Inspiring Publishers.

Virtue, P. 2018. Unpublished correspondence with author. R.W.J. Collections: Box 36B, Lamington Eruption 1951, General Correspondence 2017–19, Folder 9, sleeves 45–52.

2018: An Australian anthropologist, Victoria Stead, drew attention to local Orokaiva people recognising the historical value of Higaturu, which had been destroyed by the 1951 volcanic eruption and was the place where wartime public hangings had taken place. Higaturu's history was becoming a 'resource' like gold or oil palm that might attract outsiders and thus forms of local wealth resulting in improved lifestyles, but possibly also the risk of outside exploitation and profit from outsiders. This:

Mobilisation of history-as-resource also speaks to other concerns, including about the relationships of insiders and outsiders across time, and the proper attributions of guilt, responsibility, and entitlement within colonial and postcolonial landscapes of remembrance. (Stead 2018, 16)

Stead, V. 2018. 'History as Resource: Moral Reckoning with Place and with the Wartime Past in Oro Province, Papua New Guinea'. *Anthropological Forum* 28, 16–31. doi.org/10.1080/00664677.2018.1426439.